Scriptural Traces:
Critical Perspectives on the Reception and Influence of the Bible

27

Editors
Matthew A. Collins, University of Chester
Michelle Fletcher, King's College London
Andrew Mein, Durham University

Editorial board
Michael J. Gilmour, David Gunn, James Harding, Jorunn Økland

Library of New Testament Studies

649

Formerly the Journal for the Study of the New Testament Supplement series

Editor
Chris Keith

Editorial Board
Dale C. Allison, Lynn H. Cohick, R. Alan Culpepper, Craig A. Evans, Jennifer Eyl, Robert Fowler, Simon J. Gathercole, Juan Hernández Jr., John S. Kloppenborg, Michael Labahn, Matthew V. Novenson, Love L. Sechrest, Robert Wall, Catrin H. Williams, Brittany E. Wilson

Matthew's Account of the Massacre of the Innocents in Light of Its Reception History

Sung J. Cho

t&tclark

LONDON • NEW YORK • OXFORD • NEW DELHI • SYDNEY

T&T CLARK
Bloomsbury Publishing Plc
50 Bedford Square, London, WC1B 3DP, UK
1385 Broadway, New York, NY 10018, USA
29 Earlsfort Terrace, Dublin 2, Ireland

BLOOMSBURY, T&T CLARK and the T&T Clark logo are trademarks
of Bloomsbury Publishing Plc

First published in Great Britain 2022
This paperback edition first published in 2023

Copyright © Sung J. Cho, 2022

Sung J. Cho has asserted his right under the Copyright, Designs and
Patents Act, 1988, to be identified as Author of this work.

For legal purposes the Acknowledgments on p. vii constitute an
extension of this copyright page.

Cover image: *The Massacre of the Innocents*, c.1628-29
(oil on canvas) by Nicolas Poussin © Musée Condé, Chantilly / Bridgeman Images

All rights reserved. No part of this publication may be reproduced or transmitted in any
form or by any means, electronic or mechanical, including photocopying, recording,
or any information storage or retrieval system, without prior permission
in writing from the publishers.

Bloomsbury Publishing Plc does not have any control over, or responsibility for, any
third-party websites referred to or in this book. All internet addresses given in this
book were correct at the time of going to press. The author and publisher regret any
inconvenience caused if addresses have changed or sites have ceased to exist, but
can accept no responsibility for any such changes.

A catalogue record for this book is available from the British Library.

Library of Congress Cataloging-in-Publication Data
Names: Cho, Sung J., author.
Title: Matthew's account of the Massacre of the Innocents in light of its
reception history / by Sung J. Cho.
Description: London; New York: T&T Clark, [2021] |
Series: Scriptura l traces: critical perspectives on the reception and influence of the Bible; 27 |
Revision of author's thesis (doctoral)–Catholic University of America, 2019. |
Includes bibliographical references and index. |
Summary: "Sung Cho addresses the seeming contradiction of Herod the Great's massacre in
Matthew 2:16-18, questioning why such a tragedy had to occur, why it was included in the
good news of Jesus, and what connection it has to ancient prophecies"– Provided by publisher.
Identifiers: LCCN 2021025375 (print) | LCCN 2021025376 (ebook) |
ISBN 9780567699534 (hardback) | ISBN 9780567699541 (pdf) | ISBN 9780567699565 (epub)
Subjects: LCSH: Bible. Matthew, II, 16-18–Criticism, interpretation, etc. |
Bible–Prophecies. | Massacre of the Holy Innocents.
Classification: LCC BS2575.52 .C46 2021 (print) |
LCC BS2575.52 (ebook) | DDC 226.2/06–dc23
LC record available at https://lccn.loc.gov/2021025375
LC ebook record available at https://lccn.loc.gov/2021025376

ISBN: HB: 978-0-5676-9953-4
PB: 978-0-5676-9957-2
ePDF: 978-0-5676-9954-1
eBook: 978-0-5676-9956-5

Series: Scriptural Traces, volume 27
Series: Library of New Testament Studies, volume 649
ISSN 2513-8790

Typeset by Newgen KnowledgeWorks Pvt. Ltd., Chennai, India

To find out more about our authors and books visit www.bloomsbury.com
and sign up for our newsletters.

Contents

List of Figures		vi
Acknowledgments		vii
List of Abbreviations		viii
1	Matthew and Reception History	1
2	A Close Reading of Matthew 2:16-18	27
3	Massacre of the Innocents in Early Patristic Tradition (Second to Fifth Century)	47
4	Massacre of the Innocents from Sixth Century to 1516	89
5	Massacre of the Innocents from 1517	125
6	Visual Interpretations of the Massacre of the Innocents	161
7	Concluding Reflections	205
Appendix A: Massacre of the Innocents in Modern Commentaries		221
Appendix B: The Massacre of the Innocents in Commentaries from 1517 through the Nineteenth Century		225
Appendix C: Massacre of the Innocents in Art		229
Select Bibliography		243
General Index		275
Scripture Index		281

Figures

1. "The north (left) portal tympanum of the Strasbourg Cathedral" (*ca.* 1275)   165
2. "Grabow Altarpiece," Meister Bertram von Minden, 1378–83, Kuntstalle Hamburg   167
3. Giovanni Pisano "Pistoia Pulpit," *ca.* 1297–1301, Massacre of the Innocents, relief from the pulpit   170
4. William Holman Hunt, "The Triumph of the Innocents," *ca.* 1883–4   172
5. Giovanni Pisano "Pisa Pulpit," *ca.* 1297–1301, Massacre of the Innocents, relief from the pulpit   177
6. *Massacre of the Innocents*, Matteo di Giovanni, 1482, Museo Nazionale di Capodimonte   179
7. Matteo di Giovanni, "Massacre of the Innocents," Palazzo Pubblico, Siena, Italy   180
8. Pieter Bruegel the Younger, "Massacre of the Innocents," *ca.* 1565, Kunsthistorisches Museum, Vienna, Austria   185
9. *Massacre of the Innocents*, Guido Reni, 1611, Pinacoteca Nazionale, Bologna   187
10. Peter Paul Rubens, "The Massacre of the Innocents," *ca.* 1610, oil on panel   188
11. Marcantonio Raimondi, "Massacre of the Innocents," *ca.* 1512–13, Rijksmuseum, Amsterdam   189
12. Peter Paul Rubens, "The Massacre of the Innocents," *ca.* 1635–7, Alte Pinakothek, Bayerische Staatsgemaeldesammlungen, Munich, Germany   190
13. "The Rabbula Gospels," Florence, The Biblioteca Medicea Laurenziana, ms. Plut.1.56, f. 4v   192
14. "Codex Egberti," folio 15v, *ca.* 980, Stadtbibliothek, Trier   193
15. Nicolas Poussin, "The Massacre of the Innocents," *ca.* 1625   197
16. "St Albans Psalter," *ca.* 1120–40   199
17. Peter Paul Rubens, "The Horrors of War," *ca.* 1637–8, Gabinetto Fotografico delle Gallerie degli Uffizi   200

Acknowledgments

Reception history by its very nature is a study that is dependent on others. My work is no exception. I would like to thank the members of the faculty of the Catholic University of America School of Theology and Religious Studies who have shaped my thinking during my PhD studies. I'm especially grateful to Fr. John Paul Heil, Dr. David Bosworth, and Dr. Ian Boxall who invested in my efforts to produce my dissertation, which has been reshaped for this publication.

Dr. Boxall deserves special mention here because of his excellent teaching, scholarly example, dissertation guidance, and impetus in my publication. My work largely follows his lead and I hope to continue in the imitation of his excellent reception-historical works.

Personally, I would like to thank my wife Ye Rae for her undying support and love during my studies and my current endeavors. I could not have reached this point without her constant prayer and comfort during difficult times. Thank you.

Abbreviations

AB	Anchor Bible
ABRL	Anchor Bible Reference Library
AGJU	Arbeiten zur Geschichte des antiken Judentums und des Urchristentums
AGLB	*Aus der Geschichte der lateinischen Bibel* (= Vetus Latina: Die Reste der altlateinischen Bibel: Aus der Geschichte der lateinischen Bibel). Freiburg: Herder, 1957–2016
ALUOS	*Annual of Leeds University Oriental Society*
AnBib	Analecta Biblica
ANF	*Ante-Nicene Fathers*
BECNT	Baker Exegetical Commentary on the New Testament
BETL	Bibliotheca Ephemeridum Theologicarum Lovaniensium
BibInt	*Biblical Interpretation*
BZAW	Beihefte zur Zeitschrift für die alttestamentliche Wissenschaft
BZNW	Beihefte zur Zeitschrift für die neutestamentliche Wissenschaft
CBQ	*Catholic Biblical Quarterly*
CCCM	Corpus Christianorum: Continuatio Mediaevalis
CCSA	Corpus Christianorum: Series Apocryphum
CCSL	Corpus Christianorum: Series Latina
CH	*Christian History*
CNT	Commentaire du Nouveau Testament
ConcC	Concordia Commentary
CR	Corpus Reformatorum
CSCO	Corpus Scriptorum Christianorum Orientalium
CSEL	Corpus Scriptorum Ecclesiasticorum Latinorum
DBTEL	*A Dictionary of Biblical Tradition in English Literature*. Edited by David L. Jeffrey. Grand Rapids: Eerdmans, 1992
ECF	The Early Church Fathers
EKKNT	Evangelisch-Katholischer Kommentar zum Neuen Testament
EuroJTh	*European Journal of Theology*
FC	Fathers of the Church
FCB	Feminist Companion to the Bible
FCNTECW	Feminist Companion to the New Testament and Early Christian Writings
FRLANT	Forschungen zur Religion und Literatur des Alten und Neuen Testaments
GCS	Die griechischen christlichen Schriftsteller der ersten [drei] Jahrhunderte

HThKNT	Herders Theologischer Kommentar zum Neuen Testament
HTR	*Harvard Theological Review*
IBS	*Irish Biblical Studies*
ICC	International Critical Commentary
Il.	*Illiad*
JBL	*Journal of Biblical Literature*
JSJ	*Journal for the Study of Judaism in the Persian, Hellenistic, and Roman Periods*
JSNT	*Journal for the Study of the New Testament*
JSNTSup	Journal for the Study of the New Testament Supplement Series
JSOT	*Journal for the Study of the Old Testament*
JSS	*Journal of Semitic Studies*
JTS	*Journal of Theological Studies*
LCL	Loeb Classical Library
LNTS	Library of New Testament Studies
LXX	Septuagint
MM	Moulton, James H., and George Milligan. *The Vocabulary of the Greek Testament*. London, 1930. Repr. Peabody, MA: Hendrickson, 1997
NA²⁸	*Novum Testamentum Graece*, Nestle-Aland, 28th ed.
NAC	New American Commentary
NCBC	New Century Bible Commentary
NewDocs	*New Documents Illustrating Early Christianity*. Edited by Greg H. R. Horsley and Stephen Llewelyn. North Ryde, NSW: Ancient History Documentary Research Centre, Macquarie University, 1981–1992
NIBCNT	New International Biblical Commentary on the New Testament
NIBCOT	New International Biblical Commentary on the Old Testament
NICNT	New International Commentary on the New Testament
NIGTC	New International Greek Testament Commentary
NovT	*Novum Testamentum*
NovTSup	Supplements to Novum Testamentum
NPNF¹	*Nicene and Post-Nicene Fathers*, Series 1
NPNF²	*Nicene and Post-Nicene Fathers*, series 2
NRSV	New Revised Standard Version
NTA	*New Testament Abstracts*
NTS	*New Testament Studies*
NTTS	New Testament Tools and Studies
OBO	Orbis Biblicus et Orientalis
ODCC	*The Oxford Dictionary of the Christian Church*. Edited by Frank L. Cross and Elizabeth A. Livingstone. 3rd rev. ed. Oxford: Oxford University Press, 2005
OLA	Orientalia Lovaniensia Analecta
OTL	Old Testament Library
PG	Patrologia Graeca

PL	Patrologia Latina
RB	*Revue bénédictine*
SC	Sources chrétiennes. Paris: Cerf, 1943–
SCH	Studies in Church History
SHBC	Smyth & Helwys Bible Commentary
SP	Sacra Pagina
STI	Studies in Theological Interpretation
SubBi	Subsidia Biblica
STr	Scriptural Traces Critical Perspectives on the Reception and Influence of the Bible
T. Job	*Testament of Job*
TPINTC	TPI New Testament Commentaries
TS	*Theological Studies*
TUGAL	Texte und Untersuchungen zur Geschichte der altchristlichen Literatur
TynBul	*Tyndale Bulletin*
USQR	Union Seminary Quarterly Review
Vg.	Vulgate
WMANT	Wissenschaftliche Monographien zum Alten und Neuen Testament
WTJ	*Westminster Theological Journal*
WUNT	Wissenschaftliche Untersuchungen zum Neuen Testament

1

Matthew and Reception History

Introduction

As one opens the New Testament (NT) to the first of the four gospel books, Matthew 1 introduces a biblical world resplendent with promises of Abraham, David, virgin birth, and God with us.[1] Then, the tone dramatically shifts in chapter two as antagonists and more characters enter the storyline, supporting the theme of Jesus's kingship.[2] Suddenly, Matthew, in contrast to Luke, proves itself to be an "adult gospel" that begins in "a cruel suffering world of Herods, of plots, of children killed, of enemies and retaliation, of refugees and magi coming from afar."[3] Through these tragic narrated events and shared human experience of suffering, various connections form through history: between antiquity and the present, original audience(s) and modern reader(s), Jesus and his followers of today. Such connections are possible through diverse readings, known as receptions by some.

If one is enticed into venturing into this world of receptions, a reception historian can arrange a guided navigation. Reception history is a scholarly project that involves "selecting and collating ... reception material in accordance with the particular interest of the historian concerned, and giving them a narrative frame."[4] While various other approaches have been applied to Matthew, reception history can show the modern reader interpretations that demonstrate the culture-shaping power of a text. In addition, reception history not only embraces readers who seek original contexts and meanings, it can also embrace reader-oriented interpretations and the meanings they have derived from the text. It embraces all different points of view, either *"behind* the text (those of the author and her or his sources), *within* the text (those of explicit or

---

[1] "Matthew" will be used to designate the evangelist(s) and the gospel written by him or her, but without any implications about the specific identity or identities. For discussion about identity, see Mark Kiley, "Why 'Matthew' in Matt 9, 9–13?," *Biblica* 65 (1984): 347–51.

[2] Anthony J. Saldarini, *Matthew's Christian-Jewish Community*, Chicago Studies in the History of Judaism (Chicago: University of Chicago Press, 1994), 176.

[3] Sean P. Kealy, *Matthew's Gospel and the History of Biblical Interpretation: Book 2*, Mellen Biblical Press Series 55b (Lewiston: Mellen, 1997), 952.

[4] Jonathan Roberts, "Introduction," in *The Oxford Handbook of the Reception History of the Bible*, ed. Michael Lieb, Jonathan Roberts, and Christopher Rowland, 1–8 (Oxford: Oxford University Press, 2011), 1.

implied narrated characters), and *in front of* the text (those of interpreters from the past and present)."[5]

A modest goal of this work is to enrich the readers' reading of the massacre of the innocents through other points of view found in receptions throughout history.[6] This chapter will (1) highlight the importance of Matthew 2:16-18 in biblical studies and reception history, (2) present the most important contributions in the field of reception history of Matthew, and (3) define the present author's approach to Matt 2:16-18.

I. Matthew 2:16-18 in Biblical Studies and Reception History

Of all the chapters and passages of the NT, what is it about Matthew 2 and the particular episode in verses 16-18 that makes this study worthwhile? First, if "wisdom is justified by her works," a study of a passage is justified by its interesting readings. Secondly, reception history is the best approach for comprehensively and critically analyzing these readings.

A. Importance of Matthew 2:16-18 in Biblical Studies

As stated above, Matthew 2 is a stark and dour contrast from Matthew 1. Certainly, the use of Old Testament (OT) in the NT and Messianic prophecies continue, but the second half of the Matthean infancy narrative is filled with potential for unique and diverse readings. Arguably the most shocking and provocative story in the chapter is the massacre of the infants in 2:16-18. It is shocking because up to this point in the narrative, dangers were social (Joseph's divorce of Mary) and potential (Herod's attempt to eliminate Jesus), not physical and realized. It is provocative because it is the NT's first violent scene and only instance of infanticide. As in the OT, the profundity of human suffering is matters of theodicy and philosophy.[7]

Hermeneutically speaking, Matthew 2 and specifically verses 16-18 have potential. There are implicit correspondences between the lives of Moses and Jesus in their shared itinerary to and from Egypt. In another link with the OT, Matt 2:16-18 belongs in the history of interpretation of Jeremiah.[8] On a macro-level of intratextuality and

---

[5] Andries G. van Aarde and Yolanda Dreyer, "Matthew Studies Today—a Willingness to Suspect and a Willingness to Listen," *HTS Teologiese Studies/Theological Studies* 66:1 (2010) article #820.

[6] When referring to Matt 2:16-18 as the massacre of the "innocents," the present writer does not advance or imply a moral or a theological stance on the character or the destiny of the victims (at least for the moment) but simply accommodate to the popular title of the episode.

[7] See discussion in Dale C. Allison, *Studies in Matthew: Interpretation, Past, and Present* (Grand Rapids: Baker, 2005), 251-64.

[8] For a discussion of Jer 31:15-22 in its own literary context and the rest of HB, as well as its lasting influence, see Susan E. Brown-Gutoff, "The Voice of Rachel in Jeremiah 31: A Calling to 'Something New,'" *USQR* 45 (1991): 177-90; and Michael P. Knowles, *Jeremiah in Matthew's Gospel: The Rejected Prophet Motif in Matthean Redaction*, JSNTSup 68 (London: Sheffield Academic, 1993). For a sample of reception history of Jer 31:15, see Walter Brueggemann, *Texts That Linger, Words That Explode*, ed. Patrick D. Miller (Minneapolis: Fortress, 2000), 4-7 for his discussion of Matt 2:16-18; Emil Fackenheim, "New Heart and the Old Covenant: On Some Possibilities of a Fraternal Jewish-Christian

narrative-critical scale, careful readers note how the massacre anticipated the Jewish persecutions of the adult Jesus and his victory over death.[9]

Critical readings also lead to hypotheses concerning the Matthean community that stands behind the text. Its Jewish character can be conjectured in the study of the fulfillment citations. Furthermore, Matt 2:16-18 may reflect the vulnerable and marginalized position of the community amidst rival Christian, Jewish, and/or Gentile populations post-70 AD.[10] The malevolent reactions of Herod and Jerusalem to the Magi's arrival indicate the dividing line: the messianic identity of Jesus.[11] The analyses of tensions between the Matthean Jewish-Christian community and Jews at large must begin in earnest here before moving on to more provocative passages like Matt 23; 27:25; and 28:11-15.

Reading of the Jewish Bible Today," in *The Divine Helmsman: Studies on God's Control of Human Events*, ed. James L. Crenshaw and Samuel Sandmel, 191–205 (New York: KTAV, 1980); and Jonathan Kozol, *Rachel and Her Children: Homeless Families in America* (New York: Broadway, 2006).

[9] Jack D. Kingsbury, *Matthew as Story* (Minneapolis: Fortress, 1986), 46; John P. Heil, *Death and Resurrection of Jesus: A Narrative-Critical Reading of Matthew 26–28* (Minneapolis: Fortress, 1991), 16; David E. Garland, *Reading Matthew: A Literary and Theological Commentary on the First Gospel* (Macon: Smyth & Helwys, 1999), 30–1. For a discussion of literary or narrative criticism, its close relation to composition criticism, and contrasts with redaction criticism, see Boris Repschinski, *The Controversy Stories in the Gospel of Matthew: Their Redaction, Form and Relevance for the Relationship between the Matthean Community and Formative Judaism*, FRLANT 189 (Göttingen: Vandenhoeck & Ruprecht, 2000), 20–1; William G. Thompson, *Matthew's Advice to a Divided Community: Mt. 17,22-18,35*, AnBib 44 (Rome: Biblical Institute, 1970), 12; David R. Bauer, "The Interpretation of Matthew's Gospel in the Twentieth Century," *American Theological Library Association Summary of Proceedings* 42 (1988): 134–5; Jack D. Kingsbury, *Matthew: Structure, Christology, Kingdom* (Philadelphia: Fortress, 1975); Jack D. Kingsbury, *Matthew as Story* (Philadelphia: Fortress, 1988), 1–40; Seymour Chatman, *Story and Discourse: Narrative Structure in Fiction and Film* (Ithaca: Cornell University Press, 1978); James L. Resseguie, *Narrative Criticism of the New Testament: An Introduction* (Grand Rapids: Baker Academic, 2005), 18–19; Mark A. Powell, "Literary Approaches and the Gospel of Matthew," in *Methods for Matthew*, ed. Mark A. Powell, 44–82 (Cambridge: Cambridge University Press, 2009), 52–65; James G. Crossley, *Reading the New Testament: Contemporary Approaches* (London: Routledge, 2010), 21; Frank J. Matera, "The Plot of Matthew's Gospel," *CBQ* 49 (1987): 233–53; Mark A. Powell, "The Plot and Subplots of Matthew's Gospel," *NTS* 38 (1992): 187–204; Mark A. Powell, "Introduction," in *Methods for Matthew*, ed. Mark A. Powell, 1–10 (Cambridge: Cambridge University Press, 2009), 6–7; Ben Witherington III, *New Testament Rhetoric: An Introductory Guide to the Art of Persuasion in and of the New Testament* (Eugene: Wipf & Stock, 2009), 1–5; Mark A. Powell, *What is Narrative Criticism?* (Minneapolis: Fortress, 1990), 8–9.

[10] See theories and discussions in Douglas R. A. Hare, "Current Trends in Matthean Scholarship," *Word and World* 18 (1998): 408–9; Kenneth W. Clark, "The Gentile Bias in Matthew," *JBL* 66 (1947): 165–72; John P. Meier, "Matthew, Gospel of," in *Anchor Bible Dictionary: K-N Volume 4*, ed. David N. Freedman, 622–41 (New York: Doubleday, 1992), 625–7; Graham N. Stanton, *A Gospel for a New People: Studies in Matthew* (Louisville: Westminster John Knox, 1993), 158–9; John K. Riches, *Conflicting Mythologies: Identity Formation in the Gospels of Mark and Matthew* (Edinburgh: T&T Clark, 2000), 228; Ian Boxall, *Discovering Matthew: Content, Interpretation, Reception* (London: Society for Promoting Christian Knowledge, 2014), 6; Ulrich Luz, *Studies in Matthew*, trans. Rosemary Selle (Grand Rapids: Eerdmans, 2005), 250; Rosemary R. Ruether, *Faith and Fratricide: The Theological Roots of Anti-Semitism* (New York: Seabury, 1974), 30; Stephen C. Barton, "Can We Identify the Gospel Audiences?," in *The Gospels for All Christians: Rethinking the Gospel Audiences*, ed. Richard Bauckham, 173–94 (Grand Rapids: Eerdmans, 1998), 180–1; Mike Bird, "Bauckham's *The Gospels For All Christians* Revisited," *EuroJTh* 15 (2006): 5–13; David C. Sim, *The Gospel of Matthew and Christian Judaism: The History and Social Setting of the Matthean Community* (Edinburgh: T&T Clark, 1998).

[11] Saldarini, *Matthew's Christian-Jewish Community*, 169.

The provocative potential of Matthew 2 is also evident in diverse reader-oriented approaches.[12] For example, Herod may represent more than a Jewish population antagonistic toward Christians. Warren Carter suggests a diametric opposition between "the powerful settled center" (Herod) and "mobile margins" (the Magi, Joseph, Mary, Jesus).[13] Thus, Matthew 2 invites readers to postcolonial biblical criticism, an "existential approach, particularly through ideological criticism," with special consideration of "unequal power relations and injustice, and *for* their justice or liberation."[14] Since the king is Roman client king of Judea, the chapter has special relevance for modern readers of marginalized groups under colonization or still suffering under its residual effects.

Further inquiries concerning the role of women confront the reader rather suddenly and forcefully as the weeping Rachel appears. How does the citation of Jer 31:15 explain her significance for women in the Matthean community?[15] For certain feminist scholars resistant to the patriarchal worlds of the past and present, Rachel stands in place of the forgotten and bereaved women and "pierces the male world of power, of slaughter and of divine favour."[16] The passive role of Mary and the dramatic emotions of the matriarch invite resistant readings and dialogues concerning feminist identity.[17] For Sharon Betsworth and her cohort of women readers, the repeated yet muted designations of Jesus as a vulnerable and lowly "child" (2:8-9, 11, 13-14, 20-21) invoke sympathy and at the same time challenge adult followers of Jesus to be child-like (18:5).[18] Potential for provocative womanist reading is evident in Matthew 2.[19]

---

[12] For technical discussions of reader-oriented approaches to historical and literary criticisms, see Powell, *What Is Narrative Criticism?*, 8; Roman O. Jakobson, "Linguistics and Poetics," in *Style in Language*, ed. Thomas A. Sebeok, 350–77 (Cambridge, MA: MIT Press, 1960), 355; Murray Krieger, *A Window to Criticism: Shakespeare's Sonnets and Modern Poetics* (Princeton: Princeton University Press, 1964), 3; Hans-Robert Jauss, *Toward an Aesthetic of Reception*, trans. Timothy Bahti (Minneapolis: University of Minnesota Press, 1982), 146–7; Stanley E. Fish, *Self-Consuming Artifacts: The Experience of Seventeenth-Century Literature* (Berkeley: University of California Press, 1972), 387–8; Susan Gillingham, "Biblical Studies on Holiday? A Personal View of Reception History," in *Reception History and Biblical Studies: Theory and Practice*, ed. Emma England and William J. Lyons, 17–30, STr 6 (London: T&T Clark, 2015), 18.

[13] Warren Carter, *Matthew and the Margins: A Sociopolitical and Religious Reading*, The Bible & Liberation Series (Maryknoll: Orbis, 2000), 73.

[14] Ferry Y. Mamahit, "Postcolonial Reading of the Bible: An Asian Evangelical Friend or Foe?," paper presented at Asia Theological Association Theological Consultation Meeting, Malang, Indonesia, July 18–20, 2017.

[15] See for example, Maarten J. J. Menken, "The Quotation from Jeremiah 31 (38).15 in Matthew 2.18: A Study of Matthew's Scriptural Text," in *The Old Testament in the New Testament: Essays in Honour of J. L. North*, ed. Steve Moyise, 106–25, LNTS 189 (Sheffield: Sheffield Academic, 2000); and George Soares-Prabhu, *The Formula Citations in the Infancy Narrative of Matthew: An Enquiry into the Tradition History of Matthew 1–2*, AnBib 63 (Rome: Biblical Institute, 1976).

[16] Elaine Wainwright, "Rachel Weeping for Her Children: Intertextuality and the Biblical Testaments—a Feminist Approach," in *A Feminist Companion to Reading the Bible: Approaches, Methods and Strategies*, ed. Athalya Brenner and Carole R. Fontaine, 452–69, FCB 11 (Sheffield: Sheffield Academic, 1997), 467.

[17] For a survey of feminist criticism, see Powell, "Introduction," 7.

[18] Sharon Betsworth, "The Child and Jesus in the Gospel of Matthew," *Journal of Childhood and Religion* 1 (2010): 10–14.

[19] See for example, Amy-Jill Levine, ed., with Marianne Blickenstaff, *A Feminist Companion to Matthew*, FCNTECW 1 (Sheffield: Sheffield Academic, 2001).

Thus, the evocative topics of death, suffering, tyranny, persecution, and marginalization converge together in Matt 2:16-18 to draw readers to this passage in search of its earliest first century significance as well as contemporary significance. One may argue that this search is best accomplished through juxtaposition of more reader-oriented questions with historical-critical questions and turn to recent biblical scholarship for answers.

B. Matthew 2 and Reception History

Though one may argue that Matt 2:16-18 is a fascinating study, such uniquely Matthean passages did not garner relatively much modern interest until recent times. In the twentieth century, scholars were preoccupied with the search for original context and meaning.[20] Gospel scholars paid more attention to the Synoptic Problem, and more specifically, Mark and Q as pre-Matthean sources, and the two source theory with its presumption of Markan priority.[21] With Matthew as a passive recipient of Mark and Q, scholars concentrated on reconstructing the life of Jesus and the significance of his death and resurrection.[22]

Though redaction critical works in both the United States and Germany drew more attention to uniquely Matthean material, Raymond Brown's magisterial *The Birth of the Messiah* was significant in remedying the neglect of the birth narratives of Matthew and Luke.[23] Brown wrote in the foreword to the original edition: "In some ways the

---

[20] For an overview of NT research from Ferdinand Christian Baur (early nineteenth century) to Albert Schweitzer (early twentieth century), see Raymond Collins, *Introduction to the New Testament* (Garden City: Doubleday, 1983), 45–55. See also Bauer, "The Interpretation of Matthew's Gospel in the Twentieth Century," 119–45; Janice C. Anderson, "Life on the Mississippi: New Currents in Matthean Scholarship 1983–1993," *Currents in Biblical Research* 3 (1995): 169–218; Donald Senior, *What Are They Saying About Matthew?*, rev. and exp. ed. (New York: Paulist, 1996), 23–5; Douglas R. A. Hare, "Current Trends in Matthean Scholarship," *Word and World* 18 (1998): 405–10; Howard Clarke, *The Gospel of Matthew and Its Readers: A Historical Introduction to the First Gospel* (Bloomington: Indiana University Press, 2003), xx–xxiv; Anthony C. Thiselton, "'Postmodern' Challenges to Hermeneutics: 'Behind' and 'In Front Of' the Text—Language, Reference and Indeterminacy," in *Thiselton on Hermeneutics: Collected Works with New Essays*, 607–24 (Grand Rapids: Eerdmans, 2006); Powell, "Introduction," 1–10; van Aarde and Dreyer, "Matthew Studies Today," Article #820; Boxall, *Discovering Matthew: Content, Interpretation, Reception*, 14–15. For an example of a composition critical work of Matthew, see William G. Thompson, *Matthew's Story: Good News for Uncertain Times* (New York: Paulinist, 1989).

[21] For examples, see William R. Farmer, *The Gospel of Jesus: The Pastoral Relevance of the Synoptic Problem* (Louisville: Westminster John Knox, 1994); Christopher S. Mann, *Mark: A New Translation with Introduction and Commentary*, AB 27 (Garden City: Doubleday, 1986), 165–72; Mark Goodacre, *The Case against Q: Studies in Markan Priority and the Synoptic Problem* (Harrisburg: Trinity Press International, 2002); Michael D. Goulder, *Midrash and Lection in Matthew* (London: SPCK, 1974); Austin Farrer, "On Dispensing with Q," in *Studies in the Gospels: Essays in Memory of R. H. Lightfoot*, ed. D. E. Nineham, 55–88 (Oxford: Blackwell, 1955). For an overview, see John P. Meier, *A Marginal Jew: Rethinking the Historical Jesus: Volume 1: The Roots of the Problem and the Person*, ABRL (New York: Doubleday, 1991), 43–4.

[22] Bauer, "The Interpretation of Matthew's Gospel in the Twentieth Century," 122–5; Rudolf K. Bultmann, "New Testament and Mythology," in *Kerygma and Myth: A Theological Debate*, ed. Rudolf K. Bultmann, ErnstLohmeyer, Julius Schniewind, Helmut Thielicke, Austin Farrer, and Hans Werner Bartsch, rev. ed. Reginald H. Fuller, 1–44 (New York: Harper, 1961), 34–5; James G. Crossley, *Reading the New Testament*, 20–1.

[23] For discussions and early works of redaction criticism, see Donald A. Hagner and Stephen A. Young, "The Historical-Critical Method," in *Methods for Matthew*, ed. Mark A. Powell, 1–43

narratives of Jesus' birth and infancy are the last frontiers to be crossed in relentless advance of the scientific (critical) approach to the Gospels."[24] Critical scholars have "scouted" the narratives in the past, but because they found no historical value in them, they overlooked and treated them lightly. Ironically, the clergy they have trained in seminaries would have to deal with these passages annually during the Christmas season. As a response, Brown's work balanced comments concerning theologies and messages behind the narratives while being attentive to historical problems, technical information, and theories that assist in reconstructing the pre-Gospel history.[25]

Therefore, the growing diversity of methods and approaches brought increased attention to the original context and contribution of Matthew to Gospel studies in the twentieth and early twenty-first centuries.[26] Some, however, debated whether such intense focus is beneficial or fruitful. To them, this current state of biblical studies resembles the discipline of bonsai tree cultivation, "leaving little of its narrow remit untouched and with much repeated ad nauseum."[27] Rather, they wanted to know how modern and postmodern readers encounter and understand the ancient text, instead of hypothesizing the original intended readers and the writer(s) of the gospel.[28] Still, some engagement with historical criticism is inevitable, as Matthew assumes some amount of knowledge about first-century Pharisees, locations of Galilee and Judea, and Herod.[29] For better or worse, diversity and complexity characterize the current state of Matthean studies.

(Cambridge: Cambridge University Press, 2009), 27–9; Daniel A. Carson and Douglas J. Moo, *Introduction to the New Testament*, 2nd ed. (Grand Rapids: Zondervan, 2005), 160; Willoughby C. Allen, *A Critical and Exegetical Commentary on the Gospel according to S. Matthew*, ICC (Edinburgh: T&T Clark; New York: Charles Scribner's Sons, 1912), xiii–lxxxviii; Benjamin W. Bacon, *Studies in Matthew* (New York: Henry Holt, 1930), 125–9; Günther Bornkamm, "Die Sturmstillung im Matthäus-Evangelium," in *Überlieferung und Auslegung im Matthäusevangelium*, ed. Günther Bornkamm, Gerhard Barth, and Heinz Joachim Held, 48–53, WMANT 1 (Neukirchen-Vluyn: Neukirchener Verlag, 1960), 51.

[24] Raymond E. Brown, *The Birth of the Messiah: A Commentary on the Infancy Narratives in Matthew and Luke*, ABRL, new updated ed. (New York: Doubleday, 1993), 6.

[25] Ibid., 6–8.

[26] For example, near the end of the millennium, Donald Senior observed that attention to Matthew as literature "allies redaction criticism with literary criticism, a growing force in biblical studies." Senior, *What Are They Saying about Matthew?*, 25.

[27] Emma England and William J. Lyons, "Explorations in the Reception of the Bible," in *Reception History and Biblical Studies: Theory and Practice*, ed. Emma England and William J. Lyons, 3–13, STr 6 (London: T&T Clark, 2015), 3.

[28] See Ulrich Luz, *Studies in Matthew*, 266; Howard Clarke, *The Gospel of Matthew and Its Readers*, xiv–xv; Sean P. Kealy, *Matthew's Gospel and the History of Biblical Interpretation: Book 1*, Mellen Biblical Press Series 55a (Lewiston: Mellen, 1997), iv; Jonathan Roberts and Christopher Rowland, "Introduction," *JSNT* 33 (2010): 131; N. T. Wright, *The New Testament and the People of God* (London: SPCK, 1992), 341; Rachel Nicholls, *Walking on Water: Reading Mt. 14:22-33 in the Light of Its Wirkungsgeschichte*, BIS 90 (Boston: Brill, 2007), 17; Ulrich Luz, *Matthew in History: Interpretation, Influence, and Effects* (Minneapolis: Fortress, 1994), 6. During the last two decades, however, NT scholars have produced exegetical works with substantial aid of contemporary visual material culture. For a survey of important contributions, see Vernon K. Robbins, "New Testament Texts, Visual Material Culture, and Earliest Christian Art," in *The Art of Visual Exegesis: Rhetoric, Texts, and Images*, ed. Vernon K. Robbins, Walter S. Melion, and Roy R. Jeal, 13–54, Emory Studies in Early Christianity 19 (Atlanta: SBL Press, 2017).

[29] Boxall, *Discovering Matthew*, 29.

C. An Appeal for Reception History

While diversity and complexity in Matthean scholarship are not necessarily faulty, they nonetheless contribute to the difficulty of achieving unified dialogues.[30] Since biblical studies itself is a multifaceted discipline, different studies may champion different approaches, further increasing fragmentation.[31] In addition, sifting through vast amounts of works in the last century of biblical scholarship alone would be challenging, let alone centuries of interpretations.[32] Some consider this increasing diversity unmanageable.

Yet, a place to begin with NT scholarship may be a careful consideration of its influence in two major areas. First, outside of the boundaries of the church, the influence of the NT cannot easily be removed from the Western intellectual culture, as proven by its impact on history and politics.[33] Secondly, there is some agreement that the NT is, was, and always will be part of the church's Scriptures and its exposition one of its main tasks. Markus Bockmuehl believes that, moving forward, scholars ought to reflect on the history of the NT's influence in order to reveal the worlds in front of the text as well as the world behind it. In addition, the implied readers of the NT are, broadly speaking, not simply the early church but all followers of Christ throughout history who confess Jesus as Lord in the ecclesiastical community. In other words, the NT itself presupposes an extended readership far beyond its time of composition.[34] This broader idea of implied reader tethers the study of the NT to Christian tradition.[35] Thus, the study of the NT along with its readers and interpreters are here to stay.[36]

Even if one concedes that the implied readership of the Bible includes all generations of the church and that the Bible cannot be disentangled from the culture, why should one turn to reception history? One may find confidence in its twofold

---

[30] See discussions in Kealy, *Matthew's Gospel and the History of Biblical Interpretation: Book 2*, 953; Luz, *Studies in Matthew*, 266–70; Nicholls, *Walking on Water*, 1, 3.

[31] Douglas A. Knight and Amy-Jill Levine, *The Meaning of the Bible: What the Jewish Scriptures and Christian Old Testament Can Teach Us* (New York: HarperCollins, 2011), xviii.

[32] See critiques of Markus Bockmuehl, *Seeing the Word: Refocusing New Testament Study*, STI (Grand Rapids: Baker Academic, 2006), 30–9; Robert Evans, *Reception History, Tradition and Biblical Interpretation: Gadamer and Jauss in Current Practice*, LNTS 510, STr 4 (London: Bloomsbury, 2014), 26–31.

[33] Crossley, *Reading the New Testament*, 122–9; James G. Crossley, "The End of Reception History, a Grand Narrative for Biblical Studies and the Neoliberal Bible," in *Reception History and Biblical Studies: Theory and Practice*, ed. Emma England and William J. Lyons, 45–59, STr 6 (London: T&T Clark, 2015), 49–52.

[34] Bockmuehl, *Seeing the Word*, 61–74.

[35] Bockmuehl was not the first or the last to speak on these matters. See David P. Parris, *Reception Theory and Biblical Hermeneutics*, Princeton Theological Monograph Series 107 (Eugene: Pickwick, 2009), ix–xiv; Karlfried Froehlich, "Church History and the Bible," in *Biblical Hermeneutics in Historical Perspective: Studies in Honor of Karlfried Froehlich on His Sixtieth Birthday*, ed. Mark S. Burrows and Paul Rorem, 1–15 (Grand Rapids: Eerdmans, 1991); Gerhard Ebeling, *Wort Gottes und Tradition: Studien zu einer Hermeneutik der Konfessionen* (Göttingen: Vandenhoeck & Ruprecht, 1964); Ernst von Dobschütz, "Bible in the Church," in *Encyclopaedia of Religion and Ethics*, ed. James Hastings, 2:579–615 (Edinburgh: T&T Clark, 1909).

[36] While some may disagree with Luz's inclusive and ecumenical definition of the church, which includes all who strive to study the Scriptures, there is no denying the wider cultural impact of the Bible. Mark W. Elliott, "Effective-History and the Hermeneutics of Ulrich Luz," *JSNT* 33 (2010): 162.

nature of history and reception.[37] To refute claims that reception history is without scholarly rigor, Susan Gillingham writes that reception history is firstly a historical task that binds the "history of culture" to the "history of the text."[38] She uses an analogy of an archaeological dig: the top layer corresponds to the last century of scholarship, preoccupied mostly with historical-critical methods, but there are centuries of levels below, descending to the text's genesis.[39] So then, reception history, far from dispensing with history, expands it.[40] The reception historian reveals the cultural impact of the text in different historical contexts, as revealed in verbal and nonverbal forms of expression.[41] In addition, while remaining a *historical* task, reception history is also deeply concerned with *reception*. It can be categorized with the more recent reader-oriented methods. Reception historians are studying not only the text's meaning but also how it is meaningful to actual people over the centuries.[42] For example, one can study how Hermann Melville received the text of Matt 2:16-18 in *Moby Dick*.[43]

Thus, the practice of reception history has many possible benefits. It can allow a reader to understand the text better, identify many contact points between culture and the Bible, and unite genres of works such as scholarly, confessional, and the fine arts.[44] Yet, reception history, however it is applied, must be done critically always.[45] Reception historians must be competent in different languages and church history in

---

[37] Reception history is in reality much more multifaceted, but for simplicity's sake, its two major elements are discussed. Jonathan Morgan, "Visitors, Gatekeepers and Receptionists: Reflections on the Shape of Biblical Studies and the Role of Reception History," in *Reception History and Biblical Studies: Theory and Practice*, ed. Emma England and William J. Lyons, 61–76, STr 6 (London: T&T Clark, 2015), 62.

[38] Gillingham, "Biblical Studies on Holiday?," 18. See also Rachel Nicholls, "Is Wirkungsgeschichte (or Reception History) a Kind of Intellectual Parkour (or Freerunning)?," in conference paper, Society for the Study of the New Testament, 2005, 4.

[39] Gillingham, "Biblical Studies on Holiday?," 18; Ian Boxall, "Reception History," in *The New Cambridge History of the Bible: Volume 4: From 1750 to the Present*, ed. John Riches, 172–83 (Cambridge: Cambridge University Press, 2015), 172; William J. Lyons, "Hope for a Troubled Discipline? Contributions to New Testament Studies from Reception History," *JSNT* 33 (2010): 213–14; Crossley, *Reading the New Testament*, 132.

[40] "Examining the interpretation of the text is simply a lens through which to conduct a broader historical study." Nicholls, *Walking on Water*, 4.

[41] Reception history moves beyond "history of interpretation" to include nonverbal interpretive works such as visual arts or music or nonreligious works. For an example of the latter, see Christine Ritter, *Rachels Klage im antiken Judentum und frühen Christentum*, AGJU 52 (Leiden: Brill, 2003). The reason for this inclusion can be traced to Hans Gadamer's philosophy which is foundational to reception history. As Evans notes, "the *universality of historical consciousness* in human experience according to Gadamer's theory of understanding" properly allows reception historians to infer that exegesis should not be confined to conventional written explanatory texts but be observed in "literature, art, music, and actualizations of the texts." For a fuller treatment of Gadamer's influence, see below. Evans, *Reception History, Tradition and Biblical Interpretation*, 133–4; Roberts and Rowland, "Introduction," 132; Ian Boxall, *Patmos in the Reception History of the Apocalypse*, Oxford Theology and Religion Monographs (Oxford: Oxford University Press, 2013), 8.

[42] Wilfred C. Smith writes, "The true meaning of scripture is the solid historical reality of the continuum of actual meanings over the centuries to actual people. It is mundane, or as transcending, or both, as have been those actual meanings in the lives and hearts of persons." *What is Scripture? A Comparative Approach* (Minneapolis: Fortress, 1993), 89.

[43] Herman Melville, *Moby-Dick*, ed. John Bryant and Haskell Springer, A Longman Critical ed. (New York: Pearson Longman, 2007), 458, 465.

[44] Nicholls, *Walking on Water*, 16–17.

[45] Crossley, *Reading the New Testament*, 129–49.

order to understand many diverse contexts and readings.[46] They must be like the sons of Issachar, "who had understanding of the times" (1 Chr 12:32; translation the present author's), not just the ancient text.

Yet, an exhaustive coverage of the various readings of even three verses of Matt 2:16-18 throughout history is impossible, given the vast amount of material available.[47] The better option is to be selective, but reception historians must avoid mere cataloging. They must thoughtfully select and categorize sources. This process of discernment is precisely the task of the reception historian.[48]

Here, some may find Hans R. Jauss's idea of "summit-dialogue of authors" (*Gipfeldialog der Autoren* or *Höhenkamm der Autoren*) helpful. David R. Parris explains the analogy: the protruding peaks of a mountain range "correspond to authors or readings that define or shape the history of a text's reception."[49] This idea is helpful in at least four ways. First, there is the potential to identify multiple significant interpreters who represent "peaks" and apexes of a tradition's shape. Secondly, the summit-dialogue preserves the significant interpretative questions and answers from the past. Thirdly, a great percentage of "best evidence ... for how a passage has been interpreted, taught and applied is located at the summit-dialogue level." Fourthly, at this level are located major turning points that result in paradigm shifts and new realizations. To be a "member" of this summit, a reading must possess lasting "strength," that can be seen in its problem-solving quality and its reception.[50] In relation to Matt 2:16-18, one may argue for the inclusion of Chromatius, Theodore of Mopsuetia, and the author of the *Opus Imperfectum*.[51]

Jauss's idea may be problematic, however, when one attempts to be objective and inclusive in constructing the roster of the summit. For example, a major tradition to which a reception historian belongs may assume that a particular reading possesses lasting "strength" and problem-solving quality, while a smaller minority or a marginal group may reject that same reading. The reverse may also be true. One person's summit may look quite different from another's.

The best that a reception historian can do is to identify multiple summits from different traditions that are outside of one's own reading community, or even opposed to it. Here, Georg G. Igger's proposal to combine macro-histories and micro-histories may cure the problem of myopic subjectivity. "To rescue the unknown from oblivion," perhaps the best approach to writing a history is to give up the notion of a grand narrative or a single macro-history and instead opt for micro-histories of everyday people.[52] This approach avoids silencing the marginal receptions. Yet, a study of "broad

---

[46] James E. Harding, "What Is Reception History, and What Happens to You If You Do It?," in *Reception History and Biblical Studies: Theory and Practice*, ed. Emma England and William J. Lyons, 31–44, STr 6 (London: T&T Clark, 2015), 38, 42–3.

[47] Bockmuehl compares reception history to a "vast iceberg of Christian experience which lies very largely submerged beneath the waves of history." *Seeing the Word*, 66.

[48] Roberts, "Introduction," 1.

[49] Parris, *Reception Theory and Biblical Hermeneutics*, 216–17.

[50] Ibid., 217–22.

[51] Manlio Simonetti, ed., *Matthew 1-13*, Ancient Christian Commentary on Scripture: New Testament 1a (Downers Grove: InterVarsity, 2001), 34–5.

[52] Georg G. Iggers, *Historiography in the Twentieth Century: From Scientific Objectivity to the Postmodern Challenge* (Hanover: Wesleyan University Press, 1997), 103.

social transformations" or the wider religious climate of certain epochs cannot be dismissed, but they must be connected to individual everyday life stories.[53] If one belongs to a major tradition that influences the macro-history, the minor traditions should be included in the discussion. If one belongs to a marginal community, influential figures and ideas of the majority must be explored.[54] To expand the analogy of Jauss, a reception historian can "listen in" on multiple summit-dialogues from different traditions before determining the most important readers and readings.

Therefore, with proper critical caution, reception history is an effective approach for studying Matt 2:16-18 and its most important influential receptions. Writing a reception history of this passage broadens the parameters of text's readings beyond the twentieth and the twenty-first centuries. There may be significant moments in history in which the massacre was emphasized in texts, cited in homilies, or performed in dramatic plays. In exploring such readings of Matt 2:16-18 in the past and present, reception history can maintain its status as history with discipline and rigor without losing its emphasis on tradition- and cultural-reception.

II. Most Important Contributions in the Field of Reception History of Matthew

Reception history as a subdiscipline of biblical studies has a history of its own, albeit a short one in its formative stage. There is still plenty of debate concerning its origin and purpose.[55] Following good practice in historiography, this section presents the most important contributions in the field of reception history of Matthew.

A. Ulrich Luz

Ulrich Luz is widely known as the one who introduced *Wirkungsgeschichte* to NT studies as an integral part of his various works on Matthew, especially his contribution to the *Evangelisch-Katholischer Kommentar zum Neuen Testament* (EKK).[56] *Wirkungsgeschichte* was the operative keyword of EKK, taken over from Hans Gadamer's *Truth and Method*. It is difficult to translate into English, as alternative translations shift the emphasis between the text and its effects.[57] In the latest English edition of Gadamer's book, *Wirkungsgeschichte* is rendered as "effective history," while an earlier edition has "history of effect(s)."[58] There does not appear to be a substantial

---

[53] Ibid., 104.
[54] It is inevitable, however, that the reception historian is at the mercy of availability and accessibility of sources. Even with the best intentions to be comprehensive, certain marginal readings and readers from the past are simply unrecoverable or unknown until they become available.
[55] Gillingham, "Biblical Studies on Holiday?," 23–4.
[56] Nicholls, *Walking on Water*, 4, n. 19; Evans, *Reception History, Tradition and Biblical Interpretation*, 14.
[57] Luz, *Matthew in History*, 3.
[58] Hans-Georg Gadamer, *Truth and Method*, reprint ed., Bloomsbury Revelations (London: Bloomsbury Academic, 2013); Hans-Georg Gadamer, *Truth and Method*, 2nd ed., rev. ed. (London: Sheed and Ward, 1989). Unless otherwise noted, all citations of *Truth and Method* will be from the 1989 edition.

difference between "history of *effect*" (singular) and "history of *effects*" (plural), even though the former is a more literal rendering of *Wirkungsgeschichte*.[59] Luz explains that "effective history" emphasizes what is effective, such as events or texts, while "history of effects" focuses on "the consequences or impact" that arise from an effective source.[60] At one point, Wilheim C. Linss, who translated Luz's Matthew commentary, provided a "neutral" translation that Luz considered best: "history of influence."[61] Eventually, he would favor "effective history" as a translation of *Wirkungsgeschichte*, because an interpreter is hardly detached from history but is entrenched in it and affected by it.[62]

Luz prefers *Wirkungsgeschichte* over *Rezeptionsgeschichte* (reception history) because the latter focuses on the people who receive the text while the former describes what is most basic to him: the power of the text and its effect on its readers.[63] While Heikki Räisänen definitively divides between the "effectiveness" of a text and its "reception," Ian Boxall perceives that the difference between *Wirkungsgeschichte* and reception history is one of focus, not of content.[64] The former emphasizes the consequences of particular readings of the text while the latter emphasizes the interpreters themselves. Practically speaking, however, it is difficult to exclude effects from a study of interpreters and vice versa. In addition, commitment to reception is not mutually exclusive to careful examination of the power of a text and its effects. Thus, it seems best to use the term reception history and be especially mindful of the effects of the text and the interpreters' relationship to history.[65] In this chapter, the present author uses reception history (*Rezeptionsgeschichte*) and history of effects (*Wirkungsgeschichte*) interchangeably.

Luz began his interest in *Wirkungsgeschichte* while reflecting on his decades of teaching. In *Matthew in History: Interpretation, Influence, and Effects*, he notes how his exacerbated students were overwhelmed by the legion of scholarly works that not only conflicted with each other but also did not contribute to a personal understanding of the Bible.[66] Elsewhere, in a similar tone Luz lamented the methodological atheism and the anti-supernatural bias that accompanied the rise of the historical-critical method.[67] He saw biblical studies at the end of the twentieth century as less about dynamic divine

---

[59] Evans, *Reception History, Tradition and Biblical Interpretation*, 15.
[60] Luz, *Matthew in History*, 3.
[61] Ibid.; Ulrich Luz, *Matthew 1–7: A Continental Commentary*, trans. Wilhelm C. Linss (Minneapolis: Fortress, 1989), 11. The English translation of choice in this book is Ulrich Luz, *Matthew 1-7: A Commentary*, ed. Helmut Koester, rev. ed., Hermeneia: A Critical and Historical Commentary on the Bible (Minneapolis: Fortress, 2007).
[62] Ulrich Luz, "The Contribution of Reception History to a Theology of the New Testament," in *The Nature of New Testament Theology*, ed. Christopher Rowland and Christopher Tuckett, 123–34 (Malden: Blackwell, 2006), 125.
[63] Luz, *Matthew 1-7*, 61, 63.
[64] Heikki Räisänen, "The 'Effective History' of the Bible: A Challenge to Biblical Scholarship," in *Challenges to Biblical Interpretation*, Bible Interpretation Series 59 (Leiden: Brill, 2001), 269; Boxall, *Patmos in the Reception History of the Apocalypse*, 8–9.
[65] Boxall, *Patmos in the Reception History of the Apocalypse*, 9. Robert Morgan proceeds in a different direction. The difference between "effects" and "reception" is a matter of attitudes toward religion, with the latter term revealing more detachment. Robert Morgan, "*Sachkritik* in Reception History," *JSNT* 33 (2010): 175–6.
[66] Luz, *Matthew in History*, 1–2.
[67] Elliott, "Effective-History and the Hermeneutics of Ulrich Luz," 163.

revelation and more about an antiquated history of religion.[68] Luz's rationale was that "one does not yet understand what the subject matter of the text means if one only understands what it *has meant*."[69]

Another reflection is sourced in the aforementioned EKK project. The goal of the series was to "reflect the confessional problem—mainly, the relation of the different confessional churches to their common basis, the Bible."[70] With the application of *Wirkungsgeschichte*, the contributors perceived the Bible as an *effective* book that impacts those who live afterward in the events of history, ecclesial and/or secular. Thus, they eluded the pitfalls of "purely objectivized history of historical criticism."[71] In addition, this decision to include a *history* of effects ensured that their interpretations were not isolated from history.

According to Luz, biblical texts and *Wirkungsgeschichte* are related in two ways. First, biblical texts themselves are effects and interpretations of past events. Thus, Matthew is a result of Mark, Q, and other traditions about Jesus. Secondly, the biblical text themselves affect churches, their confessions, and the wider world. This is the world in front of the text.[72] Thus, reception history is pervasive and relevant in the pre- and post-history of the text. The biblical texts are not like a cistern with a fixed amount of water, but a constant source of new streams of effects.[73] Interpreters cannot stay offshore and study these streams, but "rather resemble men, who must investigate the water of a stream while they sit in a boat, which is carried and driven by this very same stream."[74] Establishing the specific interpreter's historical location in the stream of tradition is a building block of reception history. Thus, Luz agrees with the Gadamer's fundamental idea that "history does not belong to us; we belong to it."[75]

Gadamer and Gerhard Ebeling are the major influences on Luz's hermeneutical model.[76] He cites Gadamer who ironically states "the text that is understood historically is forced to abandon its claim that it is offering something true. We think we understand when we see the past from the historical standpoint ... and seek to reconstruct the historical horizon. In fact, however, we have given up the claim to find in the past any truth valid and intelligible to ourselves."[77] When a reader or a group of readers encounters a text, "meaning" is not necessarily discovered through the historical-critical method but located in the integral act of application of the reading.[78] Luz also

---

[68] Ulrich Luz, "Kann die Bibel heute noch Grundlage für die Kirche sein? Über die Aufgabe der Exegese in einer religiös-pluralistischen Gesellschaft," *NTS* 44 (1998): 325–6.
[69] Luz, *Matthew 1-7*, 98.
[70] Luz, *Matthew in History*, 2–3.
[71] Ibid., 3.
[72] Ibid., 23.
[73] Ibid., 19.
[74] Ulrich Luz, *Das Evangelium nach Matthäus (Mt 1-7)* 5, völlig neubearbeitete Auflage, EKKNT I/1 (Neukirchen-Vluyn: Neukirchener Verlag, 2002), 110.
[75] Gadamer, *Truth and Method*, 276–7.
[76] Parris, *Reception Theory and Biblical Hermeneutics*, xv.
[77] Luz, *Matthew in History*, 10; Gadamer, *Truth and Method*, 303.
[78] Luz, *Matthew in History*, 16. Gadamer writes, "In the course of our reflections we have come to see that understanding always involves something like applying the text to be understood to the interpreter's present situation. Thus we are forced to go one step beyond romantic hermeneutics, as it were, by regarding not only understanding and interpretation, but also application as comprising one unified process." Gadamer, *Truth and Method*, 308.

agrees with Gerhard Ebeling that Bible interpretation is not only or even mainly in words of exegesis, dogmatics, and preaching but "in doing and suffering ... in ritual and prayer, in theological work and in personal decisions, in Church organization and ecclesiastical polities ... in wars of religion, and in works of compassionate love."[79] Church history is in reality, "the history of interpretation of Holy Scripture."[80]

Wirkungsgeschichte becomes an increasingly significant dimension of Luz's EKK Matthew commentary. In the last two volumes, it amounts to nearly one-third of the material and incorporates visual art, music, and poetry. Luz's methodology is reflected in the four-fold treatise of each pericope: (1) analysis (text-critical and grammatical matters), (2) explanation, (3) history of influence, and (4) conclusion.[81] This structure reveals one attempt to reconcile the apparently different agendas of historical criticism, reader-oriented approaches, and *Wirkungsgeschichte*. Whether constrained by the format of the EKK series or by choice, Luz places traditional exegesis in a separate section from the history of influence, with the former preceding the latter. To some, this presentation appears to favor traditional historical criticism over *Wirkungsgeschichte*.[82] Robert Evans thinks that even as Luz gives weight to reception history, it still "refers to what follows *after* exegesis rather than being intrinsic to all interpretation including historical-critical reading."[83] Even his selection of "effects" reveals his prioritization of the original meanings. He favors interpretations that "offer corrections for us, especially when they approach the *original* sense of the text in a changed situation" (emphasis the present author's).[84] For Luz, while historical-critical readings used for original meanings and contexts are not superior to readings for application, the former must precede the latter.[85]

A sample of Luz's work is seen in his treatment of Matt 10:8-10 and its effects in history. He analyzes the text and notes the profound impression left on the lives of Francis of Assisi and the Waldensians, who devoted themselves to poverty.[86] A literal interpretation of the passage prevailed in polemics against luxury in the past and present.[87] Other times, when dealing with clergy compensation, interpreters such as Ulrich Zwingli called for moderation between lavish payments and zero wages.[88] Luz also considers when effects are absent in history. In Switzerland and Germany of

---

[79] Luz, *Matthew in History*, 16–17; Gerhard Ebeling, *The Word of God and Tradition: Historical Studies Interpreting the Divisions of Christianity*, trans. S. H. Hooke (Philadelphia: Fortress, 1968), 28.
[80] Ebeling, *The Word of God and Tradition*, 26.
[81] Elliott, "Effective-History and the Hermeneutics of Ulrich Luz," 166–7.
[82] Knight, "*Wirkungsgeschichte*, Reception History, Reception Theory," *JSNT* 33:2 (2010): 142.
[83] Evans, *Reception History, Tradition and Biblical Interpretation*, 46. This criticism appears to be justified in a later work of Luz: *Studies in Matthew*. While adopting Gadamer's ideas and echoing him that application is "'an integral element of all understanding,' not merely as an appendage to understanding." Luz does not depart from older terminology of "levels" and the priority of the historical-critical exegesis, even if it is only procedurally first among equal elements such as reception and application. Luz, *Studies in Matthew*, 271–4; Gadamer, *Truth and Method*, 308.
[84] Luz, *Matthew 1-7*, 62.
[85] Reception history, properly applied, does not allow for "first- and second-stage interpretations," as it might be inferred from Luz's commentary. Lyons, "Hope for a Troubled Discipline?," 214. See Gadamer, *Truth and Method*, 296.
[86] Luz, *Matthew in History*, 46.
[87] Ibid.
[88] Ibid., 46–7.

recent times, Luz notices that Matt 10:8-10 is not referenced as much as it should be in discussion of ministers' salaries.[89] In this brief survey, Luz encounters a fellow Swiss theologian Zwingli and an Italian Catholic friar, Francis of Assisi, among others, before returning to the present situation, demonstrating how reception history allows one to learn from one's own tradition as well as others.[90]

B. Sean P. Kealy

Sean P. Kealy's *Matthew's Gospel and the History of Biblical Interpretation* reinforces many of Luz's ideas. He begins by borrowing C. S. Lewis's term "chronological snobbery" to describe a widespread notion in every age that "time means progress, and that what is progressive cannot be corrected by what is earlier and that what has gone out of date is inevitably discredited."[91] One cannot presuppose that the forgotten state of an idea implies anything about its veracity or falsehood. A historical overview can assist in avoiding such a presumption.[92] Kealy's overview presents (1) the complexity of NT studies, (2) the potential for intellectual enrichment through engagement with past interpreters, and (3) cautionary tales against misunderstanding amidst exchange of diverse ideas.[93] Kealy agrees with Luz "that a major problem of historical-critical exegesis today 'lies in isolating a text in its own time and its own situation of origin and thus preventing it from speaking to the present time.'"[94]

Through the history of interpretation, Kealy demonstrates the influence of Matthew's gospel. He observes, for example, how various figures used parts or all of the Sermon on the Mount for different purposes: Marcion, to deny the authority of the OT (Matt 5:17); Constantine, to promote virtue; Chrysostom and Augustine, to describe the "true evangelical life of the monks"; Tolstoy, to oppose Russian Orthodoxy; Gandhi, to oppose the authority of the British Empire in India; Churchill, to restore the world after the Second World War; Martin Luther King Jr., to inspire the civil rights movement.[95] Kealy cites a wide spectrum of representatives among Christians, non-Christians, politicians, activists, and novelists. The Sermon on the Mount has persistently shown its ubiquitous influence.[96]

In his final reflection, Kealy considers how Matthew deals with profound themes such as existence, death, love, time, worry, family, almsgiving, prayer, and forgiveness.[97] It invites people to follow Christ, live as he lived, and to make disciples of all nations.[98] In order to better understand the gospel and its significance for all kinds of people,

---

[89] Ibid., 47.
[90] Luz, *Matthew 1-7*, 63–6.
[91] Kealy, *Matthew's Gospel and the History of Biblical Interpretation: Book 1*, i; Clive S. Lewis, *Surprised by Joy: The Shape of My Early Life* (New York: Harcourt Brace, 1955), 207.
[92] Kealy, *Matthew's Gospel and the History of Biblical Interpretation: Book 1*, i–iii.
[93] Ibid., iii–iv; James D. G. Dunn, *The Living Word* (London: SCM, 1987), 20.
[94] Kealy, *Matthew's Gospel and the History of Biblical Interpretation: Book 1*, iv–vii; Luz, *Matthew 1-7*, 96.
[95] Kealy, *Matthew's Gospel and the History of Biblical Interpretation: Book 1*, vii–viii.
[96] Ibid., ix.
[97] Kealy, *Matthew's Gospel and the History of Biblical Interpretation: Book 2*, 952.
[98] Ibid.

one must expand his or her perspective and realize that "exegesis is always condemned to be, in the main, a child of its time."[99] That is why it is so important to attend to the entirety of conversation about the gospel that took place in history and is continuing today.[100]

C. Richard Trexler

Richard Trexler's *Journey of the Magi* is next in discussion, but with an important caveat: he never explicitly espouses, recognizes, or accepts the term *Wirkungsgeschichte* as a description of his work.[101] Trexler may resemble a biblical scholar as he studies a passage's influence, but as a Professor of History, he brings to it "questions and priorities of another discipline entirely."[102] Indeed, he is concerned with "the political sociology of the magi in Christianity from their appearance in Matthew until the present."[103] While Trexler discusses historical-critical issues, he moves on to the later significance of the Nativity scene. He explains how, beyond the first century, the cult of the magi of the Orient came to the West and represented the "secular force and authority" of Europe, "a monarchist plot" during the French Revolution, and heroes of oppressed peasants and slaves.[104]

During his historical study, Trexler notes important cultural patterns and trends that impact interpretations of the magi story. For example, when he turns to early Christian art in the Roman catacombs from the time of Constantine to the mid-fifth century, he detects how the association of the magi with the Gentile world was a heuristic key to Christianity's acceptance in the mainstream.[105] In the fourteenth and fifteenth centuries, a polarity developed between the first two magi and the third in iconography, reflecting the generational and gender conflicts of the time.[106] While not directly advocating *Wirkungsgeschichte*, Trexler demonstrates the compatibility of study of effects with political science, sociology, and the history of religion.

D. Howard Clarke

Like Richard Trexler, Howard Clarke is not a biblical scholar, but a Professor of Classics, and he also does not mention Gadamer or *Wirkungsgeschichte* in his book, *The Gospel of Matthew and Its Readers: A Historical Introduction to the First Gospel*. His dissatisfaction with modern critical methods, however, sounds familiar. He begins by discerning the twofold nature of the Bible. It is at once simple in that its various parts

---

[99] Ibid., 953.
[100] Ibid.
[101] Richard C. Trexler, *The Journey of the Magi: Meanings in History of a Christian Story* (Princeton: Princeton University Press, 1997).
[102] Nicholls, *Walking on Water*, 4.
[103] Trexler, *The Journey of the Magi*, 4.
[104] Ibid., 6.
[105] Ibid., 21–2.
[106] Ibid., 123. For a work of *Wirkungsgeschichte* that deals with magi in visual art, see Martin O'Kane, "The Artist as Reader of the Bible: Visual Exegesis and the Adoration of the Magi," *BibInt* 13 (2005): 337–73.

are related, yet complex because they originate from ancient times.[107] Its complexity is demonstrated in biblical studies, "where little is certain, much is contested, and there is no shortage of reasonable alternatives, all dates are approximate, all opinions tentative, and all conclusions provisional; and those weasel words, 'seems,' 'appears,' 'probably,' 'perhaps,' and the like will run riot through the following pages."[108] Such conjectures continue in the different pictures given of the four gospels by biblical scholars.[109] Among them, Matthew stands out paradoxically and comprehensively as the "the church's gospel" and "the Jewish gospel."[110]

A sample reading of Clarke shows concerns with the influence of Matthew's text on religious and secular drama writers. For example, the description that king Herod was "exceedingly wroth" in Matt 2:16 "supplied the raging Herod of the medieval mystery cycles."[111] In some church plays, the fearful and angry Herod sent out attendants to strike clerics and worshippers in the audience.[112] Medieval churchgoers literally felt Herod's rage. In *Hamlet*, William Shakespeare mentions Herod along with a petulant deity from medieval plays named Termagant.[113] In this context, Hamlet invokes the name of Herod to warn against excessive rage during acting: "It out-herods Herod" (3.2.16).[114]

E. Dale C. Allison

After finishing a draft of his commentary on Matt 1–7, coauthored with W. D. Davies, the Matthean scholar Dale C. Allison observed how twentieth-century commentaries would often repeat questions and answers from nineteenth-century German commentaries.[115] The experience led him to a greater appreciation of patristic literature that offers "valid exegetical insights that the secondary literature, to its detriment, has forgotten."[116] Allison is persuaded that "the exegetical present is indebted to the exegetical past" and he promotes the use of older commentators.[117]

In *Studies in Matthew: Interpretations Past and Present*, he begins his study of the exegetical past with a critical look at the star the magi followed (Matt 2:1-2). Modern exegetes employ modern astronomy in their task and suppose that the star (ἀστήρ)

---

[107] Clarke, *The Gospel of Matthew and Its Readers*, xiii.
[108] Ibid., xvi.
[109] Ibid., xvi–xx.
[110] Ibid., xx.
[111] Ibid., 23.
[112] Ibid.
[113] According to Ebenezer C. Brewer, Termagant was "the name given by Crusaders and in medieval romances, to an idol or deity that the Saracens were popularly supposed to worship. He was introduced into the morality plays as a most violent and turbulent person in a long, flowing Eastern robes, a dress that led to his acceptance as a woman, whence the name came to be applied to a shrewish violently abusive virago." *Brewer's Dictionary of Phrase & Fable*, rev. and enlarged ed. (New York: Harper & Brothers, 1952), 900. See also Blanche Coles, *Shakespeare Studies: Hamlet* (New York: R. R. Smith, 1938), 147–8.
[114] Clarke, *The Gospel of Matthew and Its Readers*, 23.
[115] Allison, *Studies in Matthew*, 9.
[116] Ibid.
[117] Ibid.

is a planetary conjunction, a comet, or a supernova.[118] Allison, however, sees a major flaw in this eisegesis: assuming Matthew presupposes twenty-first-century scientific knowledge.[119]

Instead, Allison proposes that the star of Bethlehem should be interpreted as a guiding angel. Allison lists ancient texts "identifying or closely associating stars and angels" such as Ps 148:1-4, 1 En. 18:11-14, Joseph and Asenath 14:1-7, Rev. 1:20.[120] Yet this plausible interpretation of an animate heaven could not survive two major obstacles in history: (1) "guilt by association" with Origen who himself held that heavenly bodies were animated and endowed with souls and (2) the advent of modern astronomy.[121] Thus, this interpretation is largely forgotten in history. As it turns out, this equation of the magi's star with an angel provides a valid exegetical option. Without studying the exegetical past, one may not even be aware of such a reading's existence.

Allison, though concerned primarily with history of interpretation, does hint at some interest in other forms of reception. He notes how at times Christian artistic depictions of the nativity replace the star with an angel or display both.[122] So it turns out that this interpretation was not completely forgotten, at least in the visual tradition.

F. Rachel Nicholls

Another key figure in the application of *Wirkungsgeschichte* of Matthew is Rachel Nicholls. Her work, *Walking on the Water: Reading Mt. 14:22-33 in the Light of Its Wirkungsgeschichte* treats a specific passage in Matthew.[123] She first presents the disorganized state of NT studies in which some read the gospels as literary art while others search behind the text as if studying an artifact.[124] Next, she addresses the "larger task of bringing different methods into dialogue" through *Wirkungsgeschichte*.[125]

To develop her own understanding of reception history, Nicholls returns to Gadamer's metaphors of "horizon" (*Horizont*). The term does not simply describe one's thoughts and ideas, but "the total extent of what someone can envision from a particular point in space and time."[126] An individual's horizon is necessarily restricted and formed by "prejudices that we bring with us" (*Vorurteil*), but a horizon can

---

[118] Ibid., 17. See Colin J. Humphreys, "The Star of Bethlehem: A Comet in 5 BC and the Date of Christ's Birth," *TynBul* 43 (1992): 31–56; Mark Kidger, *The Star of Bethlehem: An Astronomer's View* (Princeton: Princeton University Press, 1999); Robert S. McIvor, "The Star of Messiah," *IBS* 24 (2002): 175–83.

[119] Allison, *Studies in Matthew*, 21.

[120] Ibid., 36–41.

[121] Ibid., 30–5.

[122] Ibid., 30. Christmas tree-toppers also promote this interpretation. An engraving from the 1840s depicts Queen Victoria and Prince Albert celebrating Christmas around a decorated tree, topped with an angel ornament. Emma Midgley, "Queen Victoria popularised Our Christmas traditions," *BBC Berkshire*, December 15, 2010, http://news.bbc.co.uk/local/berkshire/hi/people_and_places/history/newsid_9286000/9286971.stm.

[123] For another, later work that also similarly deals with a specific character in a passage of Matthew, see Nancy Klancher, *The Taming of the Canaanite Woman: Constructions of Christian Identity in the Afterlife of Matthew 15:21–28*, Studies in the Bible and Its Reception 1 (Berlin: De Gruyter, 2013).

[124] Nicholls, *Walking on Water*, 1–2.

[125] Ibid., 3–6.

[126] Ibid., 8.

change in shape through an encounter with the past.[127] Thus, Gadamer opposes the Enlightenment's "prejudice against prejudice" and believes in legitimate prejudices, perhaps better stated as "pre-judgments," "anticipations," or "pre-understandings."[128] Adaptation of Gadamer's ideas helps one preserve historical distance/differentiation and simultaneously avoid a naïve assumption that one's perspective is superior to others.[129]

The next stage is known as the "fusing of horizons" (*Horizontverschmelzung*), a term that implies the plurality of horizons. The second horizon is an attempt to understand the past from the present perspective. Beginning from the first horizon of the present, the second or "historical" horizon is projected before becoming fused back, much like the way "a piece of released elastic snaps back to its original shape."[130] This second horizon is "a scholarly ruse, an act of imagination to preserve the 'tension between the text and the present.'"[131]

Nicholls illustrates this idea through her own study of Peter. Her tradition has taught her that Peter is weak but relatable. Though this impression was strong, she realized that her perspective was limited and thus formed the first horizon. Then, once she understood Peter through the Protestant/Evangelical polemic against Orthodox and Roman Catholic traditions that promote his authority, she projected the second horizon. After this survey of ecclesiastical issues of authority and divisions, her old views on the "weak Peter" shifted, resulting in a "fusing of horizons."[132] She repeats the process and seeks multiple fusions of such a kind that allows her to explore many effects of the text.[133]

In her selection of "effects," Nicholls does not cover all historical periods and instead proceeds to look at "clusters of 'effects,' either within a particular historical period or produced in a particular medium."[134] This allows for a deeper analysis of the context in which the clusters exist, whether they have contributed to confessional or scholarly traditions.[135] While *Wirkungsgeschichte* does not resolve certain questions such as "What constitutes a good reading?" it precipitates the urgency of such an inquiry in the survey of diverse material.[136] Answering such questions of meaning necessitates critical methods, which *Wirkungsgeschichte* cannot replace or eliminate.[137] According to Gadamer, *Wirkungsgeschichte* does not discredit the ubiquitous "methodical spirit of science" or the "necessity of methodical work within the human sciences (*Geisteswissenschaften*)," but merely confronts the "objectives of knowledge."[138]

---

[127] Gadamer, *Truth and Method*, 306.
[128] Ibid., 270, 277; Evans, *Reception History, Tradition and Biblical Interpretation*, 3.
[129] Gadamer, *Truth and Method*, 302.
[130] Nicholls, *Walking on Water*, 10.
[131] Ibid., 10; Gadamer, *Truth and Method*, 306.
[132] Nicholls, *Walking on Water*, 11–12.
[133] Ibid., 13–14. These fusions are best "regulated" as "secondary acts" of interpretation in a series of encounters scheduled after historical exegesis. Evans, *Reception History, Tradition and Biblical Interpretation*, 46.
[134] Ibid., 21.
[135] Ibid., 21–2.
[136] Ibid., 22–3.
[137] Ibid., 24; Evans, *Reception History, Tradition and Biblical Interpretation*, 8.
[138] Gadamer, *Truth and Method*, xxix.

Without integrating the "history of effects" with exegesis, *Wirkungsgeschichte* is "simply an extra bolt-on procedure for exegetes: an interesting excursion, but no real help in reaching their destination."[139] To prevent such an aborted mission, both "definition" and "contextualization" must be accomplished together. The former involves "delineating the range of possible meanings in a text," while the latter "involves making sense of a text by connecting it with contemporary philosophical and theological tradition and culture."[140] These two tasks must become a "single reflexive process," with "definition" corresponding to the aforementioned projection of horizon and "contextualization," corresponding to the fusion of horizons.[141] In other words, it is not enough simply to list the many effects of Matthew in history. One must reexamine the text afterwards in one's own present tradition and culture.

To support this unity of the two tasks, Nicholls again borrows from Gadamer, this time his goal of "historically effected consciousness" (*wirkungsgeschichtliches Bewußtsein*). He used the term to describe both (1) the consciousness effected and determined by history and (2) the very consciousness of this phenomenon.[142] It is both open to effects of history and also brought into being by history.[143] The task of this consciousness is "to bring about the fusion of horizons in a regulated way."[144] Thus, Nicholls believes *Wirkungsgeschichte*-enriched exegesis will involve careful analysis of effects throughout history that becomes meaningful in the present.[145] The interpreter gets a glimpse of a text in action, inspiring and allowing him or her to experience both distance as a student and immediacy as a participant.[146]

G. Anders Runesson and Eve-Marie Becker

Anders Runesson and Eve-Marie Becker are the coeditors of the two-volume *Mark and Matthew*, "the teamwork of thirty-one scholars active in thirteen countries on four continents."[147] The goal of their project is to compare different perspectives in order to stimulate further research and deeper understanding of Mark and Matthew.[148] Whereas the first volume concentrate on "comparative analysis of the earliest Gospels in their first-century settings," the second deals with the two gospels' receptions in various settings across two millenniums and "specific issues raised by the diverse,

---

[139] Nicholls, *Walking on Water*, 24.
[140] Ibid.
[141] Ibid.
[142] Gadamer, *Truth and Method*, xxxiv.
[143] Ibid., xv.
[144] Ibid., 306–7.
[145] Nicholls, *Walking on Water*, 24.
[146] Nicholls termed this phenomenon the "hermeneutics of participation." Ibid., 27.
[147] Anders Runesson and Eve-Marie Becker, "Preface," in *Mark and Matthew II: Comparative Readings: Reception History, Cultural Hermeneutics, and Theology*, ed. Eve-Marie Becker and Anders Runesson, v–vi, WUNT 304 (Tübingen: Mohr Siebeck, 2013), v.
[148] Anders Runesson and Eve-MarieBecker, "Introduction: Reading Mark and Matthew within and beyond the First Century," in *Mark and Matthew II: Comparative Readings: Reception History, Cultural Hermeneutics, and Theology*, ed. Eve-Marie Becker and Anders Runesson, 1–12, WUNT 304 (Tübingen: Mohr Siebeck, 2013), 1.

culturally embedded hermeneutics involved in the production of meaning in different social, religious, political, and economic contexts."[149]

The editors further explain the ecumenical and reception-oriented nature of this second volume, *Mark and Matthew II Comparative Readings: Reception History, Cultural Hermeneutics, and Theology*. They presuppose that "the texts are silent, until we, their readers, give them voice," and that "meaning and use happen in the interplay between history and present, residing never in one place alone, but rather in the dynamic space embracing both text and reader."[150] Thus, Runesson and Becker invite reader-oriented approaches into scholarly dialogue with historical-critical approaches. Yet, considering the "radical diversity of opinions" with regard to both traditional and non-traditional approaches, "an overview of exegetical developments over time" may serve to place the different ideas and our own place in history into perspective.[151] The diverse interactions, however, span not only the centuries but also geographical locations. To expand the platform of study of the gospels and open up new ways of thinking about the texts and readers, scholars from different interpretative "guilds" and academic cultures are brought into conversation.[152]

These volumes present the fruits of these collaborative labors. In addition to Matthew's reception of the Markan gospel, the second volume also explores later writers' reception of Matthew.[153] For example, René Falkenberg observes how the author of *Sophia of Jesus Christ* rewrote, transformed, and incorporated the Great Commission in its prologue and the epilogue to grant the work an aura of authority.[154] Other chapters discuss receptions of Matthew found in works of Jerome, John Chrysostom, *Glossa Ordinaria*, twentieth-century Protestants, twentieth-century Catholics, and official church documents on Jewish-Christian relations.[155]

---

[149] Runesson and Becker, "Preface," v.
[150] Runesson and Becker, "Introduction," 2.
[151] Ibid.
[152] Ibid., 3.
[153] Eve-Marie Becker, "The Reception of 'Mark' in the 1st and 2nd Centuries C. E.," in *Mark and Matthew II: Comparative Readings: Reception History, Cultural Hermeneutics, and Theology*, ed. Eve-Marie Becker and Anders Runesson, 15–36, WUNT 304 (Tübingen: Mohr Siebeck, 2013), 25–8, 33.
[154] René Falkenberg, "Matthew 28:16–20 and the Nag Hammadi Library: Reception of the Great Commission in the *Sophia of Jesus Christ*," in *Mark and Matthew II: Comparative Readings: Reception History, Cultural Hermeneutics, and Theology*, ed. Eve-Marie Becker and Anders Runesson, 93–104, WUNT 30 (Tübingen: Mohr Siebeck, 2013), 93.
[155] Peter Widdicombe, "The Patristic Reception of the Gospel of Matthew: The Commentary of Jerome and the Sermons of John Chrysostom," in *Mark and Matthew II: Comparative Readings: Reception History, Cultural Hermeneutics, and Theology*, ed. Eve-Marie Becker and Anders Runesson, 105–19, WUNT 304 (Tübingen: Mohr Siebeck, 2013); Joseph Verheyden, "Reading Matthew and Mark in the Middle Ages: The *Glossa Ordinaria*," in *Mark and Matthew II: Comparative Readings: Reception History, Cultural Hermeneutics, and Theology*, ed. Eve-Marie Becker and Anders Runesson, 121–50, WUNT 304 (Tübingen: Mohr Siebeck, 2013); Martin Meiser, "Protestant Reading of the Gospels of Mark and Matthew in the 20th Century," in *Mark and Matthew II: Comparative Readings: Reception History, Cultural Hermeneutics, and Theology*, ed. Eve-Marie Becker and Anders Runesson, 151–67, WUNT 304 (Tübingen: Mohr Siebeck, 2013); Detlev Dormeyer, "A Catholic Reading of the Gospels of Mark and Matthew in the 20th Century," in *Mark and Matthew II: Comparative Readings: Reception History, Cultural Hermeneutics, and Theology*, ed. Eve-Marie Becker and Anders Runesson, 169–88, WUNT 304 (Tübingen: Mohr Siebeck, 2013); Anders Runesson, "Judging the Theological Tree by Its Fruit: The Use of the Gospels of Mark and Matthew in Official Church Documents on

III. Reception-Historical Approach to Matthew 2:16-18

The above survey of Matthean scholarship demonstrates the need to specify the reception-historical approach to be used for the current study. In this final major section of this chapter, the broad goal and task of reception-historical study, the organization of its contents, and the method of analysis will be defined, in preparation for a reception-historical study of Matt 2:16-18 in the remainder of this dissertation.

A. The Broad Goal and the Task

This dissertation will follow Nicholls in seeking as the goal a "historically effected consciousness." As stated above, it is (1) effected and determined by history and (2) the very consciousness of this phenomenon.[156] Throughout the following chapters, this consciousness will be essential in promoting an attitude of learning from the past and present receptions of Matt 2:16-18.

The task of the historically effected consciousness is "to bring about the fusion of horizons in a regulated way."[157] The entire process begins by recognizing the limitation of the present author's reading ("horizon") of Matt 2:16-18. Then, a second horizon is projected from this standpoint, involving a study of different traditions from the past or present. After projecting many horizons, the range of meanings of a text can be delineated ("definition"). Finally, the task requires a return trip ("contextualization") to the present, connecting the reception historically informed understanding of the text with contemporary philosophical and theological tradition and culture.

B. Organization

The goal and the task of reception history define the structure of the upcoming study. Chapter 2 will present a close reading of Matt 2:16-18, not to uncover meaning exhaustively from the present vantage point but to reveal this horizon's limitation. Personal prejudices will not be dismissed, but readily admitted and elaborated. The remaining chapters will be projections of the past and the present: studies of readings throughout history, beginning in the patristic period (Chapter 3) and proceeding chronologically to later periods. At the end of each chapter, there will be a review of receptions mapped out by a group of readers or within a specific epoch of time. The concluding chapter will constitute the return trip to the present, to connect the reception historically informed understanding of Matt 2:16-18 with the twenty-first-century philosophical and theological tradition and culture.

Jewish-Christian Relations," in *Mark and Matthew II: Comparative Readings: Reception History, Cultural Hermeneutics, and Theology*, ed. Eve-Marie Becker and Anders Runesson, 189–228, WUNT 304 (Tübingen: Mohr Siebeck, 2013).

[156] Gadamer, *Truth and Method*, xxxiv.
[157] Ibid., 306–7.

C. Method of analysis

The survey of receptions of Matt 2:16-18 will seek to avoid presenting a mere catalog of receptions. The present author intends to analyze the receptions critically and categorize the interpretative strategies. Because reception history itself is not a method, however, it cannot identify a "good" reading.[158] Thus, some scholars have indicated the need for the historical-critical methods to supplement reception history. Among them, John Lyons wishes to integrate historical-critical methods with reception history, as particular examples of receptions, while Robert Evans prefers to keep them separate.

Lyons is an example of the integration approach. He wants to advocate "wholesale relabeling of historical-critical methodologies with the terminology of 'reception history.'"[159] For example, redaction critics ought to recognize that Matthew is a real reader of Mark, while source and form critics must imagine audiences in their respective communities and *Sitze im Leben*.[160] The consequences of this yoking of reception history and historical criticism, however, reach beyond mere neologism. Adopting reception history spurns hierarchal first-stage and second-stage interpretations (i.e., treating historical-critical exegesis as foundational).[161] Without such a hierarchy, there is less chance that scholars will devalue those readings that are not formed according to their own values.[162] In addition, historical critics must admit their partiality when hypothesizing about the original audience and be aware of the "imagination's role within historical criticism."[163] Lyons is optimistic that "the broadening effect of adopting reception history's terminology offers real hope for NT studies, a discipline whose days at its current level may well otherwise be numbered."[164]

In contrast to Lyons, Evans prefers not to blur the lines between the historical-critical method and reception history. His aim is "to articulate the *distinctive* and significant role of historical-critical methodologies *within* the dialectic of a reception-historical approach."[165] He grounds this approach in Hans R. Jauss and Christopher Rowland.

Jauss articulates his proposal for the task of literary history in seven theses that allows for a proper evaluation of a work at its time of production and in historical reflection.[166] Among them, his sixth thesis is foundational to Evans: "The achievement made in linguistics through the distinction and methodological interrelation of diachronic and synchronic analysis are the occasion for overcoming the diachronic perspective—previously the only practiced—in literary history as well."[167] Here, Jauss applies Ferdinand de Saussure's distinction between synchronic linguistics (the study

---

[158] Nicholls, *Walking on Water*, 22–4; Gadamer, *Truth and Method*, xxix; Evans, *Reception History, Tradition and Biblical Interpretation*, 8.
[159] Evans, *Reception History, Tradition and Biblical Interpretation*, 43, n. 91.
[160] Lyons, "Hope for a Troubled Discipline?," 213–14.
[161] Ibid., 214–15.
[162] Ibid.
[163] Ibid., 215–16.
[164] Ibid., 217.
[165] Evans, *Reception History, Tradition and Biblical Interpretation*, 43, n. 91.
[166] Jauss, *Toward an Aesthetic of Reception*, 20–45.
[167] Ibid., 36.

of language at a specific time) and diachronic linguistics (the study of the evolution of language) to literary studies, a discipline in a state of flux in the 1960s.[168] At that time, Jauss opposed the dominance of diachronic approaches to German literary studies that did not judge the quality of the individual life and work of the writers.[169] To him, history of literature was simply "a chronological series of literary facts."[170] A better approach entails synchronically comparing and contrasting a certain literary work in its specific historical epoch with contemporary works to judge quality.[171] This way, synchronic evaluations of a work combined with the diachronic perspective to make "the literary horizon of a specific historical moment comprehensible."[172]

Christopher Rowland proposes a comparable plan. He champions a co-determinacy of meaning that comes from the text and the reader. He accordingly contests the temporal preference for the "original meaning."[173] He describes reception history as "an attempt to be truly diachronic and to appreciate the history of the text through time as a key to their interpretation."[174] For the synchronic component, he identifies in post-Enlightenment hermeneutics an interpretation in which "the exegesis of biblical texts was based on the relationship with texts which were contemporaneous with them rather than on the history of the way those texts had been interpreted within faith communities."[175] This historical comparison between a text and its contemporary texts is the *synchronic* complement to a *diachronic* reception history.

Following Jauss and Rowland, Evans understands the synchronic historical exegesis as coessential with the diachronic movement of reception history.[176] He is not merely interested in *the* historical-critical exegesis singularly focused on original meaning and context. He seeks multiple historical-critical exegeses of effects that appear throughout the reception history of a text.[177]

One could outline this process in a diachronic/synchronic matrix, resulting in diachronic horizontal "rows" of reception-historical epochs with the corresponding synchronic vertical "columns" of receptions. For example, under a row entitled "sixth century Syriac poet-theologians," receptions of Matt 2:16-18 by Jacob of Serugh and

---

[168] Evans, *Reception History, Tradition and Biblical Interpretation*, 37–8; Ferdinand de Saussure, *Course in General Linguistics*, ed. Charles Bally and Albert Sechehaye, trans. Wade Baskin (New York: McGraw-Hill, 1966).
[169] Hans-Roberts Jauss, "Limits and Tasks of Literary Hermeneutics," *Diogenes* 109 (1980): 96; Jauss, *Toward an Aesthetic of Reception*, 4–5, 36–9.
[170] Jauss, *Toward an Aesthetic of Reception*, 36.
[171] Ibid.
[172] Ibid., 37.
[173] Christopher Rowland, "Re-imagining Biblical Exegesis," in *Religion, Literature and the Imagination: Sacred Worlds*, ed. Mark Knight and Louise Lee, 140–9 (London: Continuum, 2010), 143.
[174] Roberts and Rowland, "Introduction," 132.
[175] Christopher Rowland, "A Pragmatic Approach to *Wirkungsgeschichte*: Reflections on the Blackwell Bible Commentary Series and on the Writing of Its Commentary on the Apocalypse," paper presented at Evangelisch-Katholischer Kommentar Biannual Meeting, Germany, March 21–3, 2004.
[176] Evans, *Reception History, Tradition and Biblical Interpretation*, 39.
[177] Nicholls's decision to study "clusters of effects" within particular historical periods could have allowed for synchronic exegetical analyses within a diachronic narrative framework. Nicholls, however, arranges historical-critical exegesis before reception history. Nicholls, *Walking on Water*, 13–14, 21; Roberts, "Introduction," 1.

Narsai would be listed. Then, the historical-critical method is used to compare and contrast the two poet-theologians and their receptions. Questions concerning these authors' identities, audiences, historical backgrounds, theological presuppositions, and genres are posed.

While there are strengths in both approaches, the Evans approach is preferred for the sake of clarity and the present author intends to use (1) reception history to identify influential readers and readings and (2) historical-critical methods to better understand their contemporary culture, time, place, and works. Such an approach offers a fruitful model for this book. It will attempt to move through the study of effects from Matt 2:16-18 diachronically through reception history. In addition, following Evans, it will stop at various points to study influential effects synchronically in relation to their contemporary culture, time, place, and works.

IV. Conclusion

This chapter has (1) highlighted the importance of Matt 2:16-18 in biblical studies and reception history, (2) presented the most important contributions in the field of reception history of Matthew, and (3) defined the present author's approach to Matt 2:16-18. The second chapter of Matthew and in particular verses 16-18 have potential for unique and diverse readings, as it introduces themes of death, suffering, tyranny, persecution, and marginalization into the traditional NT canon. Readers may turn to intratextual connections with Moses and Jeremiah, inquire concerning the tensions between the Matthean community and rival group, and investigate women's role within this community perhaps symbolized by the weeping Rachel. There are many provocative readings of Matt 2:16-18 to consider.

Reception history allows a regulated passage through that large span of Matthean readership. Biblical critics can be assured that reception history is sufficiently critical as it is not without scholarly rigor. In addition, reception history does not necessarily dispense with traditional historical-critical methods but can complement them, or even utilize them in fresh ways. At the same time, as a reader-oriented approach, reception history is also deeply concerned with actual (as opposed to ideal or implied) readers and audiences. While searching for influential readings, the reception historian must explore not only the major traditions but also learn from the marginal ones as well. To avoid a bias toward a major or a minor tradition, one must "attend" multiple summit-dialogues from different traditions before determining the most important readers and readings.

This chapter has also surveyed a number of recent works on Matthew that directly or indirectly use reception history (e.g., Ulrich Luz, Sean P. Kealy, Richard Trexler, Howard Clarke, Dale C. Allison, Rachel Nicholls, and the combined efforts of Anders Runesson and Eve-Marie Becker). The present work builds upon these contributions and their methodological approaches. Among them, Luz's principles are foundational. His analogy of effects and the interpreters as streams of water and boats that float upon them, respectively, primes one to identify a personal historical position instead of assuming an objective position.

Nicholls's adaptation of Hans Gadamer's goal of "historically effected consciousness" and the "fusion of horizons" is especially practical in setting this work's agenda. A learning attitude results from the realization that one's perspective is limited. Other perspectives, mostly from the past, are projected before being fused back into the present for reflection. In the midst of these projections, synchronistic historical-critical methods will be used to analyze the receptions of particular epochs, as suggested by Evans. The next chapter will consist of a personal close reading of Matt 2:16-18 that reveals the limitation of the present horizon and thus necessitates the journey of reception history.

2

A Close Reading of Matthew 2:16-18

Introduction

This second chapter is devoted to a close reading of Matt 2:16-18, which describes the massacre of the innocents. The passage will be analyzed phrase by phrase, not in an attempt to arrive at a definite position on authorial intention or exhaust the text's meaning from the present vantage point but to reveal possibilities of the text for imaginative and diverse interpretations.[1] To be clear, a text is not effective because it answers all questions readers bring to it but because of the "interpretative space" that is left by a text which later readers fill.[2] At a micro level, these potentialities arise mainly from Greek words, grammar, and syntax.[3]

This chapter will serve as a springboard to the later chapters. Even close perusals and multiple rereadings of Matt 2:16-18 will serve to reveal the limitations of the present author's historical horizon. As explored in the previous chapter, these boundaries may be largely formed by personal beliefs and/or procedural limitations (mainly from the historical-critical and the narrative-critical methods).

This chapter is an attempt at "exegesis without presuppositions," as prescribed by Rudolf K. Bultmann, which does not mean a neutral, objective stance on history. Instead, this approach entails exegesis without "presupposing the results of the exegesis" (based on dogmatism) or putting forth a specific methodology as the only one (based on methodological despotism).[4] An open admission that one's approach

---

[1] The approach taken in this chapter accords with the method used in Ian Boxall's chapter: "'I Was on the Island Called Patmos': Re-reading Rev. 1:9," in *Patmos in the Reception History of the Apocalypse*, 14–27.
[2] Ibid., 3–4.
[3] While consulting the Hebrew and the LXX versions of Jer 31:15 may be necessary, no attempt will be made to reconstruct a hypothetical pre-Matthean *Vorlage* or a catena of christological OT passages behind Matt 2:16-18. For discussion see Ulrich Luz, *The Theology of the Gospel of Matthew*, New Testament Theology (Cambridge: Cambridge University Press, 1995), 38; Maarten J. J. Menken, "The Quotation from Jeremiah 31 (38).15 in Matthew 2.18: A Study of Matthew's Scriptural Text," in *The Old Testament in the New Testament: Essays in Honour of J. L. North*, ed. Steve Moyise, 106–25, LNTS 189 (Sheffield: Sheffield Academic, 2000); Joseph A. Fitzmyer, "4Q Testimonia and the New Testament," *TS* 18 (1957): 513–37.
[4] Rudolf K. Bultmann, "Is Exegesis Without Presuppositions Possible?," in *Existence and Faith: Shorter Writings of Rudolf Bultmann*, trans. Schubert M. Ogden, 289–96 (New York: Meridian Books, 1960).

is not the only way in the study of Matt 2:16-18 expedites the prospective task of reception history: the need to learn from traditions of the past and present, familiar and foreign.[5] This learning process takes place through projections of past receptions, the task of chapter three and beyond.

I. Matthew 2:16-18 in Its Literary Context

Briefly stated, Matt 2:16-18 contributes to the overall understanding of Jesus's identity and mission. Yet, more can be said concerning the passage's unique and specific function in its literary context, concentrically in (1) the birth narratives (Matt 1-2), (2) Matthew 2, and (3) Matt 2:13-23.

A. Matthew 1-2

The structure of the birth narratives as a whole is crucial to a proper understanding Matt 2:16-18. In Matthew 1-2, Brown detects a fourfold division based on four important Christological questions.[6] The resulting outline is as follows: (1) Jesus's identity as the Son of David and the Son of Abraham, illustrated through the genealogy (*Quis*; 1:1-17); (2) Jesus's identity as the Son of God and Emmanuel, clarified through the account of virginal birth (*Quomodo*; 1:18-25); (3) Jesus's identity as the Son of David and the Son of Abraham, proved through birth in Bethlehem and the visit from the magi (*Ubi*; 2:1-12); (4) Jesus's destiny, which echoes the experiences of Moses and Israel in Exodus, set in motion by the hostility of his enemies, resulting in his movement from Bethlehem to Egypt to Nazareth (*Unde*; 2:13-23).[7] Therefore, Matt 2:16-18 contributes to the understanding of Jesus's destiny and further clarifies why Jesus, the Son of David, does not reside in Bethlehem.

B. Matthew 2

Matthew 2 is likely the combined result of two oral sources: (1) a story about the Magi and (2) a tradition recording Herod's response to the newborn king.[8] Yet Matthew retells

---

[5] Boxall, *Patmos in the Reception History of the Apocalypse*, 14.
[6] This scheme expands upon Stendahl's twofold outline that addresses two theological questions: (1) Who (*Quis*) is Christ (Matthew 1)? and (2) From where (*Unde*) does he come (Matthew 2)? Krister Stendahl, "Quis et Unde? An Analysis of Mt 1-2," in *Judentum, Urchristentum, Kirche: Festschrift für Joachim Jeremias*, ed. W. Eltester, 94–105, BZNW 26 (Berlin: Töpelmann, 1964).
[7] Brown, *The Birth of the Messiah*, 50–4.
[8] Soares-Prabhu, *Formula Quotations in the Infancy Narrative of Matthew*, 297–8; Jan van Henten, "Matthew 2:16 and Josephus' Portrayals of Herod," in *Jesus, Paul, and Early Christianity: Studies in Honour of Henk Jan de Jonge*, ed. Rieuwerd Buitenwerf, Harm W. Hollander, and Johannes Tromp, 101–22, NovTSup 130 (Leiden: Brill, 2008), 103; Steven Mason, *Josephus and the New Testament* (Peabody: Hendrickson, 1992), 97. For background information on Herod and the magi, see William D. Davies and Dale C. Allsion, *Matthew 1-7*, vol. 1, ICC (London: T&T Clark, 2004), 227–31; Abraham Schalit, *König Herodes: Der Mann und sein Werk*, 2. Auflage (Berlin: De Gruyter, 2015); Christian-Georges Schwentzel, *Hérode le Grand: Juifs et Romains, Salomé et Jean-Baptiste, Titus et Bérénice* (Paris: Pygmalion, 2011).

the stories in his own voice, pieced together with repeated Matthean vocabulary.[9] *Ubi* and *Unde* are appropriate section markers for Matthew 2, as the narrator shifts from messianic questions about "who?" and "how?" in Matthew 1 to questions of "where?" and "whence?" The Magi, Herod, the chief priests, and the scribes all seek the location of Christ (2:2, 4-6).[10] In addition, Jerusalem, Bethlehem, Ramah, Egypt, and Nazareth are locations of biblical importance, explicitly connected to the Scriptures (2:6, 15, 18, 23).[11]

Matthew's presentation of Herod as the prominent antagonist in chapter 2 is highly relevant to the study of Matt 2:16-18. His reactions to the magi mark the beginning of two key pericopae in this chapter (2:7-12, 16-18).[12] Scholars commonly identify this Herod as Herod the Great, who is thought to have died in 4 BC (2:19).[13] If the massacre is tied to his last year and the magi's star appeared at the birth of the Messiah (2:16), Jesus would be around two years old at that time.

Readers of Matthew first meet Herod as the king of Judea (2:1). Matthew provides insight about his emotional state, namely that he was disturbed (ἐταράχθη) at the thought of a rival king shared by the entire city (2:2-3).[14] Elsewhere in Matthew, the twelve disciples react similarly ("were disturbed" ἐταράχθησαν) in response to Jesus walking on the sea, initially thinking that they saw a ghost (φάντασμά) (14:26).

After consulting the chief priests and scribes to locate his rival (2:4-6), Herod ascertains the time that the star appeared (2:7, 16). The verb ἠκρίβωσεν reveals Herod's industrious investigation and malicious eagerness.[15] When he sends the magi to Bethlehem, he shows his duplicity, as he disguises his true colors by appropriating

---

[9] Examples of repeated Matthean vocabulary in Matthew 2 include ἀνατολή (2:1, 2, 9; 8:11; 24:27); βασιλεύς (2:1, 2, 3, 9); ἀστήρ (2:2, 7, 9); προσκυνέω (2:2, 8, 11, 4:9, 10; 8:2; 9:18; 14:33; 15:25; 18:26; 20:20; 28:9, 17); ἀκούω (2:3, 9, 22); ἀκριβόω (2:7, 16); πορεύομαι (2:8, 9, 20); ὅπως (2:8, 23; 5:16, 45; 6:2, 4, 5, 16, 18; 8:17; 8:34; 12:14; 13:35; 22:15; 23:35; 26:59); ἀναχωρέω (2:12, 13, 14, 22; 4:12; 9:24; 12:15; 14:13; 15:21; 27:5); πληρόω (1:22; 2:15, 17, 23; 3:15; 4:14; 5:17; 8:17; 12:17; 13:35, 48; 21:4; 23:32; 26:54, 56; 27:9, 35). See van Henten, "Matthew 2:16 and Josephus' Portrayals of Herod," 103. Note also repeated mentions of τὸ παιδίον and μήτηρ αὐτοῦ (2:11, 13, 14, 20, 21), which may demonstrate the "senselessness of Herod's paranoid brutality." Stanton, *A Gospel for a New People*, 182. Lastly, see Stephanie L. Black for discussion of Matthew's peculiar and frequent use of τότε (ninety times in Matthew; seventy-one times in the rest of the NT). Majority of the time (13/17, 76 percent) the τότε + subject + verb order in Matthew's narrative framework marks the beginning of a new theme or a section, as seen by the paragraph schemes in Nestle-Aland:[28] Matt 2:7, 16, 4:1; 15:12; 16:24; 17:19; 18:21; 19:27; 22:15; 23:1; 26:14; 27:3, 27. So then, this syntactical feature of Matthew is observed twice in Matthew 2. Stephanie L. Black, *Sentence Conjunction in the Gospel of Matthew: Sentence Conjunction in the Gospel of Matthew: καί, δέ, τότε, γάρ, οὖν and Asyndeton in Narrative Discourse*, JSNTSup 216 (Sheffield: Sheffield Academic, 2002), 218–53.

[10] Garland, *Reading Matthew*, 27–8.

[11] Daniel J. Harrington, *The Gospel of Matthew*, SP 1 (Collegeville: Liturgical Press, 1991), 46.

[12] See n. 9.

[13] Brown, *Birth of the Messiah*, 166–7, 205; Michael Grant, *Jesus: An Historian's Review of the Gospels* (New York: Charles Scribner's Sons, 1977), 71; James D. G. Dunn, *Jesus Remembered: Christianity in the Making* (Grand Rapids: Eerdmans, 2003), 324; Ben Witherington III, "Primary Sources," CH 17 (1998): 12–20; Harrington, *The Gospel of Matthew*, 45.

[14] The verb ταράσσω (to perturb) is found in various episodes in Josephus when Herod responds to threats against his rule (*War* 1:440; *Antiquities* 15:82; 16:75). van Henten, "Matthew 2:16 and Josephus' Portrayals of Herod," 114.

[15] Robert H. Gundry, *Matthew: A Commentary on His Literary and Theological Art* (Grand Rapids: Eerdmans, 1982), 30.

their pious words (cf. ἤλθομεν προσκυνῆσαι αὐτῷ in 2:2 with ἀπαγγείλατέ μοι, ὅπως κἀγὼ ἐλθὼν προσκυνήσω αὐτῷ in 2:8). This is the last word that Herod exchanges with the Magi, as they return via another route after meeting the Holy Family. All of these negative descriptions of Herod prepare the reader for his final act in Matthew: the massacre of the innocents (2:16-18).

Herod's woeful character is far-reaching in its influence. Scholars commonly note his symbolic significance as his response to the infant Jesus foreshadows Jewish leaders' response to the adult Jesus. For example, both Herod and they are "spiritually blind" (2:3; 27:63), "fearful" (2:3; 21:46), "conspiratorial" (2:7; 12:14), "guileful" and "mendacious" (2:8; 26:4; 28:13-14), "murderous" (2:13; 12:14), "wrathful" (2:16; cf. 21:15), and "apprehensive of the future" (2:16; 27:62-64).[16] Thus, oppositions and controversies surrounding Jesus's identity and mission are not limited to his ministry and crucifixion but reach back to his infancy.

In addition, Herod also prepares readers for Matthew's presentation of another, later Herod: Antipas.[17] When relating the account of the Baptist's death, Mark is careful to distinguish between Herod Antipas, who "feared John, knowing him as a righteous and a holy man, and protected him" (6:20) and his wife Herodias, "who held a grudge against John and wanted to kill him, but could not" (6:19). Herod Antipas in Mark appears conflicted about Baptist because "when Herod heard John, he was greatly perplexed yet he was listening to him gladly" (6:20). Matthew, however, only states that Antipas, "though he wanted to kill John, he was afraid of the people, because they held him as a prophet" (14:5). There is no fear or reverence of John himself, only antipathy. There is no lecture by the Baptist that befuddles Herod or delights him. Unlike Mark, Matthew's presentation of Herods, both Herod the Great and Herod Antipas, is unequivocally ruthless and violent.

C. Matthew 2:13-23

In Matt 2:1-12, the setting steadily moves from one location to another: the magi arrive in Jerusalem (2:1-8) and then proceed to Bethlehem after consultation with Herod (2:9-12). In Matt 2:13-23, the readers follow the action in a relatively frenetic pace. First, there is the move from Bethlehem (2:13) to Egypt (2:14-15). Then, the readers return to Jerusalem where Herod orders the massacre (2:16-18). After some time, readers accompany the Holy Family as they return from Egypt to Israel (2:19-21). Avoiding Judea, Joseph leads his family to Galilee, where they settle in Nazareth (2:22-23).

Even with all of these movements, there is a visible sandwich structure. The massacre of the innocents (2:16-18) is flanked by the Holy Family's departure to Egypt from Israel (2:13-15) and their return to Israel from Egypt (2:19-23). Deliberate repetitions of vocabulary and events are found in 2:13-15 and 2:19-23. The repetitions include (1) the

---

[16] Kingsbury, *Matthew as Story*, 46. See also Heil, *Death and Resurrection of Jesus*, 16; Garland, *Reading Matthew*, 30–31; van Henten, "Matthew 2:16 and Josephus' Portrayals of Herod," 104; Howell, *Matthew's Inclusive Story*, 119. See also Appendix A.

[17] For general background information on Herod Antipas, see Frederick F. Bruce, "Herod Antipas, Tetrarch of Galilee and Peraea," *ALUOS* 5 (1963/5): 6–23.

appearance of the angel in dreams (2:13, 19): "behold, the angel of the Lord appears in a dream to Joseph" (ἰδοὺ ἄγγελος κυρίου φαίνεται κατ' ὄναρ τῷ Ἰωσὴφ), (2) the angel's commands (2:13, 20): "saying: 'Rise up and take the child and his mother'" (λέγων· Ἐγερθεὶς παράλαβε τὸ παιδίον καὶ τὴν μητέρα αὐτοῦ), (3) the obedient reaction of Joseph (2:14, 21): "And he rose up and took the child and his mother" (ὁ δὲ ἐγερθεὶς παρέλαβε τὸ παιδίον καὶ τὴν μητέρα αὐτοῦ), and (4) the fulfillment of prophecy (2:15, 23): "what was spoken was fulfilled ... through the prophet(s)" (πληρωθῇ τὸ ῥηθὲν ... διὰ τοῦ προφήτου/τῶν προφητῶν).

The tone of 2:13-23 is markedly different as joyous worshipers from the East become Herod's enemies (2:10, 12, 16) and the focus shifts from a birth (1:18-25) to deaths and bereavement (2:13, 15, 16-18, 20).[18] The passage demonstrates Herod's savage nature and the reason why the magi could not return to him (2:12). The angel of the Lord predicts that Herod will make an attempt to destroy the child, justifying the Holy Family's escape to Egypt (2:13-15).[19] The next pericope (2:16-18) begins with the conjunction τότε, which connects this unit to the previous one (2:13-15), marks continuity of the topic (Herod's plot), and reintroduces participants from earlier (Herod and the Magi).[20]

II. Description of the Massacre (Matthew 2:16)

The portrayal of Herod in Matt 2:16 have promoted discussion in at least three ways: (1) the function of Herod's character in the narrative flow of Matthew, (2) similarities with other oppressors in Israelite history, and (3) comparisons with extra-biblical sources that describe Herod the Great. The first topic will be addressed in the subsection II. A, but the second and the third topics will be delayed until the following subsection (II. B), when the details of the massacre will be analyzed.

A. Τότε Ἡρῴδης ἰδὼν ὅτι ἐνεπαίχθη ὑπὸ τῶν μάγων ἐθυμώθη λίαν ...

While explaining the massacre's details would be sufficient to pass judgment on Herod's character, the narrator begins Matt 2:16 with a vivid glimpse of the king's psyche and emotion. Herod's plan to manipulate the magi fails, and he perceives himself as the mocked victim (ἐνεπαίχθη ὑπὸ τῶν μάγων) and orders the massacre in violent anger (2:16). This reaction is ironic, since he himself beguilingly hid his true intentions behind their pious words (cf. ἤλθομεν προσκυνῆσαι αὐτῷ in 2:2 with

---

[18] "Consequently, no one sings in Matthew's infancy narrative as they do in Luke's; instead they weep." Garland, *Reading Matthew*, 30.

[19] Adriana Destro and Mauro Pesce argue that the author is shaped by important cultural frames of "fight as the total annihilation of the adversary" (Herod's action) and "flight as a mechanism of salvation" (Joseph's reaction). "The Cultural Structure of the Infancy Narrative in the Gospel of Matthew," in *Infancy Gospels: Stories and Identities*, ed. Claire Clivaz, Andreas Dettwiler, Luc Devillers, Enrico Norelli, and Benjamin Bertho, 94–115, WUNT 281 (Tübingen: Mohr Siebeck, 2011).

[20] See n. 9 and Stephen H. Levinsohn, *Discourse Features of New Testament Greek: A Coursebook on the Information Structure of New Testament Greek*, 2nd ed. (Dallas: SIL International, 2000), 96–7.

ἀπαγγείλατέ μοι, ὅπως κἀγὼ ἐλθὼν προσκυνήσω αὐτῷ in 2:8). His anger is described with an intensifying adverb "exceedingly" (λίαν) and stands in contrast to Magi's "great joy" (χαρὰν μεγάλην) (2:10).[21]

According to Ross Chambers and Seymour Chatman, a narrator may comment on a narrative element in an attempt to either reinforce beliefs shared with the readers or to persuade them to agree with him or her.[22] Under narrative-critical analysis, this insight into Herod's internal state may be an example of narrator's commentary of the "judgment" type. This commentary is a moral evaluation, which "is supplied as a description of characters' attitudes which could have been deduced on the basis of their actions."[23] Even though Herod's rage could have been inferred from the resulting slaughter, Matthew provides an inside look into Herod's faulty values and rejection of Christ.[24]

Other narrative-critical insights are available by comparing Herod to other authority figures in Matthew, especially in the Passion narrative. For example, Herod can be compared with another king. The verb "mocked" ἐνεπαίχθη anticipates and contrasts with the mockery of Jesus in the Passion narrative (27:29, 31, 41).[25] Both Herod and Jesus face mockery in spite of their kingships, but the latter in a much more degrading manner (2:1; 27:27-31). Though the magi do not openly mock Herod, this king reacts in exaggeration while Jesus the true king does not retaliate or abort his mission (27:38-44). In addition, the excessive and emotional reaction of Herod to Jesus (ἐθυμώθη λίαν) anticipates the reaction of another ruler, Pontius Pilate. The latter is "exceedingly amazed" (θαυμάζειν ... λίαν) by the silence of Jesus amidst accusations (27:14).

B. καὶ ἀποστείλας ἀνεῖλεν πάντας τοὺς παῖδας ...

Matt 2:16 continues with the outworking of Herod's violent wrath. The word ἀποστείλας is connected with ἀνεῖλεν, because Herod accomplishes his killing through his sent agents.[26] Information that can be gathered from the verse includes (1) the

---

[21] Moisés Mayordomo-Marín, *Den Anfang Hören: Leserorientierte Evangelienexegese am Beispiel von Matthäus 1-2*, FRLANT 180 (Göttingen: Vandenhoeck & Ruprecht, 1998), 311. Elsewhere in Matthew, the adverb is used to describe the extreme heights where the devil tempted the adult Jesus (4:8), the terrible violence of the Gerasene demoniacs (8:28), and the profound amazement of Pilate as Jesus refuses to give a defense (27:14).

[22] Ross Chambers, "Commentary in Literary Texts," *Critical Inquiry* 5 (1978): 327-8; Chatman, *Story and Discourse*, 228.

[23] David B. Howell, *Matthew's Inclusive Story: Study in the Narrative Rhetoric of the First Gospel*, JSNTSup 42 (London: Sheffield Academic Press, 1990), 181.

[24] Ibid., 181-2.

[25] Carter, *Matthew and the Margins*, 86; Brown, *The Birth of the Messiah*, 204; Harrington, *The Gospel of Matthew*, 44; Joachim Gnilka, *Das Matthäusevangelium: I. Teil: Kommentar zu Kap: 1, 1-13*, 58, Bd. 1, HThKNT (Freiburg: Herder, 1986), 51; Gundry, *Matthew*, 35.

[26] The participle ἀποστείλας here is one example of the "graphic participles ... which express a concomitant or preceding action which is implicit in the verb to which they are added, certain idioms however adding such participles as a matter of course." Maximilian Zerwick, *Biblical Greek: Illustrated by Examples*, 9th reprint, SubBi 41 (Rome: Gregorian & Biblical Press, 2011), 126-7. See also Richard C. H. Lenski, *The Interpretation of St. Matthew's Gospel* (Columbus: Wartburg, 1943), 80.

one ultimately responsible for the massacre, (2) his character, (3) his target location, and (4) his target age. The victims are children, two years old and younger, located in Bethlehem and its vicinity. The age criterion is based on information gathered from Herod's interactions with the Magi.[27] Matthew spares his readers the gory details of the infanticide.

This tyrannical act is reminiscent of an older tragedy in Israelite history. Herod's act and the Holy Family's plight resemble Moses's birth narratives (Exodus 1–2) and accreted legends around the time of Jesus.[28] Aside from the journeys to Egypt, parallels include (1) protectors who defy the king (midwives and the Magi), (2) an unsuccessful attempt to kill one infant (Moses and Jesus), and (3) the killing of numerous infants.[29] To this list can be added the linguistic similarity of Matt 2:19-21 to Exod 4:19-20.[30] While it is difficult to pin down the exact intention of Matthew's typology, one may agree with Allison that Jesus as the "new Moses" or a "Moses-figure" possesses authority like his predecessor.[31] By extension, there are some similarities between Herod and the pharaoh in Exodus, since both attempt to do away (ἀνελεῖν) with their enemy (Exod 2:15 LXX).[32]

Besides discussions of literary features, some debate this massacre's historicity.[33] Richard T. France observes, "The detail in Matthew's story is perhaps the aspect of his

---

[27] See Appendix A for a list of commentators that attempt to explain the reasons behind the two-year calculation.

[28] Ibid.

[29] Pseudo-Philo's *Biblical Antiquities* 9.9-15 and Josephus' *Antiquities* 2:205-37 add the following details to the Moses story that have affinities with Matthew 1–2: (1) warnings through dreams to family members Miriam, pharaoh's daughter, and Amram; (2) an angelic mediator; (3) the etymological explanation of Moses's name that signifies his adult mission; (4) a note that the slaughter of innocents was actually carried out by the pharaoh; (5) a scribe who prophesies to pharaoh that a remarkable child will be born to abase the Egyptians; and (6) the mother's escape from danger. See also Harrington, *The Gospel of Matthew*, 47–8; Gareth L. Jones, "Jewish Folklore in Matthew's Infancy Stories," *Modern Believing* 52 (2011): 20–1; Christina Tuor-Kurth, *Kindesaussetzung und Moral in der Antike: Jüdische und christliche Kritik am Nichtaufziehen und Töten neugeborener Kinder*, Forschungen zur Kirchen- und Dogmengeschichte 101 (Göttingen: Vandenhoeck & Ruprecht, 2010), 211; Peter Wick, "Herodes im Matthäus-Evangelium: Messiasprätendent—Pharao—Antichrist," in *Herodes und Jerusalem*, ed. Linda-Marie Günter, 61–70 (Stuttgart: Franz Steiner Verlag, 2009); Ingo Broer, "Jesusflucht und Kindermord—Exegetische Anmerkungen zum zweiten Kapitel des Mattäusevangeliums," in *Zur Theologie der Kindheitsgeschichten: Der heutige Stand der Exegese*, ed. Rudolf Pesch, 74–96 (München: Schnell & Steiner, 1981), 83–7; For Jewish sources and legends in detail, see Louis Ginzberg, *The Legends of the Jews Volume II: From Joseph to Exodus* (Philadelphia: Jewish Publication Society, 1969), 243–72.

[30] Common words and phrases are τελέω; Αἴγυπτος; κύριος; "οἱ ζητοῦντες … τὴν ψυχήν"; and παιδίον. Allison, *The New Moses*, 142–4; Broer, "Jesusflucht und Kindermord," 84–5.

[31] Allison, *The New Moses*, 275–7; Richard T. France, *The Gospel of Matthew*, NICNT (Grand Rapids: Eerdmans, 2007), 82. Even Tadashi Saito, who disputes a Moses typology, does not deny the existence of resemblances, although he assigns them to a pre-Matthean tradition. *Die Mosevorstellungen im Neuen Testament* (Bern: Peter Lang, 1977), 18, 51–72. Daniel J. Harrington prefers to avoid the designation "new Moses," because it may imply that the "old Moses" is unimportant. Harrington, *The Gospel of Matthew*, 49.

[32] Davies and Allison, *Matthew 1–7*, 227; Garland, *Reading Matthew*, 30. For a work that deals with similarities between Jesus and David as seen in Matthew 2, see Brian M. Nolan, *The Royal Son of God: The Christology of Matthew 1–2 in the Setting of the Gospel*, OBO 23 (Göttingen: Vandenhoeck & Ruprecht, 1979), 38–46.

[33] See Appendix A for a list of works dealing with historicity of the event.

infancy narratives most often rejected as legendary."[34] Michael Grant labels the story as "myth or folk-lore," "invented, though it is based, in one respect, on what is likely to be a historical fact, since Jesus Christ was born in one of the last years of Herod's reign."[35] Opponents of its historicity insist that this massacre could not have gone unnoticed and point to the lack of extra-biblical corroboration. As Brown writes, "the double use of 'all' ('regions all around it') in this verse gives the impression of large numbers."[36] Macrobius's mention of the event (ca. AD 400) is sought as an independent support of its historicity, but it is more likely that Matthew influenced him.[37]

More significantly, Josephus makes no mention of this event, even though his interest in Herod's last years is plain.[38] Josephus, however, would likely agree with France that much of Herod's volatility comes from his "obsessive defense of his throne."[39] Herod eliminated anyone who posed a threat to him: his predecessors Antigonus and Hyrcanus, their supporters, and members of the Hasmonean family, including his closest relatives and wife.[40] He struggled with conspiracies, both real and imagined until the end of his life when he became ill and his tyrannical nature became especially apparent.[41] Perhaps the conspiracy that most closely resembles Matthew 2 is found in *Antiquities* 17:41-44, when Herod executed the Pharisees who predicted the cessation of Herod's government and the rise of Pheroras and his dynasty.[42]

These accounts convince France that Herod's execution of the children is hardly out of line with his character and the massacre is historically possible and not reported, considering that Herod's targets would be reasonably numbered around twenty at most.[43] These lower figures take into consideration Bethlehem's estimated population size, which may have been around one thousand, high infant mortality rates in antiquity, and annual birth rates.[44] So then, perhaps the event was forgotten or overshadowed considering Herod's greater evils in his last days. In addition, Nicolas of Damascus, Herod's friend and personal historian, may have excluded this account to salvage what is left of the king's denigrated reputation.[45]

---

[34] France, *The Gospel of Matthew*, 82.
[35] Michael Grant, *Herod the Great* (New York: American Heritage, 1971), 12, 228–9.
[36] Brown, *Birth of the Messiah*, 204.
[37] Macrobius, *Saturnalia* II, 4.11, ed. and trans. Robert A. Kaster, *Macrobius: Saturnalia Books 1–2*, vol. 1, LCL 510 (Cambridge: Harvard University Press, 2011), 348–9; Brown, *Birth of the Messiah*, 226.
[38] Brown, *Birth of the Messiah*, 226.
[39] France, *The Gospel of Matthew*, 84–5.
[40] Josephus, *Antiquities* 15:6, 8-10, 53-55, 173-78, 222-36, 247-51, 260-66; 16:392-94; 17:182-87.
[41] Ibid., 15:280-90; 16:387-94; 17:41-44, 148-50, 167 (cf. *War* 1.654-55), 174-78.
[42] Gnilka, *Das Matthäusevangelium: I. Teil*, 51. For discussions of similar cases of infanticide in other ancient literature, see Marie-Joseph Lagrange, *Évangile Selon Saint Mattieu*, Études bibliques, 3rd ed. (Paris: Gabalda, 1927), 34.
[43] France, *The Gospel of Matthew*, 85; David Hill, *The Gospel of Matthew*, NCBC (Grand Rapids: Eerdmans, 1981), 85; Paul L. Maier, "Herod and Infants of Jerusalem," in *Chronos, Kairos, Christos II: Chronological, Nativity, and Religious Studies in Memory of Ray Summers*, ed. E. Jerry Vardaman, 169–89 (Macon: Mercer University Press, 1998), 178, n. 25. See Appendix A for modern works that calculate the death toll.
[44] Brown, *Birth of the Messiah*, 204–5.
[45] Ibid., 226, n. 34.

C. Interpretive Possibilities of Matthew 2:16

Whether these tyrannical acts were widely known or not, a reader can safely conclude from Matthew 2 alone that this Herod is an evil king who acts violently to suppress his rival. While Jesus comes to save his people (1:21), shepherd his people (2:6), and give his life for others (20:28), Herod kills others to save himself.[46] While Jesus sends out the Twelve for acts of mercy at no cost (10:8), Herod sends out agents of destruction for selfish gains.

What seem less obvious are the specific logistics of the massacre, as described in Matt 2:16. Readers do not know the number of soldiers sent, method of execution, and, as discussed, the death toll.[47] Thereby, historical "interpretative space" is opened for later readers to fill.[48] Most modern interpreters attempt employ historical-critical methods to fill that gap by (1) asking whether the event is historically plausible and (2) speculating on numbers with the calculations of two years and the death toll.[49]

Another approach is to combine historical-critical methods with the narrative-critical method and hypothesize how biblical and extra-biblical works have informed Matthew. Recent commentators note parallels with the lives of OT figures and entities such as Moses, David, and Israel itself and look forward to the Passion of Christ and Jewish rejection and fate.[50] Herod's dominant role in Matthew 2 has some wondering about his continual symbolic significance beyond his likeness to the pharaoh of Exodus. Some commentators note parallels with the rebellious kings of Ps 2:1-3.[51] Others like Floyd V. Filson look elsewhere in the NT, to the red dragon of Revelation, ready to devour the child destined to rule all nations (Rev 12:1-6).[52] Such studies reveal concern for the text of Matthew, the world within the text, and other works of literature, biblical and extra-biblical.

A few scholars even venture beyond the text and arrive at atypical conclusions. In Frederick D. Bruner's eyes, Herod is an embodiment of human angst and need of God.[53] Even more specifically, Stanley Hauerwas warns against the fear that gripped Herod, which manifests itself in abortions and child abandonment.[54] Due to his background as a theological ethicist, Hauerwas provides insights that are different from typical biblical scholarship on Matt 2:16-18.[55] Thus, these two commentators demonstrate the

---

[46] Garland, *Reading Matthew*, 30.
[47] Gnilka, *Das Matthäusevangelium: I. Teil*, 51.
[48] Boxall, *Patmos in the Reception History of the Apocalypse*, 3-4.
[49] See Appendix A.
[50] Ibid.
[51] Ibid.
[52] Floyd V. Filson, *A Commentary on the Gospel According to St. Matthew* (London: Adam & Charles Black, 1960), 61. See also commentaries of Revelation that make similar connections, albeit without explicitly equating the dragon with Herod: Grant R. Osborne, *Revelation*, BECNT (Grand Rapids: Baker Academic, 2002), 462; John Sweet, *Revelation*, TPINTC (London: SCM, 1990), 196-7; George E. Ladd, *A Commentary on the Revelation of John* (Grand Rapids: Eerdmans, 1972), 169.
[53] Frederick D. Bruner, *Matthew: A Commentary*, rev. and exp. ed. (Grand Rapids: Eerdmans, 2004), 1:76.
[54] Stanley Hauerwas, *Matthew*, Brazos Theological Commentary on the Bible (Grand Rapids: Brazos, 2006), 41.
[55] See Boston Collaborative Encyclopedia of Western Theology, "Stanley Haeurwas (1940–)," accessed April 13, 2016, http://people.bu.edu/wwildman/bce/hauerwas.htm.

potential to explore deeper anthropological and moral issues in the person of Herod. They look beyond the historical-critical and narrative analyses to seek answers to ethical questions.

Yet Bruner and Hauerwas are exceptional in their focus on Herod. The interpretative imaginations of most commentators are often securely tethered to a Christ-oriented perspective. In their works, Herod is consistently juxtaposed with Jesus and subordinated to him. After all, Matthew is concerned with Christ's genealogy, birth, and plight. A reader, however, may encounter Matt 2:16 and speculate further about the slaughter's consequences and implications for the Holy Family. Eugene M. Boring imagines the story of the eighteen-month-old Davey, one of the twenty-one victims in Bethlehem, and his parents, Susanna and Jehoiachim, who later learn about the warnings heeded by Joseph.[56]

Readers may be challenged to provide comforting explanations.[57] In the wake of such wanton disaster, one might even pose a Johannine question: "Who sinned, these children or their parents, so that they were born to die so soon? (cf. John 9:1-2)."[58] Even after a rigorous application of the historical-critical methods and narrative-critical procedures, one must address "how the death of the children from Bethlehem can be justified for the sake of the rescue of the messianic child."[59] The following verses affirming scriptural fulfillment may hint at Matthew's own answer to this problem.[60]

III. Beginning of the fulfillment citation (Matthew 2:17)

Preliminary matters to be addressed before an in-depth analysis of Matt 2:17-18 include (1) an understanding of Matthew's "fulfillment citations," (2) their constituent parts, (3) their occurrences throughout Matthew, and (4) their special function in the birth narratives. First, the present writer prefers the title "fulfillment citation" over *Reflexionszitat*, *Kontextzitat*, and "formula citation," because it conveys what is most important to Matthew: fulfillment of Scriptures.[61] Since the thought processes behind

---

[56] Eugene M. Boring, "Matthew," in *The New Interpreter's Bible: General Articles & Introduction, Commentary, & Reflections for Each Book of the Bible Including the Apocryphal/Deuteronocanonical Books. Volume 8: General Articles on the New Testament; Matthew; Mark*, 87–506 (Nashville: Abingdon, 1995), 148.

[57] For example, Gundry turns to Luke for answers. He believes Matthew creatively reworked the material from the Lucan infancy narratives to fit his Moses typology. The slaughtered innocents and the bereaved parents correspond to the turtledoves (Luke 2:34) and the pierced heart of Mary (2:35), respectively. Thus, Gundry appears to hold to the view that the innocents are sacrifices offered to God for Christ's sake. Robert H. Gundry, *Matthew: A Commentary on His Literary and Theological Art* (Grand Rapids: Eerdmans, 1982), 34–5.

[58] William Hendriksen does not shy away from such issues. He first questions whether the victims are rightly called "innocents," because all are born with original sin. If they are truly innocent, their status comes from the merits of Christ. Secondly, Hendriksen opposes the idea that these parents are punished because they failed to acknowledge and pay homage to Christ. *Exposition of the Gospel According to Matthew*, New Testament Commentary (Grand Rapids: Baker, 1973), 180–1.

[59] "wie der Mord der Kinder von Bethlehem um der Rettung des messianischen Kindes willen gerechtfertigt werden kann." Gnilka, *Das Matthäusevangelium: I. Teil*, 52.

[60] Ibid.

[61] Luz, *Matthew 1-7*, 125, n. 1.

the various citations are the narrator's, they hold a special value to students of the Gospel.[62]

A fulfillment citation includes the following material (in order of appearance): (1) a conjunction (purposive ἵνα and ὅπως, or temporal τότε), (2) an aorist passive third person singular verb of "fulfill" (πληρωθῇ or ἐπληρώθη), (3) a substantive aorist neuter passive singular nominative participle of λέγω: "what was spoken" (τὸ ῥηθέν), (4) the agent(s) of the speech in a prepositional phrase: "through the prophet" or "the prophets" (διά...προφήτου or τῶν προφητῶν), (5) the act of prophetic speech: "saying" (λέγοντος), and (6) the placement of an OT text within the narrative and not within Jesus's speech.[63] Nine passages contain all of the six components while Matt 2:23 lacks the fifth part: "saying" (λέγοντος).[64] In five instances, either Isaiah or Jeremiah is specifically named as the prophet.[65] Twice "by the Lord" (ὑπὸ κυρίου) is added before the fourth component (1:22; 2:15). The stereotyped introductory formula probably originates from Matthew, who may have found inspiration from Mark (14:49; 15:28) and/or 2 Chr 36:21.[66] Many commentators propose theories concerning sources used by Matthew (Greek OT, Hebrew Bible, and/or Testimonia) and/or his own hand in the matter (friend of scribes, redactor, Targumist, and/or translator).[67]

While it is difficult to be dogmatic about pre-Matthean sources and the role of Matthew, some observations are in order about the final product as it appears in the Gospel. In diverse ways, all of the ten fulfillment citations relate to Christ and so appropriately and generally categorized as "Christological." Jesus's story was "an age of fulfillment, ordained and singled out by God," with Jesus and his Church corresponding to the Teacher of Righteousness and his Essene community in Qumran, respectively.[68] Thus, through christological fulfillment of Scripture, the Matthean community claims

---

[62] Donald Senior thinks the fulfillment citations are important "not because of their theology (scriptural fulfillment is characteristic of Matthew), nor even for their placement (scriptural fulfillment is asserted throughout the gospel in a variety of ways), but mainly because in these instances it is the narrator rather than other characters in the narrative world of Matthew who makes this recurring and fundamental affirmation." "The Lure of the Formula Quotations: Re-assessing Matthew's Use of the Old Testament with the Passion Narrative as Test Case," in *The Scriptures in the Gospels*, ed. C. M. Tucket, 89–115, BETL 131 (Leuven: Leuven University Press, 1997), 115. For a general discussion of Matthew's use of OT, see Stanton, *A Gospel for a New People*, 346–63; Morgens Müller, "The Reception of the Old Testament in Matthew and Luke-Acts: From Interpretation to Proof from Scripture," *NovT* 43 (2001): 318–21; Senior, "The Lure of the Formula Quotations," 103–8. Preexisting traditions and schools will not be assumed here. See n. 3.
[63] Matthew generally avoids fulfillment citations whenever Jesus himself speaks from the Bible. Otherwise, Matthew inserts prophetic fulfillment citations when appropriate. One exception is Matt 13:14. Luz, *The Theology of the Gospel of Matthew*, 39, n. 29. All of the passages Matthew cites are easily located save one: the Nazarene prophecy (2:23). For a discussion of 2:23 and the origin of its contents, see John C. O'Neill, "Jesus of Nazareth," *JTS* 50 (1999): 135–42.
[64] They are (1) Matt 1:22-23; (2) 2:15; (3) 2:17-18; (4) 4:14-16; (5) 8:17; (6) 12:17-21; (7) 13:35; (8) 21:4-5; and (9) 27:9-10. Stanton, *A Gospel for a New People*, 348; Davies and Allison, *Matthew*, 52; Luz, *Matthew 1-7*, 125–30. To these ten citations, Brown lists four more: Matt 2:5-6; 3:3; 13:14-15; and 26:56. However, he adds a qualification for each: "Imperfections in the formula create uncertainty as to whether this passage should be classified as a formula citation." Brown, *The Birth of the Messiah*, 98. I will deal with fulfillment citations that only contain all six components.
[65] Matt 2:17; 4:14; 8:17; 12:17-21; 27:9-10.
[66] Luz, *The Theology of the Gospel of Matthew*, 37.
[67] See Appendix A.
[68] Luz, *The Theology of the Gospel of Matthew*, 37.

legitimate continuity of Israel's legacy.[69] This fulfillment idea, merely incidental in Mark, is essential in Matthew, since a new program of Israel is initiated in Christ.

A. Fulfillment Citations in the Birth Narratives

Of the ten fulfillment citations, four appear in Matthew 1-2, in the short span of twenty-seven verses (1:22-2:23). Brown's explanation for this frequency is based on his comparison of the birth narratives with the Passion. While the Passion has been consistently studied "against an OT backdrop from the beginning of Christian preaching" and thus requires little didactic guidance, the readers need more help with Matthew 1-2. In other words, Matthew employed "the *nota bene* technique" and added the fulfillment citations often and early so that the readers may have a Scripture-oriented outlook to Jesus's life, especially his early years.[70] His residences in Bethlehem of Judea, Egypt, and Nazareth of Galilee are not merely logistic details but opportunities for deeper study.

The first two fulfillment citations (1:22-23 and 2:15) are closely related to the narrated action. Matthew summarizes the extraordinary events surrounding Jesus's birth (1:18-21) with the phrase, "everything happened" (τοῦτο ... ὅλον γέγονεν) in 1:22. This phrase is grammatically connected to the preceding passage through its use of the postpositive conjunction δέ. Another conjunction, the purposive ἵνα, begins the fulfillment citation of Isaiah who prophesied the virgin birth.[71]

Similarly, 2:14-15a summarizes Joseph's obedience to the angel's warning (2:13), his escape to Egypt with his family, and his sojourning there until the death of Herod the Great. In 2:15b, the formula citation once again begins with the purposive conjunction ἵνα. Jesus's geographical movement out of Egypt is the fulfillment of Hos 11:1.[72] While the Hosea's name is unmentioned, the prophecy's divine origin is explicit here as in 1:22 (ὑπὸ κυρίου). In both fulfillment citations, there is the verb καλέω, which testifies to divine presence in Christ and his sonship.

B. τότε ἐπληρώθη τὸ ῥηθὲν διὰ Ἰερεμίου τοῦ προφήτου λέγοντος

By 2:17, the reader has some idea about how a fulfillment citation works: an event relating to the life of Christ fulfills the ancient Scriptures. Much of 2:17 does not buck

---

[69] Ibid., 39-40. Brandon D. Crowe believes that the fulfillment citations display how the messianic king by his obedience reverses the sinful trajectories of Israel's history so that the eschatological blessings accrue to the messianic community. "Fulfillment in Matthew as Eschatological Reversal," *WTJ* 75 (2013): 111-27.

[70] Brown, *The Birth of the Messiah*, 98-101.

[71] Δέ is found six times in 1:18-25 to connect the sentences and signal a change in the subject. Such is its typical function. More than nine times out of ten (235/257, 91 percent) it is used to signal a subject switch in Matthew's narrative framework. In contrast, καί signals a subject change only 55 percent (183/335) of the time in the same framework. Black, *Sentence Conjunction in the Gospel of Matthew*, 167.

[72] Joel Kennedy believes that the Egypt referenced in Hosea 11:1 is not the literal Egypt, but a metaphorical one: Judea has become the oppressive Egypt in this phase of Israelite history. *The Recapitulation of Israel: Use of Israel's History in Matthew 1:1-4:11*, WUNT 2, Reihe. 257 (Tübingen: Mohr Siebeck, 2008), 131-5.

the trend, since it includes all six components of fulfillment citations. What is atypical, however, is (1) the appearance of τότε, as opposed to the purposive ἵνα or ὅπως; and (2) the mention of Jeremiah.[73]

Like the previous verse, 2:17 begins with τότε. When the conjunction precedes the subject and the subject precedes the verb (τότε + subject + verb), a new section commences, as in 2:7 and 16.[74] In 2:17, however, the verb precedes the subject (τότε + verb + subject). Thus, τότε in 2:17 does not function in the same manner as 2:7 and 16. Instead, within 2:16-18, verse 17 introduces OT material related to the event just described in 2:16.[75]

There is something else unusual about 2:17, since in eight of ten cases, either ἵνα or ὅπως begins the fulfillment citations. While the appearance of τότε does not signal a complete break from verse 16, the conjunction ought to be recognized for what it does not do: it does not connect 2:17-18 to 2:16 as a purposive clause as ἵνα or ὅπως would. In other words, while the tragedy is related to Jeremiah's prophecy, it did not occur *in order to* fulfill it.

This subtle use of τότε usually arrests the attention of commentators, who often conclude that Matthew is distancing God from the tragic event.[76] Their case for this understated attempt at theodicy is strengthened after studying Matt 27:3-10. In the midst of the Passion, Judas Iscariot regrets his actions (μεταμεληθεὶς) and returns the thirty pieces of silver to the chief priests and the elders (27:3).[77] He confesses his sin before them, but they refuse to help (27:4). He leaves the money and subsequently commits suicide (27:5). The chief priests take this "price of blood" (τιμὴ αἵματός) and use it to purchase "the Potter's Field as a burial place for foreigners" (τὸν Ἀγρὸν τοῦ Κεραμέως εἰς ταφὴν τοῖς ξένοις) (27:6-7). Matthew cites a tradition that prefers another title for the land: "Field of Blood" (Ἀγρὸς Αἵματος) (27:8).

These tragic events, which include betrayal, blood money, cold rejection, isolation, suicide, and the transaction, are not connected to the fulfillment citation in Matt 27:9-10 through the purposive clause ἵνα or ὅπως. Instead, τότε is in 27:9. Similar to 2:16-18, 27:3-10 begins with τότε in the initial verse and a second τότε within the passage starts a fulfillment citation of Jeremiah (27:9). The first nine words of 27:9 are in verbatim agreement with 2:17: "then was fulfilled the words which was spoken by Jeremiah the prophet who says" (τότε ἐπληρώθη τὸ ῥηθὲν διὰ Ἰερεμίου τοῦ προφήτου λέγοντος).[78]

---

[73] In fact, Matthew is the only book in the NT that explicitly mentions Jeremiah by name. See also Matt 16:14 and 27:9.
[74] See n. 9.
[75] Levinsohn, *Discourse Features of New Testament Greek*, 96-7.
[76] See Appendix A.
[77] In total, the verb μεταμέλομαι is found three times in Matthew, twice in the parable of the two sons and its explanation (21:28-32). The father commands his two sons to work in a vineyard. The first son initially refuses but afterwards changes his mind (μεταμεληθεὶς) (21:29). Unlike this son, the chief priests and the elders do not repent (μετεμελήθητε) (21:32). Strikingly, Judas shows more remorse than the Jewish leaders!
[78] Matt 27:9-10 has other interpretative challenges that will not be treated in detail. While the passage introduces a citation from Jeremiah, the primary reference is to Zech 11:12-13. It appears Matthew is thinking of Jeremiah's purchase of a field from Hanamel son of Shallum (Jer 32:6-15), but that transaction points to hope and restoration after exile. There is a dissonance between the field of Anathoth and the field of blood. See Knowles, *Jeremiah in Matthew's Gospel*, 15-16.

Taken together, Matt 2:17 and 27:9 contribute to a common idea. Concerning the unusual use of τότε, Allison thinks "the dual deviation from the usual form betrays a theological conviction," as Matthew "implicitly draws a distinction between what God foresees, permissively wills, and records in Scripture on the one hand, and what God actively wills and ensues will come to pass on the other."[79] As for "through Jeremiah" (διὰ Ἰερεμίου), Knowles builds his case for "the rejected-prophet motif" and "a unitary redactional purpose" that underlies the three passages that mention and/or cite Jeremiah (2:17-18; 16:14; 27:9-10).[80] More than christological, eschatological, or pedagogical purposes, references to Jeremiah have more apologetic/polemical function for the Matthean community in conflict with nonbelieving Jews.[81] Knowles argues that Matthew has highlighted the prophetic identity of Jesus as a Jeremiah-like figure "to underscore the spiritual obduracy and consequent responsibility of Israel with regard to the rejection of Jesus, on the one hand, and the destruction of Jerusalem, on the other."[82] John the Baptist, Jesus, and the Church share in the fate of rejected prophets.[83]

As early as Matt 1:11-12, there are invocations of themes from Jeremiah. The mere mention of Jeconiah in 1:11 would suffice to remind readers of the Babylonian exile, since his name is virtually synonymous with the cataclysmic event.[84] Yet Matthew proceeds further and cites the "deportation to Babylon" (μετοικεσία Βαβυλῶνος) as a key turning point in the genealogy (1:11, 12, 17). Another theme is the condemnation of Jerusalem.[85] Jerusalem is a city that rejects Jesus and shares Herod's dismay of a rival (2:3; 23:37) just as it rejected Jeremiah's oracles in the past.[86]

So then, Matt 2:17 has enough material to begin speculation on Matthean theodicy and the use of Jeremiah in the Gospel. Yet, judgment must wait until Matt 2:18 is analyzed. While Matt 2:17 contains five of the six components that make up a fulfillment citation, 2:18 contains the last component, the citation of Jer 31:15.[87]

---

[79] Allison, *Studies in Matthew*, 254–55.
[80] Knowles, *Jeremiah in Matthew's Gospel*, 95.
[81] Ibid., 161.
[82] Ibid.
[83] Ibid., 160–1. See Matt 5:12; 11:16-19; 21:33-46; 23:34-37. Luke also contains the rejected prophet motif, but Jesus's ministry therein more closely resembles the works of Isaiah, Elijah, and Elisha. See Roger Stronstad, *The Charismatic Theology of St. Luke: Trajectories from the Old Testament to Luke-Acts*, 2nd ed. (Grand Rapids: Baker Academic, 2012), 45–54; Joseph A. Fitzmyer, *The Gospel According to Luke I-IX: Introduction, Translation, and Notes*, AB 28 (Garden City: Doubleday, 1981), 213–15.
[84] See 1 Chr 3:16-17; Esth 2:6; Jer 24:1; 27:19-21; 28:4; 29:2.
[85] While Luke-Acts has the distinction of having the largest number of references to Jerusalem (about two-thirds of the occurrences appear within Luke-Acts, which makes up about one-third of the NT), it leaves open the possibility of its restoration, and there is no reference to Jeremiah. For further discussion, see J. Bradley Chance, *Jerusalem, the Temple, and the New Age in Luke-Acts* (Macon: Mercer University Press, 1988), esp. 115–38.
[86] For examples of passages where Jeremiah directly addresses Jerusalem and its sins, see Jer 4:14; 6:18; 8:5; 13:27; 15:5.
[87] See discussion above.

IV. Citation of Jeremiah 31:15 (Matthew 2:18)

The final element of the fulfillment citation formula is the OT text. Among the citations in the birth narratives, Matt 2:17-18 is the longest and perhaps the most perplexing in the entirety of Matthew.[88] There are various factors that contribute to the complexity. For example, scholars speculate whether Matthew makes use of a Hebrew or a Greek source and attempt to reconstruct Matthew's text of Jer 31:15 cited in Matt 2:18, which has both similarities and dissimilarities with the MT and the Septuagint (LXX).[89]

Whence Matt 2:18 may have come, it is now part of Matthew. The primary concern in the following discussion will be the function of Matt 2:18 in the infancy narratives and the rest of Matthew. Of immediate concern are (1) geographical difficulties, which arise from the non-proximity of Ramah and Bethlehem and multiple traditions about the location of Rachel's tomb, and (2) the tonal dissonance between the broader joyful context of Jeremiah 31 and the terrible gloom of this massacre. All of these issues will be addressed in what follows.

A. Φωνὴ ἐν Ῥαμὰ ἠκούσθη, κλαυθμὸς καὶ ὀδυρμὸς πολύς ...

The first words of Jer 31:15 in Matt 2:18 paint a picture of audible agony. The citation does not begin with "thus says the Lord," as found in LXX (οὕτως εἶπεν κύριος) and corresponding to the MT (כה אמר יהוה).[90] Since Matt 2:17 implies that God spoke through the prophet Jeremiah (τὸ ῥηθὲν διὰ Ἰερεμίου τοῦ προφήτου), the introductory formula is superfluous. Besides, just as he used the temporal conjunction τότε instead of the purposive ἵνα or ὅπως to distance God from the massacre, Matthew may have tactfully omitted those words. The omission serves to lay the emphasis on one voice, that of the grieving Rachel.

The tone of "voice" (φωνή) is largely dependent on the immediate context, since it is used elsewhere to describe John the Baptist's exultant voice in concert with Isaiah (3:3), and God the Father's heavenly voice of approval (3:17; 17:5). Here, "weeping" (κλαυθμός) and "great mourning" (ὀδυρμὸς πολύς) contextualizes the voice. "Mourning" (ὀδυρμός) is a rare word, occurring in only one other place in the NT (2 Cor 7:7).[91] "Weeping" (κλαυθμός), however, is found throughout Matthew. Every other

---

[88] France writes, "This is one of Matthew's most elusive OT quotations, and few claim with any confidence to have fathomed just what he intended, but the creativity which he displays in many of his formula-quotations perhaps encourages us to believe that in giving so prominent a place to Jer 31:15 he had more in mind than simply to point out that there was a precedent for sorrow arising out of the loss of children, even if we now lack the key to unlock the fuller meaning that some of his readers may have been able to draw from the quotation." *The Gospel of Matthew*, 88. See also Martin Hengel and Helmut Merkel, "Die Magier aus dem Osten und die Flucht nach Ägypten (Mt 2) im Rahmen der antiken Religionsgesschichte und der Theologie des Matthäus," in *Orientierung an Jesus: Zur Theologie der Synoptiker, Für Josef Schmid*, ed. Paul Hoffmann, Norbert Brox, and Wilhelm Pesch, 139–69 (Freiburg: Herder, 1973), 139.

[89] See n. 3.

[90] Jer 31:15 in the MT corresponds to Jer 38:15 in the LXX.

[91] In 2 Macc 11:6, when Lysias invaded Judea, Maccabeus, his companions, and the rest of the Jews "began begging the Lord with mourning and tears" (μετὰ ὀδυρμῶν καὶ δακρύων ἱκέτευον ... τὸν

instance of it in the Gospel is paired with "gnashing of teeth" (ὁ βρυγμὸς τῶν ὀδόντων) and describes the painful expulsion from the kingdom of heaven.[92] This terror is reserved for those who share the lot with hypocrites (τὸ μέρος ... μετὰ τῶν ὑποκριτῶν) (24:51) in the outer darkness (τὸ σκότος τὸ ἐξώτερον) (8:12; 22:13; 25:30) and the fiery furnace (τὴν κάμινον τοῦ πυρός) (13:42, 50). So then, Rachel's voice is closer to the voice of Jesus on the cross (27:46, 50), filled with agony and pain.

The voice's location is in Ramah, which is a stumbling block for interpreters. As commentators often point out, Ramah is located approximately six miles north of Jerusalem, while Bethlehem is about six miles south of Jerusalem.[93] Since the massacre occurs near Bethlehem, some wonder what Ramah has to do with the tragedy.[94] According to Genesis, Rachel was buried "on the way to Ephrath, that is Bethlehem" after giving birth to Benjamin (35:19; 48:7). These passages would affirm that Rachel's tomb is in Judah's territory. In another tradition, however, Rachel's tomb is located in Benjaminite territory, either at Zelzah or Ramah, where captives gathered before their transport to Babylon (1 Sam 10:2; Jer 31:15; 40:1).

Various solutions are offered. Some scholars surmise that the tomb originally existed in the north near Ramah, but Judah later appropriated it to enhance its prestige.[95] Joachim Gnilka thinks the move took place because Ephrathah was absorbed into the Bethlehem region (Mic 5:2) and all other matriarchs are buried in the land of Judah.[96] Yet, curiously, the citation of Mic 5:2 in Matt 2:5 does not mention this absorption.

In another place, Robert H. Gundry proposes the following: Matthew may have sidestepped the issue because he understood "in Ramah" (ברמה) as "in the height" (ἐν (τῇ) ὑψηλῇ or *in excelso*), as found in some Greek and Latin versions.[97] To strengthen Gundry's case, the Masoretes pointed the preposition (ב) in Jer 31:15 with sheva instead of a qamets, revealing their understanding that "Ramah" here is not a place name.[98] If God simply heard the voice "in the height" of heaven the geographical problem no longer exists.

Yet the LXX and Matthew himself clearly records "Ramah" not "heights." Whether Matthew opts for an etymological wordplay as in 2:23, made a geographical error, or did not care so much about exact locations is hard to determine. While "Ramah"

κύριον) so that a good angel might come to save Israel. For uses of the corresponding verb in extra-biblical sources, see MM, 439.

[92] See also Luke 13:28 where "weeping" (κλαυθμός) is again used in context of expulsion from the kingdom and Acts 20:37, where elders from Ephesus weep after Paul tells them that they would not see his face again.

[93] See Appendix A.

[94] One can make the case that the voice of the grieving Bethlehemite mothers, who are represented by Rachel, is so strident and loud that it is heard as far as Ramah, but Ramah's significance still requires explanation.

[95] Frederick M. Strickert, *Rachel Weeping: Jews, Christians, and Muslims at the Fortress Tomb* (Collegeville: Liturgical Press, 2007), 61–2; Jules F. Gomes, *The Sanctuary of Bethel and the Configuration of Israelite Identity*, BZAW 368 (Berlin: Walter de Gruyter, 2006), 92.

[96] Gnilka, *Das Matthäusevangelium: I. Teil*, 53.

[97] See Codex Alexandrinus, Codex Sinaiticus, Aquila, and the Vulgate. Gundry, *Matthew*, 35.

[98] Everywhere else in the MT the place name Ramah appears with the article. Jack R. Lundbom, *Jeremiah 21-36: A New Translation with Introduction and Commentary*, AB 21b (Garden City: Doubleday, 2004), 436.

creates some problems for interpreters (or interpretative space that offers interesting potential), the voice is undoubtedly full of gloom. Yet, one can be sure that the voice was heard (ἠκούσθη), "so that it reached the Lord."[99] The next part of Jer 31:15 provides more details about the voice.

B. Ῥαχὴλ κλαίουσα τὰ τέκνα αὐτῆς, καὶ οὐκ ἤθελεν παρακληθῆναι ὅτι οὐκ εἰσίν

In the second portion of Jer 31:15, the readers learn that Rachel is behind the voice. She is "crying over her children, and she does not want to be comforted, because they are no more." Some believe that certain words in Matt 2:18 function proleptically in the broader narrative of Matthew. For example, the mention of slain "children" (τὰ τέκνα) here may be foreshadowing the disaster that will befall the descendants of those who reject Jesus (27:25).[100] In addition, the use of "comfort" (παρακαλέω) in this sad context prepares readers for 5:4, where Jesus declares that "blessed are those who mourn, because they will be comforted (παρακληθήσονται)."

Like Herod before her, Rachel's symbolic significance is a topic of much debate. One question concerns whether Rachel represents the northern Israel or the southern Judah. Depending on the answer, she is weeping over either the eighth-century Assyrian captivity or the sixth-century Babylonian captivity.[101] If Rachel represents Joseph's sons, Manasseh and Ephraim, then she is a representative of the northern tribes. If, instead, her name is synonymous with the "Daughter of Zion," the emphasis may be on the southern kingdom.[102]

These options, however, may not be mutually exclusive. Jack R. Lundbom thinks that the words of Jer 31:15-17 may very well have been spoken to northern Israel originally, but had continual profound application and impact on exile-bound Judahites later.[103] Furthermore, every time her children suffer, as the innocents do in Matt 2:16-18,

---

[99] Johann A. Bengel, *Gnomon of the New Testament by John A. Bengel*, now First Translated into English with Original Notes Explanatory and Illustrative, trans. and ed. Ernest Bengel, Johann C. F. Steudel, and Andrew R. Fausset, vol. 1 (London: T&T Clark, 1858), 132.
    See also Jer 31:16-17, where God's response is given. *Pace* Richard J. Erickson, it seems unnecessary to wait until the voice of Rachel is answered by the voices of God (3:17) and John the Baptist (3:3). "Divine Injustice? Matthew's Narrative Strategy and the Slaughter of the Innocents (Matthew 2:13-23)," *JSNT* 64 (1996): 5–27.

[100] Whether Matthew purposefully translated בניה as τὰ τέκνα αὐτῆς or his *Vorlage* already did so for him is of little consequence. What matters is how these words prepare readers for the remainder of Matthew. Luz states that Matt 2:18 has "proleptic depth dimension." *Matthew 1–7*, 122. See Appendix B for a list of commentators who detect a foreshadowing of Jewish rejection of Jesus and its consequences. See also Eugene E. Park, who thinks that the "least of these" in Matt 25:40, 45 refer to the slaughtered children who are vindicated at the *Parousia*. "Rachel's Cry for Her Children: Matthew's Treatment of the Infanticide by Herod," *CBQ* 75 (2013): 473–85.

[101] Daniel A. Carson, "Matthew," in *The Expositor's Bible Commentary: Matthew-Mark*, ed. Tremper Longman III and David E. Garland, 23–670, rev. ed., Expositor's Bible Commentary 9 (Grand Rapids: Zondervan, 2010), 122; Brown, *The Birth of the Messiah*, 205–6; Lenski, *The Interpretation of St. Matthew's Gospel*, 81–2.

[102] Lenski, *The Interpretation of St. Matthew's Gospel*, 82. See Jer 4:31; Lam 2:1, 4, 10, 18.

[103] Lundbom, *Jeremiah 21–36*, 438. See also Barnabas Lindars, "'Rachel Weeping for Her Children'—Jeremiah 31:15–22," *JSOT* 12 (1979): 53.

Rachel weeps. Instead of citing Jer 31:15 out of context as Pierre Bonnard proposes, Mathew may be recognizing the typological significance of Rachel as a representative of all parents who grieve the loss of children.[104] Rachel gives voice to sorrowful people in three major moments of tragedy.

C. Interpretative possibilities of Matthew 2:17-18

If Herod is at the center of attention in Matt 2:16, Rachel functions the same way in 2:17-18. As Herod is characterized by rage, Rachel is a picture of sorrow. The uncertainty of her burial location sets the agenda for historical-critical discussions of geography, but Matthew clearly presents her poignant voice. It is her representative power that spoke for victims of Assyrian invasion originally and later allowed her to be recast in the Babylonian exile and the massacre of the innocents. Matriarch Rachel has been cast in three different tragedies in the history of Israel.

So then, if Sarah is a model of faith and holiness (Heb 11:11; 1 Pet 3:6), Rachel may be a model of intercession and sympathy. As the suffering, bereaved mother, she shares a pathos with Tamar, Rahab, Ruth, the wife of Uriah, Mary, and the marginalized members of the society like the bereaved parents of Bethlehem and the deceased children.[105] Since Rachel's cry is heard, others in dire straits can hope to be heard by God as well. She gives voice to the voiceless. Rachel is not unlike the outcasts and the weak of the society whom Jesus helps in his merciful role as the "Son of David."[106]

Less prominent, but nonetheless important, is the role of God the Father in this story. As Benedict T. Viviano writes, the study of God in Matthew is already fraught with difficulties, but it is even more pronounced in the infancy narratives, with its dearth of direct references to God.[107] Throughout the Gospel, the activity of God is usually veiled behind divine passives and the person of Jesus Christ.[108] Locating God's

---

[104] Pierre Bonnard, *L'évangile selon Saint Matthieu*, CNT 1 (Neuchâtel: Delachaux et Niestlé, 1963), 29.

[105] E. Anne Clements writes about the four women in the genealogy: "the inclusion of these women serves to signal the importance of those on the margins in the ministry of the Messiah and to anticipate Matthew's rhetoric concerning the broadening of Israel's boundaries to include Gentile outsiders." *Mothers on the Margin? The Significance of the Women in Matthew's Genealogy* (Eugene: Pickwick, 2014), 4. If these four women are marginalized, certainly Mary and Rachel can be categorized under the same heading. Mary is in danger of marginalization through divorce though she has done nothing wrong (Matt 1:18-25), and Rachel represents the bereaved parents.

[106] "Son of David" is not a title that simply brings to mind promises made to the political and military liberator of the past. Even if that was the expectation at the time, Matthew shows throughout his Gospel that "Son of David" is a champion of the simple, uneducated, and marginalized. As Luz finds, "Son of David" is modified from a political level to a human one. *The Theology of the Gospel of Matthew*, 70–5. Aside from the crowd, characters that recognize Jesus as the "Son of David" are four blind men (9:27; 20:30-31), the Canaanite woman (15:22), and children at Jerusalem (21:15). These characters are recognized by Jesus and appear in a positive light in contrast to the Jewish leaders who question, doubt, and fail to acknowledge Jesus by that title (21:15-16; 22:41-46). This ministry of margins is anticipated as early as verse one of Matthew when "Son of David" first appears.

[107] See Benedict T. Viviano, "God in the Gospel According to Matthew," *Interpretation* 64 (2010): 341–54.

[108] Viviano concludes, "Matthew is the gospel of Jesus the Emmanuel—God-with-us, the presence of the Transcendent in our world in a human way, horizontally, we might say." Ibid., 341.

intentions and his lack of activity in the massacre of the innocents is imperative in constructing a Matthean theodicy.[109]

This present author's search for a solution begins at the surface level of Matthew's text, but advances to the motifs and the fulfilled Scriptures. The motifs evoked are mainly the Exodus motif (Hos 11:1 in Matt 2:15 and 2:16) and the Exile motif (Jer 31:15 in Matt 2:17-18), which symbolize the greatest trials in Israel's history. In this single event narrated in Matt 2:16-18, Matthew ingeniously combines the Exodus motif with the Exile motif.[110]

To discover God's role in the massacre, one may explore parallels between Matthew 2 and the Exodus. In Exodus 2, Moses is rescued from danger and grows up in the pharoah's household. As an adult, he retreats from Egypt and settles in Midian. He marries Zipporah and has a son whom he names Gershom, being resigned to his fate as "a stranger in the land" (Exod 2:22). Exodus 2 begins with the infant Moses in Egypt, but it ends with him in Midian. Leaving behind Moses, the narrative shifts back to Egypt in Exod 2:23. While Moses lives on, the king of Egypt dies and the enslaved Israelites continue to cry out to God. Their cry goes up to God and he hears and remembers his covenant with Abraham, Isaac, and Jacob (2:23-24). God sees them and takes notice of them (2:25). Exodus 3-4 is the answer to those cries, as God prepares Moses for his return to Egypt.

If Moses is God's answer to Israel's cries and groans, then Jesus is more so. Just as the king of Egypt killed the children of Israel, Herod massacres the innocents of Bethlehem (Exod 1:22; Matt 2:16). In the same way that pharoah's death opened the way for Moses's return, Herod's death opens the way for Jesus's return.[111] The use of τελευτή and τελευτάω to describe Herod's death harmonizes with the description of pharoah's death, also reported twice (Exod 2:23; 4:18; Matt 2:15, 20). Just as the cries of the enslaved Israelites went up to God's ears, God hears the cry of Rachel (Exod 2:24-25; Matt 2:17-18).[112] Just as God's concern for the groaning Israel prompted Moses's return, God's concern for weeping Rachel prompts Jesus's return (Exod 3:1-4:31; Matt 2:19-23). So as Herod fits the role of the *pharaoh recidivus*, and Jesus is the new Moses, God hears the cries of his people and sends his deliverer.

Whether this answer to the theodicy question is the correct one remains to be seen. It is merely one attempt to bridge a need raised by the weeping Rachel whose voice beckons hearing: the God of Exodus sends his Son as the new Moses in reply. The method used employed some imagination after comparison of two texts:

---

[109] Since one conjunction (τότε) in 2:17 cannot explain the entirety of Matthean theodicy, Allison looks further on for themes such as "eschatological vindication" in the Beatitudes (5:3-12) and "Christological suffering" in the Passion narratives, where the innocent Son of God suffers just as the innocents. Allison, *Studies in Matthew*, 258-9, 263-4. See also Anna Case-Winters for a discussion of retributive justice, character building, human freedom, and divine love. *Matthew. Belief: A Theological Commentary on the Bible* (Louisville: Westminster John Knox, 2015), 38-9.

[110] Brown writes, "His ingenuity lies not so much in connecting the two events, as in relating them to what happened at Bethlehem." *The Birth of the Messiah*, 215.

[111] Kennedy, *The Recapitulation of Israel*, 120.

[112] If indeed Matthew is interpreting "Ramah" (רמה) as "heights" or the higher, heavenly plane where the voice of Rachel is heard, there is more agreement between Matt 2:18, Jer 31:15, and Exod 2:23. Gundry, *Matthew*, 35-6.

Exodus and Matthew. The fact that this passage may complicate convictions of God's benevolence is a major motivation for the present author. It is not far-fetched to suspect that Matt 2:16-18 has challenged other readers in history who also look to defend God's goodness.

V. Prospectus for Matt 2:16-18

This chapter began with the admission that the present author's readings of Matt 2:16-18 are largely informed and guided by basic presuppositions, such as the belief in God's goodness. The common title of this passage, however, begs the question of theodicy: "If God is good, how can he allow massacre of the innocents to take place?"[113] Studying Exodus and noting parallels between divine activity there and Matt 2:16-18 may produce one answer. It would be prudent to learn how others in history have wrestled with this passage to maintain, modify, or abandon their conviction that God is good.

Modern commentators and works of historical-critical and narrative-critical nature fill the "interpretative space" left by Matt 2:16-18. Such details include Herod's psychological state and the death toll. On the other hand, narrative critics discuss similarities between Moses and Jesus as well as anticipate the coming Passion. They maintain a close association with the person of Christ, as he is the main character of the Gospel. Yet, some scholarly works have moved peripherally out of the Christological focus of this passage to explore the symbolic significance of other characters like Herod. Whether there is similar potential with Rachel is worth exploring, since she has already served as a representative of two groups of exiles (Israel and Judah) and the bereaved parents of Bethlehem. Since Matt 2:16-18 spotlights "supporting actors" in the drama of Matthew, perhaps readers in its reception history can help in understanding how they fit into the greater story of Jesus, who is "God with us" (1:23).

---

[113] One can, of course, challenge the assumption that the children are innocent. Hendriksen, *Exposition of the Gospel According to Matthew*, 180.

3

Massacre of the Innocents in Early Patristic Tradition (Second to Fifth Century)

Introduction

This present reception-historical study of Matt 2:16-18 begins in the foundational early patristic period, lasting from the second to the fifth century. There are many works on Matthew to consider during this time. Matthew was prominent not only because it was regarded as apostolic in origin and the earliest gospel, but also because the early church found in it key passages for studying the Trinity, relationship of the OT with the NT, and the apostolic office.[1] With special attention paid to the Sermon on the Mount and the Great Commission in sermons, commentaries, and other works, one may venture to call this period "the beginning of Matthean priority."[2]

In addition to Christian works, certain post-NT Jewish writings may have relevance to this discussion.[3] Since the scope of this study, however, is circumscribed by Matt 2:16-18, certain methodical limitations are necessary. Only when Jewish literature on Rachel and Jer 31:15 has clearly influenced exegesis of the massacre will there be any mention of them. Tracing the line of influence and ascertaining the coexistence of NT and oral traditions can be a difficult endeavor.[4] It is assumed that Christian streams of traditions do not converge with others unless there is clear evidence to the contrary.

---

[1] Charles Kannengiesser, *Handbook of Patristic Exegesis: The Bible in Ancient Christianity*, The Bible in Ancient Christianity 1 (Leiden: Brill, 2006), 336–43; Graham N. Stanton, *The Gospels and Jesus*, 2nd ed., Oxford Bible Series (Oxford: Oxford University Press, 2004), 58–9.

[2] Already, a large number of secondary literature on Matthew overwhelmed Jerome. Thomas P. Scheck, "Introduction," in *Jerome: Commentary on Matthew*, trans. Thomas P. Scheck, 3–47, FC 117 (Washington, DC: Catholic University of America Press, 2008), 19–20, 56–7.

[3] For example, in some treatises on Genesis, Jacob buries Rachel on the way to Ephrath because he foresees that Israelites would need her intercession on their behalf when they are driven to exile (*'Ag. Ber.* 35:19; *Gen. Rab.* 82:11). At the Babylonian exile, the supplications of patriarchs and Moses fail to move God, but Rachel's pleas are heard by God as she appeals to her self-abnegation with regard to Leah's marriage to Jacob. God grants her request and promises the restoration of Israel (*Lam. Rab.*, Petiḥta, 25). If one opts for an earlier date of Targum Pseudo-Jonathan, the replacement of "Rachel" with "House of Israel" (בית ישׂראל) is also a tantalizing discovery.

[4] For example, D. Adolf Schlatter argues the following: the living community of faith in the first century believed that they were connected to the ancient patriarchs and matriarchs like Rachel, whose intercessory powers reach beyond limitations of space and time. Schlatter, however, cites support for such belief from *Lam. Rab.*, even though it is later than Matthew. *Der Evangelist*

As for Christian works, apocryphal and liturgical works exist alongside a large number of homilies, commentaries, and theological treatises. With so many works for exploration, it is difficult to predict what type of readings will be uncovered. While this chapter will not be exhaustive, best attempts will be made to fairly represent both major and minor traditions that have encountered this passage. All translations are the present author's unless otherwise indicated.

Both the synchronic historical-critical method and the diachronic reception history are crucial to this study. Synchronically, it is important to study the readings in respective historical contexts to see how they relate to their contemporary culture, time, and place and evaluate the worth of these readings in their unique historical horizon. Diachronically, the readings will be presented in the order of occurrence. The advantage of such an approach is that it will be easier to trace how many have received a particular reading of Matt 2:16-18. At the end of this chapter, the receptions will be reviewed and organized, in preparation for the following chapter. This process will be repeated in subsequent chapters, before a final encounter with the text of Matt 2:16-18 at the end of this work.

I. Major Strands of Reading

In the early patristic period, many works deal with the massacre as a whole, Herod as an individual, Rama as a significant place, the weeping Rachel, the victims, and lesser-known characters such as Herod's executioners and the victims' parents. Particularly prominent is discussion of Herod and the victims. The massacre as a whole is discussed in relation to Luke, Isaiah, and theodical discussions. Some compare Herod with other evil kings of the Bible, depicting him as a pawn of greater evil that ultimately ruins himself and those close to him. He becomes a symbol for later persecutors of Christ and his followers. The victims also receive much attention, mainly praised as martyrs and sacrifices offered to God. Finally, Rama's location concerns some writers, as do the reasons for Rachel's weeping.

II. The Massacre in Harmonization of Matthean and Lucan Infancy Narratives

With so much discussion on the massacre, the appropriate place to begin may be in its synoptic relationship to other events in the Matthean and Lucan infancy narratives. The ancient writers looked to harmonize Matthew and Luke as they addressed theological challenges to incarnation, differences between the two nativity scenes, and doubts about the massacre's historicity.

Matthäus: Seine Sprache, sein Ziel, seine Selbständigkeit: Ein Kommentar zum ersten Evangelium (Stuttgart: Calwer, 1929), 43–4. For a similar conflation of ideas derived from Jewish and Christian sources, see Mark F. Whitters, "Jesus in the Footsteps of Jeremiah," *CBQ* 68 (2006): 229–47.

A. Tertullian

In a polemical work, *de Carne Christi* (ca. 205) Tertullian (ca. 155-240) argues against Marcion, who likely held a Docetic view of Christ and a pessimistic view of the material world (1:2; 4:1-2).[5] Tertullian promotes the reality of Christ's flesh and his "two substances": both "born and unborn ... fleshly and spiritual ... weak and strong ... living and dying."[6] According to Tertullian, Marcion has denied Christ's nativity in order to deny his flesh, as the two of them are intimately connected (1:2).[7]

In 2:1-9, Tertullian mocks Marcion by listing the various characters and settings involved in the nativity stories of Matthew and Luke. While the heretic would likely do away with them, Tertullian mixes together and presents as a unit individual episodes found in both infancy narratives. He places the massacre episode after the events of Matt 1:18-2:12 and Luke 1:26-2:20, with the exception of events related to the Baptist's birth. He omits the flight to Egypt (Matt 2:13-15), perhaps due to the charges that Jesus fled in fear.[8] He inserts the massacre just before the circumcision, Simeon's blessing, and Anna's words (Luke 2:21-38). Gregory of Nazianzus and Jacob of Serugh present the massacre in their presentation of Christ's nativity in similar ways.[9]

B. Fragment 23

The second or third century author of *Fragment 23* harmonizes Matthew and Luke as Tertullian did, but uses a specific detail of Matt 2:16 ("from two years and under") for that purpose.[10] The magi did not appear immediately after Jesus's birth and the presentation at the Temple. Instead, they arrived two years later when the Holy Family was in Bethlehem, as they were "dwelling in the house of a stranger for many days." The rest of the fragment narrates the subsequent flight to Egypt, the massacre, and the return from Egypt.

Unlike Tertullian's reading, which simply lists the different nativity episodes, the author of *Frag. 23* exegetically attempts to reconcile the differences and chronologically organize the individual episodes. Eusebius of Caesarea and Epiphanius of Salamis make similar attempts.[11] The writer of *Protoevangelium of James* offers an alternative

---

[5] Geoffrey D. Dunn, *Tertullian*. ECF (London: Routledge, 2004), 37. Later, Augustine deals with Faustus and Manicheans who dismiss or deny the veracity of Matt 2:16 along with other nativity story episodes. See *Faust*. 22.62.
[6] Dunn, *Tertullian*, 37; See *de Carne Christ* 5:7.
[7] See also Origen, *Contra Celsium* 1.61.
[8] Hence, ancient writers give more space and ink elsewhere to the theological necessity of the flight. See Origen, *Contra Celsium* 1.61; Eusebius of Caesarea, *Proof of the Gospel* 9.4; Leo the Great, *Sermon 33: On the Feast of the Epiphany* 2; Fulgentius of Ruspe *Sermon 4: Concerning Epiphany, and Concerning the Murder of the Innocents, and the Gifts of the Magi*, 7; Eusebius of Caesarea, *Commentary on Psalm 72:15*; Chromatius, *Tractate 6 on Matthew 2:13-18*, 2; and Peter Chrysologus, *Sermon 150: Concerning the Flight of the Lord into Egypt*, 8.
[9] See Gregory of Nazianzus, *Oration 38:17* and Jacob of Serugh, *Prose Homily on the Epiphany*, 20-1.
[10] In GCS 12, the authorship of this Greek fragment is disputed between Eusebius of Caesarea and Origen. Thus, no conclusion can be established about its origins, except for a second or third century range. GCS 12: vii-ix, 25.
[11] See Eusebius of Caesarea *Quaestiones Ad Stephanum 16* and Epiphanius of Salamis, *Panarion 51.22.12-13*.

view: the star appeared before Jesus's birth so that the magi had sufficient time to travel and find him very soon after birth.[12]

III. The Massacre through the Lens of Isaiah 7-8

An early method of studying Matt 2:16-18 involves Isaiah 7-8. By claiming the titles therein, the inert Matthean Jesus is projected into the dynamic Isaianic warrior sovereign who arranges and participates in the events of Matthew 2. This empowering of Jesus through Isaiah is influential among the early readers of the massacre.[13]

The ancient writers may have found inspiration from the fulfillment of Isa 7:14 in context (Matt 1:23), so that some of them ventured to speculate on the fulfillment of other prophecies from Isaiah in the early life of Jesus. They may have also been spurred on by the frequency of fulfillment citations in Matthew 1-2, frequent citations from Isaiah in the rest of the Gospel, and the *Ascension of Isaiah*.[14] In addition to the name of Immanuel, which means "God with us," Jesus takes on the name of Maher-Shalal-Hash-Baz to signify Christ's might. Even though the role of the infant Jesus is quite passive in Matthean infancy narratives, these interpreters imbue Jesus with power and majesty even at his young age.

A. Justin Martyr

In Justin Martyr's (*ca.* 100-165) *Dialogue with Trypho* (*ca.* 160), Trypho the Jew argues that "the systemic meaning of the Scriptures is the law, while Justin argues that their systemic meaning is Christ."[15] *Dial.* 32-110 is the lengthiest section, where Justin explores Christological themes such as the two advents, divinity, death, and resurrection while offering arguments from the fulfillment of OT prophecies.

In chapter 78, Justin tells the events of Matthew 2 and Luke 2:1-7 without much deviation in content. He, however, adds that the Magi's actions prove Jesus's worth

---

[12] While the author of this fragment observes that the magi came to a house (Matt 2:11), the author of *Protoevangelium of James* narrates that the magi arrived at the cave. For second-century discussions of Jesus's birth in a cave (σπήλαιον), see Justin Martyr, *Dial.* 78.5 and *Protoevangelium of James*, 18-21.

[13] Typology in general was popular in the second century, especially when the types involve Jesus. Alan J. Hauser and Duane F. Watson, "Introduction and Overview," in *A History of Biblical Interpretation. Volume 1: The Ancient Period*, ed. Alan J. Hauser and Duane F. Watson, 1-54 (Grand Rapids: Eerdmans, 2003), 43. For a discussion of the complexity in defining and distinguishing between typology and allegory, see Frances Young, "Alexandrian and Antiochene Exegesis," in *A History of Biblical Interpretation. Volume 1: The Ancient Period*, ed. Alan J. Hauser and Duane F. Watson, 334-54 (Grand Rapids: Eerdmans, 2003), 335-8, esp. 337.

[14] For discussion of fulfillment citations in Matthew, see above Chapter 2, III. A. Following are the citations of Isaiah in Matthew: Matt 3:3 (Isa 40:3); 4:14-16 (Isa 9:1-2); 8:17 (Isa 53:4); 12:17-21 (Isa 42:1-4); 13:14-15 (Isa 6:9-10); 15:7-9 (Isa 29:13); 21:13 (Isa 56:7); and 24:29 (Isa 13:10). Either the whole of *Ascension of Isaiah* or its parts have origins in first and/or second century, contemporaneous with Justin Martyr and Irenaeus of Lyons. "Isaiah, Ascension of," in *ODCC*, 854-5.

[15] Bruce Chilton, "Justin and Israelite Prophecy," in *Justin Martyr and His Worlds*, ed. Sara Parvis and Paul Foster, 77-87 (Minneapolis: Fortress, 2007), 79; Erwin R. Goodenough, *The Theology of Justin Martyr* (Jenna: Fromman, 1923), 89.

as Christ. Before this chapter, Justin cites Isa 8:4 together with 7:10-17 and avers that Jesus fulfills this prophecy because he was born of a virgin, while Trypho and the Jews believe that the prophecy refers to Hezekiah who is born of a young woman (*Dial.* 43:6; 66:3; 71:3; 77:1). Justin agrees to Trypho's request for an explanation but first asks for proof that Hezekiah fulfills Isa 8:4 (*Dial.* 77:2). If the conquest of Damascus and Samaria in the presence of the king of Assyria takes place "before the child knows how to call father or mother," Hezekiah would be too old to qualify (*Dial.* 77:3).

Christ, however, does qualify because he fulfills Isa 8:4 at a very early age and subdues enemy nations as Lord.[16] To arrive at this reading, Justin matches the principal characters of Isa 8:4 with the principal characters of Matthew 2. According to typological interpretation, Herod's "wicked ungodliness" qualifies him as an antitype of the king of Assyria (77:4), while the magi from the orient correspond to the wealth and spoil of Damascus and Samaria.[17] Thus, the Magi's defiance against Herod fulfills Isa 8:4 (Matt 2:16).

Through this Isaianic typology, Matt 2:16 is no longer simply an outcome of the Magi's defiance of Herod. Even as infant Jesus wins the loyalty of Gentiles and orchestrates revolts against rival authorities. The main contribution of this particular strand of reading is that Christ is not a passive character in his infancy but combative against the king of Assyria, who is a type of Herod. Later, Pope Peter I, the author of the *Opus Imperfectum*, and Peter Chrysologus further this interpretation.[18]

B. Irenaeus

Irenaeus's (*ca.* 130–200) *Adversus Haereses* (*ca.* 185) is a meticulous attack on Gnosticism. In 3.16.1-6a he opposes the Valentinians and others who assert a multiplicity of "Saviors" and "Christs" by asserting the one and the same Christ attested by Matthew, Paul, Mark, Simeon (who appears in Luke 2:25-35), and accounts of the Passion and resurrection.[19] In 3.16.4, Irenaeus dwells on Simeon, with particular stress on his words in 2:29-32. After citing Simeon, Irenaeus expounds on the child's significance. He particularly focuses his revelatory work as the "light of men," described in terms of conquest similar to Justin Martyr's use of Isaiah 8:

---

[16] Goodenough, *The Theology of Justin Martyr*, 204.
[17] Justin specifies the Magi's origins "from the east" (ἀπὸ ἀνατολῶν; Matt 2:1) and matter-of-factly states that they are from Arabia (*Dial.* 77:4). Since Damascus is part of Arabia at one point in history, the magi represent both places (78:10). However, by coming to Jesus to worship him, the magi defied the "power ... that belongs to the wicked demon that dwells in Damascus" (δύναμιν ... τὴν τοῦ πονηροῦ δαίμονος, τοῦ ἐν Δαμασκῷ οἰκοῦντος ...) whose name "in parable ... one calls Samaria" (ἐν παραβολῇ ... Σαμαρείαν καλεῖ) (78:9-10). The adoration of the magi is not a mere diplomatic homage, but rebellion against spiritual authorities.
[18] See Pope Peter I of Alexandria's *Canons of Penitence 13*, *Opus Imperfectum: Second Homily*, and Peter Chrysologus's *Sermon 150: Concerning the Flight of the Lord into Egypt 9*.
[19] Matthew C. Steenburg, "Introduction," in *St. Irenaeus of Lyons: Against the Heresies: Book 3: Translated and Annotated with an Introduction and Further Revisions*, trans. Dominic J. Unger, 1–26, ACW 64 (New York: Paulist, 2012), 21.

The newborn whom he was carrying in the hands, Jesus the one born from Mary, confessing him as Christ, the Son of God, Light of men and glory of Israel, not only peace but also the refreshment for those who have come into rest. For already on one hand, he despoiled [ἐσκύλευε] men removing their ignorance, but on the other hand, as he was bestowing his own knowledge to them he was making booty [προνομὴν ἐποίει] of those who know him, just as Isaiah says, "Call his name: quickly despoil, swiftly plunder [Ταχέως σκύλευσον, ὀξέως προνόμευσον]." But these are the works of Christ.

Next, this conquering Christ is the same as the Christ adored by many in the infancy narratives. They include the shepherds, John the Baptist before birth, and the Magi. The Magi, whose gifts were mentioned earlier in *Haer.* 3.9.2, defy King Herod to follow the way of Jesus the eternal king. They also depart from their loyalty to the Assyrians:

Therefore, this same one was Christ; whom Simeon carrying was blessing the Most High; whom the shepherds beholding were glorying God; whom John while he was still in the womb of his mother and the other one in the womb of Mary, recognizing as the Lord, as he was leaping was saluting; whom the Magi beholding and worshipping and bringing aforementioned gifts and returning themselves to the eternal king through another way they went, no longer going back through the way of the Assyrians, since "before the child knows how to call father or mother, he will take the power of Damascus and the spoils of Samaria before the king of Assyria," secretly indeed, but powerfully disclosing that "with a secret hand the Lord was making war with Amalek."

While Irenaeus follows Justin Martyr in using Isa 8:4 to interpret the Magi's defiance as Christ's victory, the former does not interpret the "power of Assyrians," "Samaria," or "the king of Assyria" typologically. By citing Exod 17:16 (LXX), however, Irenaeus highlights God's covert battles against the nations that the infant Jesus subtly yet powerfully executes. The Lord conquers "with the hidden hand," which is understood to be the incarnate Word.[20]

Next, Irenaeus explains the fate of the slaughtered children. The victims belong to the Davidic house, fortunate to be peers of Christ, called martyrs (for the first time in reception history; see section IX. Victims as Martyrs below) and slain in accordance with Scriptures:

Wherefore he also removed the children who are in the house of David [τοὺς ἐν οἴκῳ Δαυίδ] who were fortunate to be born around that time, in order that he may send them ahead [προπέμψῃ] into his own kingdom, he himself being an infant

---

[20] Dominic J. Unger, trans., *St. Irenaeus of Lyons: Against the Heresies: Book 3: Translated and Annotated with an Introduction and Further Revisions*, ACW 64 (New York: Newman, 2012), 162, n. 37; D. Jeffrey Bingham, *Irenaeus' Use of Matthew's Gospel in Adversus Haereses*, Traditio Exegetica Graeca 7 (Leuven: Peeters, 1998), 114–15.

preparing infants of men to be martyrs on account of Christ who was born in Bethlehem of Judea in the city of David slain according to the Scriptures.

Here, the dark tone of Matt 2:16-18 is radically modified. Irenaeus extends his reading of Isaiah beyond the Christ child to the massacred children. The victims belong to the royal household due to their residence near and in Bethlehem, the town of David, and perhaps even their lineages royal, though Irenaeus does not specify. At any rate, he extends the Isaiah typology with the "house of David," so that the infants directly benefit from the promises of Immanuel and Maher-Shalal-Hash-Baz (Isa 7:2, 13).[21]

In addition, Irenaeus heads the long list of ancient writers who call the victims "martyrs." Christ, far from being passive, makes a "sovereign arrangement" to send his peers ahead into God's kingdom.[22] This key concept of "sending ahead" (προπέμπω) appears again later in *Haer.* 4.31.3 and 4.33.9 as Irenaeus presents the Church sending her martyrs ahead to heaven.[23] Thus, Irenaeus's triumphant Isaianic image of Christ includes a comforting commentary on the slain.

C. Jerome

In Jerome's (*ca.* 340-420) *Commentary on Isaiah* (*ca.* 410), Isa 7:15 provides an occasion to discuss the incarnation of Christ and his divinity (3.17). First, Jerome reviews Isa 7:14 and the need for the Davidic house to invoke the name of Emmanuel for salvation. Continuing to verse 15, Jerome adopts the phrase "he will eat butter and honey" to combat docetic views on Christ and reinforces this idea by citing Luke 2:52. Jerome navigates the verse and discovers the spiritual sense through an ecclesiological analysis of the OT, which pays attention to how a biblical passage speaks concerning the struggle of the Church.[24]

The next phrase, "to know to reject evil and to choose good," describes the infant Jesus's mental capacity. Human limitations do not circumscribe Christ's divine knowledge since "the infancy of the human body was not prejudicial to divine wisdom." On the contrary, he demonstrates the ability to choose good by inviting the shepherds from the field and the magi from the east (Luke 2:7, 12; Matt 2:1-12), while rejecting the evil Herod, the scribes, and the Pharisees "who for the sake of one infant have slaughtered many thousands [*multa parvulorum milia*] of newborns" (Matt 2:16). Jerome not only holds Herod responsible for the massacre, but also the scribes (Matt 2:4) and the Pharisees (though not mentioned in Matthew 1-2).[25]

---

[21] See a similar treatment in Jacob of Serugh, *Sixth Homily: Concerning the Star Which Was Seen by the Magi and the Killing of the Children*, in *Homiliae selectae Mar-Jacobi Sarugensis*, ed. P. Bedjan, 1:84–152 (Paris: Harrassowitz, 1905), 142. The present author is indebted to Nora Macabasag for her help in translation of this work.

[22] Bingham, *Irenaeus' Use of Matthew's Gospel in Adversus Haereses*, 156–7.

[23] Unger, *St. Irenaeus of Lyons*, 162, n. 38. See also Eusebius, *Hist. eccl.* 5.1.55.

[24] Aline Canellis, "Jerome's Heremenutics: How to Exegete the Bible?" in *Patristic Theories of Biblical Interpretation: The Latin Fathers*, ed. Tarmo Toom, 49–76 (Cambridge: Cambridge University Press, 2016), 74.

[25] Note the use of "qui" (nominative plural) and "trucidarunt" (perfect third-person plural of trucido).

In addition, he contrasts the one infant Jesus with the "many thousands of newborns." Whether this figure is a dramatic exaggeration or based on some data is unknown. Since interpreters embellish the victims with images from Revelation early and often (e.g., crowns and palms), the 144,000 figure may have influenced Jerome.[26]

Like Justin Martyr and Irenaeus before him, Jerome sees the nativity events through the typological lens of Isaiah. Beyond the prophecy of Isa 7:14, the verses in context such as 7:15 and 8:3-4 provide an opportunity to present an active infant Jesus through Christological analysis.[27] While Matthew 1–2 and Luke 1–2 are mainly concerned with active obediences of Joseph and Mary, respectively, an Isaiah-infused reading of Matthew 2 introduces the sovereign Immanuel and the despoiling Maher-Shalal-Hash-Baz. He does not sit idle, but works against Herod and works for the martyred victims of Matt 2:16. Later Augustine, Leo the Great, Fulgentius of Ruspe, and Quodvultdeus also observe this activity of Christ.[28]

IV. Theodical Explanations of the Massacre

The readings above indicate a deep concern of the early church to defend the goodness of the Christian faith. Still, some major theological conundrums remain unsolved as interpreters assert Christ's sovereignty over the Magi, Herod, the victims, and the massacre event itself. One may challenge God's character, as Jesus flees to Egypt while his peers perish. According to some, Christ ought to be blamed for the deaths of the children. For example, the author of the fourth-century *Acts of Pilate* lists his birth as the principal cause of the massacre (2:3), though, for whatever reason, he does not directly address the problem. For other writers, the role of Christ and God the Father is important in attending to the theodical discussions.

A. Gregory of Nyssa

In the twenty-ninth chapter of his *Catechetical Oration* (ca. 384), Gregory of Nyssa (ca. 335–395) grapples with the apparent delay of Christ's first advent. God's wisdom is similar to a physician who waits for the manifestation of the disease before applying the cure. In the same manner, God did not "apply the cure [τὴν θεραπείαν] to humanity" at the first sight of its depravity, when Cain murdered Abel. Further, God waited after the passing of wicked contemporaries of Noah, lawlessness of Sodom, belligerence of Egypt, the pride of Assyrians, and persecution of Jews. At the end of this series of sinful acts stands "Herod's lawless killing of children," along with other recorded and unrecorded acts of evil. Only after "the root of evil burst forth in diverse manners in the

---

[26] See discussion below and Rev 2:10; 3:11; 4:10; 7:9.
[27] Canellis, "Jerome's Hermeneutics," 74.
[28] See Augustine, *Sermon 373 on the Epiphany*, 3; Leo the Great, *Sermon 32: On the Feast of the Epiphany 2*, 1; Fulgentius of Ruspe, *Sermon 4: Concerning Epiphany, and Concerning the Murder of the Innocents, and the Gifts of the Magi*, 6; and Quodvultdeus, *Contra Iudaeos* 10.9-12.

intentions of men ... evil has reached the uttermost limit," and "no form of wickedness among men was not dared still," God applied the cure for humanity by sending his Son.

Interestingly, Matt 2:16 is the last specific manifestation of evil before the cure. The massacre is also the only definite event from the NT corpus Gregory mentions, as "the bloodthirstiness of the Jews against the saints of God" immediately preceding it likely refers to the persecution of OT prophets like Jeremiah. Gregory places Herod in the most nefarious and notorious company of evil in salvation history and arguably the worst of them all, because his wickedness at last leads to God's cure.

B. John Chrysostom

The first three sections of John Chrysostom's (*ca.* 349–407) ninth homily on Matthew (*ca.* 393) deal with Matt 2:16-18. Chrysostom is aware of various reactions to this passage, including charges of "injustice," "perplexity," and "madness." His initial answer is an analogical comparison of the massacre to Acts 12:18-19. There another Herod kills unjustly, his target the soldiers who unsuccessfully guarded Peter in prison though his escape was no fault of theirs. Herod Agrippa I should have prudently inferred from the strange circumstances that a supernatural event has taken place and that the soldiers were innocent. The tyrant does not sensibly submit to God who "leads [χειραγωγῆσαι] the king to the truth through these things" and "manage [πραγματευόμενον] all things to do good." Likewise, his predecessor Herod the Great is willfully stubborn despite the sufficient evidence from the chief priests, scribes, Micah, the star, and the Magi.

After proving that the wicked Herod is the culprit, there is still the issue of injustice, which eventually leads to the topic of suffering Christians. In the second section, Chrysostom swiftly provides an answer: "For whatever we may suffer from anyone, either God reckons to us that injustice for the dissolution of sins [εἰς ἁμαρτημάτων διάλυσιν] or for recompense of rewards [εἰς μισθῶν ἀντίδοσιν]." He illustrates this principle with a story of a servant greatly indebted to his master. When the servant is robbed, the master has the option of reckoning the loss of the servant toward what is owed to the master. Such a transaction is beneficial to the servant. The master could also recompense the servant beyond what he has lost. This grace would also be beneficial. In the same way that the master recompenses the victimized servant, God remembers the suffering believers.

Chrysostom cites 1 Cor 5:5 as an example in which death is beneficial to the sufferer. Furthermore, David's pious acceptance of Shimei's curse (2 Sam 16:11) and his enemies' animosity (Ps 25:18-19) results in catharsis that comes from unjust affliction. Lazarus also enjoyed the same benefits (Luke 16:19-31). Then Chrysostom (1) clarifies that the children are paragons of suffering of innocents who are rewarded and (2) assures his audience that God would not have removed them if they would have grown up to accomplish great deeds.

At the beginning of the third section, Chrysostom concludes his teaching on Matt 2:16. While there are other greater mysteries, the audience ought to trust God "by yielding such things to him" who "knows such things with precision" and "orders [οἰκονομῶν] them himself." Meanwhile, believers ought to bear pain nobly.

Chrysostom regards Herod as the one guilty of the massacre. Theodore of Mopsuetia also attempts to exonerate Christ this way.[29] Just as Peter should not be blamed for escaping the prison and Herod Agrippa's wrath, Jesus should not be condemned for escaping Bethlehem and Herod the Great's wrath. As for the victims, Chrysostom tells his audience that their suffering is like the righteous suffering in the Bible. Believers who experience similar pain can trust God who accurately decides the children's fate.

V. Herod in Comparison with Evil Kings of the Bible

In the minds of ancient readers of Matt 2:16-18, Herod is important as the proper locus of blame. Since Herod is not the first (or the last) political ruler to persecute the saints, he has drawn comparisons to other evil kings of the Bible, both implicitly with behavior corresponding with Joash's and explicitly with cited names, such as pharaoh, Saul, and the kings of Psalm 2. Owing to these typological associations, Herod stands in the long line of evil authorities.

A. *Protoevangelium of James*

The portion of *Protoevangelium of James* (PJ; *ca.* 145) that directly relates to the massacre is PJ 22-24, known as the "Secret of Zechariah" (*Apocryphum Zachariae*).[30] After the magi depart via another route in accordance to the divine warning, Herod becomes angry and orders the killing of those two years old and younger. From this starting point, the writer develops the story imaginatively, freely, and elaborately.[31] In this version of events, Mary is still in Judea and she successfully hides her child in an ox-stall. Elizabeth takes John and flees to the hill-country where a mountain opens and hides them. Meanwhile, her husband Zechariah is serving at the temple. There, Herod's officers who ask for John's location apprehend him. Zechariah replies that he is the servant of God in holy things who is constantly at the temple and he does not know John's whereabouts. The officers report this reply to Herod who is enraged and threatens Zechariah's life. At around daybreak the priest is slain and his congealed blood is found soon afterwards by the altar.[32]

---

[29] See Theodore of Mopsuetia's *Fragment of Matthew 9*.

[30] Apocryphum Zachariae may be a later addition or from a different source with post-second-century origins. James K. Elliott, *A Synopsis of the Apocryphal Nativity and Infancy Narratives*, NTTS 34 (Leiden: Brill, 2006), xii; Édouard Massaux, *The Influence of the Gospel of Saint Matthew on Christian Literature Before Saint Irenaeus Book 2: The Later Christian writings*, trans. Norman J. Belval and Suzanne Hecht, New Gospel Studies 5/2 (Macon: Mercer University Press, 1993), 227-8.

[31] In this manner, PJ, even though it is a prose, anticipates the use of *ekphrasis*, a descriptive method in which a preacher begins from a biblical passage and garnishes it with lively dialogues, monologues, and vivid descriptions. See discussion in J. H. Barkhuizen, "Romanos Melodos, 'On the Massacre of the Innocents': A Perspective on *Ekphrasis* as a Method of Patristic Exegesis," *Acta Classica* (2007): 29-50.

[32] This account is known by Pope Peter I of Alexandria and Ephrem the Syrian. See *Canons of Penitence*, 13 and *Commentary on Diatessaron*, 3.3.

At this point, strange signs take place (PJ 24:1-4). A voice is heard, "Zechariah has been slain, and his blood shall not be wiped away until his avenger comes."[33] The ceiling panels of the temple wail as fellow priests split their clothes from top to bottom. His body goes missing, but his blood turns into stone. When the news of Zechariah's demise spreads, all the tribes of the people mourn over him three days and three nights.[34] They appoint in his stead, Simeon, the man who was promised that he would not see death until he sees Christ in flesh (Luke 2:25-35).

This treatment of Zechariah the priest builds on Matt 23:35, which states the "righteous blood ... of Zechariah the son of Barachiah," was shed between the temple and the altar. This polemical statement is the climax of the seventh woe presented in Matthew 23 against the Jerusalem leaders.[35] While it is unclear whether the allusion refers to the post-exilic prophet (Zech 1:1) or the son of the priest Jehoiada (2 Chr 24:20-22), PJ uses the agreement in names to present John's father as a martyr. Appropriately, Zechariah replies to Herod who threatens him, "I am a witness of God" (Μάρτυς εἰμὶ τοῦ Θεοῦ) (23:3).

Zechariah and Herod renew a rivalry between wicked kings and the righteous prophets. This confrontation borrows from recurring strife between the OT saints and kings, who are types of NT kings and rulers who oppose Christ and the church saints. To be more specific: like Joash before him, divine vengeance looms over Herod for the righteous blood that is shed in the holy temple.

B. Ephrem the Syrian

While PJ implicitly shows Herod's likeness to evil OT kings by his behavior, Ephrem the Syrian (ca. 306-373) explicitly identifies and names wicked rulers of the past in his *Commentary on Tatian's Diatessaron* (ca. 369). Ephrem vests Herod with unflattering appellatives, such as "a seed of Canaan, and an Ashkelonite" (3.3).[36] He compares the king to Cain, Gehazi, and Judas Iscariot (3.5). In particular, Herod is "a second Pharaoh." He, like his predecessor, attempted to destroy the single Hebrew redeemer among other children (3.3, 5; Matt 2:16).[37] Like Moses, Jesus escapes to a foreign land until the king's death, and God hears cries of his people (Ex 2:15, 23-25; 4:19-20; Matt 2:13-21).[38]

Herod also follows the way of King Saul (3.3). Just as Saul persecuted David and the priests, Herod persecuted Jesus and the children. In the same manner in which Abiathar, who eventually supplanted the house of Eli, escaped the massacre of priests, John, the one who concludes OT prophecy, escaped the massacre of infants (3.3; PJ).

---

[33] See PJ 24:2. Translations of PJ and reference numbers are from James Elliott, *The Apocryphal New Testament: A Collection of Apocryphal Christian Literature in an English Translation* (Oxford: Oxford University Press, 1993).
[34] There seems to be some parallel with the Passion of Jesus as well.
[35] This idea is repeated in Luke 11:51, albeit in a different context.
[36] The English translations of Ephrem's commentary comes from Carmel McCarthy, trans., *Saint Ephrem's Commentary on Tatian's Diatessaron: An English Translation of Chester Beatty Syriac MS 709 with Introduction and Notes*, JSS Supplement 2 (Oxford: Oxford University Press, 1993).
[37] Cf. Josephus, *Ant.* 2.9.2.
[38] See Chapter 2 for detailed discussion.

Herod had enough knowledge to recognize Jesus as the Messiah, but he was blinded by jealousy like Saul, "who, when it was in the hollow of his hand [to have] a drink of David's blood for which he was thirsting, did not recognize that David was within his grasp" (1 Sam 24; 26) (3.4).

Thus, Ephrem the Syrian finds many typologies between evil OT kings and Herod. Gregory of Nyssa, the author of the *Opus Imperfectum*, and Quodvultdeus also look for such similarities.[39] By naming specific kings, they go beyond the implicit typology of PJ.

C. Augustine

In his *Exposition of Ps 48 (LXX 47)* (ca. 400), Augustine (ca. 354–430) dwells on the image of kings gathered at Zion (vv. 4-7). He locates a parallel idea in Psalm 2, which warns kings to acknowledge the divinely installed king destined to possess all of the earth. Kings of the earth have reason to fear losing their kingdoms "just as the wretched Herod feared, and for the child [*pro parvulo*] killed children [*parvulos*]."[40] Thus, these cowering kings of the Psalms are types of Herod. If Herod had adored Jesus along with the Magi, "he would not have destroyed the harmless [*innocentes perderet*] ones and perished as harmful [*nocens periret*] by wrongly seeking the kingdom."[41] Here, Augustine is not necessarily declaring the infants to be guiltless, but Herod is clearly at fault.[42] Herod in his folly is the antithesis of people who suffer the "pangs of repentance" and come together to the Lord's mountain to submit to his rule in the cornerstone, that is Christ (Ps 48:6; Isa 2:3; Eph 2:20). Augustine repeats the idea in his *Sermon 200 on the Epiphany*.

VI. Herod as a Pawn of Demonic Forces

While Herod is liable for the deaths, certain interpreters believe unseen forces are at work behind him. Specifically, as early as Justin Martyr, they thought demons stood behind him during the events of Matthew 2.

---

[39] See Gregory of Nyssa, *Oration on the Birthday of Christ* (Sennacherib, Nebuchadnezzar, Joash), *Opus Imperfectum: Second Homily* (Solomon's persecution of Jeroboam), and Quodvultdeus, *The Book of Promises and Prophecies of God* 1:32 (Pharaoh).

[40] Note the play on words. In the fifth century, Caelius Sedulius penned a hymn used on Vespers for Epiphany *Hostis Herodes Impie*, which begins by asking why Herod would fear Christ's coming. The hymn is a continuation of another hymn used for Lauds during the Christmas season, *A solis ortus cardine*.

[41] Note again the play on words.

[42] In *Conf.* 1.7.11, Augustine bewails the sin that plagues the universal mankind, even infants who live a short time. As innocent as they look, infants are not without evil desires. They are simply not capable of manifesting them yet. Augustine uses word play to explain: "The weakness of infant limbs is innocent, not the will of the infant" (*imbecillitas membrorum infantilium innocens est, non animus infantium*). In due time, the bodily powers of the child can adequately express the desires of the sinful soul.

A. Origen

In his *Contra Celsum* (*ca.* 248) 1.61, Origen (*ca.* 185–254) opines that Herod's futile conspiracy is credible "because wickedness is in a certain sense blind and wishing, as if it is stronger than fate, to conquer it [fate]."[43] He was "agitated by the blind and wicked devil" to slay the Christ child. Both Herod and the devil are blinded by their own wickedness so that they cannot perceive the shield over the infant Jesus, who is worthy to be king. This work contains one of the earliest mentions of Satanic activity behind Herod, an idea the author of the *History of Joseph the Carpenter*, Apponius, and Basil of Seleucia support.[44]

B. Optatus

Optatus (died *ca.* 385) is among the writers who broke the silence of Latin patristic works on Herod and his involvement on the slaughter.[45] In his *Sermon on the Festival of Holy Innocents*, he sharply contrasts the Magi's joy with the insane Herod's reaction: "Truly indeed the dejected Devil in Herod grieves over the church which is snatched away from his chasms and adjoined to God. However, with crafty subtleties he feigns himself as if he will adore the king, in order that he may kill the man mixed with God, if it could be done." The complexities of Satan's emotions are on display: his disappointment, grief, and self-delusional determination.

C. Jacob of Serugh

Jacob of Serugh's (*ca.* 451–521) *Second Homily on the Nativity* builds on the images of infant Christ's power and Satan's despair to narrate the plot to destroy the infant Christ. In line 215, the demonic counsel wonders, "If the new born babe subdues you, the great one, and you did not know Him, what will he do to us after a while, as you say?"[46] The evil one forms a detailed plot:

> Until the arrival of the Magi let us keep quiet about the affair but once they have arrived I will arouse the sword on account of them. I have envy and Herod has the sword. I will give him envy and he will give his sword also. I will murmur to him: "This child will be King, and He will carry off your kingship from you if you will disregard Him." I will secretly temper him with envy and I will intoxicate him and I will make him to sharpen the sword against the infant. I have wiles and means, guiles and treachery as well as the snares of iniquity and next of falsehood.

---

[43] Τυφλὸν γάρ τι ἐστὶν ἡ πονηρία καὶ βουλομένη ὡς ἰσχυροτέρα τοῦ χρεὼν νικᾶν αὐτό.
[44] See *History of Joseph the Carpenter* 8:1; Apponius, *Explanation of Song of Songs*; and Basil of Seleucia, *Oration 37 on the Children Who Were Killed by Herod in Bethlehem*, 2.
[45] M. J. Mans, "The Early Latin Church Fathers on Herod and the Infanticide," *Hervormde Teologiese Studies* 53 (1997): 94.
[46] The English translations of Jacob of Serugh's *Second Homily on the Nativity* are from Thomas Kollamparampil, ed. and trans., *Jacob of Serugh, Select Festal Homilies* (Rome: Centre for Indian and Inter-Religious Studies and Dharmaram, 1997).

> I will not be negligent, neither will I be silent, nor will I stay quiet from the new born, until I have subdued Him, if I can. (lines 251–62)

Another demonic being named "Error" follows the paradigm set by Satan and Herod by recruiting conspirators who will persecute Christ. Among them is "the daughter of Hebrews," likely a soubriquet for the Jerusalem leaders, responsible for all the righteous bloodshed upon earth (Matt 23:33-39). This recruiting prepares for the upcoming Passion of Christ:

> Error said, "As for me, I am concerned from now on about the infant and I am planning and plotting, and I will conquer Him. I have a dear friend who hates truth like me, the daughter of Hebrews, who loves to kill all kinds of good people. She is instructed in blood and sets her sword against the innocent. She is trained in deceit and is skilled in falsehood. I am proposing to her a way because she can perform all my desires and, as is the custom, she will encounter the child and put it to rest. She stoned Hur and through Aaron she cast the calf. She reviled Moses and threw Jeremiah into the well." (lines 277–86)

Thus, spiritual forces use human pawns in attempts to thwart Christ's works. Jacob envisions a counsel not unlike the one in Psalm 2, but demonic in its composition. Just as Herod shares with Jerusalem common anxiety concerning infant Jesus, multiple demonic forces coalesce to battle Christ's converting power.[47] Peter Chrysologus and Leo the Great also perceive the spiritual warfare behind Herod's plot.[48]

VII. Herod's Family Punished

A common belief was that Herod received his due penalty for his part in the massacre.[49] Some interpreters associate Herod's uxoricide and filicide with divine justice. Others heap the faults of Antipas and Agrippa upon Herod the Great. Either way, the result is a vilification of Herod that goes beyond his role in Matt 2:16-18.

A. Eusebius of Caesarea

In Eusebius of Caesarea's (*ca.* 260–340) *Ecclesiastical History* (*ca.* 324) 1, 8, the topic of discussion is Herod's plan to destroy Christ in the massacre. Eusebius attaches Josephus's account to Matt 2:16-18 like a denouement of the story:

---

[47] Jacob of Serugh repeats this idea in *Sixth Homily*, 141.
[48] Peter Chrysologus's *Sermon 150: Concerning the Flight of the Lord into Egypt* 9; Leo the Great's *Sermon 35: On the Feast of the Epiphany* 5; and *Sermon 36: On the Feast of the Epiphany* 6.
[49] See Origen, *Frag.* 32; Basil of Seleucia, *Oration 37 on the Children Who Were Killed by Herod in Bethlehem*, 2; Peter Chrysologus's *Sermon 152: Concerning Herod and the Infants*, 1–5, Augustine's *Exposition of Ps 48 (LXX 47)*; Quodvultdeus's *De Symbolo 3*, 4.15-18.

Now, the sacred scripture of the Gospel also teaches this, but it is worth noting in this connection the result of Herod's crime against Christ and those of like age with Him; for immediately, after not even a short delay [ὡς παραυτίκα μηδὲ μικρᾶς ἀναβολῆς γεγεννημένης], divine justice [ἡ θεία δίκη] overtook him while he was still in this life, exhibiting a prelude [προοίμια] of what was to be his lot after his departure hence. How, then, he beclouded the so-considered glories of his reign by the successive calamities within his household, by the foul murders of wife and children and of the rest who were especially close in family relationship and most dear to him, it is not possible to recount in detail now, for the account of these events, which Josephus has detailed at length in the history of Herod, overshadow any tragic drama. But it is better to hear from the words of the writer how, as soon as Herod plotted against our Saviour and the other infants, a scourge sent by God seized him and drove him to his death, according to words of him who write in Book 17 of the Jewish Antiquities as follows.[50]

Eusebius proceeds to cite various misfortunes of Herod and his family, according to Josephus's *Antiquities* and *Jewish Wars*.[51] While modern commentators have used Josephus's Herod to deny or question the historicity of Matt 2:16-18, Eusebius has linked them and formed a continuing narrative. Divine justice (ἡ θεία δίκη) is swift and immediate as the tragedies surrounding his family follow closely behind his destruction of many families of Bethlehem. Herod's punishment begins in his earthly life as a prologue to justice in the afterlife. Ephrem the Syrian, Macrobius, and the author of the *Opus Imperfectum* connect Matthew and Josephus in the same manner.[52]

B. *History of Joseph the Carpenter*

In the fourth- or fifth-century *History of Joseph the Carpenter* (HJC) 8:1, Satan takes counsel with Herod the Great, whom the writer of HJC fuses with Herod Antipas and credits with the beheading of John the Baptist.[53] Herod the Great seeks to kill Jesus supposing that his kingdom was from this world (8:2; cf. John 18:36). Joseph, warned in a vision, takes the Holy Family to Egypt for a year. Salome, initially skeptical, accompanies them and becomes the first witness of the virgin birth after the midwife and possibly the later follower of Christ (PJ 24:14-21; Mark 15:40; 16:1). They stay until worms eat Herod, "because of the blood he shed of the sinless little children" (HJC 8:3).[54] Again Herod the Great is amalgamated with another Herod, this time Agrippa

---

[50] The English translation of Eusebius is from Roy J. Deferrari, trans., *Eusebius Pamphili: Ecclesiastical History, Book 1-5*, The Fathers of the Church: A New Translation 19 (Washington, DC: Catholic University of America Press, 2005), 65-6.

[51] Josephus, *Ant.* 17.168-170, 187, 191; J.W. 2.1.656-60, 662, 664-65.

[52] See Ephrem the Syrian, *Commentary on the Diatessaron* 3:1; Macrobius, *Saturnalia* 2.4.11; and *Opus Imperfectum: Second Homily*.

[53] The dating of *History of Joseph the Carpenter* (HJC) ranges from fourth century to seventh century. James K. Elliott settles for an Egyptian provenance, within a fourth- to fifth-century time frame. Elliott, *The Apocryphal New Testament*, 111; Bart D. Ehrman and Zlatko Pleše, eds. and trans., *The Other Gospels: Accounts of Jesus from Outside the New Testament* (Oxford: Oxford University Press, 2014), 79; Elliott, *A Synopsis of the Apocryphal Nativity and Infancy Narratives*, xvi.

[54] The translations of HJC are from Ehrman and Pleše, eds. and trans., *The Other Gospels*.

I (Acts 12:23). Apponius, Pope Peter I of Alexandria, and Augustine treat the Herods similarly.[55]

VIII. Herod as a Symbol of Later Persecutors

Just as Herod is closely related to evil rulers of the OT and NT, his role is analogous to later persecutors of Christians, even those outside the Scriptures. At times, interpreters read their extra-biblical circumstances into Matt 2:16-18, a practice Christopher Rowland and Judith Kovacs describes as an "actualization" of the text.[56] While the passage can be simply a description of the past (typical of post-Enlightenment historical-critical methods), actualization either (1) moves beyond "one particular personage or circumstance" for comparisons with present circumstances and application or (2) allows the details of the passage to be reexperienced or reinterpreted.[57] The first type of actualization is the primary concern of the following interpreters.[58]

A. Origen

Currently, the portion of Origen's *Commentary on Matthew* (ca. 248) that deals directly with Matt 2:16-18 is missing, though it is possible that *Frag.* 23 belongs to it. Book 17, on Matt 21:23–22:33, however, does mention the passage. In 17:11, Origen comments on the farmers who plan to kill the heir, the son of the master of the house (Matt 21:38). These violent men are likened to Jews who do not perceive Jesus as Christ. They are conflicted concerning Jesus's identity, some believing him to be Christ, while others having questions about his origins (John 7:27). Based on the miracles alone, they are inclined to think that Jesus is from God just as the farmers could respect the owner's son. Yet, they do not confess Jesus as Christ, even though they know him and where he is truly from (7:28).

Even with knowledge of Christ's origins, they "plot [ἐπιβεβουλευκέναι] something worse against him." They act like Herod, who after learning of Christ's birth, found Bethlehem as the city of birth and recruited the magi to pinpoint the location of the child. Herod was "not ... faithless in every way" (οὐκ ... πάντῃ ἀπιστῶν) when he ordered the massacre, because he believed that Jesus was the prophesied Christ.

---

[55] See Apponius, *Explanation of Song of Songs*; Pope Peter I of Alexandria's *Canons of Penitence* 13; and Augustine's *Sermon 375 on the Epiphany*, 1.

[56] Judith Kovacs and Christopher Rowland, *Revelation: The Apocalypse of Jesus Christ*, Blackwell Bible Commentaries (Oxford: Wiley-Blackwell, 2004), 7–11.

[57] Ibid., 9–10.

[58] Actualization also differs from "decoding" since the latter interprets the symbolic language of the Bible with an eschatological focus while the former presents the struggles of the Church in a hostile world. Natasha F. H. O'Hear, *Contrasting Images of the Book of Revelation in Late Medieval and Early Modern Art: A Case Study in Visual Exegesis* (Oxford: Oxford University Press, 2011), 218. Later, Christopher Rowland preferred "analogy" over "actualization" to describe the process of illuminating current situation by means of a biblical passage. "The Interdisciplinary Colloquium on the Book of Revelation and Effective History," in *The Way the World Ends? The Apocalypse of John in Culture and Ideology*, ed. William J. Lyons and Jorunn Økland, 289–304, The Bible in the Modern World 19 (Sheffield: Sheffield Phoenix, 2009), 299.

In the same way, the Jews plot against Jesus even while recognizing him as Christ, just as Herod and the farmers plot against the infant Jesus and the son of the owner, respectively.

Thus, Herod's persecution of the infant Jesus foreshadows the Jews who persecute the adult Jesus later. Hilary of Poitiers, Ephrem the Syrian, Theodore of Mospuetia, Augustine, and Jacob of Serugh also make similar observations.[59] This early reading of Matt 2:16-18 anticipates modern narrative-critical readings that connect the Matthean infancy narratives with the Passion narratives.[60]

B. Hilary of Poitiers

Hilary (ca. 315–67/68), born in Gaul, was an educated convert from paganism, elected bishop of Poitiers ca. 350, and he subsequently became mired in Arian disputes.[61] Condemned at the Synod of Biterrae (356), Emperor Constantius exiled him to Phrygia for four years before he could contend for orthodoxy at the Council of Seleucia.[62] Even though the date of its writing is disputed, Hilary's commentary on Matthew has the distinction as the first full Latin commentary on Matthew with a nearly complete text.[63]

In chapter 1.6, Hilary juxtaposes the flight to Egypt with the massacre of the innocents near Bethlehem. This move of the Holy Family foreshadows the gospel's movement from persecuting Jews to ignorant pagans devoted to futility:

> While Herod was arranging the slaughter of the newborns, Joseph is warned by the angel to transfer him to Egypt, the same Egypt which is full of idols and venerates monstrosity of every kind of god. In the present, after the persecution of the Jews and the agreeing of the wicked common people in extinguishing him, Christ passes over to the people devoted to empty pieties and forsaking Judea, he who is about to be worshipped is presented to a world ignorant of him, while Bethlehem, that is Judea, is overflowing with the blood of the martyrs [*martyrum sanguine redundante*]. Indeed the fury of Herod and the killing of infants are a pattern of the Jewish people raging against Christians [*populi Iudaici in Christianos saevientis*

---

[59] See Hilary of Poitiers, *Commentary on Matthew* 1:6; Ephrem the Syrian, *Commentary on the Diatessaron*, 3:1–3; Theodore of Mospuetia, *Fragment 9 of Matthew*; and Jacob of Serugh, *Second Homily on the Nativity*, 277–86.
[60] Kingsbury, *Matthew as Story*, 46; Heil, *Death and Resurrection of Jesus*, 16; Garland, *Reading Matthew*, 30–1.
[61] "Hilary of Poitiers," in *ODCC*, 744; D. H. Williams, "Introduction," in *Hilary of Poitiers: Commentary on Matthew*, trans. D. H. Williams, 3–38, FC 125 (Washington, DC: Catholic University of America Press, 2012), 4.
[62] "Hilary of Poitiers," in *ODCC*, 744.
[63] At times, the Arian controversy has provided the lens through which Hilary's commentary on Matthew has been read. Modern scholars have theorized different conclusions from Hilary's texts and interpretations, ranging from vague acquaintance of subordinationist issues to full exposure to Arius's writings. Correspondingly, some scholars date the commentary closer to Hilary's exile while others date the work earlier in the decade. Even without pinpointing the exact year of its composition, the work is a helpful puzzle piece "in reconstructing the exegetical and intellectual history of the West during the 350s." Williams, "Introduction," 3–4, 21–3.

est forma], estimating for themselves that from the massacre of the blessed martyrs they are able to extinguish the faith and profession of the name of Christ among all.

Here, Hilary moves beyond Origen's narrative-critical linking of persecutors of infant Jesus and the enemies of the adult Jesus. Now the attention turns beyond the text to Jews in subsequent salvation history. The gospel moves past Israel, responsible for the "overflowing of martyrs' blood," to the ignorant Gentiles. In the present, the massacre of the innocents stands as a microcosm of ongoing antagonistic Jewish-Christian tensions. Just as Herod's plot fails to destroy Christ, however, the Jews' plan to destroy the Christians and their profession also fails.

This actualization of Matt 2:16 may not provide a comprehensive picture of Jewish-Christian relations in Poitiers, but one can observe at least Hilary's personal perspective on the Jews. Later in chapter 12.22, Hilary comments that the devil possessed Jews before the Law and after their rejection of Christ. Such charges lend credence to Venantius Fortunatus's biographical accounts of Hilary that depict him ignoring and avoiding Jews in public (*Vita Sancti Hilarii* 3). Hilary's treatment of Jews may have left a lasting harmful influence beyond the pages of his commentary.[64]

C. Lucifer of Cagliari

Not much is known concerning Lucifer of Cagliari before the 350s, when he emerges during the Arian controversies. When Athanasius of Alexandria was seemingly condemned at a church council at Arelate, Gaul (353), Pope Liberius asked Lucifer to request a new impartial imperial council.[65] The result, however, remained the same at the first session of Council of Milan (*ca.* 354). Lucifer opposed Athanasius's condemnation with such force that the Arians convinced Emperor Constantius to confine him for three days in the Imperial Palace.[66] His vehemence continued with haranguing polemical writings intended to provoke Constantius and court martyrdom.[67] Even after the succession of Julian led to his release in 362, he had no interest in reconciling with the repentant Arians at Antioch and consecrated the Eustathian Paulinus in opposition to Meletius, creating further schism.[68]

In his two-part work "On St. Athanasius" (*de S. Athanasio*; *ca.* 358), Lucifer's relentless diatribes include association of Constantius with the pro-Arian Constantine (whom he claimed was backed by the Devil and pursued harmful policies), Nero, and Maxentius (whom Constantine defeated at the Milvian Bridge).[69] Lucifer was not

---

[64] James E. Seaver, *The Persecution of the Jews in the Roman Empire (300-428)*, Humanistic Studies 30 (Lawrence: University of Kansas Press, 1952), 21.

[65] "Lucifer (bishop of Cagliari)," *Encyclopaedia Britannica Online*, accessed October 26, 2016, https://www.britannica.com/biography/Lucifer-bishop-of-Cagliari.

[66] Richard Flower, *Emperors and Bishops in Late Roman Invective* (Cambridge: Cambridge University Press, 2013), 84; "Lucifer," in *ODCC*, 1008.

[67] The letters are *de non conveniendo cum haereticis, de regibus apostaticis* and *de S. Athanasio*.

[68] "Lucifer," in *ODCC*, 1008.

[69] See I. 2:1-4; 29:20-27, 45-48; 43:3-4; II. 2:35-39; 14:74; 30:12. Flower, *Emperors and Bishops in Late Roman Invective*, 93–4. The full title of the work is "That no one while absent ought to be judged or condemned, or on Athanasius" (*Quia absentem nemo debet iudicare nec damnare, sive De Athanasio*).

above sarcasms, mocking Constantius as "most pious" (I. 30:12; II. 24:1), "most holy" (II. 4:32), "most fair" (I. 14:1), "most just" (I. 24:1), and "the most wise" (I. 6:20-21; 36:36; 40:41; II. 29:1; 6:39).[70]

In *de S. Athanasio* I, Lucifer probes the OT for figures and passages and weaves them together to depict Constantius as both imitator and heir of ancient evil (I. 20:10; 25:12).[71] The Scriptures have foretold the origins and the arrival of Arians and Constantius. Meanwhile, Lucifer and other anti-Arians belong to the "genealogy of orthodoxy" traced to the patriarchs.[72] In *de S. Athanasio* II. 3:45-53, Lucifer continues a similar line of thought with a comparison to Herod the Great:

> You will not be able to deny, such as it has been shown, to show you what concerns us, that the same Herod, with whom you are found to be partner [*esse inveniris college*] in butchering rage and in sacrilege and in regal dignity, we read about in the Gospel with regards to those who are killed as newborns for God, the son of God. You have found undoubtedly what is written about the cruelty of Herod, which now you deign to display [*quam nunc tu dignaris exhibere*], in the perspective of Matthew the Evangelist: "Herod, when he saw that he was tricked by the Magi, he was exceedingly enraged and sent to kill all the infants in Bethlehem and in all its boundaries from age of two years and below according to the time which he inquired from the Magi." Perhaps you do not notice yet you are the unjust one stirred against us who are workers of God, just as the Herod had stirred against those newborns [*sic te iniuste contra nos dei cultores motum, ut contra illos parvulos fuerit motus Herodes*]. Why do you deign to be dangerous to us? Indeed, because we confess ourselves as Christians who have not rejected what is just by being deceived by you who are overburdened with accusations.

Lucifer, like Origen before him and Hilary of Poitiers his contemporary, reads the massacre account with Herod filling the role of the persecutor(s) and the victims as the persecuted Christians. While Origen and Hilary are general in their polemics, targeting the Jewish population, Lucifer directly assaults a specific individual in political authority. The persecution pattern that began early in Christ's life continues in the fourth-century church life through actualizations of Matt 2:16.

D. Gregory of Nazianzus

In two separate works, Gregory of Nazianzus (*ca.* 329-390) discredits the immature and his contemporary rivals. In the theological poem on *Cursory Definitions* ('Ὀροι παχυμερεῖς), elements of the nativity story signify greater concepts for those learning

---

[70] Flower, *Emperors and Bishops in Late Roman Invective*, 100-4.
[71] Ibid., 110-11. The references include the serpent, Cain, Saul, Jezebel, Ahab, and Rabshakeh. The order of the quotations matches the order of the OT. See also II. 20:30.
[72] Flower, *Emperors and Bishops in Late Roman Invective*, 201-3. See I. 5:13-14; 6:3; 11:22-23; 40:73-74; 43:23-24; II. 3:21; 29:18; 34:48-49.

the Scriptures.[73] For example, the running star signifies creation's worship and the magi hastening to Christ symbolizes Gentiles' entrance (2.34.198-99). "And the murder of children" stands for the "rejection of patterns of the immature" (νηπίων ἄρσις τύπων) (2.34.197). Gregory reinterprets the tragic massacre tropologically so that it symbolizes the rejection of immaturity that characterizes the uninitiated or the carnal Christians.[74]

In *Oration 36*, the tone is harsher. Gregory responds to those who opposed his appointment as bishop of Constantinople. In 36:5 he excoriates "envy" that ruined Lucifer, Adam, Cain, the antediluvian world, Sodom, Dathan, Abiram, Miriam, the prophets, Solomon, Judas, and Pilate. Herod is also mentioned as the "killer of children." The work of envy continues beyond the life of Christ: scattering Israel, persecuting and dividing the Church, and blinding those who fail to comprehend the Trinity. Like Hilary and Lucifer, Gregory is employing actualization of Matt 2:16 to discredit his opponents.

E. Apponius

After Gregory of Nazianzus, a shadowy figure named Apponius emerges with a similar actualization of Matt 2:16-18 in his *Explanation of the Song of Songs* (ca. 410) 4.16-17. He is thought to be a member of the Roman Church and a combatant of fourth-century heretics.[75] Apponius arrives at Song 2:15 and interprets the foxes that ruin the fruits of the warmer seasons as "the heresies of corrupt ones, the most caustic dogmas." Using the word "fox" (*vulpes*), Apponius strings together OT passages to prove that their tongue is evil and they are destined for the place of damnation where the angels of punishment dwell (Ps 63:10; 68:23).

In the NT, Jesus rebukes a destructive foe of the church in Herod and mocked him as a fox (Luke 13:32). Apponius conflates Herod the Great with this Herod Antipas to analogize the ways false teachers target neophytes to the way the king targeted the infants. He writes,

> Therefore it is shown: just as the Devil had the children in flesh killed through Herod, who because of unbelief was certainly the same killer of John the preacher, thus also through heretics he [the Devil] does the same to children in the gospel teachings [*parvulos in doctrina Evangelica*], as if he is destroying vineyards [*quasi vineas exterminate*]. For foxes more easily destroy young hitherto new vineyards [*parvulas adhuc novellasque vineas facilius*], in order that they may not rise up high hitherto from the ground [*ut quae non alte adhuc a terra surgant*].

---

[73] Gregory wrote poems partly for promotion of Christian literature, possibly for use at schools. Denis M. Meehan, "Introduction," in *Saint Gregory of Nazianzus: Three Poems: Concerning His Own Affairs, Concerning Himself and the Bishops, Concerning His Own Life*, trans. Denis M. Meehan, 1–21, FC 75 (Washington, DC: Catholic University of America Press, 1987), 20.
[74] See Rom 2:20; 1 Cor 3:1-4; 13:11; Gal 4:1; Eph 4:14; and Heb 5:11-14.
[75] Johannes Quasten, *Golden Age of Latin Patristic Literature from the Council of Nicea to the Council of Chalcedon, Patrology*, vol. 4 (Westminster: Christian Classics, 1986), 4:565–6.

So then, according to this ecclesiological analysis, true teachers must vigilantly shepherd new believers.

F. Augustine

As stated above, Hilary of Poitiers did more than illuminate the Scriptures. He, along with Augustine, may have encouraged an openly antagonistic attitude toward Jews in the fourth century.[76] Augustine's reading of Matt 2:16-18 in particular is an interesting study due to various converging factors: the confluence of his biblically crafted understanding of Jews and Judaism; his interactions with actual contemporary Jews; and his lasting influence in church history.[77] Quodvultdeus, in turn, is a direct heir of Augustine's conception of the Jews in relation to the Church, going as far as blaming them for the children's death in the massacre.[78]

Augustine's sermons on the Epiphany provided public occasions for comparing and contrasting the believing magi who worshipped Christ and the unbelieving Jews who helped Herod. In *Sermon 199 on the Epiphany*, he reflects on the recent celebration of Jesus's birth among the Jews (the shepherds) before speaking on the day when Gentiles (the Magi) adore him (199:1; John 4:22; Isa 49:6). Jesus unites the Jews and the Gentiles in the sphere of worship (Eph 2:14-17).

Jewish leaders however, relinquish their choice between the examples of the magi and Herod: "Between the pious love of the Magi, and the cruel fear of Herod, those ones [the Jewish leaders] have vanished" (199:2). The Jewish leaders reemerge later in Matthew as persecutors of the adult Jesus, proving that their prior knowledge of Jesus did not lead to acceptance of his truths. Like Origen, Augustine condemns the Jews of Matthew 2 en bloc with the later ones. Augustine concludes that "happy rather is the ignorance of the infants," who could suffer for him, though unable to confess Christ.

In *Sermon 375 on the Epiphany*, Augustine contrasts the Jews with the Magi. The magi follow the way of the star and demonstrate knowledge of Christ in the manger, like the donkey in Isa 1:3 (375:1). The Jews in contrast are like the troubled Herod who supposed that Jesus sought to establish an earthly kingdom.

Though Jewish leaders are not mentioned in Matt 2:16-18, Augustine nonetheless implicates them because they had the knowledge to revere Christ but chose to do nothing or joined Herod in anxiety. This emphasis on their co-guilt not only accords with narrative-critical anticipations of Christ's later persecutions. Augustine also actualizes the text to reinforce antagonistic attitudes toward Jews during Epiphany.

---

[76] See Mans, "The Early Latin Church Fathers on Herod and the Infanticide," 92–102.
[77] For a discussion of the "hermeneutical Jew," which is the output of Augustine's biblical and theological understanding of Jews that is also influenced by his definition of the Church and the Jews of fourth and fifth century, see Franklin T. Harkins, "Nuancing Augustine's Hermeneutical Jew: Allegory and Actual Jews in the Bishop's Sermons," *JSJ* 36 (2005): 41–64.
[78] See *de Symbolo* 1. 5.14-19; 2. 4.21-22; 3. 4.10-14.

IX. Victims as Martyrs

At least as much as Herod and Jews are derided as foes, the victims of the massacre are celebrated as martyrs. As mentioned above, Irenaeus was the first to identify them as such while also identifying them as members of David's house and claimants of Isaianic promises (*Adv. Haer.* 3.16.4). Other interpreters advance the same idea, albeit in different ways. They defend the victims' character by offering epithets, scriptural support, and theological explanations.

A. Tertullian

In *De Anima* (*ca.* 210) chapter 19, Tertullian addresses "those who deprive the soul [*animam*] from the intellect [*intellectu*] even for a small amount of time." He continues, "They wish that infancy be comprised of soul alone, in so far as it merely lives, not in order that it may equally discern, because neither do all things that live discern" (19:1).[79] Proponents of this view use trees as an example, but Tertullian counters that the innate "vital instincts of the tree" (*animationem arboris*) and the young vines' inborn knowledge guide their growth and incline them to cling and spread out to safe areas (19:2-6). If young plants "know" how to act, infants also possess knowledge, as evidenced by their cries at birth (19:7). They even discern between different caretakers "from the spirit" (*spiritu*).[80] He writes,

> Furthermore from the spirit [*spiritu*] he also inspects [*probat*] the mother and from spirit he examines [*spiritu examinat*] the wet nurse and from spirit he recognizes [*spiritu agnoscit*] the waiting maid, while fleeing strange breasts and refusing unknown beds, desiring nothing except what is experienced. Whence for him is the judgment of newness and custom [*iudicium novitatis et moris*], if he did not have discernment? How could he be vexed and be soothed, if he did not understand? It would be surprising enough that infancy is naturally animated without having soul and naturally is affectionate not having reason [*intellectum*]. But for Christ, praise being experienced "from the mouth of sucklings and young ones," he has proclaimed neither childhood nor infancy dull [*hebetes*]. One of which, with rushing applause could offer testimony for him, while the other one being slaughtered on behalf of him certainly perceives violence (19:8-9).

Tertullian ends 19:9 with an argument from Ps 8:2, quoted in Matt 21:16. He interprets "sucklings and young ones" (*lactantium et parvulorum*) as two different references of praise. One refers to the children at the triumphal entry (Matt 21:15-16) while the other refers to the children massacred by Herod (2:16). Both are instances of worship from conscious individuals who can "offer testimony" (*testimonium ... offerre*)

---

[79] *Volunt infantiam sola anima contineri, qua tantummodo vivat, non ut pariter sapiat, quia nec omnia sapiant quae vivant.*
[80] In chapters 10 and 11, Tertullian has not only equated the "soul" (*anima*) with "spirit" (*spiritus*) but also defined the former as a term of substance and the latter as a term of function.

and "sense violence" (*vim sensit*) like their adult counterparts. Since Christ accepts their sensible acts of worship, infants possess not only souls but also knowledge.

Thus, Tertullian thinks an infant possesses enough instinctual capabilities to worship Christ. Unlike Irenaeus, the massacred infants are not voiceless victims.[81] He finds support for his argument from nature and Jesus's use of Ps 8:2 in Matt 21:16. Epiphanius of Salamis, Chromatius of Aquileia, Augustine, and Quodvultdeus also find support from Ps 8:2.[82]

B. Origen

The recurring imagery of the victims with palms and/or crowns in heaven begins in Origen's *Homily 4 on Psalm 37 (36 LXX)*, which deals with Ps 37:23-29.[83] In 4:2, Origen directs his attention on the phrase in Ps 37:24: "though he may stumble, he will not be confounded." He thematically strings together other verses that also deal with stumbling and encourages Christians who resemble struggling athletes that win their crowns.[84] Even younger saints, such as Daniel, Jeremiah, and Jacob in utero, can be crown-qualifiers. He also presents the victims of the Bethlehem massacre: "Thus are not those boys in youth regarded by you as crowned because of agony [*in puerile agone coronati*], those who near Bethlehem, from two years and below, have seized the palm of martyrdom for the name of the Lord [*pro Domini nomine palmam cepere martyrii*]? You see how in boyhood, we have examples of crowns [*in pueros coronoarum habemus exempla*]." Though they may stumble, their ultimate fate is not humiliation.

Crowns and palms were common and enduring emblems of victory. Jesus's triumphal entry in the Gospels, the exhortations in the epistles, and the visions in Revelation all contributed to their popularization in Christian circles.[85] In particular, the Apocalypse likely had lasting influence on readings of Matt 2:16-18 with regard to figures of victims, which amount to thousands and tens of thousands in Byzantine and Syrian liturgies.[86] Outside of the NT, crowns were bestowed on the *triumphus* while *palma* could be used as a metonym for victory in the battlefield or the court of law, and it could also stand for the ensuing peace.[87] Long before NT times, Solomon's temple and Ezekiel's temple contained carvings and ornaments of palm trees, signifying the blessings of God's presence (1 Kings 6-7; Ezekiel 40-41). Later writers and artists also employed the imagery of palms and/or crowns.[88]

---

[81] See Irenaeus, *Adv. Haer.* 3.16.4; Candida R. Moss, *Ancient Christian Martyrdom: Diverse Practices, Theologies, and Traditions* (New Haven: Yale University Press, 2012), 4.

[82] See Epiphanius of Salamis, *Panarion* 67, 4:4; Chromatius, *Tractate 6 on Matthew 2:13-18*, 2; Augustine, *Sermon 375 on the Epiphany*, 1; and Quodvultdeus, *The Book of Promises and Prophecies of God*, 3:9.

[83] This homily is only available in Latin.

[84] E.g., 1 Cor 9:26; Eph 6:12, 15; 1 Tim 4:7; 2 Tim 2:5; James 3:2.

[85] See John 12:13 (cf. Matt 21:8; Mark 11:8); 2 Tim 4:8; Heb 2:7, 9; James 1:12; 1 Pet 5:4; Rev 2:10; 3:11; 4:4, 10; 7:9.

[86] Brown, *Birth of the Messiah*, 205.

[87] Guillermo Galán Vioque, *Martial, Book VII: A Commentary*, trans. J. J. Zoltowski (Leiden: Brill, 2002), 61, 205-6, 411.

[88] Examples include works of/from Cyprian, Optatus, Epiphanius, John Chrysostom, Theodore of Mopsuetia, Peter Chrysologus, Augustine, Prudentius, *Opus Imperfectum*, Leo the Great, and Quodvultdeus.

C. Cyprian of Carthage

Cyprian of Carthage (*ca.* 200–258) was elected as bishop in 249 AD, only to face ten tumultuous years until his death.[89] In the autumn of 249, the Decian persecution forced Cyprian to flee, but he ruled his church from exile by letter.[90] He returned to Carthage in 251, but a plague broke out in 252 and Christians were blamed and held responsible. Aside from these trying external circumstances, Cyprian also dealt with internal conflicts on various issues including the reconciliation of the lapsed and baptism.[91]

Cyprian wrote three letters in 253 that are linked together: letters 56, 57, and 58. Letter 56, written around Easter, raise questions on penitence to be reviewed at the next council meeting in May.[92] Letter 57 is a conciliar document that resulted from major shifts in penitential discipline in light of prophesied trials to come.[93] These imminent persecutions link letters 57 and 58 in chronological proximity (*ca.* May 253), and in letter 58, Cyprian is forced to announce the cancellation of his planned trip to Thibaris.[94] Though unable to be present with the people of Thibaris, the severity of the coming persecutions warrants a pastoral exhortation. Using models from the OT as well as the NT, Cyprian encourages vigilance and steadfastness.[95] Cyprian writes in Letter 58.6.2 concerning the slaughter of the victims, whom he calls "innocent":

> As soon as there was the nativity of Christ, there were the martyrdoms of infants, so that on account of his name those who are from two years and below would be killed. Though not yet at an age apt for combat, it is suitable for a crown [*Aetas necdum habilis ad pugnam idonea extitit ad coronam*]. Innocent infancy [*infantia innocens*] is killed on account of his name, in order that those who are killed because of Christ may appear as innocent. It is exhibited that no one is immune from the peril of persecution [*neminem esse a periculo persecutionis inmunem*], when even such ones have endured martyrdom.

Cyprian bestows honor on the victims by calling their tragic massacre a martyrdom of "innocents," becoming one of the earliest writers to refer to the massacre victims by that title. Their suffering not only amounts to rewarding of crowns but also a warning for future martyrs: If such innocuous individuals can be killed, Christians in Thibaris should not expect to escape. Cyprian offers an actualization of the innocents' story as his audience in anticipation of prophesied persecutions. Ephiphanius of Salamis,

---

[89] "St. Cyprian," in *ODCC*, 444–5.
[90] Ibid.
[91] Ibid.
[92] G. W. Clarke, "Introduction," in *The Letters of St. Cyprian of Carthage: Translated and Annotated: Volume III: Letters 55–66*, trans. G. W. Clarke, 1–29, ACW 46 (New York: Newman, 1983), 29.
[93] Ibid.
[94] Cf. Letter 57.2.1; 5.1; 5.2 with Letter 58.1.2; 2.2; 7.1.
[95] G. W. Clarke, trans., *The Letters of St. Cyprian of Carthage: Translated and Annotated: Volume III: Letters 55–66*, ACW 46 (New York: Newman, 1983), 226.

Chromatius of Aquileia, Basil of Seleucia, Peter Chrysologus, and Fulgentius of Ruspe also bestow that same epithet on them.[96]

D. Chromatius

In *Tractate 6 on Matthew 2:13-18*, Chromatius (died ca. 406), like Cyprian, call the children "innocents who died for Christ" but adds "first martyrs of Christ [*primi Christi martyres*]." While others before him have labeled the victims martyrs, Chromatius is the earliest known writer to call them "first" martyrs, favoring them over Stephen for the title (Acts 7:54-60). Herod, "the wicked king" (*rex iniquus*), fails against the "king of heaven" (*regem caelorum*) while the blessed infants "last for all time" because they die first for Christ.

In *Sermon 14: On the Healing of the Paralytic and Baptism* (ca. 396) Chromatius begins with discussions on baptism's importance. The rite is so significant that the Holy Spirit spoke of it to the Church in Song 5:12. In that verse, the white milk corresponds to the baptismal water while the purified eyes correspond to apostles or martyrs of the church. To further this point, Chromatius cites Paul (1 Cor 3:2) as an example of apostles, since "rightly, he who is washed with milk provides milk" (*Merito praebet lac, qui lacte lotus est*). As for the example of martyrs, the massacred infants are "the eyes of the Church" (*Oculi ecclesiae*), no less than Paul. He explains, "For those ones were truly washed by milk [*vere lacte loti sunt*], who while still not yet weaned [*qui cum adhuc lactentes*], were entitled to die for Christ. Therefore they, who were washed by milk while nursing at the mothers' breasts [*Lacte ergo loti sunt, qui sugentes ubera matrum*], had borne the martyrdom for Christ."

Here, Chromatius builds upon Origen's earlier readings of the Song of Songs to honor the victims. In his typological interpretation of Song 1:15, Origen matches the dove-like eyes to the eyes of the Church, endowed with the spiritual understanding of the Scriptures and its mysteries (*Comm. Cant.* 3.1). Thus, if any member of the Church would be an eye, one would expect it to be the apostles like Paul or bishops. Indeed Apponius, Chromatius's contemporary, affirms this in his *Explanation of the Song of Songs* 3.19. Chromatius, however, surprisingly affirms that the infant victims are just as qualified to guide the Church as the sagacious adult teachers. While the infants do not teach with lectures or epistles, their character ought to be imitated. Apponius stops short of making this connection, but he does exalt those who lead the Church by exemplary gentleness, simplicity, and purity (*Explanation of the Song of Songs* 7.1-34). In addition, the bloodshed from martyrdom washes them with the milk of baptism, equivalent to normal baptism.[97] Thus, Chromatius continues the sermon with the words of Jesus, who connects baptism with martyrdom in Luke 12:50.

---

[96] See Epiphanius of Salamis, *Panarion* 67 4:4; Chromatius, *Tractate 6 on Matthew 2:13-18*, 2; Basil of Seleucia, *Oration 37 on the Children Who Were Killed by Herod in Bethlehem*, 4; Peter Chrysologus, *Sermon 146: Concerning the Birth of Christ (second)*, 8; *Sermon 152: Concerning Herod and the Infants*; and Fulgentius of Ruspe, *Sermon 4: Concerning Epiphany, and Concerning the Murder of the Innocents, and the Gifts of the Magi*, 6.

[97] "Martyr," in *ODCC*, 1052-3.

E. Prudentius

Aurelius Prudentius Clemens (*ca.* 348–413) was a Christian poet, whose *Hymn for the Epiphany* (*ca.* 400) records an epithet for the victims. After a graphic and gory description of Herod's massacre, he writes, "Flowers of martyrdom [*flores martyrum*], all hail! Of rising morn pure blossoms frail! By Jesus' foe were ye downcast, like budding roses [*nascentes rosas*] by the blast." (125–8).[98] Similar to Chromatius before him, Prudentius, then declares in line 129 that the victims are "the first victims offered up for Christ" (*prima Christi victima*).[99] He also borrows from the pervasive Greek mythological symbolism: life or identity of a tragic dying figure transfers to a flower.[100] Quodvultdeus also combines the Scriptures with the flower in *The Book of Promises and Prophecies of God* 3:9.

Elsewhere, Prudentius penned a hymn for a martyr entitled *Discourse of the Martyr St. Romanus against the Pagans* (*ca.* 405). Romanus was a deacon of Caesarea, who was martyred in the Diocletianic persecution in *ca.* 304. Eusebius, his contemporary, writes about him in *de Martyribus Palaestinae* 2, which later writers embellished. Prudentius himself speaks of a boy who shares Romanus's suffering, revered later as Barulas.[101]

In this discourse, the martyred infants' strong resolve sets a model. During a debate with Galerius, Romanus shifts his strategy and asks that a child be brought, seven years old or less, to ask if worshiping idols or Christ is appropriate (lines 656–70). When the child speaks in support of Romanus's argument for worship of God, the ruler tortures him before his mother to the point of severe thirst (lines 671–720). The mother does not relent but encourages her child to obtain "that living fountain at hand, which forever flows" (line 727).[102] In the present, she exhorts the child, who must drink a bitter cup:

> This is the chalice that you now must drink, my son, of which a thousand babes in Bethlehem once drank: Their tender years, unmindful of the flowing breasts, were fed from bitter cups that soon to nectar changed, partaking of the blood as sweet as honey dew ... Essay to follow that example, valiant child, the noble scion of your race, your mother's pride. The Father has decreed that every age excel in deeds of courage and has barred no time of life, according triumphs even to the crying babe [*omnes capaces esse virtutum Pater mandavit annos, neminem excepit diem,ipsis triumphos adnuens vagitibus*]. (lines 736–45)

More examples of martyrs follow (Gen 22:6-10; 2 Maccabees 7) before the child is killed along with Romanus. Aside from the influence of the mother and her seven sons

---

[98] The line numbers and the translation of this hymn come from R. Martin Pope, trans., *The Hymns of Prudentius* (London: J. M. Dent. 2005).
[99] The translation of line 129 is the present author's.
[100] See Ovid, *Metamorphoses* X, 519–741. The blood of Adonis and the grief of Aphrodite mix to form the rose.
[101] "St. Romanus," in *ODCC*, 1422.
[102] The translations of Prudentius's *Discourse of the Martyr St. Romanus against the Pagans* are from H. J. Thomson, ed. and trans., *Prudentius*, LCL 387 (Cambridge: Harvard University Press, 1949), 275–7.

in 2 Maccabees 7, Prudentius borrows from Tertullian. The latter cited Ps 8:2 with Matt 2:16-18 in support of the argument that infants are spiritually capable of worshipful suffering even at a young age. Prudentius's hymn lauds the infants' character on the special occasion of Epiphany.

F. Augustine

Augustine's *Sermon 202 on the Epiphany* extols the victims' character. In this homily, Augustine explains the reason for joy on the day of Epiphany. He explains that the magi frightened King Herod with their announcement (202:1). Their journey and worship fulfill Isa 8:4 since even as an infant, Jesus was despoiling Samaria, a symbol of idolatry (202:2). Even his flight to Egypt is a demonstrative teaching of Matt 10:23, as the Word in flesh was appointed to die at a later time.

In addition to the Magi's gifts, the massacred victims are also moral object lessons for Augustine's congregation: "Furthermore, he shows in the infants whom Herod killed how innocent, how lowly are such people who would die for his name. For in this way, their age of two years signified those number of precepts from which the whole Law and the Prophets depend." (Lev 19:18; Deut 6:5; Matt 22:40). Using numerology, Augustine teaches that their two years of age signifies moral excellence in fulfilling the commands to love God and the neighbor.

Herein displays Augustine's principle of interpreting "ambiguous figurative signs" in action: "anything in the divine discourse that cannot be related either to good morals or to the true faith should be taken as figurative" (*On Christian Doctrine* 3.10.14).[103] "Good morals" and "true faith" correspond to (1) the two greatest love commandments and (2) sufficient concern for God and the neighbor, respectively. Since everything in Scripture does not promote love and faith in the literal sense, other senses are needed "with the reign of love" (3.15.23), as is the case here.[104]

G. Peter Chrysologus

Peter Chrysologus's (*ca.* 400–450) *Sermon 152: Concerning Herod and the Infants* deals directly with Matt 2:16-18 and extols the infants' character, as Augustine did. In 152:6, Chrysologus asks concerning them, "Whose speech is silent, eyes see nothing, ears hear nothing, hands perform nothing, and with whom no one has done anything": "where is the guilt?" They do not even know how to live and their only "crime" is that they were born in Herod's land. By dying, "they were returning the loan of birth" and "because of them the condition of the seller was exacted."[105] Next, Chrysologus asks how Christ,

---

[103] Translations of Augustine's *On Christian Doctrine* are from Tarmo Toom, "Augustine's Hermeneutics: The Science of the Divinely Given Signs," in *Patristic Theories of Biblical Interpretation: The Latin Fathers*, ed. Tarmo Toom, 77–108 (Cambridge: Cambridge University Press, 2016), 102–3.

[104] Toom, "Augustine's Hermeneutics," 103. It is also possible that since two is the pivotal number needed for valid testimony, the two fulfilled commandments stand in approval of the infants' innocence (cf. Deut 17:6; 19:15; Matt 18:16, 20; 2 Cor 13:1; Rev 11:1-14).

[105] *Et revera, quomodo non redderent naturae creditum, a quibus causa exigebatur auctoris?*

who knows all things can allow this tragedy to happen (152:7). After all, the victims are "his soldiers of innocence," "his peer," and "those pruned from their own cradles." Chrysologus answers: instead of abandoning them, Christ has given them their rewards in advance.[106] Christ "has sent ahead" (*praemisit*), "not lost" (*non amisit*), "taken back" (*recepit*), "not abandon" (*non reliquit*) them.

Thus, the massacre is paradoxically a happy event. In 152:8, Chrysologus uses "happy" (*beatus*) five times in the span of six sentences. Happy are those "born for martyrdom not worldliness" and "those who transform labors into rest, pains into cooling, mourning into joy." Chrysologus exclaims, "They live, they live, because those who merit to die for Christ truly live." The grieving mothers also have reasons to rejoice. Happy are the "wombs," "breasts," and even "tears," "which being shed in weeping have gathered together for such ones for the grace of baptism" (*quae pro talibus fusae flentibus gratiam baptismatis contulerunt*). The paradoxical chain of "happy" victims evokes memories of Jesus's beatitudes (Matt 5:3-12).

The mothers and the sons are thus baptized in tears and blood, respectively, because the sword that penetrated the children's members reaches the mothers' hearts. "It is necessary," then, for the mothers to be "kindred of the prize" since they are "sharers of suffering." While the young victims laugh at their slayers, are consoled by the sword, pay attention to the horror, and take joy in death, the mothers shed "tears of martyrdom" (*martyrii lacrimas*), so they will not lack the "joy of martyrdom" (*martyrii gaudio*). This sermon's ultimate lesson is that martyrdom is a grace, not a merit, owing nothing to self, since these innocents did not voluntarily give up their lives (152:9).

Peter Chrysologus continues with this theme in *Sermon 153*, another sermon concerning Herod and the infants, preached during the Christmas season of another year. The children are "divine warriors [*praelia*]" and "an arising cohort [*Coorta regi cohors*] delighted to die prematurely for their own king rather than die with him at the same time" (153:1-2). Chrysologus uses various military and heroic images to honor their courageous martyrdom.[107]

He is, however, careful to designate them as "martyrs of grace." Just as the virgin who is ignorant of corruption received the privilege of motherhood, the infants who

---

[106] Christ "has granted them to triumph before living" (*quibus dedit ante triumphare quam vivere*), "appointed to capture victory without controversy" (*fecit capere sine concertatione victoriam*), "bestowed crowns before limbs" (*donavit coronis ante quam membris*), "wished to disregard faults because of courage, possess heaven before earth, not to be included with things human before things divine" (*voluit virtutibus vitia praeterire, ante caelum possidere quam terram*) (152:7).

[107] These "soldiers dedicated to Christ" (*Christo dicati milites*) display their precocious prowess as they begin "fighting before living" (*ante militare quam vivere*), "combating before playing" (*ante pugnare quam ludere*), and "pouring out blood before drinking up breasts of milk" (*fundere ante sanguine quam lactis ubera perpotare*). Their "burning souls did not endure delays of the body" (*Ardentes animae moras corporis non tulerunt*) as they move from "bosoms ... to raging flanks of enemies" (*e gremio ad furentes hostium cuneos*). They "receive in advance" (anticipant) "courage before blandishments" (*virtutibus blandimenta*), "wounds before kisses" (*vulneribus oscula*), and "sword before ointments" (*unguenta ferro*). Thus, they are granted the dwelling of heaven before earth, the rewards of the spirit before those of the flesh, because they brought back triumphs before they learned how to feed themselves. They "confess while silent, combat while unknowing, conquer while unaware, die while not knowing, they raise up palms while ignorant, snatch crowns though being ignorant" (*confitentur tacentes, nescientes pugnant, vincunt inscii, moriuntur inconscii, ignari tollunt palmas, coronas rapiunt ignorantes*). See also Jacob of Serugh, *Sixth Homily*, 144.

do not know pain receive rewards of martyrdom. Chrysologus concludes the sermon by stating that "intimate love," not fear, led to Christ's flight to Egypt (153:3). If Christ stayed and the children lived, "the synagogue would have them as sons [*haberet eos synagoga filios*], while the Church would not have them as martyrs [*hos ecclesia martyres non haberet*]." With such statement, Chrysologus does not quell the anti-Jewish sentiments that Hilary of Poitiers and Augustine may have incited in their reception of this passage.

Thus, Peter Chrysologus emphasizes slaughtered victims' rewards and grace. Unlike Cyprian of Carthage and Lucifer of Cagliari, no specific struggle appears to have occasioned these sermons. Following Tertullian's thought that even young children can exercise great faith (*De Anima* 19:1-9), perhaps Chrysologus wished to inspire courage in all Christians in Ravenna, whether young or old. Following him, Fulgentius of Ruspe, and Quodvultdeus all cast a hopeful outlook for the children, relying on Christ's grace to redeem them.

H. Basil of Seleucia

In *Oration 37 on the Children Who Were Killed by Herod in Bethlehem*, Basil of Seleucia (died *ca.* 459) condemns Herod's crime while explaining Christ's sovereignty over the tragedy and his flight to Egypt. Christ is the "Lord of all" who has punished the "cruel schemer of impious crimes." Christ, "after hiding [ἐναποθέμενος] the souls of innocent infants in the arms of father Abraham [τοῖς τοῦ πατρὸς Ἀβραὰμ κόλποις]," went down to Egypt with authority to purge impiety, idolatry, and pride therein. The massacre is a Pyrrhic victory, because the devil destroys "very few Jewish boys" while Christ sacks an entire city by fulfilling Isa 19:1.

Basil of Seleucia continues the strand of reading that emphasizes Christ's sovereignty over the infancy narrative events through the lens of Isaiah. Unlike, however, the triumphant images of palms and crowns, the tender sight of "Abraham's bosom" evokes the memory of poor Lazarus who suffer during the lifetime but find mercy after death, carried away by angels (Luke 16:19-22). Herod and the devil, on the other hand, are destined to suffer like the condemned rich man (16:23).

I. Pope Leo the Great

In his tropological *Sermon 37: On the Feast of the Epiphany 7*, 3-4, Pope Leo the Great (*ca.* 400-461) praises the humility that Christ demonstrates in his incarnation and shares with the victims. Childlikeness is required to enter heaven (Matt 18:3). Christ loves the "childhood" which he took up in soul and body, and equates it with "the teacher of humility," "the rule of innocence," "the image of gentleness."[108] He directs older people in its direction. Paul, however, demonstrates with 1 Cor 14:20 that not every aspect of childhood is fitting for adults. Appropriate aspects befitting them are

---

[108] The English translations are from Jane P. Freeland and Agnes J. Conway, trans., *St. Leo the Great: Sermons*, FC 93 (Washington, DC: Catholic University of America Press, 1996).

quick return to peace, "no memory of offences, no desire for importance," love for sharing and equality. Pope Leo continues,

> Our Savior, the child worshipped by those wise men, suggests this pattern of humility (*humilitatis formam*) to you. In order to show what glory he has prepared for those who imitate him, he has consecrated with martyrdom those who came forth at the time of his appearance. Begotten at Bethlehem, where Christ was born, they became participants in his Passion by sharing his age.[109]

J. Quodvultdeus

Before his election as Bishop of Carthage in 437, Quodvultdeus (died *ca.* 450) exchanged correspondences with Augustine whose teachings heavily influenced him.[110] Like his predecessor, Quodvultdeus wrote a statement on grace bestowed on the massacre victims in two of three creedal homilies delivered in the mid-430s, just before his appointment as bishop.[111] Their chronological order is likely *De Symbolo 2, 1*, and then *3*.[112]

In *De Symbolo 2*, Quodvultdeus builds on the idea of Christ's sovereign activity as an infant, found earlier in Justin Martyr, Irenaeus, and Jerome. The infant Jesus lying in the manger defeats the devil because he assimilates the "sons of enemies" into "the number of adopted ones," though they soon die unknowingly for Christ as martyrs and witnesses (4:14-15). The raging Herod is ignorant of these truths and his unwitting role in the greater plan to save the children (4:16). Quodvultdeus addresses the evil king and reveals the plan: "You send ahead [*praemittis*] for him such a great army—many thousands—of white-robed infants even prior to the [arrival of] kingdom of heaven" (4:17).[113] Just as Irenaeus and Peter Chrysologus, *Sermon 152:7* taught that Christ "sent ahead" (προπέμψῃ; *praemisit*) the children, here, Quodvultdeus teaches that Christ uses Herod as an agent for the same purpose.

Next, Quodvultdeus locates the children in the visions of Revelation: "The Apocalypse of blessed John the apostle points to this throng, saying: 'I see a great crowd from every tribe that no one could count, standing in God's presence; and they were clothed in white robe, and palms were in their hands'" (4:18). The victims are honored with the adoption into God's family and the white-robe attire. Unlike his predecessors, Quodvultdeus explicitly cites Rev 7:9, instead of merely alluding to it. In addition, he amplifies the victims' number beyond the few mentioned by Basil of Seleucia to match the description in the Apocalypse.

---

[109] Elsewhere, Pope Leo says that the myrrh brought by the magi indicate "the confession of mortality" (34:3), perhaps anticipating the Passion to come.
[110] Sara Petri, "Quodvultdeus of Carthage," in *The Oxford Guide to the Historical Reception of Augustine* 3, ed. Karal Pollman and Willemien Otten, 1629–30 (Oxford: Oxford University Press, 2013), 1629.
[111] Thomas M. Finn, "Introduction," in *Quodvultdeus of Carthage: The Creedal Homilies: Conversion in Fifth-Century North Africa: Translation and Commentary*, trans. Thomas M. Finn, 1–22, ACW 60 (New York: Newman, 2004), 3.
[112] Ibid.
[113] *tu illi prior ad regnum caelorum tot millia candidatorum infantum innumerabilem praemittis exercitum.*

In *de Symbolo 2*, 4:19-20, Quodvultdeus continues to extol the grace given to the slaughtered children, who are granted victory in heaven.[114] He again mocks Herod as Christ's pawn: "Thus, you have hurried them along to their life [*accelerasti ad eorum vitam*], lest with their parents they might have killed True Life [*occiderent veram vitam*]" (4:21). Thus, Quodvultdeus does not relent from his diatribe against the martyrs' parents, fomenting more anti-Jewish sentiments. Christ "freed their souls from the destructive society of their parents, and he left you alone, empty in crime" (4:22). Anti-Jewish sentiments of Hilary of Poitiers and Augustine found in their actualizing readings of Matt 2:16 have come to fruition in Quodvultdeus and Chrysologus.

Quodvultdeus returns to the martyrs and explicates how divine grace saved them. They were "by nature children of wrath, just like the others" but grace "plucked them out from the power of darkness" (4:22-23). Christ "provided" (*praestitit*) the twofold grace: (1) their death on behalf of Christ and (2) their cleansing "from original sin" (*ab orginale peccato*), "through his own blood" (4:23).[115] Indeed, "they were born for death [*Nati sunt ad mortem*], but immediately death returned them to life [*eos mors reddidit vitae*]."

In Quodvultdeus's mind, Christ's blood resolves the problem of the children's original sin and the problem of actual sin is precluded. While Chromatius and Chrysologus located the source of the infants' grace in the blood of martyrdom, Quodvultdeus points to Jesus's blood. Without its cleansing power, the children would die in their original sin before the grace of baptism comes into effect.[116] The blood shed at Christ's adulthood benefits the victims in Christ's infancy, albeit anachronistically.[117] While Augustine is vague concerning the infants' salvation (*On the Freedom of the Will* 3:68), Quodvultdeus sets out a logical soteriological scheme for them.

De Symbolo 1 develops similar ideas in *de Symbolo 2*, by berating "the wicked land of the Jews" and extolling the infants (5:13). The massacre serves as Jews' punishment because the victims are Jews themselves (5:14-15). Their deaths also testify to Christ's innocence (5:16). While the Jews are bereaved, Quodvultdeus assures them that the children are rewarded in heaven with the "glory of immortality" (5:17). While helping Herod kill God's son, Herod in fact killed their sons, but Christ made the victims "heirs" of God (5:18). Christ, simultaneously dwelling in heaven while lying helpless as a babe on earth mocks the Jews and their king (5:19).

---

[114] See Peter Chrysologus, *Sermon 152* and *Sermon 153*.

[115] Note the double use of "provided" (*praestitit*): "Christ has provided for them so that they might die for Christ, and provided so that by his own blood they may be cleansed from their original sin" (*praestitit eis christus ut pro christo morerentur, praestitit ut suo sanguine ab originali peccato diluerentur*).

[116] Augustine's view of original sin does not except the infants, who need the grace of baptism like their adult counterparts. See Augustine, *De pecc. mer.* 1.9-15.20, *Sermo* 293.11, 294.3, *Contra Iulianum* 5.11.44, *De nupt. et. conc.* 2.18.33, 2.33.56. Yet he does not make clear teaching in *On the Freedom of the Will* 3.68, *Letter 166 to Jerome: A Treatise on the Origin of the Human Soul* 16-18, and *Exposition of Ps 48 (LXX 47)*, when the occasion arises for him to discuss how grace overcomes the original sin of the infant victims he calls "innocent."

[117] See Leo the Great, *Sermon 31: On the Feast of the Epiphany 1*, 3; *Sermon 33: On the Feast of the Epiphany 3*; Fulgentius of Ruspe, *Sermon 4: Concerning Epiphany*, and *Concerning the Murder of the Innocents, and the Gifts of the Magi*, 7.

X. Victims as Sacrifices

Another strand of reading uses the language of sacrifice to describe the victims' deaths. The images invoked include grapes used for wine, firstfruits, and sacrificial lambs.

A. Ephrem the Syrian

Ephrem the Syrian's *Commentary on Tatian's Diatessaron* mentions the massacred victims in the context of Matt 21:15-16, where Ps 8:2 is cited. He writes,

> That is, "If these praises do not please you, make them keep silent." At his birth and at his death children were intertwined in the crown of his sufferings. The infant John jumped for joy within the womb on meeting him and children were slain at his birth. They were [like] the grapes of his wedding feast. It was also children who proclaimed his praise when the time of his death drew near.

Like Tertullian before him, Ephrem references two groups of infants based on Jesus's use of Ps 8:2. Interestingly, the infants' massacre counts as "praise" as much as John the Baptist's joy in Elizabeth's womb. Their slaughter is elevated to a heavenly wedding banquet where their sacrifice contributes to the joyous occasion. Jesus later speaks of the kingdom of heaven as a wedding feast in Matt 22:1-14 and 25:1-12, but the idea may be more Johannine. Jesus begins his ministry and manifests his glory at the wedding at Cana (John 2:1-12). The marriage supper of the Lamb arrives at the eschaton (Rev 19:7-10). Jacob of Serugh shares Ephrem's view that the children are grapes for wine of the marriage feast.[118]

The language of sacrifice continues in the *Hymn on the Nativity 7*. It contains thirteen verses with the worship and offerings from watchers (v. 1), shepherds (vv. 2-3, 5-8), lambs (v. 4), young women (v. 9), elderly women (v. 10), old men (v. 11), and chaste and bereft women (vv. 12-13).[119] Verse 12 records, "The chaste women said, 'The blessed fruit blessed the fruits. Let there be given you the firstfruits [ܪܝܫܐ].' The [women] boiled over [ܪܬܚܝ], prophesying [ܐܬܢܒܝ] about their children, who although being killed would be harvested [ܡܚܨܕܝܢ] by him as the firstfruits [ܪܫܝܬܐ]."[120]

The use of firstfruits again evokes the eschatological visions of Revelation. The infants are likened to the 144,000 marked singers, virgin followers of the Lamb, purchased and offered as first fruits to God and the Lamb, and blameless in speech (14:1-5). Whether part of the multitude from every tribe or part of the 144,000, they worship before God in heaven. This idea is repeated in Augustine's *Sermon 375 on the Epiphany*, 1 and Jacob of Serugh, *Sixth Homily: Concerning the Star Which Was Seen by the Magi and the Killing of the Children*, 145-6, 150.

---

[118] See Jacob of Serugh, *Sixth Homily*, 145.
[119] CSCO, 186, 55-8. The present author is indebted to Morgan Reed for his help in translation of this work.
[120] Ibid., 58.

B. Gregory of Nazianzus

In this *Oration 38*, Gregory exhorts his audience to worship Christ on the occasion of the festival of his "divine appearance" (θεοφάνια) or "birth" (γενέθλια). This ambiguous title leaves doubts as to whether the oration was delivered on Christmas of 380 or January 6, 381.[121] Much of the work deals with divine mystery, his creation of the immaterial and material world, and Christ's incarnation that reversed Adam's fall. The audience ought to leap like John the Baptist in the womb, revere the enrollment into heaven, honor the small Bethlehem, worship the manger by which the ox and the ass are fed God's Word, run with the star, bear gifts with the Magi, glorify Christ with the shepherds, and sing with the angels (38:17). Disciples of Christ must "travel without fault" through all of Christ's life stages via participation in the liturgical feasts.[122] Not every act, however, should be imitated. Herod's "child murder" must be despised (Matt 2:16), while the children in Bethlehem should be revered as "the sacrifice of Christ's peer which is slain in place of the new victim."[123]

The infants' massacre and Christ's Passion are brought together in ritual vocabulary. Both deaths are seen as sacrifices. While substitutionary sacrifice is normally associated with Jesus, here the infants die on behalf of the infant Christ, because their sacrifices would allow for the Jesus's ultimate sacrifices once he reaches adulthood. Jacob of Serugh shares similar ideas.[124]

C. Prudentius

As mentioned before, Prudentius's *Hymn for the Epiphany* describes the infants in glowing epithets, such as "flowers of martyrdom" (line 125) and "first victims offered up for Christ" (line 129). Another significant title is "a tender flock of pure sacrifice before his altar" (*grex inmolatorum tener, aram ante ipsam simplices*). Like Basil of Seleucia, Prudentius equate the children with lambs, but he clearly depicts an altar scene.[125] Leo the Great also uses a similar motif, appropriating the promises of Rom 8:35-36 for the victims, while Jacob of Serugh calls them "beloved lambs" and "innocent lambs."[126]

XI. Herod's Executioners and the Victims' Parents

The gory details of the slaughter or its aftermath are unrecorded in Matt 2:16-18, even though the fourth-century *Hymn to the Virgin Mary* makes a brief mention of the bereft mothers.[127] Some interpreters, however, lead their audiences to the streets and the victims' homes, revealing the horrifying scenes that may have taken place. Others

---

[121] *NPNF*² 7:344.
[122] See *Oration* 30:21. Brian E. Daley, *Gregory of Nazianzus*, ECF (London: Routledge, 2006), 229–30.
[123] τὴν ἡλικιῶτιν Χριστοῦ θυσίαν τοῦ καινοῦ σφαγίου προθυομένην.
[124] Jacob of Serugh, *Sixth Homily*, 147, 150.
[125] Basil of Seleucia, *Oration 37 on the Children Who Were Killed by Herod in Bethlehem*, 3.
[126] Leo the Great, *Sermon 36: On the Feast of the Epiphany* 6; Jacob of Serugh, *Sixth Homily*, 143, 146.
[127] "Every mother was lamenting for her son. The infant lay hidden with his mother" (om[n]is mater pro filio plorabat. Latebat infans cum matre) (lines 84–5).

are more meditative, reflecting on the massacre's impact on the parents. While the preponderance of mothers' pain is evident, the fathers and other bereaved members of the family are also considered.

A. Gregory of Nyssa's *Oration on the Birthday of Christ*

Gregory of Nyssa (ca. 335-394) is the possible writer of *Oration on the Birthday of Christ* who presents details of the slaughter. The city of Bethlehem was "filled with executioners" among mothers, infants, and fathers. The families' grieving sounds mix with the executioners' cruel threats. Mothers throw their necks to the sword, unable to look at deathblows to their children. One attack of the sword is enough to kill both the mother and the child, so that "one stream of blood from the wound of the mother and from the fatal wound of the child was running mixed."

Herod's calculation of two years leads to the double punishment of some mothers. Gregory describes one mother who in that span of time bore two sons. In one scene, there are "two executioners occupied around one mother, and one nearby snatched the running son, but another pulled from the lap of the mother an infant still not weaned." The mother is "torn apart by natural instincts" (σχιζομένης τῆς φύσεως) with her "maternal viscerals" (μητρῴοις σπλάγχνοις) moving toward both of her children.

Gregory of Nyssa uses his imagination to dramatize Matt 2:16. While the verse does not cite the number of dispatched soldiers, he envisions the city filled with them. Mothers and fathers appear in the scenes, adding to the children's cries and the soldiers' violent noise. Prudentius, Basil of Seleucia, Narsai, Peter Chrysologus, Quodvultdeus, and Jacob of Serugh also supplement Matt 2:16 with similar details.[128]

B. Ephrem the Syrian

In two verses of Ephrem the Syrian's *Hymns on the Nativity 7*, the bereaved women emerge from the massacre to "boil over" (ܢܒܥܝ) and "prophesy" (ܐܬܢܒܝܢ) that their deceased children became firstfruits for God (verse 12) and to seek mercy (verse 13). The verse 13 records, "The bereft had brooded to hatch him, they cherished [Christ] saying, 'Blessed fruit [formed] without marriage, bless our wombs more than marriage. Have mercy on our bereavement, wondrous child of virginity.'"[129] In Ephrem's interpretation, the bereaved women are no longer helpless victims but prophetesses, worshipers, and prayerful. They perceive that the infant Jesus comes from a virgin birth and cherish him. Unlike Gregory of Nyssa, their stories continue as they find hope in Christ.

---

[128] See Prudentius, *Hymn for the Epiphany*, 99-124; Jacob of Serugh, *Sixth Homily*, 146-7; Basil of Seleucia, *Oration 37 on the Children Who Were Killed by Herod in Bethlehem*, 2-4; Narsai, *Memra on the Birth of Our Lord*, 92; Peter Chrysologus's *Sermon 146: Concerning the Birth of Christ (second)*, 8; *Sermon 152: Concerning Herod and the Infants*, 2; Quodvultdeus, *De Symbolo 2*, 4:12.

[129] CSCO, 186:58.

C. Augustine

In *On the Freedom of the Will* 3:68, Augustine makes clear that the suffering children are sinless and their pains are a means of "correction of the parents," as "they will either become better, if corrected by the temporal troubles they have chosen to live more rightly, or they will have no excuse in the punishment of the coming judgment, if in spite of the anguishes of this life, they are unwilling to turn their desire to eternal life." Through their sufferings the parents' "hardness is bruised, faith is exercised, or compassion is proved." God may indeed have a reward for them "in the secret of his judgments." These children have done no right or wrong but deserve exaltation: "Furthermore, truly not without cause that the Church commends those infants, who were slain when our Lord Jesus Christ was being sought by Herod to be killed, having been received in honor of martyrdom."

Augustine explains with pastoral guidance what Ephrem has shown in hymnody. The loss of the children leaves a profound positive impact on the grieving parents' faiths. The children are not being punished for wrong, but the parents need the experience to increase their devotion to God.

D. *Opus Imperfectum*

In the second homily of the *Opus Imperfectum* (OI; ca. 405), the anonymous author differentiates between "wailing" (*ploratus*) and "loud lamentation" (*ululatus*) (Matt 2:18). The former refers to the children separated from their mothers. The latter refers to the bereft mothers who cry, "as if their own heart [*viscera*] had been torn out of them." The surviving mothers face "greater grief" since the children did not even fear death but died in an instant. The women, however, suffer twice: (1) they see their children die and (2) they are bereft. The children face a "blessed death" that ended their sorrow, but the mothers live with the painful memory.

XII. Ramah as a Distant Place

Ramah is a common geographical name, which could signify at least three places in Joshua 18–19 alone: (1) one near Gibeah of Benjamin (Josh 18:25), (2) a town on the border of Asher (19:29), and (3) a city of Naphtali (Josh 19:39). A tomb attributed to Rachel on a common path to Bethlehem did not garner significant interest among pilgrims or writers until the first Muslim period began.[130] The most interesting readings from this era, however, have little to do with specific locations. Ramah is closely related to the voice that is heard either by foreigners in Arabia or God in the heavens.

---

[130] Frederick M. Strickert, *Rachel Weeping: Jews, Christians, and Muslims at the Fortress Tomb* (Collegeville: Liturgical Press, 2007), 71–83. Egeria (late fourth century) mentions nothing about the tomb while speaking of Bethlehem. The Bordeaux Itinerary and *Onamasticons* (worked on by Origen, Eusebius, Jerome) mention the location of Rachel's tomb along the way to Bethlehem, but without much detail.

A. Justin Martyr

In *Dial.* 78:8, Justin does not struggle with the distance between Bethlehem and Ramah. The epicenter of Rachel's weeping voice is not the Benjaminite city located north of Jerusalem, but Bethlehem, where Rachel has been buried (τέθαπται). From there, the bereaved women's pained voice echoes far into foreign territory. The voice is "about to be heard from Ramah, which is in Arabia, for there is also until the present time a place in Arabia called Ramah."[131]

Earlier in 77:4, Justin has pinpointed the Magi's home "from the east" as Arabia (Matt 2:1; *Dial.* 77:4). Thus, just as the magi carry gifts from there, Rachel's voice carries the families' grief to there. Damascus (see III. A above) and Ramah are cities in Arabia that are significant in the interpretation of Matthew 2 as they represent the heightened drama of the infancy narratives.

B. *Fragment 34*

The author of *Fragment 34* (GCS 12: 29) is believed to be Origen, and if that were true, he would be the pioneer of the etymological reading of Ramah. Like Justin, the author detects the non-proximity between the Benjaminite Ramah and the Judahite Bethlehem. His solution is that Rama is not actually a physical location on earth, but it means "the highest" (τῇ ὑψηλῇ). Whether this reading was a common one cannot be determined for certain, but Jerome reflects familiarity with this reading in book one of his *Commentary on Matthew*. Narsai may also be alluding to it in *Memra on the Birth of Our Lord*.[132]

C. *Opus Imperfectum*

In the second homily of OI, the author explains Ramah's significance. Ramah is the city of Saul, not of David, but Saul was from the tribe of Benjamin, Benjamin is the son of Rachel, and Rachel was buried near Bethlehem. In addition, Ramah's distance from Bethlehem is not a problem when the former is understood as "on high" (*in excelso*). The author of OI builds on Origen and Jerome's etymological reading of Ramah by citing Sirach. The mourning voice over the children rises to heavens just as "the voice of the poor pierces the clouds, and it does not depart until it is heard" (Sir 35:21). While Jer 31:15 and Matt 2:18 are vague about the audience of Rachel's voice, the verse from Sirach turns it into a prayer that reaches God, imbued with humility and power that penetrates the heavens. Thus, the author of OI teaches a tropological lesson on the power of humble prayer.

---

[131] ... ἔμελλεν ἀκούεσθαι ἀπὸ Ῥαμᾶ, τοῦτ᾽ ἔστιν ἀπὸ τῆς Ἀρραβίας ἔστι γὰρ καὶ μέχρι τοῦ νῦν τόπος καλούμενος ἐν Ἀρραβίᾳ Ῥαμᾶ.

[132] He writes, "He [Christ] will recompense them new salvation in the highest kingdom [ܪܘܡܐ ܕܡܠܟܘܬܐ]" Narsai, *Memra on the Birth of Our Lord*, 93.

XIII. Rachel's Reasons for Weeping without Comfort

Already in the considerations of the "voice" and "Ramah," ancient writers hint at Rachel's importance. While early commentators such as Fortunatianus of Aquileia would be foundational in analogizing Rachel and Leah as the Church and the synagogue, respectively, other thinkers develop that idea further or shift the details.[133] They look closely at the tragic figure of Matt 2:18 to inquire the reasons for her weeping.

A. Fragment 34

In Origen's *Fragment 34*, the women represented by Rachel refuse to be comforted "for they were not yet educated [μεμαθηκότες] concerning the resurrection of the dead by the one able to show visibly his resurrection, because such considerations are not for those weeping and mourning." This learning occurs later when Jesus's ministry and mission are fulfilled, not in the present, while the bereaved still grieve. In a similar reading, Gregory of Nyssa believes a more festive day is coming even though Rachel weeps bitterly at the moment.[134]

B. Hilary of Poitiers

A more enlightened and confident Rachel emerges in Hilary's commentary of Matt 2:18. In chapter 1.7 of his commentary, Hilary immediately notes how Rachel in Jer 31:15 cannot be Jacob's wife literally. She did not grieve over her sons, Joseph and Benjamin, since they did not die during her lifetime. Rather, Rachel represents the Church. The Church weeps over the strife between Jews, who should have been her firstborn sons, and Christians, her younger children. The true cause of her grief is the strife between the two, not the deceased children. There is no need to comfort Rachel the Church for her Christian children who are glorified as martyrs:

> But a glorious honor is restored to the slain among them through the prophet who said: "A voice is heard in Rama, weeping and great lamentation, Rachel weeping for her children, and she did not want to be comforted, because they are no more." Rachel the wife of Jacob, had been barren for a longtime, but she had lost none of those she gave birth to [*sed nullos ex his quos genuit amisit*]. In fact, this one was presented in Genesis as a type of the Church [*Ecclesiae typum*]. It is not therefore her voice and weeping that is heard, since she did not possess any sorrow over lost children, but it is that of the Church, barren for a long time, but now truly fruitful [*diu sterilis nunc vero fecundae*]. This weeping over children is heard, not because she was grieving those destroyed, but because they were being annihilated by those whom she had wished to preserve as firstborn sons [*quos primum genitos*

---

[133] Fortunantius of Aquileia, *Commentary on the Gospels: English Translation and Introduction by H. A. G. Houghton*, CSEL Extra Seriem (Berlin: De Gruyter 2017), 28; For this reason, the reception of Hilary of Poitiers, his contemporary, was judged to be more relevant to the current study.

[134] Gregory of Nyssa, *Oration on the Birthday of Christ*.

filios retinere voluisset]. Thereafter she did not want to be comforted for what she was grieving. For those who are dead are not thought about, for they were brought to success of eternity through the glory of martyrdom, but consolation is provided as a matter of losing, not enriching.

C. Jerome

In book 1 of his *Commentary on Matthew*, Jerome discusses 2:17-18. He begins with a question about Rachel's relationship with Bethlehem: "Benjamin, to whose tribe Bethlehem does not belong, was born of Rachel. Therefore it is asked, how Rachel mourns for the children of Judah, which is Bethlehem?" Jerome offers two solutions: (1) Rachel was buried in Ephratha, which is near Bethlehem, and (2) the massacre affected not only Bethlehem in the territory of Judah but also its neighboring region of Benjamin.

Jerome also offers two reasons for Rachel's rejection of comfort: (1) the children are considered perpetually lost ("dead for eternity") or (2) "she knows that they will live."[135] This latter interpretation is close to Hilary's position, but Jerome does not commit to either one. This speculation on Rachel's thinking reveals an interest in not only the matriarch but also the young victims.

D. Augustine

Augustine compiled a list of Bible questions called *Questions from the Old and New Testament*. The sixty-second question concerns Matt 2:18: "Why is it that with the killings of sons of Leah, who were from the tribe of Judah, Rachel is said to bewail her sons?" He begins by precluding the possibility that Rachel could weep over children of Judah. After all, Rachel's sons are Benjaminites who were decimated in the Gibeah tragedy (Judges 19–20), not Bethlehemite sons of Leah. As for Leah, she has no reason to weep for her massacred children, because they are (1) innocent and (2) rewarded by God in heaven:

> However much it pertains to history, Rachel's sons are from the tribe of Benjamin. Furthermore, for their own crimes, namely the works of Sodomites, and the apathy that they had against the concubine of the Levite man, they were extinguished and eradicated from the surviving tribes (Judges 19-20). Wherefore, she [Rachel] is precluded from even wanting to receive consolation, knowing nothing about the hope for those [Rachel's sons] who are known to have perished [already]. But the sons of Leah, in the first years, were killed for the sake of the Savior. Nowhere does she want the reason for wailing them added: because they who are innocent were killed and because of God, from whom without doubt, is grace of reward, they have been given eternal life.

---

[135] "*Victuros*" could be derived from either "*vinco*" (to win or conquer) or "*vivo*" (to live). But the latter contrasts better with "*mortuos*" just mentioned.

The true reason for Rachel's weeping is due to her envy of Leah's sons. While Rachel's sons are lost forever due to their sins at Gibeah, Leah's sons inherit eternal life. Rachel weeps as she remembers her sons who are gone forever:

> Wherefore he speaks to connect bewailing with Rachel's sons, who are eradicated both in present and in future [*qui et in praesenti et in future erasi sunt*]. However, those [sons of Leah] are bewailed in body were consoled in spirit [*carnaliter plancti, spiritualiter consolati sunt*]. But the sons of Rachel who were dwelling carnally will be consumed with spiritual flames [*carnaliter conversati, flammis spiritualibus consumentur*]. But for that reason, the evangelist testifies that the bewailing of Rachel was fulfilled by the killing of Leah's sons, because then she [Rachel] began to bewail her own sons, when she saw the sons of her sister killed for such cause, so that they may appear as heirs of eternal life. For to something opposite she arrives, because of the fruitfulness of the other [Leah], she grieves her more miserable unfavorable state.

Here, Augustine resists the common preferential treatment given to Rachel as the interceding matriarch of Israel or a type of the Church. This is remarkable since in Judaism, midrashic literature honors Rachel above even the patriarchs for her role as an intercessor for the exiled captives.[136] As early as Justin Martyr (*Dial.* 134.6) and Irenaeus (*Adv. Haer.* 4.21.3), Rachel has been interpreted typologically as the Church among Christians.[137] Augustine, however, foregoes these ideas and creatively incorporates geography, OT themes, and storytelling imagination to solve an interpretative problem that arises concerning Matt 2:18. Leah and Rachel's rivalry continues as their descendants' fates are juxtaposed throughout history.

XIV. Concluding Thoughts

Much has been written and spoken concerning Matt 2:16-18 from the second century to the fifth century. This chapter has dealt with twelve major strands of reading. In broader schemes, some discuss the passage while attempting to harmonize Matthean and Lucan infancy narratives (Sec. II). Another major interpretative scheme is to read Matt 2:16-18 through the lens of Isaiah 7–8 (Sec. III). Thirdly, the massacre raises theodical issues that certain readers attempt to address (Sec. IV). As for Herod, he is juxtaposed with other evil earthly authorities in Scripture (Sec. V) and manipulated or influenced by demonic ones (Sec. VI). Other readers form a continual narrative for Herod that results in punishment of his family (Sec. VII). Herod also becomes a symbol for later persecutors of Christians (Sec. VIII).

As for the victims, they are most often celebrated as martyrs (Sec. IX). Their deaths are not in vain but amount to sacrifices offered to God (Sec. X). Other readers fill in untold details involving Herod's executioners and the victims' parents (Sec. XI).

---

[136] See n. 3 for sources.
[137] See also Hilary of Poitiers, *Commentary on Matthew*, 1.7.

Finally, other interpreters consider the name of Ramah (Sec. XII) and Rachel's reasons for weeping (Sec. XIII).

The readings and interpretations are diverse as the passage reveals itself as a rich quarry for typological readings, tropological applications, and actualizations. While retelling the story (PJ) or reimagining the massacre through the Christological lens of Isaiah (Justin Martyr and Irenaeus), second-century readings focused relatively less on implications for the victims, Rama, and Rachel. As stated above, Christological fulfillment of Isaiah is a speculation encouraged in extrabiblical literature and the Gospel itself. In the third and fourth centuries, the details of the passage receive more attention, as readers employ exegetical methods similar to those used by modern historical critics and narrative critics. For example, Eusebius connects the story with Josephus, not unlike what scholars do today. Origen reads Matthew as a unified whole and notices how Herod the persecutor of the infant Jesus adumbrates later persecutors of the adult Christ.

The more imaginative interpretations of Matt 2:16-18, however, would prevail, especially when they were concerned with Herod and the victims.[138] For example, Origen introduces demonic forces behind Herod and Ephrem the Syrian explicitly compares him to wicked OT kings. Unlike Pilate, there is little ambivalence concerning Herod's fate or character. This vilification of Herod, however, is not completely radical considering that Matthew presents Jesus's enemies in mimicry of the Devil. For example, just as Satan began his temptation of Jesus in the wilderness with the protasis, "If you are the Son of God" (εἰ υἱὸς εἶ τοῦ θεοῦ), the onlookers at the crucifixion mock Jesus verbatim (Matt 4:3, 6; 27:40).

King Herod's reputation heads toward a deplorable trajectory, while the victims rise to the other end of the spectrum. They receive more honor than Matt 2:16-18 would warrant. Irenaeus is the first among many to call them martyrs while Tertullian and Origen deem them capable of worship, testimony, and struggle that reward them with crowns and palms. Like the association of the Devil with Herod, Matthew's Gospel itself provides grounds for the praise of the infants. For example, Tertullian finds support for infants' noetic ability in his observation about Matt 21:16, which cites Ps 8:2. The massacre story is furnished with ideas that add complexity to the narrative.

Herod and the victims (the martyred children and Rachel), however, are not simply confined to the past as a villain and heroes, respectively. Through actualization and tropological applications, the victims inspire perseverance in the Church under persecution (Cyprian), Christians in contact with Jews (Hilary of Poitiers, Augustine, Quodvultdeus), and defenders of orthodoxy and Christian virtues (Lucifer, Gregory of Nazianzus, Apponius, and Pope Leo the Great). Finally, meditation on Matt 2:16-18 also has theological implications. Gregory of Nyssa and John Chrysostom address questions concerning God's timing, goodness, and providence. Quodvultdeus crystallizes how the infants can be saved in spite of their inborn original sin, an idea promoted by his own hero, Augustine. Indeed, the students of Matt 2:16-18 from the second century to

---

[138] While interesting readings concerning Rama and Rachel exist, they seem to have been less influential than certain interpretations of Herod and the victims.

the fifth century were faced with a passage laden with lasting potential for imaginative storytelling, springboards for difficult theological conundrums, and paradigmatic living.[139]

---

[139] Paul Middleton writes, "The central character is not the most important element in the creation of martyrdom; it is the narrator." *Martyrdom: A Guide for the Perplexed*, T&T Clark Guides for the Perplexed (London: T&T Clark, 2011), 30. If Middleton is right, reception history of Matt 2:16-18 can provide glimpses into how various traditions handle human evil and suffering. Furthermore, these matters are relevant not only for Christendom but also for faith-seekers in general. In Os Guinness's view, "issue of human dignity and worth, and the problem of evil and suffering" are two issues that highlight the differences between the three major systems of faith: Eastern, secular, and Abrahamic. He continues, "Run those two issues through the lenses of the three families of faith and the results are starkly different, and they highlight the choices dramatically." Os Guinness, *Fool's Talk: Recovering the Art of Christian Persuasion* (Downers Grove: InterVarsity, 2015), 243.

4

Massacre of the Innocents from Sixth Century to 1516

Introduction

For organizational purposes, the fifth century was a convenient point to conclude the previous chapter. One reason was practical: to prevent it from becoming too lengthy. A weightier reason was the timely emergence of the pivotal *Calendar of Carthage* (ca. 505-23) and the *Veronese Sacramentary* (or *Leonine*; ca. 600).[1] These were the first known Western church documents to formalize an annual commemoration of the victims on December 28, the *Festival of the Innocents*. In the East, the Syrian Orthodox Church and the Eastern Orthodox Church also celebrate this feast, on December 27 and 29, respectively. The fifth-century Basil of Seleucia's *Oration 37 on the Children Who Were Killed by Herod in Bethlehem* is the earliest extant Greek sermon commemorating the victims.[2] While it is unlikely that all churches observed an annual celebration immediately, there are various indications that Matt 2:16-18 was growing in importance in liturgical practice from the sixth century onward.[3]

---

[1] Cassian Folsom argues that this work is not really a sacramentary, but a collection of booklets containing many prayers and formularies or a kind of liturgical resource book from which a celebrant could choose. In addition, while it contains formularies of Leo the Great, the entirety of the work is not his. Cassian Folsom, "The Liturgical Books of the Roman Rite," in *Handbook for Liturgical Studies Volume 1: Introduction to Liturgy*, ed. Anscar J. Chupungco, 245-314 (Collegeville: Liturgical Press, 1997), 245-7.

[2] Paul A. Hayward, "Suffering and Innocence in Latin Sermons for the Feast of the Holy Innocents, c. 400-800," in *The Church and Childhood: Papers Read at the 1993 Summer Meeting and the 1994 Winter Meeting of the Ecclesiastical History Society*, ed. Diana Wood, 67-80, Studies in Church History 31 (Oxford: Blackwell, 1994), 67-8, n. 3.

[3] While the fourth-century Philocalian Calendar mentions December 25 as Christmas, there is no mention of the *Feast of the Innocents*. The veneration of the children began as early as Irenaeus of Lyons, but the most formative stage in the development of the cult of the innocents is the fifth to sixth century. See Hayward, "Suffering and Innocence in Latin Sermons for the Feast of the Holy Innocents, c. 400-800," 67-8. For a more general discussion of liturgy in the first four centuries, which tended to be unfixed, see Cyrille Vogel, *Medieval Liturgy: An Introduction to the Sources*, rev. and trans. William Storey and Niels Rasmussen (Portland: Pastoral, 1986), 31-8.

Significant consequences follow. The reading of Matt 2:16-18 did not need to be confined to Christmas or Epiphany.[4] The massacre would receive more attention as an individual event, not as an addendum to the magi story.[5] This development corresponds to the increase in post-fifth-century works that devote more content to the massacre.[6] Visual representations of the massacre also begin to make their appearance from the fifth century onwards.[7] Thus, marking the transition at the end of the fifth century is appropriate.

I. Complexities of Reception History of Matthew 2:16-18 sixth century and beyond

Some inherent complexities of the reception history from the sixth century onwards require explanation. First, many works depend on the foundational readings of Matt 2:16-18 prior to the fifth century. Secondly, in addition to sermons, commentaries, and hymns, the reception historian of Matt 2:16-18 encounters art, pilgrimages, meditations, and dramas. Thirdly, an acceptable length of the current chapter needs proper demarcation.

While the extant sources for reception of Matt 2:16-18 in the sixth century and beyond are more numerous, many interpreters are indebted to their patristic predecessors. Examples abound. Like Eusebius of Caesarea and the *History of Joseph the Carpenter* before them (see Chapter 3, VII), *Cursor Mundi* (ca. 1300), Giovanni Boccacio of Certaldo's *De Casibus Virorum Illustrium* (ca. 1360), and John Lyndgate's *The Fall of Princes* (ca. 1431–8) narrate Herod's ignoble end. The creative interpretation of Matt 2:16 in *Protoevangelium of James* (PJ) continues in the *Gospel of Pseudo-Matthew* (GPM) and the *Arabic Gospel of the Infancy of the Savior* (AIG). Romanos the Melodist borrows from the descriptive content and styles of Ephrem the Syrian, Prudentius, Gregory of Nyssa, and Basil of Seleucia.[8] The tropological illustrations of

---

[4] For discussions of Matt 2:16-18 in hymns, orations, and sermons delivered on Christmas or Epiphany, see Chapter 3, VIII. F; IX; and X.

[5] Karl Young writes, "The association of the two events was maintained for a time in the Roman liturgical calendar, for during the early Christian centuries they were commemorated in a single feast, the separate celebration of the *Massacre of the Innocents* on December 28th being unknown before the fourth or fifth century." *The Drama of the Medieval Church* (Oxford: Clarendon, 1967), 2:102.

[6] For example, fourth- and fifth-century hymns such as Prudentius's *Hymn on the Epiphany* and Caelius Sedulius's *Hostis Herodes Impie* (used for Vespers on Epiphany) deal with Matt 2:16-18 tangentially. Later, Romanos the Melodist's sixth-century *Hymn on the Massacre of the Innocents*, the Venerable Bede's eighth-century *Hymn for Martyrs*, and Notker the Stammerer's ninth-century *Praise to you Christ* cover it more in depth. Another example is the emergence of independent dramatic units dealing with the massacre in the eleventh and the twelfth centuries from kernels in the Epiphany plays in the ninth and the tenth centuries. Young, *The Drama of the Medieval Church*, 2:109.

[7] See Chapter 6. Gertrud Schiller, *Iconography of Christian Art*, trans. Janet Seligman (Greenwich: New York Graphic Society, 1971), 1: 114–17.

[8] Barkhuizen, "Romanos Melodos, 'On the Massacre of the Innocents,'" 29–50. Borrowed ideas include Herod's likeness to the pharaoh and king Saul (Ephrem the Syrian), victims as flowers (Prudentius), Herod giving elaborate instructions to his soldiers and graphic details of the slaughter (Gregory of Nyssa), and fathers mourning with the mothers and the victims in the bosom of Abraham (Basil of Seleucia).

Isidore of Seville, Rufus of Shotep, Venerable Bede, Thomas Kerameus, Hildegard of Bingen, Radulfus Ardens, and Thomas Aquinas are reminiscent of Origen, Optatus, Jacob of Serugh, Apponius, and Gregory of Nazianzus.[9] It is difficult to overstate the predecessors' importance, especially when commentators like the ninth-century Rabanus Maurus cite block quotations from Jerome and Hilary of Poitiers verbatim.[10] In some cases, next to nothing is unique or determinable about the medieval writers themselves except their use of patristic sources.[11]

Other times, post-fifth-century interpreters compile past works to stimulate critical thinking during Bible lectures.[12] Joseph Verheyden opines that the *Glossa Ordinaria* is "a prominent representative of a kind of approach that typifies medieval exegesis: firmly rooted in the Patristic tradition and arguing above all on the model of *auctoritas*."[13] In his *Catena Aurea*, Thomas Aquinas collects (though he does not synthesize) the readings of Matt 2:16-18 from *Opus Imperfectum* (OI), Augustine, and the more recent Rabanus Maurus and the Venerable Bede. These citations supply theodical approaches, interpretative options (e.g., calculation of two years), and tropological lessons.

So then, the real value of the reception of Matt 2:16-18 from the sixth century onwards is not in content but in various innovative genres. In addition to the traditional sermons, orations, and hymns, at least four more forms grew in importance: (1) pilgrimages to Rachel's tomb, (2) meditations on Christ's life, (3) visual arts, such as

---

[9] Venerable Bede comments on the worse state of the "impious" compared to the "iniquitous" in Prov 21:18: The impious Herod is held to a greater standard of judgment than the iniquitous. *Commentary on Proverbs*, 21:18. In *Homily 52 on the Holy Infants*, Thomas Kerameus teaches that the age of four in which Christ returns to Judea represents four cardinal virtues, which can be obtained only after the mindset of the flesh, the earthly mindset, the purposes of the flesh, and the earthly members are purged from the immature Christian (Rom 8:13; Col 3:5; Heb 5:11-14). Herod's massacre of the infants and the flight to Egypt, allegorically speaking, are suffering experiences that allow an immature believer to move on from the foundation to growth. Jesus sympathizes not only with the mature but also those less developed as he himself increased in growth (Luke 2:52). In *Allegoriae Quaedam Scripturae Sacrae* 137 (PL 83: 118), Isidore of Seville highlights Herod's typological role of the devil and other enemies of Christ. See also Susan Boynton's discussions of Radulfus Ardens, who says Rachel is the Church weeping over the rude and uneducated souls destroyed by the Devil. "Performative Exegesis in the Fleury Interfectio Puerorum," *Viator* 29 (1998): 52. In contrast, Hildegard of Bingen in her *Homily 10: The Eve of Epiphany 1* analogizes Herod's massacre to Satan's plot to destroy simple reverence for God's precepts and wisdom through idolatry. Herod's action is in line with the golden calf at Horeb (Exod 32:2) and Jeroboam's two calves in Dan and Bethel (1 Kg 12:28-29). *Homily 11: The Eve of Epiphany 2* similarly condemns the devil's deceptive plan to promote prideful self-righteousness among people. The cure for this problem is reliance upon God, not self-reliance spoken by God.

[10] Rabanus Maurus, *Commentary on Matthew 1*, 2:3.

[11] For example, there are some doubts about whether the anonymous author of *Liber Questionum in Euangeliis* (LQE) relied on an Irish writer named Frigulus from the late seventh/early eighth century. Cf. CCSL 108F and Michael M. Gorman, "Frigulus: Hiberno-Latin Author or Pseudo-Irish Phantom? Comments on the Edition of the Liber Questionum In Euangeliis (CCSL 108F)," *Revue d'Histoire Ecclésiastique* 100 (2005): 425–56.

[12] Marie A. Mayeski, "Early Medieval Exegesis: Gregory I to the Twelfth Century," in *A History of Biblical Interpretation Volume 2: The Medieval through the Reformation Periods*, ed. Alan J. Hauser and Duane F. Watson, 86–112 (Grand Rapids: Eerdmans, 2009), 100–1.

[13] Joseph Verheyden, "Reading Matthew and Mark in the Middle Ages: The *Glossa Ordinaria*," in *Mark and Matthew II: Comparative Readings: Reception History, Cultural Hermeneutics, and Theology*, ed. Eve-Marie Becker and Anders Runesson, 121–50, WUNT 304 (Tübingen: Mohr Siebeck, 2013), 130.

drawings, paintings, and sculptures, and (4) performance arts, such as plays.[14] Since visual arts relate to the text in complex ways, a separate chapter on it is necessary.[15]

First, more pilgrims paid heed to the site of Rachel's tomb near Bethlehem. Detailed descriptions of the tomb replaced the earlier brief mentions in the *Bordeaux Itinerary* and *Onomastica* (worked on by Origen, Eusebius, and Jerome). Local congregations and visitors identified a physical space to remember Matt 2:16-18.

Secondly, after the rise of monasticism, meditations on the episodes of Christ's life became prominent in spirituality and shaped the readings of Matt 2:16-18.[16] One example is the influence of *Meditationes Vitae Christi* (likely of Franciscan origin from the fourteenth century), which spanned several traditions. The Carthusian Nicholas Love translated and expanded upon the work. Another Carthusian, Ludolph of Saxony, heavily cited the Infancy and the Passion portions.[17] In turn, Ludolph's work influenced the *Devotio Moderna*, Ignatius of Loyola, and Teresa of Ávila.[18] Alongside individual works are monastic ideas such as the use of imagination and uniform monastery architecture, designed to aid mental prayer.[19] So then, the genre of monastic meditation adds to the growing complexity of the massacre's reception history.

The third and fourth genres are best discussed together: visual and performance arts, for both of which the *Meditationes Vitae Christi* was especially influential. Its picturesque words formed by "lively imagination and refined sensibility" influenced important scenes recorded in Italian iconography (e.g., Giotto) and the fifteenth-century mystery plays.[20] In some of these performances, Herod sent out his soldiers to

---

[14] To this list one can add Geoffrey Chaucer's stories (*The Miller's Tale* and *The Prioress's Tale*), but they do not contribute greatly to the current reception history. Performance arts necessarily involve literature (e.g., script) and visual arts (e.g., costumes and props), which will be considered.

[15] Paolo Berdini comments on the unique nature of "visual exegesis": "Not one that replaces the reading of the text; the viewer may well return to the text after seeing the picture, for that matter. A picture is not a sermon or any other form of text; it can only put the viewer in contact with the text, tell the viewer something about Scripture that may concern him. What visual exegesis describes is the new encounter with the text made possible by the image, not its substitution, much in the same way as the painter's reading of the text should not be taken as a substitution for ours." *The Religious Art of Jacopo Bassano: Painting as Visual Exegesis* (Cambridge: Cambridge University Press, 1997), 14.

[16] "Meditation," in Christian tradition means at least four things: (1) memorizing/reciting Scripture; (2) keeping truths or inspirations in mind during the day; (3) pondering on things, emphasizing "intellectual rigour, acuteness of perception, or devotional fervour"; and (4) applying the mind and often the imagination to the truths of faith, especially to episodes of Christ's life. The fourth type (which I focus on this chapter) became a part of various methods of prayer. "Meditation," in *ODCC*, 1072.

[17] Mary Immaculate Bordenstedt, *The Vita Christi of Ludolphus the Carthusian: A Dissertation*, The Catholic University of America Studies in Medieval and Renaissance Latin Language and Literature 16 (Washington, DC: Catholic University of America Press, 1944), 30–1; Michelle Karnes, *Imagination, Meditation, and Cognition in the Middle Ages* (Chicago: University of Chicago Press, 2011), 145.

[18] See Alister E. McGrath, *Christian Spirituality: An Introduction* (Oxford: Wiley-Blackwell, 1999), 84–7; and ElenaCarrera, *Teresa of Avila's Autobiography: Authority, Power and the Self in Mid-sixteenth-century Spain*, Legenda (London: Modern Humanities Research Association and Maney, 2005), 28.

[19] Bordenstedt, *The Vita Christi of Ludolphus the Carthusian*, 31; MaryCarruthers, *The Craft of Thought: Meditation, Rhetoric, and the Making of Images, 400–1200*, Cambridge Studies in Medieval Literature 34 (Cambridge: Cambridge University Press, 1998), 254–7.

[20] Emile Mâle, *Religious Art in France: The Late Middle Ages: A Study of Medieval Iconography and Its Sources*, trans. Marthiel Matthews, Bollingen Series 90:3 (Princeton: Princeton University Press, 1986), 28–48.

strike some members of the audience, who thereby experience the "wrath of Herod" in Matt 2:16 in a visual and tactile manner.[21] The people no longer simply read or heard about the massacre in feasts, but experienced it in plays. By the fourteenth to fifteenth centuries, the dramatic presentations of Matt 2:16-18 moved outside the church to the streets and fields of large European towns.[22] The great influence of this genre is observed in Geoffrey Chaucer's characterization of the prideful Absolon, who "somtyme, to shewe his lightnesse and maistrye, He pleyeth Herodes upon a scaffold hye (*Miller's Tale*, 1.3384-5).

Though mystery plays enjoyed popularity in Europe by means of guild and circuit performances through the sixteenth century, changing religious, political, and economic conditions, not least the Reformation, led to their gradual decline.[23] According to Alan E. Knight, the mystery plays would survive as "dramatic mirrors" for unified communities under the Catholic faith. Yet the same performances in less unified communities led to widespread diffusion and acceptance of essentially different religious ideas, which began to expose community divisions.[24] For example, Elizabeth's anti-Catholicism and the French wars of religion affected the types of plays performed.[25] Since the Reformation is a major event that affects this major type of reception of Matt 2:16-18, 1516 is the appropriate end date for this chapter. This decision also coheres somewhat with the emergence of many post-1516 Renaissance artworks (e.g., Pieter Bruegels (the Elder and the Younger), Guido Reni, Peter Paul Rubens, Nicolas Poussin et al.).

II. Major Strands of Reading

While the number of diverse genres complicates the reception-historical study of Matt 2:16-18 from the sixth century to 1516, the strands of readings themselves are not so diverse. As before, literal readings of the massacre inspire some to harmonize its details with other accounts by using explanatory additions. Tropological readings continue to interpret Herod, the victims, and Rachel as symbolic figures. Many works dramatize Herod's role, but of particular interest is his role as the dragon's pawn in Revelation and a symbol of secular rule opposing God.

The emphasis on the rewarded martyrdom and innocent sacrifice continues from the sixth century to 1516. Often, by recontextualizing Matt 2:16 alongside more hopeful passages, the children's role transforms from that of helpless victims to triumphant

---

[21] Clarke, *The Gospel of Matthew and Its Readers*, 23.
[22] Mâle, *Religious Art in France*, 35; Meg Twycross, "The Theatricality of Medieval English Plays," in *The Cambridge Companion to Medieval English Theatre*, ed. Richard Beadle and Alan J. Fletcher, 26-74, 2nd rev. ed. (Cambridge: Cambridge University Press, 2008). For the discussion of a modern reenactment, see Roland Reed, "The Slaughter of the Innocents," *Early Theatre* 3 (2000): 219-28.
[23] Karen Rall, *Medieval Mysteries: A Guide to History, Lore, Places and Symbolism of Twelve Medieval Mysteries* (Lake Worth: Nicolas-Hays, 2014), 120-1.
[24] Alan E. Knight, "Faded Pageant: The End of the Mystery Plays in Lille," *Journal of the Midwest Modern Language Association* 29:1 (1996): 3-4.
[25] Ibid., 4.

victors and offerings acceptable to God.[26] Most frequently various interpreters visualize the innocents in triumphant visions borrowed from the Apocalypse and other sources.[27] The tropological and the anagogical senses reimage them as models for the present and afterlife.

Closely related to the innocents is Rachel who continues to represent the Church. As before, she stands for those grieving in Bethlehem, but as pilgrims frequent her supposed tomb at a specific fixed location nearby, there is less emphasis on Ramah as a distant place (see Chapter 3, XII). Many works contain dialogues between Rachel and others in her grief, opening up interpretative space for her allegorical role as the Church, tropological lessons about her martyrs, and anagogical teachings about her ultimate triumph.

III. The Massacre in Harmonization with Other Accounts

The previous chapter surveyed some works that harmonized the Matthean and Lucan infancy narratives (see Chapter 3, II). Notably important was the PJ, which differs somewhat from Matt 2:16-18 in its narration of the massacre. While the author of *Frag. 23* (*ca.* second or third century, see Chapter 3, II. B) observes that the magi came to a house (Matt 2:11), PJ narrates that the magi arrived at the cave, very soon after the birth of Jesus, who was still in swaddling clothes. Thus, PJ implies that the star appeared before Jesus's birth.[28] In his seventh homily on Matthew, Chrysostom follows PJ and explains that for precaution's sake Herod adds two years to the calculation of the age range.[29] PJ also records that during the massacre, Mary hides Jesus in an ox-stall, mountains conceal Elizabeth and John the Baptist, and Herod has Zechariah killed in the temple.[30]

---

[26] This idea of "recontextualization" borrows from Thomas Blackstone's study of hermeneutics in the Epistle to the Hebrews. Blackstone believes that a "living voice" guides the community to interpret OT texts in either (1) static, (2) surface, or (3) fluid recontextualization. While the first does not deviate from the original context, surface recontextualizations are "modernizations," in which close links to the original context are maintained. Fluid recontextualizations are "accommodations," where the new circumstances guide the meaning more than the original. Thomas L. Blackstone, "The Hermeneutics of Recontextualization in the Epistle to the Hebrews" (PhD diss., Emory University, 1995).

[27] There is a variety of figures for the death toll, including 1,800 and 2,000 in the *Book of the Bee*, 39; 2,200 (140 in Bethlehem) in *Leabhar Breac*; 3,000 in *Martyrdom of Matthew*; 14,000 in the Byzantine liturgy; and 64,000 in Syrian tradition. The connection between Matt 2:16-18 and Revelation no doubt influenced these high totals, though the mathematical logic behind these numbers is not clear. Dionysius Exiguus (*ca.* 470–544) however, comments on the total of 64,000, which is the product of the following formula: Herod sends forty leaders, each with forty executioners, who in turn killed forty children each. Brown, *The Birth of the Messiah*, 205.

[28] See discussion in Chapter 3, II. B.

[29] See also Ernest A. W. Budge, trans., *The Book of the Cave of Treasures: A History of the Patriarchs and the Kings Their Successors from the Creation to the Crucifixion of Christ*, translated from the Syriac Text of the British Museum Ms. Add. 25875 (London: Religious Tract Society, 1927), 203; *Book of the Bee*, 38; Christian of Stavelot, *Exposition on Matthew the Evangelist*, 2:155–67.

[30] The sixth-century apocryphal *Cave of Treasures* also records the demise of Zechariah but with less detail than PJ and the *Book of the Bee*. *The Book of the Cave of Treasures*, 217–18. The repeated references to Matthew 23 are likely due to the pervading influence of PJ.

Just as PJ has expanded upon Matt 2:16-18, three notable additions build upon both PJ and Matt 2:16-18: (1) Herod's trip to Rome just before the execution of his plot, (2) the Holy Family's narrow escape out of Judea, and (3) the continual flow of Zechariah's blood along with Nathanael's survival of the massacre. While the effect of each episode is different, all of them fill the imaginative narrative space created by the massacre account.

A. Maximus the Confessor

Maximus the Confessor (*ca.* 580–662) was a Greek theologian and a prolific ascetical writer.[31] One of the works attributed to him is the *Life of the Virgin*, the earliest complete biographical treatise on the Virgin Mary, originally written in Greek but surviving only in an Old Georgian translation.[32] Some later manuscripts evince its use in liturgical readings of monastic communities, anticipating later meditations on Christ's life.[33] Sections 42–5 deal directly with Matt 2:16-18. Familiar features include censures of Herod, consumed by envy to the point of killing children, the innocents and even his own (sec. 43); Benjaminite ownership of Ramah and Rachel's burial near Bethlehem (sec. 44); the virtuous martyrdom and the sacrifice of the innocents (secs. 44–45); and the foreshadowing of Jesus's Passion (sec. 45).[34]

Maximus builds upon the PJ-Chrysostom chronology so that (1) the magi arrive soon after Jesus's birth, (2) they return home without reporting to Herod, (3) a year passes after the events of the Lucan infancy narratives (circumcision, presentation at the temple, encounter with Simeon, etc.), and (4) Herod finally executes his massacre plan (secs. 38–41). So then, in section 42, Maximus anticipates the following questions: Why did Herod not act immediately? Why did the magi not take the Holy Family to safety? Why did the Holy Family themselves flee right away?

The answer is that, when the magi visited, a great tumult in Herod's family "took place through Providence from above, which did not allow him the opportunity to search for the newborn king and Lord of all." Herod successfully killed his wife, but he needed the emperor's consent to kill his sons. After travelling to Rome to obtain Augustus's permission and prevailing over his sons, he remembered the magi and the infant and raged anew. Since considerable time had passed, he slaughtered children two years and younger from Bethlehem and its environs.

Thus, Maximus connects Herod's family troubles to the time leading up to the massacre, intensifying his murderous rage and envy. The Confessor's acknowledgment of Providence and incorporation of material from Josephus are reminiscent of Eusebius of Caesarea (see Chapter 3, VII. A).[35] Herod's journey to Rome is also

---

[31] "Maximus the Confessor, St.," *ODCC*, 1061–2.
[32] Stephen J. Shoemaker, trans., *The Life of the Virgin: Maximus the Confessor: Translated with an Introduction and Notes* (New Haven: Yale University Press, 2012), 1–2.
[33] Ibid., 3.
[34] All chapter markers and translations of *The Life of the Virgin* are Shoemaker's.
[35] See also *The Book of the Cave of Treasures*, 217–19; Ishodad of Merv, *A Commentary on St. Matthew*, 2:18; and Theophanes Kerameus, *Homily 52 on the Holy Infants*.

found in *Leabhar Breac*, Aelfric of Eynsham, the *Golden Legend*, and Denis the Carthusian.[36]

B. The *Speckled Book*

PJ not only depicts the magi close to the time of Jesus's birth, it also locates the Holy Family in Judea during the massacre, setting the stage for a narrow escape. Some works fill the details. For example, in AIG 9 and GPM 17:2, the angelic warning comes to Joseph just a day or so before the calamity befalls Bethlehem and its surroundings.[37] Another example is a fifteenth-century manuscript known as the *Speckled Book* (*Leabhar Breac*), a collection likely compiled by Murchadh Ó Cuindlis, an Irish scribe at Duniry.[38] It contains "an Infancy Gospel (known in other manuscripts) of much earlier date," evidently of ninth-century origin.[39]

The portion most relevant to Matt 2:16-18 extends from *Speckled Book* 97–123.[40] It notes that some writings locate Christ, Mary, and Joseph in the land of Judah at the time of the massacre and follows these sources (120).[41] The Holy Family escapes from

---

[36] Leabhar Breac 107–10; Aelfric of Eynsham, *Homily 5: The Nativity of the Innocents*; Jacobus de Voragine, *The Golden Legend: Readings on the Saints: Translated by William G. Ryan with an Introduction by Eamon Duffy* (Princeton: Princeton University Press, 2012), 56–8; Denis the Carthusian, *Exposition on Chapter 2 of Matthew*, 5.

[37] AIG is a work indebted to PJ, but with additional material from the *Infancy Gospel of Thomas* and a possible Syrian archetype (fifth or sixth century) that has connection to the *Syriac History of the Virgin*. Mary is the main character, and the core of the work deals with miracles in Egypt during the sojourn of the Holy Family. Ernest A. W. Budge thinks that this Syrian translator had access to Infancy material as early as fourth century. *The History of the Blessed Virgin Mary and the History of the Likeness of Christ*, Luzac's Semitic Text and Translation Series 5 (London: Luzac, 1899), viii. GPM is a Latin reworking of PJ, along with various additions and omissions, emphases and de-emphases. De-emphases include minimal references to Jewish customs and practices, while emphases include Mary's asceticism and willful devotion to virginal purity. These redactions suggest that the author is a Latin-speaking monk in the early seventh century, when monastic orders were beginning to expand in the West. Constaine von Tischendorf initially thought that the book's attribution to the disciple Matthew was part of the original text, but it turned out to be a later addition. Another title is *Liber de ortu beatae Mariae et infantia Salvatoris*. Ehrman and Pleše, eds. and trans., *The Other Gospels*, 37–40; Elliott, *The Apocryphal New Testament*, 100; Elliott, *A Synopsis of the Apocryphal Nativity and Infancy Narratives*, xvii.

[38] Hence the alternative title "Great Book of Duniry" (*Leabhar Mór Dúna Doighre*). *Oxford Concise Companion to Irish Literature*, ed. Robert Welch, Oxford Paperback Reference (Oxford: Oxford University Press, 2000), 191.

[39] Elliott, *A Synopsis of the Apocryphal Nativity and Infancy Narratives*, xiv–xv, xviii. For a detailed discussion of relationships between *Leabhar Breac*, the *Liber Flavus Fergsiorum Infancy Narrative*, and the "J Compilation" that make up this "special source," see MartinMcNamara and Jean-Daniel Kaestli, "The Irish Infancy Narratives and Their Relationship with Latin Sources," in *Apocrypha Hiberniae I, 1: Evangelia Infantiae*, ed. Martin McNamara, Caoimhín Breatnach, John Carey, Máire Herbert, Jean-Daniel Kaestli, Brian Ó Cuív, Pádraig Ó Fiannachta, and Diarmuid Ó Laoghaire, 41–134, CCSA 13 (Turnhout: Brepols, 2001).

[40] It is apparent that the writer borrows from Matthew, Josephus, and Eusebius of Caesarea, but other sources are more obscure, making dating difficult. The works of Josephus and Eusebius are *Historia ecclesiastica* I, 6 and *Antiquities* 14–16. The *Speckled Book* also borrows from the eighth-century LQE, which specifies names of twenty plains where Herod dispatches his soldiers. Eighteen of twenty plains are named after specific individuals among the sons of Canaan (111). CCSA 13: 374–84; McNamara and Kaestli, "The Irish Infancy Narratives and their Relationship with Latin Sources," 44.

[41] All Irish texts and English translations of the *Speckled Book* are from CCSA 13.

the patrolling soldiers in Bethlehem and its environs to reach Nazareth (121–4). Then, following the warning of the angel, Joseph becomes the protector of Mary and the child as they flee to Egypt (124).

Yet Jesus's role, not Joseph's, is paramount during the escape. During the flight, a large troop apprehends the Holy Family, at which point Mary asks the child Jesus for instructions (121). Jesus directs Mary to tell the troops that she is carrying wheat, not a child. Mary follows Jesus's words and then the soldier finds wheat in place of Jesus. The narrator cites a tradition that claims the Greeks offer wheaten grain as offering because Jesus's body is made of wheat (122).[42] In a similar episode, Jesus tells Mary to be forthright and tell the troop that she is carrying the one they seek (123). The incredulous troops, however, dismiss them, because she would not admit the truth. Jesus's active role in the escape is a significant departure from Matthew's account, where Joseph is the dominant actor.

These close encounters with Herod's troops in the *Speckled Book* are similar to the dangers faced on the flight to Egypt in GPM 18–22. In both accounts, the Holy Family meets deadly foes: dragons, lions, panthers, wolves, and other creatures in GPM 18–19 and Herod's troops in *Speckled Book* 121–3. In both stories, Jesus is actively vocal in protecting the group. In addition, miracles involve the aid of plants: the palm tree in GPM 20–1 and wheat in the *Speckled Book* 121–2. Thus, the action in the *Speckled Book* dramatizes Matt 2:16-18 and reinforces the idea of Jesus's sovereignty known since the second century (see Chapter 3, III).

C. Book of the Bee

Little is known about Solomon, the author of the *Book of the Bee*, except that he was a native of Akhlât, a Nestorian, and appointed bishop of al-Basra in 1222.[43] The Syriac work is a compilation of Bible stories and legends, stretching from creation to the final resurrection. Chapters 33–40 deal with the events found in the Matthean and Lucan infancy narratives.

In chapter 39, twelve Persian kings (divided into three groups of four, each carrying one of the three gifts) find their way to the cave of Jesus's birth after first visiting Herod.[44] A sage named Longinus reports this event to Augustus, who asks Herod for more details concerning the child.[45] Herod feels mocked and destroys about two thousand children from Bethlehem and its surroundings, two years and younger (Matt 2:16). Herod searches for John the Baptist, but Zechariah takes him to safety after conferring the priesthood on him. As in PJ, Herod's men kill Zechariah near the altar.[46]

---

[42] Perhaps the author was also influenced by the Eucharist and the miracle of the corn in the *Infancy Gospel of Thomas*, 10.
[43] Ernest A. W. Budge, ed. and trans., *The Book of the Bee* (Oxford: Clarendon, 1886), iii.
[44] *Cave of Treasures* names only three kings. The twelve priest-kings in the Syriac *Revelation of the Magi* likely influenced the *Book of the Bee*. All chapter markers and translations of the *Book of the Bee* are Budge's.
[45] This Longinus appear to be unrelated to the Roman soldier who was bestowed the same name in the *Acts of the Pilate* (Matt 27:54; Mark 15:39).
[46] See the discussion of Matt 23:35 in Chapter 3, V. A.

Like Eusebius of Caesarea and Maximus the Confessor, the *Book of the Bee* confirms that Herod received his due for this evil (ch. 40).

At the close of chapter 39, the compiler contributes two noteworthy addendums. First, he cites a tradition concerning John's father: "They say that from the day when Zechariah was slain his blood bubbled up until Titus the son of Vespasian came and slew three hundred myriads of Jerusalem, and then the flow of blood ceased." Here, the *Book of the Bee* combines Jewish extra-biblical sources with PJ and the fall of Jerusalem in AD 70.[47] At the time of the Babylonian siege, Nebuzaradan, the captain of Nebuchadnezzar's guard, arrives in Jerusalem to destroy the temple. When Zechariah's blood begins to bubble, the captain inquires the leaders concerning it and they deceitfully reply that the bubbling blood came from sacrifices. The captain disproves them, and on the threat of torture, he demands to know the truth.[48]

They confess that the blood is from Zechariah the son of Jehoiada, whom they killed.[49] Seeking to appease the blood, the captain slays priests and others until the number reached 940,000.[50] Nebuzaradan wonders aloud whether he must destroy every single individual in the nation. At these words, the blood ceases to boil and, in the Babylonian versions, Nebuzaradan becomes a convert to Judaism.

So then, the *Book of the Bee* sets up an analogy between (1) Joash and Herod; (2) Zechariah, the son of Jehoiada and Zechariah, the father of John the Baptist; (3) the invasion of Babylonians and the invasion of Romans; and (4) Nebuzaradan and Titus the son of Vespasian. In both cataclysms of Jerusalem, Zechariah's blood demands retributive justice. The differences are also telling. In certain Jewish sources, Nebuzaradan's conversion to Judaism and his dismay at the extensive killing indicate some hint of mercy for Israel. In the *Book of the Bee*, however, there is no mention of Titus' hesitation to kill, conversation with the blood, or conversion. It is interested only in justice for Herod's crimes and those he represents.

Another note in the book concerns John 1:48: "The father of the child Nathanael also took him, and wrapped him round, and laid him under a fig-tree; and he was saved from slaughter. Hence our Lord said to Nathaniel, 'Before Philip called thee, I saw thee, when thou wast under the fig-tree.'" Like John the Baptist, Nathanael survives the slaughter through the protective agency of his father to become a follower of Jesus as an adult. Jesus's supernatural knowledge of Nathanael extends far beyond

---

[47] See *y. Taan.* 69; *b. Git.* 57b; *b. Sanh.* 96; *Lam. Rab.* 4:13. Michael D. Swartz thinks that this story could have originated outside rabbinic circles, perhaps in Jewish Christian circles, but later modified for non-Christian Jews. Whatever the origins, the legend may have been well known. *The Signifying Creator: Nontextual Sources of Meaning in Ancient Judaism* (New York: New York University Press, 2012), 83.

[48] In the Palestinian versions, the captain places them on gallows, while in the Babylonian versions he threatens to tear their flesh with iron.

[49] Though not cited explicitly in the *Book of the Bee*, the author may have been familiar with the Palestinian Talmud and *Lam. Rab.* 4:13, texts that identify seven sins that elevate the gravity of their evil: (1) murder of a priest, (2) murder of a prophet, (3) murder of a judge, (4) spilling of innocent blood, (5) pollution of the Temple Court, (6) Sabbath violation, and (7) violation on the Day of Atonement.

[50] In the Babylonian versions, the greater and lesser courts of Sanhedrin, young men and women, and school-age children are also included in the slaughter.

the time of their encounter in Bethsaida to their infancy. Thus, the book heightens Jesus's prophetic power.

IV. Herod as the Dragon's Pawn

As seen in the previous chapter, early interpreters imagine demonic forces influencing Herod to carry through the massacre plot (see Chapter 3, VI). Later, this strand of reading Matt 2:16-18 would converge with the readings of Revelation 12 to project Herod as the dragon's pawn.

A. Oecumenius

Just as some works supplement readings of Matt 2:16-18 with contents of the Apocalypse, some commentaries on Revelation refer to Matthew. One source is the oldest Greek commentary on Revelation, written by the mysterious sixth-century Oecumenius.[51] His "exposition, vigorous, modest, but uneven, accepts the Apocalypse as a divinely inspired canonical Book, relevant not only for its immediate situation but for the understanding of the past and the future."[52]

In *Commentary on the Apocalypse* 7:7-10, Oecumenius deals with Rev 12:3-6, which relates to the past.[53] The scene in which the dragon stands ready to devour the child of the woman in labor refers to Satan's plan to destroy Christ, who is born of the Virgin, through the manipulation of Herod (7:7, 9; Rev 12:4). Satan is aware that the child will fulfill Isa 8:4, the prophecy of his demise (see Chapter 3, III). When Oecumenius urges John to reveal the male child more clearly, John answers that he is destined to rule the nations with the iron rod (7:8; Rev 12:5). Oecumenius responds that the child is the "savior and Lord, Jesus the Messiah," who fulfills Ps 2:8-9. The final phrase of Rev 12:5 continues the drama of Matthew 2: just as "her child was caught up to God and to his throne," the "forethought of the Father" leads to the escape of the child. The escape is possible through Joseph's obedience and Satan fails in his plan to kill the child through the massacre (*Commentary on the Apocalypse* 7:9). Rev 12:6 guarantees the Virgin's protection alongside Jesus in Egypt, where the Holy Family stays for three and a half years ("one thousand two hundred and sixty days") (7:10).

By juxtaposing Matthew 2 with Rev 12:4-6, Oecumenius places the massacre of the innocents in the midst of a cosmic struggle between God and Satan. God is present and active so that the male child and the Virgin find solace with God (Rev 12:5-6). Simultaneously, Satan manifests his dragon-like monstrosity in his desperate attempt to destroy Christ.

---

[51] Oecumenius "appears to be a contemporary and a supporter of Severus of Antioch ... not to be confused with Oecumenius, the Bishop of Tricca in Thessaly (10th century)." "Oecumenius," *ODCC*, 1182.
[52] Ibid.
[53] The English translations of Oecumenius are from John N. Suggit, trans., *Oecumenius: Commentary on the Apocalypse*, FC 112 (Washington, DC: Catholic University of America Press, 2006).

B. John of Euobea

The mid-eighth-century John of Euboea similarly connects Revelation 12 to Matt 2:16-18 in his *Sermon on the Innocents Killed in Bethlehem and Rachel*. He recalls familiar images, such as the victims as lambs, grapes of harvest, and the desperate attempts of mothers to protect their children (2–4).[54] Even the victims plead futilely with Herod's soldiers (4). John then bewails the demonic cause of the massacre:

> O transgression of the dragon of the deep sea (τοῦ βυθίου δράκοντος), not satisfied even after eating up the flesh of the guiltless infants! For even after the merciless infanticide took place, he was still seeking the born king with cowardice and folly. And he did not stop groaning and trembling (στένων καὶ τρέμων), until his life was removed from him.[55]

Like Oecumenius, John evokes dragon-related visions of the Apocalypse but adds the curse of Cain, who was "groaning and trembling" on earth after God judged him (Gen 4:12, 14 LXX). Just as the Devil induces Cain to be the first OT murderer, so he also provokes Herod to be the first NT murderer (1 John 3:12). So then, Satan's sentence is fittingly Cain's.

V. Herod as Symbol of Secular Rule Opposing God

Medieval dramas are often complex amalgams of liturgy and art, as well as a variegated repository of Scripture readings. Though their origins are somewhat obscure, certain plays, known individually as the *Play of the Star* (*Officium Stellae*), depict Herod as symbol of secular rule, thwarted by Christ and the innocents.[56] One specific play was performed in late-eleventh-century Freising. Freising was a city with cathedral schools influenced by the Ottonian Renaissance, which spurred the "impulse to unite classical and Christian language" for an audience of "highly cultivated milieu."[57]

---

[54] John appears as a bishop of Euboea in some texts, but no bishopric existed there. In addition, the corpus of his works is not clearly defined. *The Oxford Dictionary of Byzantium*, ed. Alexander P. Kazhdan, Alice-Mary Talbot, Anthony Culter et al. (Oxford: Oxford University Press, 1991), 2: 1065.

[55] All translations of John of Euboea are mine and derived from the Greek text in P. Michaelis Lequien, ed., *John of Damascus, John of Nicæa, Patriarch John VI of Constantinople, Joannes of Eubœa*, PG 46 (Paris: Petit-Montrouge, 1864) 1501–8.

[56] Peter Dronke warns against a "monolithic answer" in search for the genesis of the medieval drama, and earlier, including sources, original purpose, and development. *Nine Medieval Latin Plays*, Cambridge Medieval Classics I (Cambridge: Cambridge University Press, 1994), xxxi. The performance of the play and the interpretation of the script in specific social location are what counts. As Johann Drumbl writes, "The composition with which the history of the theatre in the early Middle Ages takes its beginning shows itself as the product of the *schola*, and we do not know whether it was originally destined for liturgical use. Unexpectedly the study of the diffusion of the *Play of the Star* has taught us that what we can study of medieval theatre is not its origin, but only the moment at which it enters and becomes a part of 'culture.'" *Quem quaeritis: teatro sacro dell'alto Medioevo*, Biblioteca teatrale 39 (Roma: Bulzoni, 1981), 326.

[57] Dronke, *Nine Medieval Latin Plays*, xxii–xxiii. Karl Young and Peter Dronke disagree concerning the condition and the value of the text. The former thinks it is irrecoverably fragmentary while the latter

Peter Dronke divides the Freising *Play of the Star* into twelve scenes, with the first introducing Herod's evil reign.[58] Scenes 2-11 follow Matt 2:1-12, but adapt the timeline of PJ; incorporate the shepherds of Luke 2:8-20; and add secondary and tertiary characters such as the Jerusalem citizens, messengers, the shield bearer, knights, interpreters, and the midwives. The magi entered before the high altar in the cathedral (East) where the nativity scene and the choir stood. The magi would pass through the nave where the audience doubled as Jerusalem citizens. Herod's throne was fittingly located in the northern transept, since the North is Lucifer's region. The shepherds, who crossed paths with the Magi, were stationed on the platform near the opposite transept.[59]

The finale (scene 12) takes place at Herod's palace. When the messenger informs Herod that he has been mocked by the Magi, the king responds, "I shall quench my blaze of rage by a cataclysm," a mimicry of the Roman conspirator Catiline's outburst at accusations of treason, as recorded by Sallust (line 119).[60] Such intermingling of Christian and classical texts, by an early Christian and the earliest known Roman historian, respectively, likely intrigued educated audiences.[61] The shield bearer urges Herod to expiate his "just" anger through a massacre of male infants and kill Christ along the way (lines 120-3). Herod uses four lines from Prudentius's *Hymn on the Epiphany* when he commands the execution of the plan (124-8).[62]

Unprecedented in this play is the abrupt closing before the actual massacre (lines 129-36).[63] Immediately after Herod's order, an instruction follows for a paean: "Let the boys in the King's procession sing these verses." Herod may think that his subjects are praising him, when in fact they are praising his rival king Christ.[64] They exclaim,

> Let's sing "hurrah!"—this yearly feast brings with it royal praises! This day has given us what the mind could not have hoped: it's truly brought a thousand joys in answer to our prayers, restored this kingdom to its King, and peace too to the world, to us it's brought wealth, beauty, singing, feasting, dancing. It's good for him to reign and hold the kingdom's scepter: he loves the name of King, for he adorns that name with virtues.

The mention of the "yearly feast" returns the audience from the biblical scenes to the life of the Church. At times, the *Feast of Fools* (*festum stultorum*) fell during the *Feast of the Innocents* on December 28. In the former, "play with every kind of freedom was

---

finds it not only recoverable but at the apex of its genre. Young, *The Drama of the Medieval Church*, 2:92, n. 5; Dronke, *Nine Medieval Latin Plays*, 24, 30-1.
[58] Translations, scene divisions, and line numbers are Dronke's and from *Nine Medieval Latin Plays*, 34-49.
[59] Dronke, *Nine Medieval Latin Plays*, 25.
[60] "Since I am hounded by enemies on every side, I'll quench my blaze of rage by a cataclysm."
[61] Dronke, *Nine Medieval Latin Plays*, 28, 30. This line is also found in a play at Einsiedeln.
[62] "Let every male child die! Search the bosoms of the nurses [101-2] lest any, furtively, withhold a child of manly kind [107-8]."
[63] Later in twelfth century, a playwright from Bilsen (Belgium) adopts these lines for the opening of his *Ordo Rachelis*. Young, *The Drama of the Medieval Church*, 2:75.
[64] Dronke, *Nine Medieval Latin Plays*, 30.

allowed, and a boy was invested with the sceptre of authority who could, in jest, turn the established world upside-down."[65] Since the cathedral boys took on the innocents' role, Herod, and the King's procession, the play ends in a "symbolic ritual reversal," in which the boys pay their true homage to Christ, not Herod or the boy taking his role.[66] These same boys also sing *Letabundus*, which celebrates Christ's birth and challenges the Synagogue to recognize him (136–7).[67]

In this way, the Freising *Play of the Star* also subversively challenged secular political establishments of its day that opposed Christ. This challenge, however, took place without violence and with hopes of eschatological reversal. Even if the play appears to end in frenzy, Max Harris argues that such medieval dramas do not promote societal misrule or "deliberate inversion of established order," but "celebrate the overthrow of disordered power."[68] If there is a violent disorderly protester, it is ironically Herod himself, who in his angst imitates Catiline, the conspirator against the Roman Republic. Only with their nonviolent praise do the victims challenge their enemy, just as children in Jerusalem defend Jesus (Ps 8:2; Matt 21:15-16).

Herod's fall also looks to the future when the weak will rule in place of the strong. The *Feast of Fools*, with its frequent references to Luke 1:52, overlapped with the *Feast of the Innocents* and the *Play of the Star*, not only in time but also conceptually.[69] The joyful message that follows is this: Herod represents the fallen mighty while the innocents represent the humble, who will ultimately be exalted. This message is not only taught or preached but also celebrated and performed.

VI. Victims as Martyrs

Many readings of Matt 2:16-18 from the sixth century onwards continue and build on the legacy of the innocents as martyrs. They continue to incorporate passages from Revelation and project the victims as positive role models for the Church.

A. The Sacramentaries of the Roman Rite

As stated at the beginning of the chapter, the *Veronese Sacramentary* is a historically significant work in the reception history of Matt 2:16-18. While it contains many familiar readings from the past, discussion of such a work here introduces the complexities of liturgy: of its various forms of prayers, participants, and traditions.[70]

---

[65] Ibid., 29. For a brief overview of the *Feast of Fools* and its origins, see Francs X. Weiser, *Handbook of Christian Feasts and Customs: The Year of the Lord in Liturgy and Folklore* (New York: Harcourt Brace, 1958), 124–6.

[66] Dronke, *Nine Medieval Latin Plays*, 29.

[67] The insertion of *Letabundus* in place of the traditional *Te Deum* is another innovation of the Freising *Play of the Star*. Ibid., 30.

[68] Max Harris, *Sacred Folly: A New History of the Feast of Fools* (Ithaca: Cornell University Press, 2011), 48–9.

[69] Ibid., 49.

[70] For example, in the *Veronese Sacramentary*, there are two sets of Mass prayers scheduled with two prefaces detailing the slaughter. In addition to the priest or bishop, there are other books used for Mass that includes lectors (the lectionary) and the cantors (the antiphonary). Also, while Eastern

For the sake of simplicity, this present author will delimit his treatment of liturgy to the Western reception of Matt 2:16-18 and begin with the sacramentary material, used by priests or bishops at the Mass.[71] Three works to consider are the *Veronese*, the *Gelasian*, and the *Gregorian Sacramentaries*. Mass prayers therein elaborate on themes associated with the massacre of the innocents, mixing literal and tropological readings of Matt 2:16-18. Since much of the *Gregorian Sacramentary* repeats the first two, an in-depth coverage of it is not necessary.

The first prayer in the *Veronese Sacramentary* appeals to God's grace, which pardons the ignorant and unconfident.[72] This plea is appropriate in remembrance of the victims. Herod has killed an "immense amount with the savagery of the beast," but their "precious deaths" were for the sake of the infant Christ. Like Peter Chrysologus (see Chapter 3, IX. G), the *Veronese Sacramentary* emphasizes grace, which excels over the will. In addition, the innocents confess without speech, suffer before others, and witness for Christ without recognizing him. As Quodvultdeus similarly taught (see Chapter 3, IX. J), Christ's blood efficaciously regenerates the infants so that they are rewarded the martyr's crown. This triumph of mercy is a cause for celebration because God's compassion also sustains the present worshipers with their attendant "human fragility."

The second prayer continues the emphasis on grace. It begins with praise of God who works "wonderful things more gloriously in the smallest ones" though he could be "great through great ones" (see also the *Gregorian Sacramentary*). Much of the following content echoes Pope Leo the Great's *Sermon 37: On the Feast of the Epiphany 7*, 3-4 and Augustine's *Questions from the Old and New Testament*, 62 (see Chapter 3, IX. I and XIII. D). For example, there is a plea to imitate the innocents' sincerity, humility, and simplicity (1 Cor 14:20). God's grace rewards Christ's peers with the "glorious palm of martyrdom" and surpasses their lack of intelligence and maturity. If weak infants are thus revered, Jesus ought to be venerated as an infant as well. Since this grace only extends to Leah's offspring, Rachel weeps in envy for her uncrowned children.

Like the *Veronese Sacramentary*, the *Gelasian Sacramentary* presents the Church with the example of crowned innocents, who in their death confessed Christ though ignorant and voiceless. Their sincerity, innocence, and piety are worthy of imitation. Unlike the *Veronese Sacramentary* but similar to Gregory of Nazianzus (see Chapter 3, VIII. D), a tropological reading reinterprets the slaughter to inspire the mortification of

---

and Western liturgies are equally rich, the former, with Byzantine, West Syrian, East Syrian, Armenian, and many other churches, is too variegated for an adequate survey here. David M. Hope, *Leonine Sacramentary: A Reassessment of Its Nature and Purpose*, Oxford Theological Monographs (London: Oxford University Press, 1971), 37; Folsom, "The Liturgical Books of the Roman Rite," 245.

[71] The present author is indebted to Dominic E. Serra for help with locating and organizing this liturgical material.

[72] All translations of the sacramentaries are mine and derived from the Latin texts in Charles L. Feltoe, ed., *Sacramentarium Leonianum: Edited, with Introduction, Notes, and Three Photographs* (Cambridge: Cambridge University Press, 1896), 166-7; Leo C. Mohlberg, Leo Eizenhöfer, and Petrus Siffrin, eds., *Liber Sacramentorum Romanae Aeclesiae Ordinis Anni Circuli: (Cod. Vat. Reg. Lat. 216/Paris Bibl. nat. 7193, 41/56): (Sacramentarium Gelasianum)* (Roma: Herder, 1960), 12-13; Jean Deshusses, ed., *Le Sacramentaire Grégorien: Ses Principales Formes D'Après Les Plus Anciens Munscrits: Edition Comparative* (Fribourg: Editions universitaires, 1971), 110-11.

sins (see also the *Gregorian Sacramentary*): "God, whom the innocents have confessed with the martyr's proclamation today, not in speaking, but in dying, mortify all vices in us, in order that in our conversation our life may express thy faith." The *Gelasian Sacramentary* prescribes a prayer that signifies innocents' deaths as both speechless martyrdom and Christian struggle for pure speech.

Thus, the three sacramentaries show familiarity with past influential works or at least their methods of reading Matt 2:16-18. The literal sense (i.e., Herod's rage, age of the victims, Rachel's weeping) serves as a springboard for various tropological lessons, proving the worth of the passage as a source of inspiration.

B. The *Comes of Würzburg*

Just as the sacramentaries were books for the priests and bishops, the lectionaries were books for lectors. The oldest extant witness of the Roman lectionary system is the *Comes of Würzburg* (ca. 600-50), which prescribes the reading of Rev 14:1-5.[73] This reading, paired with Matt 2:16-18 on the *Feast of the Innocents*, is an important source for the high death toll (i.e., Jerome, Prudentius, Quodvultdeus) and their identification as "firstfruits" (Ephrem the Syrian) (see Chapter 3, III. C; IX. E, J; and X. A). In addition, the pairing of Rev 14:1-5 and Matt 2:16-18 recontextualizes a dark passage of infanticide into a happy conclusion for the victims.

C. The Roman Antiphonals

Just as the celebrants and the lectors reflect upon Matt 2:16-18 through prayers and lections, respectively, cantors possess the antiphonaries, which exist for the Mass, the Office, or both.[74] In the following, one antiphon from each antiphonal will be discussed.[75]

The most ancient texts of the Mass antiphonary date from the eighth and ninth centuries. In the Mass antiphonary, alleluia verses usually accompany the gradual responsories (chanted as the lector ascended to the pulpit), offertories, and the communion antiphons throughout the year. Yet, the introit antiphon for the *Feast of the Innocents* begins with the following heading: "'Glory to God in the highest' is not sung, nor 'Alleluia,' but as if because of sorrow, it is taken away in those days."[76] Yet Psalm 8, which follows, compensates for the missing alleluia. Ps 8:2 clarifies God's

---

[73] Folsom, "The Liturgical Books of the Roman Rite," 256. The manuscript of the *Comes of Würzburg* (ca. 700) exists in two parts: (1) the epistolary, which prescribes Rev 14:1-5 and (2) evangeliary, a later work, which prescribes the reading of Matt 2:13-23 for the *Feast of the Innocents*. The focus will be on the former. See G. Morin, "Liturgie et Basiliques de Rome au Milieu du VIIe Siècle d'après les Listes D'Évangiles de Würzburg," *RB* 28 (1911): 297; and "Le Plus Ancien *Comes* ou Lectionnaire de L'Église Romaine," *RB* 27 (1910): 47.

[74] Folsom, "The Liturgical Books of the Roman Rite," 270.

[75] Ibid., 260. They are collected in René-Jean Hesbert, ed., *Antiphonale Missarum Sextuplex: D'après le graduel de Monza et les antiphonaires de Rheinau, de Mont-Blandin, de Compiègne, de Corbie et de Senlis* (Herder: Rome 1967).

[76] The translations are mine and based from the Latin texts in Hesbert, ed., *Antiphonale Missarum Sextuplex*, 20-1 and PL 78:739-41.

purpose for the innocents' deaths, which aligns with the triumphant theme of God's renown (Ps 8:1, 9). This use of Psalm 8 is not extraordinary since Matthew contains Ps 8:2 (Matt 21:16) and Tertullian had already associated Ps 8:2 with Matt 2:16-18.

The more innovative feature of this antiphon is the connection to Psalm 124. This community hymn is one of the Songs of Ascents, sung by pilgrim worshipers attending Jerusalem festivals.[77] This psalm employs perilous images such as a snared sparrow, swallowed prey, and torrential waters to describe the plight of Israel under oppressors. God, however, is present with them to liberate and protect them. For the communion, the antiphon cites Matt 2:18.

In this Mass antiphon, the following reflections are in order: (1) God is sovereign yet cares for his people, (2) God's people are in distress from their enemies, and (3) God's people can praise him and trust in his vindication. So then, the worshiper can be confident that the sovereign God cares for the innocents and Rachel. Though they are distressed because of Herod and his soldiers, they can praise (in fact the innocents do, according to Ps 8:2) and hope for vindication.

The second work is from the Office antiphonary. Like earlier works, *Under the Altar of God* (*Sub altare Dei*) of the Matins of the Innocents continues to associate visions from the Apocalypse with Matt 2:16-18. It begins with the words of Rev 6:9: "Under the altar of God I heard the voices of those killed." The innocents are like the souls under the altar. Verses 10 and 11 follow so that the complaint and the reason for the delayed vindication are explicit: the number of their brothers must reach its limit. Like the Mass antiphon above, a Psalm adds an aquatic image: the blood of the saints is poured out like water and their corpses are unburied (Ps 79:3). An imprecatory prayer based on Deut 32:43 and Rev 19:2 follows: "Avenge, Lord, the blood of your servants which was poured out." Repeated mentions of blood and appeals for vengeance give voice to the silent victims of Matt 2:16-18.

The Office antiphon ends with a triumphant image. As past works identified the victims as the great multitude in white with palms (Rev 7:9), they are likened to the twenty-four elders in Rev 4:10-11, as "they adore him who lives forever, casting their crowns before the throne of the Lord their God." In addition, "they go forth exultantly carrying their bundles." This agricultural imagery borrows from another psalm among Songs of Ascents, Ps 126:6. The sowing in the fields, accompanied by tears and weeping, eventually leads to reaping, homecoming, songs of joy, and sheaves of wheat. *Under the Altar of God* serves as a prologue to the Limoges *Lamentation of Rachel*. Many other antiphons adorn Matt 2:16-18 with other scriptural passages/phrases to furnish a happier context.[78]

---

[77] Nancy de Claissé-Walford, Rolf A. Jacobson, and Beth LaNeel Tanner, *The Book of Psalms*, NICOT (Grand Rapids: Eerdmans, 2014), 906.

[78] For example, the Office antiphon for Lauds augments Matt 2:16, 18 with assurance that "their angels always see the face of the Father" (Matt 18:10), the vision under the altar, and the new song of the 144,000 (Rev 14:2-3). Yet another antiphon associates the innocents with (1) the worthy ones of Sardis who walk with Christ in white and whose names are recorded in the book of life (Rev 3:4-5) and (2) the 144,000 virgins who follow the Lamb wherever he goes without deceit or blame (Rev 14:4-5).

D. Ambrose Autpert

Another work that connects the massacre victims to the Apocalypse is the Apocalypse commentary of Ambrose Autpert, an eighth-century monk of St. Vincent, near Capua, Italy, and later an abbot.[79] His commentary became a standard Latin work, characterized by its "clean break with eschatological speculation," lack of "references to actual times and places," and "a vision of the Church universal, transcending time and space."[80] These features are manifest in the exposition of Revelation 7.

The number of the sealed in Rev 7:4 provides an opportunity to discuss the massacre of the innocents.[81] Autpert responds to those who doubt whether the figure 144,000 is the number of killed infants. Herod never ruled over all of the twelve tribes, and the massacre only affected Benjamin and Judah. "Therefore," according to Autpert, "it can only be that according to the sense of the explanation sent ahead in time [*praemissae expositionis sensum*], they have known that the sum of all the elect [*omnium electorum summam*] is included in them."

Autpert admits the inherent difficulty of calculating 144,000 as the massacre death toll, at least literally. By employing the anagogical sense, the victims are not only martyrs but also the chief among the elect. This reading promotes the victims beyond the status of "eyes of the Church" as found in Chromatius (see Chapter 3, IX. D). While apostles and martyrs share that office as church coleaders, Ambrose Autpert promotes the victims beyond them as the first ones sealed in the universal Church.

E. *Martyrdom of Matthew*

While the apocryphal *Martyrdom of Matthew* borrows from the ancient works such as the *Acts of Andrew* and the *Acts of Andrew and Matthias*, no ancient manuscript of the original survives.[82] Since Latin manuscripts of the Greek original exist from the eighth and ninth centuries, Els Rose conservatively suggests an early medieval composition.[83]

The story begins as Matthew is praying and resting in the mountain, where Jesus comes to him "in the likeness of the infants who sing in paradise" and greets him.[84] Matthew regrets that he cannot offer proper hospitality, but the child assures him that a good talk is better than good food. The child introduces himself with many titles, including, "the boast of the widowed" and "defence of the infants." Matthew receives comfort from these words. The next exchange deals directly with Matt 2:16-18:

---

[79] "Autpert, Ambrose," *ODCC*, 137.
[80] Ibid.
[81] All translations of Ambrose Autpert are mine and derived from the Latin text in CCCM 27: 299.
[82] Elliott, *The Apocryphal New Testament*, 520; Els Rose, *Ritual Memory: The Apocryphal Acts and Liturgical Commemoration in the Early Medieval West (c. 500-1215)*, Mittellateinische Studien und Texte 40 (Leiden: Brill, 2009), 167.
[83] Rose, *Ritual Memory*, 168. While the *Passio Matthaei* in the Latin collection of Pseudo-Abdias shares certain themes with subject matters with the *Martyrdom of Matthew*, they are different in content.
[84] The translations are from Alexander Walker, trans., *Apocryphal Gospels, Acts, and Revelations*, Ante-Nicene Christian Library 16 (Edinburgh: T&T Clark, 1870).

"And that indeed I saw thee in paradise when thou didst sing with the other infants who were killed in Bethlehem, I know right well; but how thou hast suddenly come hither, this altogether astonishes me. But I shall ask thee one thing, O child: that impious Herod, where is he?" The child says to him: "Since thou hast asked, hear his dwelling-place. He dwells, indeed, in Hades; and there has been prepared for him fire unquenchable, Gehenna without end, bubbling mire, worm that sleeps not, because he cut off three thousand infants, wishing to slay the child Jesus, the ancient of the ages; but of all these ages I am father."

After assuring Matthew of Herod's eternal demise, the child gives him his rod and commissions the apostle to plant the stick near the church in Myrna that Andrew and another apostle previously founded among man-eaters.[85] The child ascends to heaven, and Matthew obeys in spite of demonic opposition from some members of the city's royal family.

The child Jesus appears throughout the story to aid Matthew. While Matthew evangelizes, Jesus and a bishop named Plato accompany him. The planted rod miraculously becomes a bountiful tree producing vines, honey, fruits, and water. When the king becomes angry and intends to kill Matthew, Jesus comforts him with promises of his presence and power. When the king orders ten man-eater soldiers to cannibalize Matthew and Plato, Jesus runs toward them and burns out their eyes. The king continues his assault despite repeated failures.

Eventually Matthew is martyred. The child Jesus leads Matthew's spirit by the hand into heaven and crowns him before twelve men wearing shining garments and golden crowns. These men likely represent twelve patriarchs, representing the Israelite tribes. Next, Plato and other Christians see Matthew standing on a crystal sea flanked by the twelve men and the boy Jesus in front of them. Finally, the boy moves Matthew's coffin behind the king's palace to its final location. Plato baptizes the amazed king, celebrates the Eucharist with him, and gives each member of the king's family new names.

While the massacre of the innocents is just one of many biblical references and/or allusions included in the *Martyrdom of Matthew*, it holds special significance for four reasons. First, Jesus's appearance as a massacred innocent is appropriate as the introductory vision for Matthew, given that he is the only evangelist to mention the innocents. Secondly, the writer wishes to emphasize the innocents' triumph more than their massacre. When Jesus appears as one of them, Matthew recognizes his place in heaven alongside other victims and learns that Herod's damnation is also certain. No doubts remain concerning their fates.

Thirdly, the *Martyrdom of Matthew* also teaches that an infant can have authority in the kingdom (see, e.g., Matt 18:3). The prominent apostle Matthew takes his order from Jesus, but the latter appears as a child. Just as God instructs Moses and Aaron about their staffs and performs miracles through them (Exodus 4; Numbers 17), the

---

[85] This foundation took place in an earlier work called the *Acts of Andrew and Matthias* (or *Matthew*). It is unclear from the manuscripts of whether Andrew worked with Matthew the writer of the first Gospel or Matthias the replacement of Judas Iscariot. The oldest manuscript indicates the latter, while four or five has the former. *Apocryphal Gospels, Acts, and Revelations*, xvii, 348.

child commands Matthew to use the rod similarly. Just as Jesus promises his presence and power while commissioning the Eleven (Matt 28:16-20), the child comforts the endangered Matthew.

Finally, the *Martyrdom of Matthew* sets the infant as a paradigm for Christ-like character and humility. Matthew obeys and imitates the heavenly child who suffered before him. It is the child, not the twelve men, who crowns Matthew in heaven. What Jesus teaches in Matt 18:1-5 the *Martyrdom* narrates: the eschatological reversal for all child-like humble ones. This idea is similar to the theme of the *Feast of the Fools*, where children switch roles of authority and submission with adults. The *Martyrdom of Matthew* uses salient features and unique passages from Matthew's Gospel to undergird lessons on humble endurance (2:16-18; 18:1-5; 21:15-16).

F. Fleury *Play of Rachel*

A playbook from Fleury (*ca.* twelfth century) contains an independent *Play of Rachel* (*Ordo Rachelis*). There is much in this work for Karl Young to commend it. It stands out from other plays that deal with Matt 2:16-18 due to its "enlargement of familiar elements" and "addition of new roles," resulting in "a highly successful composition, both in its arrangement and in its completeness."[86] It is also "a mosaic of passages from the service-books and the Vulgate" with liturgical passages "chosen with skill and appropriateness."[87] Finally, "the sequence of events is smooth and orderly, and the utterances of the chief personages are not wanting in force and vividness."[88] A careful observation of its opening confirms this evaluation:

> At "The Slaying of the Boys," let the Innocents be costumed in white stoles, and singing joyfully through the church, let them pray to God saying: "O how glorious is the kingdom, in which with Christ rejoice all the saints! Vested in stoles and albs, they follow the lamb wherever he goes." Then the Lamb appears suddenly, carrying a cross, and goes before them, hither and yon, and they follow, singing: "Send forth the Lamb, O Lord, Ruler of the earth, from stony desert to the Mount of the Daughter of Zion! On the throne of David, and over his kingdom he will preside forever. Alleluia!" Meanwhile let some Armiger offer the enthroned Herod his scepter, saying: "On the throne of David, and over his kingdom he will preside forever. Alleluia!"[89]

From the onset, the writer seamlessly incorporates three antiphons: (1) *O quam gloriosum* (Vespers for the Vigil of All Saints), (2) *Emitte agnum* (Lauds in Advent), and (3) *Super solium David* (Lauds of the second Sunday before Christmas).[90] As in

---

[86] Young, *The Drama of the Medieval Church*, 2:114.
[87] Ibid., 2:116.
[88] Ibid.
[89] Translations of the Fleury *Play of Rachel* are from Fletcher Collins Jr., ed. and trans., *Medieval Church Music-Dramas: A Repertory of Complete Plays* (Charlottesville: University of Virginia Press, 1976), 145–64.
[90] Young, *The Drama of the Medieval Church*, 2:113.

liturgical works, (see VI. A–C above) the victims participate in heavenly visions of the Apocalypse (Rev 7:9; 14:4), worshipping the Lamb who was slain. Furthermore, the eschatological vision of the Lamb fuses with the ancient prophecy of Isa 16:1, interpreted as foretelling the first advent of Christ. As the innocents praise the true Davidic king in heaven, the armiger echoes the same words as he hands the scepter to the pretender Herod on earth.

After the flight to Egypt, the magi escape and Herod is enraged to the point of suicide. He regains his composure and mimics Catiline's outburst as in the Freising *Play of the Star* (see V. above). Immediately the script instructs,

> Meanwhile let the innocents, still in a line behind the Lamb, sing: "To the Lamb so holy, for us slaughtered, the splendor of the Father, the splendor of virginity, we offer to Christ under this banner of light. In many ways the wrath of Herod that has sought us, by the Lamb we'll be saved from in Christ, we will die."[91]

With these words, the victims exercise faith in Christ and voluntarily become martyrs. When the armiger prompts Herod to kill the boys, the king bestows the sword to him to carry out the massacre.

The following massacre scene again binds together disparate parts. The next script states, "Meanwhile, as the killers are approaching, the Lamb leaves, while the innocents hail him." The innocents cry: "Hail, Lamb of God! Hail, you who take away the sins of the world! Alleluia!" This adaptation of the liturgical invocation *Agnus Dei* presents at least two different ideas. First, the victims' sacrifice for Christ foreshadows Christ's sacrifice for the world. Secondly, since the *Agnus Dei* is closely tied to the fraction of the Host at the Mass, the Fleury play may suggest that the innocents fully participate in the life of the Church before their demise. Their twofold "hail" (*salve*), not found in John 1:29 or the liturgical *Agnus Dei*, signifies their sincere respect for Christ. The hails echo Gabriel's greeting of Mary (Luke 1:28) but stand in contrast to the impious mockery of Christ (Matt 26:49; 27:29; Mark 15:18; John 19:3).

The victims' mothers implore the killers to spare the children to no avail. Next, the Archangel admonishes the innocents from a distance with words from the Vulgate, Isa 26:19: "You who in dust are, rise up and shout." The prostrate innocents, who wait eagerly for the future resurrection and divine vengeance, respond with lyrics from *Under the Altar of God*: "Why did you not defend our blood, God of ours?" The angel too responds from it: "Here stay for a little while, until you are reunited in the company of your brothers." They eventually rise after Rachel's lamentation.[92]

Next, the Archangel sings the antiphon for Lauds of Innocents Day, *Sinite parvulos*: "Suffer little children to come unto me, for such is in fact the kingdom of heaven." At this command, the innocents rise and enter the choir area while singing

---

[91] While "splendor of virginity" is juxtaposed with "splendor of the Father" to highlight Jesus's deity and virgin birth, Christ also may serve as a paragon for the innocents who follow the Lamb as virgins, purchased from mankind and offered as firstfruits (Rev 14:4).

[92] This portion of the Fleury play will be covered later in this chapter (see IV. F.). The Laon *Play of the Star* also contains same or similar material dealing with the massacre, including the *Agnus Dei*, portions of the *Under the Altar of God*, and a lament of Rachel.

a part of the Christmas sequence of Notker the Stammerer, *Festa Christi*: "O Christ, how many in the Father's army of youth learned in battles the most! To the people a warning, as they huddle together, darkness suggesting by so much misery." The play ends with Herod's death, Archelaus's succession, and the Holy Family's joyous return from Egypt, during which Joseph as cantor sings the hymn *Te Deum*.

The Fleury *Play of Rachel* is a collage of liturgical pieces and Bible passages, sewn together with dramatic acting. Its treatment of the innocents is comprehensive and thoughtful, as both a narrative and a theological work. They are not passive victims but triumphant central characters whose appearances bookend the script. They inspire with their unwavering piety but are relatable in their pained plea for vengeance. The play remembers the martyrs of the past, encourages participation with Christ's suffering in the present, and hopes for the future resurrection.

VII. Victims as Sacrifices

After the fifth century, the massacred victims continue to appear not only as martyrs but also as sacrifices offered to God. While martyrdom and sacrifice are closely related, each evokes different set of ideas and images. John of Euobea and a Sahidic manuscript contain memorable readings of the victims as sacrifices.

A. John of Euobea

In his *Sermon on the Innocents Killed in Bethlehem and Rachel*, John of Euboea considers Bethlehem blessed by the innocents' blood. Aforementioned Maximus the Confessor anticipated this idea and derived it from patristic origins: Bethlehem observed the Passover through the blameless innocents' sacrifice (*Life of the Virgin*, sec. 44). John, however, goes beyond Maximus and declares: "O holy [ἁγία] Bethlehem, because you were not only sanctified [ἡγιάσθης] by the king born, but also by the blood of children unjustly killed, you received doubled sanctification [διπλοῦν τὸν ἁγιασμὸν ἐκομίσω]" (2). Later, he explains Bethlehem's two sanctifications in contrast to the mad and pilloried Jerusalem, which killed prophets. John styles his rhetoric like Jesus's lamentation (Matt 23:37-39; Luke 13:34-35):

> Bethlehem, Bethlehem, in whom was born Christ the great king, who for the sake of the royal purple and fine linen, welcomes the blood of the happy infants, indeed you were sanctified (ἡγιάσθης) first in your borders when he was born, and the one coming not in your borders, but in you yourself, in order to save the world, those proceeding out of the flanks of virgins first welcome the firstborn of all creation (ἐκ παρθενικῶν λαγόνων προελθόντα πρώτη πρωτότοκον πάσης τῆς κτίσεως), and the producer of all things. And as the second consecration (δεύτερον ἁγιασμὸν) you receive the blood of the blameless and happy children (5).[93]

---

[93] Note the continual emphasis on Holiness (ἁγιασ-roots) and the alliteration.

Concerning this "second consecration," John enthusiastically likens the children to sacrificial animal victims such as lambs, young turtledoves, pigeons, and calves:

> For they are truly blameless (ἄμωμοι) the blood of such ones like pure lambs (ὡς ἀρνίων ἀκάκων) was poured out for the one who made us. O happy are those blameless ones who though they do not read the law of the Lord, even in his law come to him! O the wise thoughts of the young turtledoves (νεοσσῶν λογικῶν σοφῶν τρυγόντων) and undivided pigeons (ἀκεραίων περιστερῶν), which are not offered to God in accordance with the Law, but by the grace of Christ, poured out for him their blameless blood (τοῦ ἀμωμήτου τοῦ αἵματος αὐτῶν)! O after the calves (μοσχαρίων), who are prophetically about to pass through their bonds are dedicated (ἀνεθέντων) and skip around in joy (ἐν ἀγαλλιάσει σκιρτούντων), with them Christ God will give to us our part and lot; because to Him is proper glory, honor, worship and splendor, now and forever, and completion of ages, Amen (5).

While Herod ravages Bethlehem, the innocents fulfill various OT sacrifices through their death and elevate the humbled city above Jerusalem.[94] In another critique of Jerusalem, John writes that Bethlehem's victims are offerings of grace that do not operate under the Law. The pastoral and idyllic picture of free, skipping calves encapsulates the victims' present bliss (Mal 4:2). Thus, John elaborately praises Bethlehem who can boast of their sanctifications through the innocents' sacrifice. The victims die soon after birth but become heroes of the city of David's birth.

B. Sahidic MS 36

Among text collections of Coptic Apocryphal Gospels, certain Sahidic fragments of the *Life of the Virgin* exist from medieval times.[95] Like PJ, Lord Crawford's Sahidic MS 36 relates that Herod targets the young John the Baptist but fails even after cornering his father.[96] After a discussion of Rachel and a lacuna, the fragment ends with another mixture of legend and Scriptures, this one about the phoenix and Abel:

> There is a bird called phoenix. *As for* this *bird*, when the fire came from heaven and consumed the sacrifice of Abel the righteous—now *as for* that bird, the fire of that sacrifice burnt it, and made it ashes. On the third day, a little worm came forth from the ashes of the bird, and advanced little by little; until it put forth wings and

---

[94] In an interesting contrast to John of Euboea, Eusebius Gallicanus in *Homily 11 on Blandina Lugdunensis*, 2-3, argues that Lyons deserve more recognition than Bethlehem, because the former can boast of Blandina and her company, who suffered greater than the slaughtered infants from the latter, who died without consciousness of martyrdom.

[95] Forbes Robinson does not attempt to date these or the Bohairic manuscripts. Fragment III of the *Life of the Virgin*, however, shares content with the seventh-century GPM. Thus, only the *terminus post quem* is certain. Forbes Robinson, *Coptic Apocryphal Gospels: Translations Together with the Texts of Some of Them*, TS 4, No. 2 (Cambridge: Cambridge University Press, 1896), xx, 198.

[96] Departing from other accounts, Zechariah's remains are hidden, along with the corpses of the victims.

again became even as it was. Every five hundred years the phoenix, the bird, comes flying in the height, and goes into the temple to the altar *where* they offer.

The author is likely familiar with Clement's use of the phoenix legend to boost confidence in the OT promises of resurrection (Ps 3:5; 28:7; Job 19:26; 1 Clement 24–27). The itinerary of Clement's pagan phoenix is from Arabia to Heliopolis, but Sahidic MS 36's antediluvian bird, first making its appearance in Genesis 4, arrives at the temple from heaven. While it is not completely clear how the phoenix legend relates to the victims, the bird's regeneration likely complements the sacrificial language and Abel's piety, supplying hope for the bereaved. Perhaps the author envisions the innocents suffering as burnt sacrifices for God, who will raise them in the future resurrection.

VIII. Rachel as a Representative of the Church

Unlike the earlier period, post-fifth-century works devote more space to the subject of Matt 2:18.[97] Yet interpreters often simply aggregate and evaluate past interpretations without much innovation.[98] Emerging in significance is Rachel's representation of the Church, which relates to the innocents' role as martyrs. One may venture to say that if the innocents who die serve as the Church's ideal in paradise, Rachel who weeps is the Church's source of sympathy on earth.

A. Rufus of Shotep

Rufus served as the bishop of Shotep, a town in Upper Egypt, during the last quarter of the sixth century.[99] Only two sets of his homilies survive, one on Matthew and the other on Luke.[100] J. Mark Sheridan opines, from limited data, that Rufus is primarily concerned with his flock's spiritual growth during a stable time of fruitful literary activity in Egyptian churches.[101] In his *Homily on the Gospel of Matthew*, Rufus exhibits familiarity with earlier readings of Matt 2:16-18. For example, he imitates Gregory of Nazianzus (see Chapter 3, VIII. D) when he exhorts his audience tropologically to flee

---

[97] For a survey of some representative works, see Boynton, "Performative Exegesis in the Fleury Interfectio Puerorum," 50–3.

[98] As early as the beginning of the sixth century, Dionysius Exiguus's *Clear and Learned Explication of the History of Our Blessed Saviour Jesus Christ* collected multiple strands of readings of Matt 2:18: (1) Rachel typifies the children since the rewards mentioned in Jer 31:16 belong to innocent victims, not guilty captives of Babylon; (2) geographical and tribal relationships between Bethlehem, Ramah, Benjamin, Judah, and Rachel; and (3) the appropriateness of Rachel as the representative of bereaved mothers. This pattern follows in Ishodad of Merv, *A Commentary on St. Matthew* 2:18; Dionysius Bar Salibi, *The Holy Gospel, The Vivifying Announcement of Our Lord Jesus Christ Proclaimed by Apostle Matthew, One of the Twelve*, 2; Thomas Aquinas, *Commentary on the Gospel according to Saint Matthew*, 2:18.

[99] J. Mark Sheridan, *Rufus of Shotep: Homilies on the Gospels of Matthew and Luke: Introduction, Text, and Commentary*, Corpus dei Manosritti Copti Letterari (Roma: Centro Italiano Microfiches, 1998), 12–14.

[100] Ibid., 14.

[101] Ibid., 49–58.

from the infant stage of maturity, since they have already passed over the foundation and avoided Herod's wrath (5).[102]

Next, Rufus engages in a dialogue with Rachel after citing Matt 2:17-18. First, he asks her why she is sorrowful and she replies that Herod's men killed her children. She pronounces a woe to herself as her womb and senses suffer (cf. Jer 4:19). In reply, Rufus offers hope:

> To you also, O Rachel, I give relief to your voice from your sobbing and as for your eyes, let them cease producing tears. Your children have been killed through violence. We will not abandon them. As for the Father of the one for whose sake they were killed, it is he who will raise them up. You indeed are grieving over the fruit of your womb because it has been taken from the earth but they are alive in the bosom of Abraham (Luke 16:22). Do not weep because they have been taken in infancy. Their time of life will be fulfilled through the care-free ages. If Bethlehem has abandoned them, yet the altar … (4 lines broken) (6)

Rufus comforts Rachel despite her refusal to be comforted (Matt 2:18). When he assures her that "we will not abandon them," he likely means that he and his church will remember them in liturgy, as they also recall resurrection promises, rest in Abraham, eternal life, and the sacrificial significance of their lives (see Chapter 3, IX–X).[103] After four broken lines, a phrase "to the glory," and another broken line, Rufus urges his audience to build upon the "literal meaning" and elevate their mind to discover Rachel's true identity:

> This voice which cries out is that of Rachel, this (name) that is interpreted "the lamb." The lamb is weeping and is mourning because the wolf has destroyed her children. It is in Rama that her voice is heard, that is the place. Beloved, a voice was heard in Rama (Matt 2:18) What is the lamb? Rachel is the church, the little sister of Lea, that is, the synagogue, whose womb was shut up and she did not bring forth all this long while (cf. Gen 29:31). It is she who is weeping for these little children whom Herod killed, that is, the blood of martyrs which has been shed. Her voice was heard indeed on high. (9 lines broken or missing)

While Rachel's rivalry with her sister and the meaning of her name are familiar (see Jerome, *The Book of Hebrew Names*, 15), the interpretation of Rachel as lamb in the context of Matt 2:18 is not. In the Early Church, etymological studies focus on Christ as Immanuel and Maher-Shalal-Hash-Baz or Rama (Matt 1:23; Chapter 3, III and XII). Now, Rachel's name meaning garners interest. If struggles between lamb and wolf align allegorically with the Church and the Synagogue, Rufus may have in mind

---

[102] All of the translations and section divisions are Sheridan's.
[103] It is difficult to determine how these homilies functioned in the life of the Coptic Church. Sheridan laments, "The existence of these manuscripts and a few notations on them make it clear that these homilies were later used in liturgical services but it is not possible to determine exactly what these were." Sheridan, *Rufus of Shotep*, 49.

false teachers that hinder the Church like Apponius (Chapter 3, VIII. E). It is difficult, however, to pinpoint the controversy. Evidence points to major theological concerns of the day involving Marcionism, Manicheanism, and Chalcedonian controversies but not Judaizers.[104]

Thus, Rufus is a representative of Coptic tradition that devotes fuller attention to the weeping Rachel. He directly dialogues with her, vows to remember her children, and spiritually interprets her name and her struggles.

B. Arculf

Interplays of readings of Matt 2:16-18 and archaeology ensure Rachel's relevance even at a time when Mary eclipses all other biblical women figures.[105] One contributing factor is the Gaulish monk Arculf, whose travels to the Holy Land formed the core of Adamnán of Iona's work entitled *Concerning Holy Places* (*De locis sanctis*; ca. 698). Arculf may not have intended to comment on Rachel in Matt 2:18 directly, but his detailed eyewitness account of Rachel's tomb near Bethlehem provides two major clues about the local understanding of the matriarch.[106]

First, at some point, the Bethlehem locals accept Archelaus's pyramid tomb as Rachel's. Arculf's account of the tomb's structure reveals its likely origins. He notes how it was "assembled with cheap work ... having no adornment," but the most significant detail is that it was "surrounded by a stone pyramid" (*lapidea circumdatum pyramide*). There is also an inscription ascribing it to the matriarch Rachel.[107] Frederick Strickert concludes, (1) Arculf's pyramid description does not match Jacob's original stone pillar design (Gen 35:20); (2) the pyramid structure is characteristic of the Hellenistic-Roman era; (3) the pyramid shape matches Jerome's description of tomb of Archelaus, Herod's son who would have been afforded a dignitary's burial; and finally (4) the similarity in pronunciation between Archelaus and Rachel (with the hard Semitic "ch") and the increasing importance of Matthew's Gospel would facilitate the transfer of names.[108] The locals continually remember Rachel, while Archelaus's name fades.

---

[104] Ibid., 49–58.

[105] The sixth-century anonymous Piacenza Pilgrim's account located (1) Rachel's tomb near a water spring and a church and (2) a tomb for all the massacred infants near David's tomb in Bethlehem, but his/her testimony was not as influential as Arculf's, which Bede popularized. The anonymous pilgrim has been misidentified as "Antoninus of Piacenza" and expectantly confused with the fourth-century Saint Antoninus of Piacenza. His work, however, is unrelated to the Antonine Itinerary, *Itinerarium Antonini Piacentini*, 28–9; Gideon Avni, *The Byzantine-Islamic Transition in Palestine: An Archaeological Approach*, Oxford Studies in Byzantium (Oxford: Oxford University Press, 2014), 1, n. 1. Rachel's tomb does not have direct correlation with the Milk Grotto, located near the Church of the Nativity and appearing in sources from twelfth century and later. The grotto is believed to be a rest stop of the Holy Family where Mary spilt some milk while feeding Jesus. To this day, some believe the wall powder possesses power to increase lactation. Susan Starr Sered, "Rachel's Tomb and the Milk Grotto of the Virgin Mary: Two Women's Shrines in Bethlehem," *Journal of Feminist Studies in Religion* 2 (1986): 9–10.

[106] For discussion of two traditions regarding the location of Rachel's tomb, see Chapter 2, IV. A.

[107] P. Donatus Baldi, *Enchiridion Locorum Sanctorum* (Jerusalem: Tupis PP Franciscanorum, 1955) 110.7.

[108] Strickert, *Rachel Weeping*, 82–3.

Secondly, this appropriation helps Rachel's memory survive until around the late seventh and early eighth century, when locals conduct annual memorial services at Rachel's tomb on July 18.[109] As dilapidated as it was by Arculf's time, Rachel's tomb is still a recognizable landmark.[110] With the help of his report, directly cited by Bede, non-local Christians also spiritually "arrive at" the tomb to vivify her memory in worship.[111] Later, Johannes of Würzburg, Theodoricus, Rabbi Benjamin of Tudela, and John Phocas similarly note structural details and improvements before the end of the Crusades.[112]

C. Sahidic MS 36

The most noteworthy inclusion in the Sahidic MS 36 is a legend related to Rachel's weeping. Unlike other works that focus on Rachel the matriarch or Jeremiah 31, the story here centers on another Rachel from Moses's time. Forbes Robinson summarizes,

> Rachel was the wife of a man of the tribe of Levi named Eleazar, who lived at the time when the children of Israel were in Egypt. He was diseased in his feet, and unable to work at making bricks. The taskmasters struck his wife, and compelled her to work. She was in a state of pregnancy, and the work was beyond her strength. Her child was prematurely born. The next night God smote the firstborn, and the Egyptians in fear sent the Israelites forth. The Israelites were joyful; but Rachel was weeping for her child in the midst of the children of Israel, and no one could comfort her. As God smote Pharaoh and his multitude, so He smote Herod and all his servants.[113]

While this story is questionable in historical value, it has an explanatory value for the massacre of the innocents. At least two ideas are present. First, the triumphant Exodus meta-narrative of Israel does not eclipse the smaller tragedy in Eleazar's family. The liberated Israelites do not isolate or ignore the recently bereaved Rachel, but attempt to comfort her, to no avail. In the same way, the Magi's great joy (Matt 2:10) does not engulf Rachel's great sorrow (Matt 2:18), but they coexist in the same season. With this uneasy coexistence of jubilation and sorrow, the writer underscores the incongruity of a fallen world. The liturgical calendar also displays this admixture, since Christmas, celebrating Christ's birth, and the massacre, commemorating Rachel's

---

[109] *Kalendarium Hieroslymitanum saec. VII-VIII.* Baldi, *Enchiridion Locorum Sanctorum*, 112.
[110] By no means is Rachel's memory solely or primarily dependent on this transfer of names. Mary Carruthers observes how the Bordeaux pilgrim can remember holy sites of Jerusalem despite Hadrian's effort to destroy and replace the city. In addition, pilgrims recollect memories from Scripture despite problems with historicity and geographical accuracy. Carruthers, *The Craft of Thought*, 42.
[111] Strickert, *Rachel Weeping*, 85–6. Bede never traveled to Palestine, so he necessarily relied on eyewitnesses for his *De locis sanctis*.
[112] Ibid., 89–93.
[113] All summaries and translations are Robinson's. Robinson, *Coptic Apocryphal Gospels*, xxiii.

sorrow, are in the same week.[114] So then, the Sahidic MS 36 Rachel legend and its Exodus motif provides some hope of vindication: Herod receives due punishment just as the pharaoh did.

D. Rupert of Deutz

Rupert of Deutz was a passionate supporter of traditional Benedictine monasticism and papal reform in the twelfth century.[115] As a theologian, however, his "irremediable ignorance of dialectic" and "impudent new interpretations of Scripture" did not gain him a favorable rating among schoolmen.[116] For example, his thoroughgoing Marian interpretation Song of Songs and appeal to visions as source for his teachings caused controversy.[117] Yet in sheer number of copies, his works surpass or rival fellow Benedictine contemporaries such as Guibert of Nogent, Godfrey of Vendôme, Peter Abelard, Bruno of Segni, and Anselm of Cantebury.[118]

In some ways, Rupert of Deutz's *Concerning the Glory and the Honor of the Son of Man, Commentary on Matthew* (*De Gloria et Honore Filii Hominis super Mattheum*; ca. 1127) unswervingly continues the exegetical traditions of the past.[119] The distinctive feature of the commentary is his elaborate treatment of Rachel in relation to details of Jeremiah 31 and other passages.[120] Rupert begins with a rationale for equating Rachel with the Church: "namely because she is the mother of the first one [Joseph] from the time of the promise who suffered persecution on account of righteousness."[121] He finds support for this idea in the patriarchal history of Psalm 105, where it is recalled that Abraham, Isaac, and Jacob were protected (v. 15), but Joseph was enslaved (vv. 17-18). Saints also weep over "the ruins of Joseph" and their righteous suffering (Ps 105:18; Amos 6:5-6; Matt 5:10). So then, they ought to imitate Rachel's weeping and self-denial of comfort, which "can be felt through experience better than through the hearing of reading alone." It is better to weep now than later (Ps 42:3).

At this point, Rupert raises an interesting exegetical question. If the weeping of Matt 2:18, citing Jer 31:15, is good, what about the injunction in Jer 31:16-17 to stop? He replies that the forbidden weeping is not the same as the *vox in excelso* in Jer 31:15. The weeping in verse 15 is godly sorrow from God's Spirit while the weeping in verse 16 is worldly sorrow from the world's spirit (1 Cor 2:12; 2 Cor 7:10). The right kind of

---

[114] Rabanus Maurus considers a possibility that Herod did actually carry out the slaughter on December 28, a year and three days after Jesus's birth on December 25. *Commentary on Matthew* 1, 2:3.
[115] John H. van Engen, *Rupert of Deutz* (Berkeley: University of California Press, 1983), 3.
[116] Ibid.
[117] Bernard McGinn, *The Growth of Mysticism*, The Presence of God: A History of Western Christian Mysticism 2 (New York: Crossroad, 1994), 328–33.
[118] van Engen, *Rupert of Deutz*, 3–6.
[119] For example, like Ephrem the Syrian (see Chapter 3, V. B), he observes similarities between the pharaoh and Herod (Exod 1:16, 22; Matt 2:16). Also, the victims are martyrs and firstfruits, while Rachel stands for the Church (see Chapter 3, IX–X and XIII. B).
[120] Dionysius Exiguus also mentions Jer 31:16. Rupert also connects Jer 31:22 to the virgin birth.
[121] All translations of Rupert of Deutz are mine and derived from the Latin text in CCCM 29: 46–8.

weeping is neither hopeless nor forbidden, but truly blessed (*beatificat*) by God (Matt 5:5; 1 Thess 4:13-14, 18).

Rupert then explains the reason for Rachel's godly sorrow: "It is because her children have not obtained immutability in heaven." The heavenly Jerusalem is a material city filled with resurrected saints (Ps 122:3). Rachel's children, however, are not there yet, because they are still sleeping, that is, without glorified bodies: "Although the souls of the saints are in heaven, they do not belong there completely, because evidently their bodies still sleep in dust" (Job 21:26). "Part of them still sojourn in this world," and "those not born yet [*adhuc nascituri*] belong to their number." In due time, the children "will return to their land" (*revertentur ad terminus suos*) (Jer 31:17) when God brings up those asleep in Jesus and they see him as he is (1 John 3:2).

Rupert's explanation of Matt 2:18 continues speculations into reasons for Rachel's weeping that began with Origen (see Chapter 3, XIII). His connections to Jeremiah 31 are significant because he anticipates certain modern discussions regarding that chapter's generally joyous tone, which initially appears incompatible with the gloom of Matt 2:16-18.[122] Rupert, however, utilizes the Rachel/Church typology and the anagogical sense to harmonize Israel's restoration in Jeremiah 31 with the martyred infants' eschatological redemption.

E. Hildegard of Bingen

Hildegard of Bingen (1098–1179), "the only known female systematic exegete in the Middle Ages," composed a book of fifty-eight homilies expounding twenty-seven gospel periscopes for liturgical use on Sundays and feast days.[123] The Benedictine learned under the holy woman Jutta for nearly three decades before becoming a *magistra*, founding Rupertsberg, and receiving exegetical mandates in three visions.[124] Her monastic exegesis explores the spiritual meaning of Scriptures according to the allegorical, tropological, and anagogical senses, common among patristic and medieval authors.[125]

According to Beverly M. Kienzle, Hildegard at times "expounds the gospel texts in such a way as to create dramatic readings that engage the virtues and vices in conflict and dialogue."[126] Her homilies delivered on the Epiphany Eve (10 and 11) employ such readings of Matt 2:16-18. Spiritual battles in the context of Israelite history, as seen in the struggle between Herod and the children, culminate in the suffering church, pictured as Rachel weeping.[127] Hildegard also portrays Rachel as embodiment of Wisdom, Innocence, and Holiness.[128]

---

[122] See for example, Keener, *The Gospel of Matthew*, 111–12; France, *Gospel of Matthew*, 87; Carter, *Matthew and the Margins*, 87; Hagner, *Matthew*, 1:38; and Bonnard, *L'évangile selon Saint Matthieu*, 29.
[123] Hildegard of Bingen, *Homilies on the Gospels*, trans. with introduction and notes by Beverly M. Kienzle, Cistercian Studies 241 (Collegeville: Liturgical Press, 2011), 1–2.
[124] Ibid., 3.
[125] Ibid., 8.
[126] Ibid., 11–12.
[127] Ibid., 23, n. 76. See n. 9 above for the discussion of tropological readings of Matt 2:16, set in the context of Israelite history.
[128] All translations of Hildegard of Bingen are Kienzle's.

In Homily 10, Hildegard personifies Wisdom as Rachel weeping, similar to Wisdom calling in the streets (Proverbs 8). The scene moves beyond Herod's massacre to cosmic dimensions, as Rachel-Wisdom grieves the dishonor of God-rejecting humans, not the massacred children. She is indignant over the vain idolatries that venerate the devil. Yet, she is not hopeless. Rachel-Wisdom refuses comfort as she begs God to restore them "into the bosom of his redemption through his own Son." Consolation is only necessary when all other options are unavailable. Since this possibility of restoration exists through the "redemption of Christ's blood," Rachel-Wisdom spurns consolation, just as friends awaiting the liberation of a captive fellow friend would do the same. A more concrete example is David who mourned his ill son, but ceased to grieve after his passing (2 Sam 12:15-23). Rachel-Wisdom, though aggravated by Satan's works, stands as mediator between idolatrous humanity and the Redeemer God, hopeful of restoration because it is not too late.

In Homily 11, the voice in Ramah expresses miseries heard "above" while "wailing and much lamentation" signify distressful sadness when "Pride oppressed Innocence by striking it." This struggle is reminiscent of Prudentius's fifth-century poem *Psychomachia*, where seven virtues and seven vices, signified by women characters, war against one another, with one of them Pride.[129] Rachel signifies Holiness, "because the eyes of its knowledge brought forth weeping." For the church to know Holiness, it must know the pain of losing her children. Though these martyrs lose their lives and inheritance, "the innocent lamb demanded them back with his own blood." Like Rachel-Wisdom of Homily 10, Rachel-Holiness here refuses comfort because there is hope that Holiness can lead humans to repentance, even after their post-Fall loss of innocence. Thus, Innocence finally triumphs because of the innocent lamb's blood and Rachel-Holiness's efforts.

The message in both homilies is that the Church, like Rachel, ought to grieve idolatry and pride. It embodies Wisdom, Innocence, and Holiness, struggles against satanic forces, and overcomes through the blood of the Son, the innocent lamb. As long as there are tears to be shed and humans to be redeemed, the Church must continue to weep for the lost.

F. Limoges *Lamentation of Rachel*

Among works that elevate the massacre of the innocents to the medieval stage is the anonymous poem *Lamentation of Rachel* (*ca.* eleventh or twelfth century), from the monastery of St. Martial, Limoges.[130] Yet it is unclear whether the poem is a play script, tied to a liturgical feast, or intended for lay audiences.[131] After beginning with *Under the Altar of God*, an elaborate and dramatic trope follows:

> O sweet children, whom I have now brought forth,
> have I, who was once called mother, kept that name?

---

[129] Hildegard of Bingen, *Homilies on the Gospels*, 66, n. 13.
[130] Young, *The Drama of the Medieval Church*, 2:109–10.
[131] Ibid.

Once through pledges, I was called a woman in labor,
now I am miserable, deprived of sons.
Oh! Have pity on me! While I may be able to live,
because I see sons destroyed before me,
and further mutilated insufficiently cut off.
Impious Herod, filled with rage,
excessively proud, kills my offspring.[132]

The poet likely considered the charge to endure from *Under the Altar of God* inadequate or incomplete. Even if there is assurance for the innocents in heaven, Rachel requires comfort on earth. The angel immediately urges:

Do not, Rachel, weep over the pledges.
Why do you grieve, and beat the breasts?
Do not cry, but rather rejoice,
in that those born live happier.
Therefore rejoice!
Son of the Most High Eternal Father,
this is that one whom he seeks to destroy,
who makes you all live eternally.
Therefore rejoice!

Like Rufus of Shotep, the angel here dialogues with Rachel to encourage her. Three times the angel exhorts her to rejoice (*gaude*) and provides a rationale. In contrast to Rufus who scripts Rachel a mere line of complaint, the Limoges Rachel chants an elaborate dirge, expressing her sorrow and condemning Herod. Such poignant words have influenced the Laon *Play of the Star* and perhaps the "Lamentation of the Four Women" from the *Speckled Book*, 116–19.[133]

G. Freising and Fleury *Plays of Rachel*

Though about 900 kilometers apart, Freising and Fleury both produced *Plays of Rachel* (*ca.* eleventh to twelfth century) that feature Rachel as a type of Virgin Mary, so they are treated together here. The Freising version takes priority, since the Fleury version has been discussed already earlier (see VI. F. above).

About a decade or two after the Freising *Play of the Star*, an independent *Play of Rachel* emerged.[134] This play begins somewhat abruptly with the shepherds in

---

[132] All of the translations of Limoges, *Lamentation of Rachel* are the present author's and derived from the Latin text in Young. Ibid., 2:109.
[133] According to Edith A. Wright, "the author of the Laon play or its original was probably acquainted with the Limoges *Ordo Rachelis* and used it, along with the sequences *Celso pueri melodia* and *Misit Herodes innocentum*." *The Dissemination of the Liturgical Drama in France* (Geneve: Slatkline Reprints, 1980), 84. See also *Selections from Ancient Irish Poetry*, trans. Kuno Meyer (London: Constable, 1911), 113; and II. B. above.
[134] Dronke, *Nine Medieval Latin Plays*, xxx. See III. D. above.

Bethlehem and progresses through flight to Egypt, Herod's failure to capture the Magi, and Herod's command to kill the infants.[135] A single soldier carries out the order, uttering, "Learn to die, boy," while the victims and their parents are silent.[136] After the angel reports that Christ is safe, the chorus condemns Herod with the lyrics of the fifth-century Sedulius's hymn *Hostis Herodes impie*. The play concludes with Rachel's lamentation:

> Rachel weeping over the sons says: "O sorrow! O changed joys of fathers and mothers; pour forth a flood of tears for the plaintive lamentations mourning the lovely flower of the Judean fatherland! Alas, tender sons whose lacerated limbs we behold! Alas, sweet sons killed by rage alone! What have you done, that you have had to suffer such things? Why did the malice of Herod take away your life, which you did not yet truly know you had? Alas, whom neither mercy nor age checked! Alas wretched mothers, who are forced to see such things! Why must we suffer to have survived our murdered sons? At least let us accompany them in an equal death."

Like the Limoges Rachel, the Freising Rachel addresses her sons as "sweet sons" and condemns Herod. Yet, it also intensifies and fills Rachel's lament with sorrowful interjections, soaking tears, gory descriptions, unanswered questions, and painful recollections. Also, Rachel represents "fathers and mothers" and "wretched mothers." Its Fleury counterpart reproduces much of the same content and overall effect.

In response to the grief, one consoler (Freising) or a few (Fleury) enter(s) and dialogue(s) with the distraught matriarch. The Fleury version contains more lines of dialogue in which the consoler-mothers support her as she faints, and urge her to stop her tears. They entreat her to rejoice instead because her children "live above the stars, and are blessed," but Rachel continues with another lament.[137] Due to the extra material, the Fleury play contains three exchanges while the Freising has two. After this first exchange in Fleury, the two versions converge with the following lines from Notker the Stammer's poem *Quid tu virgo*:

---

[135] The Fleury version adds, "Then let Herod, as if a broken man, drawing his sword, prepare to kill himself, but let him be prevented by some of his people, and calmed down."

[136] Translations of the Freising *Play of Rachel* are partially mine and derived from the Latin text and notes in Young, *The Drama of the Medieval Church*, 2:117–20 and partially from Susan Boynton, "From the Lament of Rachel to the Lament of Mary: A Transformation in the History of Drama and Spirituality," in *Signs of Change: Transformations of Christian Traditions and Their Representation in the Arts, 1000–2000*, ed. Nils Holger Petersen, Claus Clüver, and Nicolas Bell, 319–40, Textxet: Studies in Comparative Literature 43 (Amsterdam: Rodopi, 2004), 324, and partially from *Medieval Church Music-Dramas: A Repertory of Complete Plays*, 145–64, where texts overlap with the Fleury *Play of Rachel*.

[137] The extra exchange is as follows: "Mothers (supporting her as she faints): 'Do not, virgin Rachel, do not, dearest mother, for the killing of the children your tears of woe stop, but as you bewail exult in your tears, because your children live above the stars, and are blessed.' Rachel (rallying in response to them): 'Alas, alas, alas! How can I rejoice when these dead limbs I see? When so torn up I am in my whole body? For me, in truth, they create, these boys, without end grief. O sorrow! O how changed is the joy of the parents to sad lamenting! Of tears in floods pour out, Juda's flower, the country's sorrow, bewailing.'"

[Consoler(s):] "Why do you weep, lovely virgin mother Rachel, whose face Jacob chose? As if the bleariness of the eyes of your younger sister pleased him!"[138] Dry, mother, your flowing eyes.[139] How do rivers on your cheeks adorn you?" [Rachel:] "Alas, alas, alas. Why do you accuse me of having poured forth my lament in vain, when I am deprived of the son, who alone would have cared for my poverty, who would not have ceded to the enemies the scanty lands that Jacob acquired for me? And to the stolid brethren what cause for grief were borne to the grave anytime?"[140] [Consoler(s):] "Is he to be mourned who possesses the celestial kingdom, and who helps his brothers with prayers in the house of God?"

Here, the Freising version ends abruptly as it began with the *Te Deum*. In contrast, the Fleury version concludes with a proper denouement in dramatic flair.[141] Rachel staggers toward the innocents and says: "Anxious is my spirit within me. Turbulent is my heart in me." The consolers lead Rachel away, the Archangel and the innocents occupy heaven, Herod dies, Archelaus succeeds his father, the Holy Family joyfully returns from Egypt, and Joseph sings.

The Fleury and Freising *Plays of Rachel* both innovatively incorporate the ninth-century *Quid tu Virgo* to add to the depth of Rachel in the Limoges *Lamentation of Rachel* and the Laon *Play of the Star*.[142] Notker did not intend his sequence to be for the *Feast of the Innocents* but for general reflections on martyrs. The gist is that Rachel is the Church who lost her son, a courageous martyr distinguished from the "stolid brethren."[143] When the play writers tie *Quid tu Virgo* to Matt 2:18, Rachel's representation moves beyond the bereaved mothers: she is also the figure of the Church weeping for martyrs and superior over her sister, the Synagogue.

Furthermore, the Freising and Fleury writers encourage the audience to envisage Rachel through the lens of Mary in the Passion. "Virgin mother" from Notker immediately suggests the blessed mother, so that not only does Rachel stand as a type of the Church but Mary as well. In addition to the provocative title, Rachel's actions here foreshadow Mary's at the cross. In various versions of the *planctus Mariae*, contemporaneous with the *Plays of Rachel*, Mary weeps over her offspring as associates nearby attempt to console her, not unlike Rachel.[144] The Rachel-Mary typology is also evident in one *planctus* that displays Mary's desire to die in place of Christ or with him, resembling the Freising Rachel, who pleads, "At least let us accompany them in

---

[138] In the Freising version, the consoler wipes Rachel's eyes before the next line.

[139] In the Freising version, "dry" is repeated.

[140] This line is missing in the Freising version. In its place is an erasure covering two or three words. In the Fleury version the mothers to raise up the Innocents before the next line.

[141] After the *Te Deum* in the Freising play, "the remaining five lines on the page are largely blank. The few passages of text are irrelevant or mostly illegible. One illegible passage appears to begin *Iterum Rachel*." Young, *The Drama of the Medieval Church*, 2:120, n. 4.

[142] Peter Dronke stresses the importance of *Quid tu virgo* and goes as far as to say that the Rachel sequences of eleventh-century dramatists are direct responses to it *Nine Medieval Latin Plays*, xxviii–xxx.

[143] Ibid., xxx.

[144] James Monti, *The Week of Salvation: History and Traditions of Holy Week*, Our Sunday Visitor Books 532 (Huntington: Our Sunday Visitor, 1993), 188.

an equal death."¹⁴⁵ The Fleury Rachel has even clearer parallels to Mary, since both sing the antiphon of Lauds on Good Friday: "Anxious is in me my spirit. In me turbulent is the heart of me."¹⁴⁶

Around this time, works dealing with Rachel in a Marian context usually refer to Genesis narratives, not Matt 2:18 (or Jer 31:15). When comparisons of Mary and the weeping Rachel do take place, they are either implicit or unexplored.¹⁴⁷ The Fleury play, however, explores the rich potential of Rachel-Mary typology by aligning three senses of Scripture with the three exchanges between Rachel and her consolers.¹⁴⁸ The first exchange mostly focuses on the literal interpretation and Herod's gory destruction. Yet the consolers assure the victims' place in heaven and call Rachel a "virgin," foreshadowing the full typology to follow. The second exchange is allegorical. The consolers cite *Quid tu virgo* so that the Rachel-Leah-Jacob love triangle frames the Church-Synagogue-Christ dynamic, respectively. The Church, represented also by Mary, emerges as the favored one of Christ. Finally, in the third exchange, the tropological sense guides the interpretation of Jacob's acquisition of property for Rachel and her son, who helps his brothers with prayers. The Church does not need to fear losing the blessings that Christ has won for her. The innocents in heaven assist and intercede for her members below.

IX. Concluding Thoughts

This chapter was an attempt to navigate the reception history of Matt 2:16-18 from the sixth century to 1516, with its attendant complexities (Sec. I). Six major strands of readings have been selected for detailed discussion. As before, a group of works attempts to harmonize the massacre with other accounts (Sec. III). One strand of reading sees the dragon of the Apocalypse standing behind Herod (Section IV), while another sees Herod standing for secular rule opposing God (Sec. V). With regard to the victims and the bereaved, the familiar readings of martyrdom (Sec. VI), sacrifice (Sec. VII), and the Church (Sec. VIII) continue from the previous centuries.

At the beginning of the chapter, the present writer hinted at a thesis as a summary: various types of interpretation, methods, and media from this period plumb the depths of meaning in Matt 2:16-18. As a test of this thesis, one can point to the abundant use of all four senses of Scripture. The literal sense of Matt 2:16-18 is foundational and stimulates the work of harmonizing the massacre with the "calculation of two years" (Maximus the Confessor) and the flight to Egypt (*Speckled Book*). Also important is the allegory of Rachel as the Church (Rufus of Shotep; Hildegard of Bingen). Building on the literal and allegorical senses are (1) the tropological readings that denigrate Herod (Oecumenius, John of Euobea, Freising *Play of the Star*) and

---

[145] Boynton, "From the Lament of Rachel to the Lament of Mary," 325.
[146] Boynton, "Performative Exegesis in the Fleury Interfectio Puerorum," 57–8.
[147] Ibid., 57.
[148] Boynton, "From the Lament of Rachel to the Lament of Mary," 326.

(2) the anagogical readings that elevate the victims among the elect (Ambrose Autpert) or Rachel as recipient of eschatological promises (Rupert of Deutz).

If the existence of such diverse readings proves the deep interpretive potential of Matt 2:16-18, the application of certain methods such as recontextualization and characterization can also serve as litmus tests. From the sixth century to 1516, the Matthean episode is most frequently recontextualized in the Apocalypse, heightening the drama of the event as well as lightening the mood of the passage with blissful images (Oecumenius, the sacramentaries, *Comes of Würzburg*, *Under the Altar of God*, John of Euobea, Ambrose Autpert, *Martyrdom of Matthew*, and Limoges *Lamentation of Rachel*).

Also, by borrowing from modern narrative-critical concepts like characterization, one can appreciate the narrative richness of these later texts. According to E. M. Forster's division of characters, Herod, the victims, and the mothers in Matt 2:16-18 are relatively minor or flat characters at best, while the Holy Family is not even mentioned.[149] Yet, these characters become rounder and more complex in later works. In the *Speckled Book*, Mary and Jesus take the leading role in their escape to Egypt, not Joseph. Herod rages like Catiline, the victims sing liturgical lyrics, and Rachel and the consolers dialogue like Job and his friends in the Freising and Fleury plays.

In addition, according to reader response critical methods, Rachel's enriched character has potential to invite an emotional "participatory response" from sympathetic readers of Matt 2:18 who are familiar with the recovery process of bereavement.[150] This idea that maternal grief has a particular influence, however, is not novel or artificial. Biblical and extra-biblical works attest that a bereaved mother in the ancient world draws the attention of gods, human social groups, and authorities.[151] Accordingly, God instantly responds to the weeping Rachel (Jer 31:16), and such an immediate reply is all the more striking considering that the intercessions of Moses and Samuel fail to save their people (15:1).[152] Imagination amplifies the roles of lesser-known characters in the Matthean infancy narratives and even introduces new characters.

Lastly, various media attest to the pervasiveness of Matt 2:16-18 from the sixth century to 1516. Intentionally or unintentionally, various interpreters pluralized their teachings on the passage according to "multiple intelligences."[153] According to Howard Gardner, intelligence is not measured by a single dominant ability but by at least seven sensory modalities.[154] Prayers, readings, sermons, commentaries and theological

---

[149] E. M. Forster, *Aspects of the Novel* (San Diego: Harcourt Brace Jovanovich, 1927), 67–78.

[150] See the discussion of Bathsheba in a similar plight in David Bosworth, "'David Comforted Bathsheba': Gender and Parental Bereavement," in *Seitenblicke: Literische und historische Studien zu Nebenfiguren im zweiten Samuelbuch*, ed. Walter Dietrich, 238–55, Orbis Biblicus et Orientalis 249 (Göttingen: Vandenhoeck and Ruprecht, 2011).

[151] Ekaterina E. Kozlova, *Maternal Grief in the Hebrew Bible*, Oxford Theology & Religion Monographs (Oxford: Oxford University Press, 2017), 205–6.

[152] Ibid., 159.

[153] For an explanation of differences between terms "intelligence," "style or learning style," and "senses," see Valerie Strauss, "Howard Gardiner: 'Multiple intelligences' are not 'learning styles,'" *Washington Post*, October 16, 2013, accessed August 1, 2017, https://www.washingtonpost.com/news/answer-sheet/wp/2013/10/16/howard-gardner-multiple-intelligences-are-not-learning-styles/?utm_term=.ee7cede43814.

[154] Howard Gardner, *Frames of Mind: The Theory of Multiple Intelligences* (New York: Basic Books, 1983).

treatises may appeal to verbal-linguistic and logical-mathematical intelligences. The antiphonals may prove useful to the musical-rhythmic and harmonic intelligence. Visual-spatial and bodily-kinetic intelligences are important for actors who play Herod, the innocents, and Rachel on stage, and for their audiences. Intrapersonal intelligences are vital in monasteries where meditations and scheduled readings take place.

5

Massacre of the Innocents from 1517

Introduction

To prevent Chapter 4 from becoming too lengthy, the present author set 1517 (oft-cited as the beginning of the Reformation) as the chronological limit before discussing post-fifth-century readings of Matt 2:16-18 (see Chapter 4, I). Though the Italian Renaissance begins earlier in the fourteenth century, more significant are the sixteenth-century developments that have direct impact on the massacre's reception history. Erika Rummel argues that Renaissance humanism affected biblical studies of early modern Europe through (1) "the privileging of classical antiquity over the 'dark' Middle Ages" and (2) "a preference for rhetoric and language studies over the traditional academic core subject, Aristotelian logic."[1] She also observes, "Under the influence of humanistic philology, sixteenth-century exegetes broke away from the medieval pattern of interpreting the text according to the four senses (historical, figurative, tropological, anagogical) and focused on the grammatical and historical sense."[2] This hermeneutical shift and the call for *ad fontes* are evident in later readings of Matt 2:16-18.

In addition, 1517 is a significant marker considering Rachel's tomb.[3] Pilgrimages to Rachel's tomb decreased noticeably with the end of the Crusades (see Chapter 4, VIII. B), the Ottoman Empire's conquest of the Mamluk Sultanate of Egypt (1517), and the Protestant reformers' disapproval of pilgrimages.[4] Even the pilgrims who

---

[1] Erika Rummel, "The Renaissance Humanists," in *A History of Biblical Interpretation. Volume 2: The Medieval through the Reformation Periods*, ed. Alan J. Hauser and Duane F. Watson, 280–98 (Grand Rapids: Eerdmans, 2009), 280.

[2] Ibid., 294. This trend, however, was not universal. A Catholic scholar like Cornelius à Lapide would draw upon aspects of the medieval four senses. See Thomas W. Mossman, trans., *The Great Commentary of Cornelius à Lapide: S. Matthew's Gospel—Chaps. I. to IX* (London: John Hodges, 1876).

[3] The architectural development of Rachel's tomb near Bethlehem includes the first-century Greco-Roman architect's pyramid structure, the twelfth-century Christian Crusaders' pillars and dome, Muslim renovations in the fourteenth and seventeenth century, and, most recently, Jewish contributions in the nineteenth and twentieth century, beginning with Moses Montefiore. The Jewish state currently prohibits its use by other faiths. Strickert, *Rachel Weeping*, 109–23, 132–7.

[4] Andrew C. Hess, "The Ottoman Conquest of Egypt (1517) and the Beginning of the Sixteenth-Century World War," *International Journal of Middle East Studies* 4 (1973): 55–76; Hunt Janin, *Four*

did travel there could not enjoy a full experience. In the late sixteenth century, the Franciscan Father Bernadino Amico sketched the sepulcher and provided its first visual representation, but he could not measure it accurately due to its limited accessibility to Christians.[5] Only a single witness in 1697 described the tomb until the mid-nineteenth century, when visitations restarted.[6] This general Muslim exclusivity of access explains a defining characteristic in this era of reception history.[7] For centuries, Christians were unable to make detailed observations of the tomb.

While such historical factors limited one mode of understanding Matt 2:16-18, other developments broadened access to new ways of reading the passage. For example, the invention of the printing press led to almost immediate and widespread proliferation of ideas.[8] While music has always been important, Thomas Sharp's timely publication of the *Coventry Carol* before the nineteenth-century destruction of its original manuscript and its subsequent popularity add another layer of depth into the reception history of Matt 2:16-18.[9] Liturgical readings developed outside the Roman Catholic tradition in the Episcopal *Book of Common Prayer* and the *Evangelical Lutheran Worship*.[10]

With such increasing variegated diversity, the approach in this chapter is necessarily different than the previous ones. Receptions are grouped under broader genre headings rather than themes and readings. There are at least two advantages to this approach. First, there is much repetition of older material that aligns with the spirit of *ad fontes*. Recent works most often rely on the literal-grammatical sense or draw from a vast repository of older ideas, just as the post-sixth-century materials owe much to works that predate them.[11] Secondly, imagination and innovation are less remarkable

---

Paths to Jerusalem: Jewish, Christian, Muslim, and Secular Pilgrimages, 1000 B.C.E. to 2001 C.E. (New York: Harper & Row, 2002), 149.

[5] Strickert, *Rachel Weeping*, 95-7.

[6] Ibid., 98-100. There is one noteworthy account of a pilgrimage by Moses Margoliouth, a Jewish convert to Christianity. On May 1848, he and missionaries of the London Jewish Society stopped at Rachel's tomb. After examining Moses Montefiore's building over it, Margoliouth says, "We chanted, in a melancholy strain, the words of Jeremiah, quoted by St. Matthew: 'A voice was heard on high, lamentation, and bitter weeping; Rachel weeping for her children,' (I translate the word Ramah; leaving it in the original, gives a wrong idea to the English readers of the Bible), and then we proceeded along the Valley of Rephaim to Bethlehem." Moses Margoliouth, *A Pilgrimage to the Land of My Fathers* (London: Richard Bentley, 1850), 400-1.

[7] Strickert, *Rachel Weeping*, 139. Nonetheless, the image of Rachel and her weeping over children continues to have universal appeal as an enduring symbol for social justice, giving voice to homeless families, abused women, and aborted children. See James T. Burtchaell, *Rachel Weeping and Other Essays on Abortion* (Toronto: Life Cycle Books, 1990); Kozol, *Rachel and Her Children*; Denise M. Rowe, *The Voice of Rachel Weeping: A Creative Journey of Compassion, Healing, and Hope for Abused Women* (Maitland: Xulon, 2016). See also the survey of allusions in English literature in Linda Beamer, "Rachel," in DBTEL, 651-2.

[8] Estimations of Luther's publications (mostly German), for example, amount to over 2,200 by 1530 and 3,183 by the end of his life (1546). Mark U. Edwards, *Printing, Propaganda and Martin Luther* (Berkeley: University of California Press, 1994), 20-7.

[9] Robert Croo's manuscript (1534) was destroyed in a fire in the nineteenth century, but not before Thomas Sharp published the lyrics and the musical notations. Richard Rastall, *Minstrels Playing, Music in Early English Religious Drama 2* (Cambridge: D.S. Brewer, 2001), 179.

[10] Gail Ramshaw, "The Holy Innocents, Martyrs, December 28," in *New Proclamation Commentary on Feasts, Holy Days, and Other Celebrations*, ed. David B. Lott, 42-7 (Philadelphia: Fortress, 2007), 42.

[11] For examples, see Chapter 4, I.

in the contents, but more noteworthy in the contents' presentations. For example, the *Coventry Carol* and Herman Melville's *Moby Dick* utilize imagination to exploit the intricacies of tonality and subversive allusions latent in music and Melville's writing style, respectively. With the genre of commentary, however, a thematic organization is most sensible due to the vast amount of data.

Yet some presentations or genres do not contain enough interesting or original readings to warrant extensive discussion. As mentioned earlier, there is the decrease of pilgrimages. As seen in the last chapter, there is the decline of mystery plays, a key development in the reception history of Matt 2:16-18. This shift marked a change in Herod's depictions in drama. For example, Herod is no longer the central antagonist, though playwrights like William Shakespeare, George B. Shaw, and William B. Yeats evoke his name as the paradigmatic wrathful tyrant that readily compares to other evil despots and terrorists of history (see Chapter 2, VIII).[12]

Thus, this chapter presents the readings under the following headings: (1) liturgical material, (2) verse (3) novels, and (4) commentaries. According to this order, the present writer bookends this chapter with more traditional ways of reading Matt 2:16-18 (liturgical works and commentaries) while discussing more secular works in the middle (verse and novels). Under each genre, either the most influential individual receptions (liturgical works, verse, novels) are identified and/or findings from a large sample, with appropriate examples (sermons, commentaries), are summarized.

I. Liturgical Material

History of liturgy is complex and deserving of an independent study, so it is prudent to highlight only major developments and representative samples with direct relevance to Matt 2:16-18 and the *Feast of the Innocents*. Combined with coverage of the liturgical readings are sermonic homilies, postils, and discourses, since they correspond to each other in content and/or settings.[13] Also needed is some attention to non-Roman Latin rites and the Orthodox Church *Menaion* to encompass a broader perspective on liturgy.

A. Roman Missals and Liturgical Readings

Much of the original and most important liturgical material comes from sacramentaries, lectionaries, and antiphonals from the seventh to ninth centuries (see Chapter 4, VI. A–C). In the second millennium, tracing the multidirectional developments of different liturgical books becomes increasingly difficult. For example, despite various syntheses and consolidations, Cassian Folsom believes the lectionary remained stable

---

[12] See William Shakespeare's *Henri V* (ca. 1599) and *Antony and Cleopatra* (ca. 1606); the preface of George B. Shaw's *Major Barbara* (1905); and William B. Yeats's *Cat and the Moon* (ca. 1924).

[13] The word "postil" (also "apostil" and from Latin *post illa*, probably meaning "after those ... (words of Scripture)") was used of a gloss of a Scriptural text in the Middle Ages (e.g., Nicholas of Lyra) but later developed to mean a homily on the Gospel or Epistle for the day or a homily book (e.g., Martin Luther). "Postil," in *ODCC*, 1321.

through the centuries until its massive reform in 1970.[14] But the antiphonal and the history of chant entered a "period of decadence" from the end of Middle Ages to a nadir during Trent, until restoration in the nineteenth century.[15]

Simplifying this fragmented history and reducing diversity is the rising prominence of the Roman Missal, which conveniently combines the sacramentary, lectionary, and antiphonal into one volume. The Missal has its own stages of development: synthesis (ninth to twelfth centuries), variety (thirteenth century), post-Tridentine, and post-Vatican II.[16] This division scheme reveals that the Councils of Trent (1545–63) and Vatican II (1962–65) would serve as important turning points in the period after 1517. In the aftermath of both, a commission was appointed to revise the Roman Missal.[17] The post-Tridentine Missal of Pius V (1570) attempted to fix problems (avarice, irreverence, and superstition) and promoted uniformity in practice and conformity to Roman customs of saints' feasts celebrated before the eleventh century.[18]

This Tridentine appeal for uniformity and return to ancient tradition was echoed in Vatican II.[19] Like Pius V before him, Pope Paul VI grounded the post-conciliar liturgical reform on the discovery and publication of ancient sources (*Missale Romanum* 4, 1969). Yet, the Second Vatican Council also attempted to improve upon the earlier reforms by directing, among other things, more Scripture readings, the restoration of the homily, calendar revisions, development of liturgical singing, adaptation to modern times, the use of the mother tongue, and more lay participation.[20]

The encouragement of more Scripture readings and homilies has direct impact on the current reception history (*Sacrosanctum Concilium* ch. I., III., 35.). The pre-Vatican II Roman Missal, which remained essentially the same over four centuries (1570–1947), prescribes two readings for the *Feast of the Innocents* (Rev 14:1-5 and

---

[14] Folsom, "The Liturgical Books of the Roman Rite," 257.
[15] Ibid., 261.
[16] Ibid., 264.
[17] Reinold Theisen, "The Reform of Mass Liturgy and the Council of Trent," *Worship* 40 (1966): 565.
[18] Ibid., 567–74, 581. To be sure, these reforms did not immediately or even uniformly produce the desired changes in the *Feast of the Innocents* everywhere. Even before Trent, authorities attempted to disassociate the *Feast of the Fools* from the *Feast of the Innocents*, due to the growing unchecked revelry of the former (see Chapter 4, V). Only with the efforts of Pope Benedict XIV in his 1748 encyclical *Super Bacchanalibus* did the vestigial remains of the *Feast of the Fools* finally cease. In addition, local traditions and superstitious elements continued to persist in the celebrations of the *Feast of the Innocents*. For example, in central Europe, stick-wielding children went from house to house to bless girls and women with a cultic fertility wish. In some German-speaking countries, some believe that unbaptized children's souls can escape from Lady Hel and join the innocents, if one can discern their cries and shapes during storms and chant their Christian names. See also description of Els Enfarinats in Ibi, Spain: Shaena Montanari, "In This Town, the Weapons of War Are Flour and Eggs," *National Geographic Society*, September 14, 2017, accessed December 8, 2017, https://www.nationalgeographic.com/photography/proof/2017/09/you-won_t-believe-this-bizarre-celebration-in-spain/. Adding to this complexity is the eleventh-century transfer of the March 12 *Boy Bishop's Feast*, the feast day of Gregory I the patron of schools and choirs, to the Innocents' Day on December 28. In many places, the *Boy Bishop's Feast* was frequently confused with the *Feast of Fools* and all of its excesses. In the fourteenth century, the *Boy Bishop's Feast* was moved again to December 5, the eve of the Feast of Saint Nicholas, the patron saint of children. As a result, the feast avoided the fate of the *Feast of Fools*, finally suppressed in the fifteenth century. Weiser, *Handbook of Christian Feasts and Customs*, 126, 132–3.
[19] Paul Bird, "Living Liturgy: The Vision of Vatican II," *Australasian Catholic Record* 91 (2014): 338–40.
[20] Ibid., 340.

Matt 2:13-18), a prescription that dates from the seventh century (Chapter 4, VI. B). In contrast, the post-Vatican II *Lectionary for the Mass* (LFM) lists 1 John 1:5–2:2, verses from Psalm 124 (2-3; 4-5; 7b-8), and Matt 2:13-18 as the first reading, the responsorial psalm (in response to the first reading and often sung as a musical interlude before the next reading), and the Gospel reading, respectively. This Psalm had been used in the earlier Roman Mass antiphon for the *Feast of the Innocents* (Chapter 4, VI. C).[21]

While liturgical texts from the first millennium and a half consistently revere the victims of Matt 2:16 as martyrs and sacrifices, the post-Vatican II readings favor a more general representative role.[22] Verses from Psalm 124 exhort the distressed to trust in the sovereign God without strong connection to martyrdom. 1 John 1:5–2:2 explicitly refers to "little children" (τεκνία), but the exhortations to walk in the light, confess sin, avoid sinning, and remember Christ the propitiation are only loosely related to Matt 2:16-18. Without connections to Rev 6:9-11; 7:9; and 14:1-4, the victims do not receive special recognition as slain martyrs under the altar, the triumphant multitude, or the 144,000 firstfruits, respectively.[23]

B. Sermons, Homilies, Postils, and Discourses

Closely related to liturgical readings are homilies based on Matt 2:16-18.[24] They are important sources for its popular reception, not only recently in the post-Vatican II era but also from the Protestant Reformation onwards. The latter movement placed special emphasis on reviving preaching as an identifying marker of the Church.[25] The Counter-Reformation would reshape the Catholic sacred oratory as well. A notable shift took place in the papal court and beyond: from the scholastic, syllogistic, and thematic methods prescribed in the medieval *Artes Praecandi* to sermons based on the text for the day, stressing the literal and the moral senses, and communicated with classical language.[26] With the proliferation of preaching manuals promoting classic

---

[21] Other feast-observing churches with ties to the Roman Catholic Church use works like the Lutheran *Evangelical Lutheran Worship* (ELW, 2006) and the Episcopal *Book of Common Prayer* (BCP, 1979). They also prescribe Psalm 124 for the feast, but add Jer 31:16-17, thereby lessening the ambiguity of this fulfillment citation. The last image from Jeremiah 31 is not a picture of Rachel weeping for her children. Instead, there is hope that her children will return from the enemy's land to their own territory. God speaks words of comfort three times in response to Rachel's refusal to be comforted: "Thus says the LORD" (כה אמר יהוה) in Jer 31:16 and "Declaration of YHWH" (נאם יהוה) in Jer 31:16, 17. Like Dionysius Exiguus, Dionysius Bar Salibi, and Rupert of Deutz (see Chapter 4, VIII. D), ELW and BCP expand the discussion of the tragedy beyond the confines of Matt 2:16-18 by considering the verses that immediately follow Jer 31:15. Ramshaw, "The Holy Innocents, Martyrs, December 28," 42-7.

[22] Ibid., 42.

[23] The same is true with ELW and BCP, though the latter prescribes a passage from the Apocalypse. 1 Pet 4:12-19 in ELW speaks of glorious Christian suffering without necessitating martyrdom. Rev 21:1-7 in BCP envisions the New Jerusalem, where God's people experience comfort in eternal bliss. The New Jerusalem under God welcomes Christ the bridegroom (Rev 21:2), while the old Jerusalem under Herod dreads him (Matt 2:3). Ramshaw, "The Holy Innocents, Martyrs, December 28," 46-7.

[24] The present writer does not sharply distinguish between sermons, homilies, postils, and discourses.

[25] Earle E. Cairns, *Christianity through the Centuries: A History of the Christian Church* (Grand Rapids: Zondervan, 1996), 349-53.

[26] Frederick J. McGinness, "Preaching Ideals and Practice in Counter-Reformation Rome," *Sixteenth Century Journal* 11:2 (1980): 115-17.

oratory during the sixteenth century, the sermon became a means to persuade the entire person's mind, heart, and soul, not merely to teach.[27] While relatively more difficult to locate than commentaries, presented next is a representative sample of available sermons from each century from 1517 onwards from various traditions and figures.

While deviating from Roman Catholicism, the Protestants did not necessarily avoid festival sermons. Martin Luther used them to draw the laity away from veneration of past saints toward veneration of Christ and the service of living saints.[28] He limits his postil notes on December 28, *The Feast of the Holy Innocents* to a general theodical discussion, exhorting faith in God's fatherly compassion and providence that preserved Christ.[29] In cases like this infanticide, where the paternal care appears lacking, Luther simply accepts the truism of Christian suffering in the world, citing 1 Cor 4:9-13.[30] The massacred victims are examples of persecuted Christians. He refrains from further comment lest the discussion diminishes the day's celebration; personal reading and meditation on the historical facts of the massacre are sufficient.[31] Thus, as is typical of many sixteenth-century exegetes, Luther prioritizes the historical sense at the exclusion of other senses (see introduction above).

Yet, not every preacher followed Luther's muted example. In addition to offering comforting words, other reformers used the pulpit to denigrate their opponents. For example, John Calvin (1509-1564) elaborates extensively on God's goodness and providence and actualizes the passage in the ecclesial struggle between the papacy and the Protestants.[32] Similarly, the German Lutheran reformer Philip Melanchthon (1497-1560) exalts the victims to the status of "sons of the Church" and "heirs of eternal life," and contrasts them with the condemned Anabaptists.[33] Initially, this invective may seem to appear uncharacteristic, especially since Melanchthon's gentle temperament contrasted sharply with Luther's rough polemical style.[34] Melanchthon's disdain for the Anabaptists, however, can hardly be overstated.[35] This type of actualization is similar to the readings of the early church preachers/commentators who directed the story against their opponents.[36] While Melanchthon does not equate the Anabaptists

---

[27] So then, the orator is not only obligated to teach (*docere*) but also to move (*movere*) and delight (*delectare*). Ibid., 117-19.

[28] Joel R. Baseley, "Some Notes on the Text," in *Sermons of Martin Luther: The Church Postils: Sermons for the Main Festivals and Saints Days of the Church Year; Winter and Summer Selections*, trans. Joel R. Baseley (Dearborn: Mark V, 2005). "Why the Festival Sermons, para. 1."

[29] Joel R. Baseley, trans., *Sermons of Martin Luther: The Church Postils: Sermons for the Main Festivals and Saints Days of the Church Year; Winter and Summer Selections* (Dearborn: Mark V, 2005), 174.

[30] Ibid., 174-5.

[31] Ibid., 175.

[32] John Calvin, Sermon 36 in CR 74:439-52.

[33] Philip Melanchthon, *Annotations in the Gospel of Matthew* 2:11 in CR 14:548.

[34] John Schofield, *Philip Melanchthon and the English Reformation*, St. Andrews Studies in Reformation History (Aldershot: Ashgate, 2006), 29-30.

[35] For a survey and a bibliography of Melanchthon's polemical writings against the Anabaptists, see John S. Oyer, "The Writings of Melanchthon against the Anabaptists," *Mennonite Quarterly Review* 26 (1952): 259-79.

[36] For example, Hilary of Poitiers envisions Christian-Jew relations through the lens of Matt 2:16-18 (Chapter 3, VIII. B). See also the actualizations of Lucifer of Cagliari, Gregory of Nazianzus, Apponius, Augustine of Hippo, and Cyprian of Carthage (Chapter 3, VIII. C-F and IX. C).

explicitly with Herod or his troops, he nevertheless damages their reputation while extolling the saints.

Counter-Reformation homilists do not necessarily pointedly respond in kind to the Reformers when preaching from Matt 2:16-18. One example is their early leader and archbishop of Milan Charles Borromeo (1538-1584) and his sermon during the *Feast of Holy Innocents* at the Metropolitan Basilica in 1583. He embellishes Matt 2:16-18 with familiar ideas from the past: exhortation from Jer 31:16-22 (based on Rom 15:4), an ecclesial interpretation of Rachel, the infants as martyrs (Rev 6:10-11), the nearby location of Rachel's tomb, grim details of the slaughter, comparison of Herod with Athaliah (2 Kings 11), the demonic forces behind Herod, and Josephus's account of Herod's demise.[37] He, however, does not condemn his enemies. Francis de Sales (1567-1622), the mild-mannered Counter-Reformation leader and Bishop of Geneva, characteristically avoids inflammatory remarks while preaching on Matt 2:16-18. In a sermon plan for January 4, 1609, the octave of the Holy Innocents, he only equates Satan with Herod who "lets loose a foul thought or flatteries."[38] He makes no direct commentary on the massacre, choosing to focus on Matt 2:13-15.

During the seventeenth and eighteenth centuries, feast-observing English churchmen used the occasion to emphasize the victims' sainthood (martyrdom and sacrifices), defend God's goodness, denigrate Herod and other evil rulers (e.g., Saul, Nero, Diocletian), cite ancient church authorities (e.g., Tertullian, Chrysostom, Augustine), and seek historical corroborations (Josephus, Macrobius).[39] While these ideas are generally familiar in reception history, some innovative features include comparison of the victims to heavenly stars (Digby Cotes; cf. Dan 12:3) and care for

---

[37] Homily 86 in Charles Borromeo, *Sancti Caroli Borromei S.R E. Cardinalis Archiepiscopi Mediolani Homiliae CXXVII. Ex MSS. Codicibus Bibliothecae Ambrosianae Ordine Chronologico In Lucem Productae* (Veith: Augustae Vindelicorum, 1758), 823-34. Early examples of the same or similar readings in Chapter 3 include Irenaeus of Lyons (III. B), Ephrem the Syrian (V. B), Eusebius of Caesarea (VII. A), Gregory of Nyssa (XI. A), Justin Martyr (XII. A), Fortunatianus of Aquileia (XIII). See also Rupert of Deutz (Chapter 4, VIII. D).

[38] See sermon LXXVI in Francis de Sales, *Oeuvres Complètes de Saint François de Sales, Évêque et Prince de Genève et Docteur de L'Église: Tome Huitième: Sermons IIe Volume* (Annecy: J. Niérat, 1892), 33-7.

[39] See George Horne, *Discourses on Several Subjects and Occasions*, 5th ed. (Oxford: Printed for J. Cooke and G.G. and J. Robinson, T. Cadell, and F. and C. Rivington, 1795), 1:285-316; Digby Cotes, *Fifteen Sermons Preach'd on Several Occasions* (Oxford: printed at the Theatre for Ant. Peisley Bookseller and are to be sold by J. Knapton, W. Meadows, and T. Combes, Booksellers in London, 1721), 93-112; Robert Neville, *Goodness Proved to Be the Best Protection from the Arrests of All Harmes: In a Sermon Preached before the University, upon Innocents Day, in Great St. Maries Church in Cambridge* (London: Printed for Benj. Billingsley, 1687), 1-25; Thomas Fuller, *A Fast Sermon Preached on Innocents Day* (London: Printed by L.N. and R.C. for John Williams at the signe of the Crowne in St. Pauls Church-Yard, 1642), 3; Peter Hausted, *Ten Sermons, Preached Vpon Seuerall Sundayes and Saints Dayes: 1 Vpon the Passion of Our Blessed Savior. 2 Vpon His Resurrection. 3 Vpon S. Peters Day. 4 Vpon S. Iohn the Baptists Day. 5 Vpon the Day of the Blessed Innocents. 6 Vpon Palme Sunday. 7 and 8 Vpon the Two First Sundays in Advent. 9 and 10 Vpon the Parable of the Pharisee and Publicane, Luke 18. Together with a Sermon Preached at the Assises at Huntington. by P. Hausted Mr. in Arts, and Curate at Vppingham in Rutland* (London: Printed by Miles Flesher, Bernard Alsop, and Thomas Fawcet for John Clark and are to be sold at his shop under S. Peters Church in Cornhill, 1636), 83-96.

impoverished children (John Killingbeck).[40] Nineteenth-century preachers continue to reiterate familiar theodical arguments as before.[41] For example, the influential English clergyman Charles Simeon demonstrates from this passage "how early our Lord's suffering began," the futility of man's designs against God, and the certainty of future recompense (Discourse 1281).[42]

In the twentieth century and beyond, the reception history of Matt 2:16-18 in a homiletical context is necessarily tied to the post-Vatican II liturgical renewal. As stated above, the increase of Scripture readings at the feast was a conscious point of emphasis, but the victims took on a more general representative role standing for suffering Christians. At the same time, preaching on this passage in certain contexts would also occasion a specific tropological corrective to the American commodification of Christmas and the accompanying frenzied consumerism.[43] For example, a homilist at the 2010 Jesuit Formation Meeting, St. Louis, Missouri, decries a monochrome, gleeful view of Christmas, because in actuality the entire advent liturgical season is a complicated mixture of penitent purple, joyful blush, and bloody red.[44] Following the Holy Family in the twenty-first century requires acceptance of pains that accompany Christ's coming.[45]

C. Non-Roman Latin Liturgical Material

While it is difficult to cover all of the diverse liturgical material outside of the Roman tradition, a few illustrative examples from the Latin West have been included for a brief study.[46] The Ambrosian and Mozarabic rites could have been introduced in earlier chapters, since they have their roots in the early church. Owing to their survival, however, were the Council of Trent and Vatican II, as they were more recent watershed conciliar moments. For example, the Missal of Pius V, even while promoting uniformity, respected these two provincial rites because they had existed for more than two centuries.[47] More recently, Vatican II also elevated them to the same status as the Roman rite with some revisions.[48] Other factors that contributed to the continual existence of Mozarabic and Ambrosian rites include the local (Milanese and Toledans)

---

[40] Cotes, *Fifteen Sermons Preach'd on Several Occasions*, 95; John Killingbeck, *The Blessedness and Reward of Charity Asserted: In a Sermon Preach'd in the Parish-Church of St. Peter's in Leeds, December 28. 1709. (Being Innocents-Day) for Promoting the Charity-School Erected There* (London: Printed for H. Clements at the Half-Moon in St. Paul's Church-Yard, 1710).

[41] W. F. Adeney, P. C. Barker, J. A. Macdonald, and R. Tuck, "Matthew 2," *Pulpit Commentaries*, accessed November 13, 2017, https://www.studylight. org/commentaries/ tpc/matthew-2.html.

[42] Charles Simeon, *Horae Homileticae: Matthew*, vol. 11 (London: Holdsworth and Ball, 1832), 15–16.

[43] Patrick Cox, "Christmas," in *The Wiley Blackwell Encyclopedia of Consumption and Consumer Studies*, ed. Daniel T. Cook and J. Michael Ryan, 77–8 (Oxford: John Wiley & Sons, 2015), 78.

[44] "Feast of the Holy Innocents: A Homily," whosoeverdesires.wordpress.com (blog), January 2, 2011 (11:01 a.m.), https://whosoeverdesires.wordpress.com/2011/01/02/feast-of-the-holy-innocents-a-homily/.

[45] Ibid.

[46] The present writer is indebted to Frs. Dominic E. Serra and Michael G. Witczak for their guidance in locating sources and organizing this section.

[47] Theisen, "The Reform of Mass Liturgy and the Council of Trent," 581.

[48] Raúl R. Gómez, "Blurring the Line between Liturgy and Popular Religion: An Example from the Hispano-Mozarabic Rite," *Journal of Hispanic/Latino Theology* 10 (2002): 18.

loyalty to them and the support of St. Charles Borromeo (Ambrosian) and Cardinal Francisco Ximénes de Cisneros (Mozarabic).[49] Thus, while their influence may not be widespread geographically, they have a long diachronic mark on reception history.[50]

1. Ambrosian Rite

The Ambrosian rite's beginnings reach back to its namesake, St. Ambrose (ca. 337–397). It developed creatively until it became relatively stable in the fifth century.[51] Among the early salient features are the prefaces that contain the name and shape of the Eucharistic prayer, not only as prayer of thanksgiving but also in unique combination of "theology and lyrical image."[52] The preface for the *Feast of the Innocents*, December 28 is similar in content to the prayers in the *Veronese* and *Gelasian Sacramentaries* (Chapter 4, VI. A): the victims are martyrs, crowned and baptized by blood before they are able to speak through their "precious deaths" for the sake of Christ.[53]

The Ambrosian lectionary prescribes Jer 31:15-20, Rom 8:14-21, and Matt 2:13-18.[54] The gospel and the prophetic readings are not remarkable (see Chapter 4, VIII. D), but the epistolary reading incorporates new themes: adoption through the Spirit as God's children (*filii Dei*), inheritance (*haeredes*), and glory (*gloria*). Paul outlines future benefits that relegate present sufferings to a negligible state (Rom 8:18). Perhaps the intended effect is the same for this epistolary reading on the memorial day of the massacre. Unlike the simple anagogical reading of Rev 14:1-5 in the *Comes of Würzburg* (Chapter 4, VI. B), the Ambrosian reading of Rom 8:14-21 stresses the didactic and the moral.[55]

Such "centonation" of biblical ideas and imagery is also in the liturgical pieces of the Divine Office and the Mass.[56] The Ambrosian rite repeats familiar themes from the Roman sacramentaries and antiphonals: innocents' sincerity, mortification of vices, silent confession, martyrdom (esp. Rev 6:9), and vindication (Chapter 4, VI. A and C). It offers more thematic connections through antiphons of Matins that string together psalms that relate to the theme of the day: testimony (Ps 92:5), instruction of babes (Pss 18:8; 118:30), association with innocence (Ps 24:21; 25:6), children's triumph (Pss 8:3; 63:8), and God's goodness (Ps 30:20).[57] With such variety of concatenations, the

[49] Lancelot C. Sheppard, *The Mass in the West* (New York: Hawthorn, 1995), 29, 39.
[50] Currently, the Ambrosian rite is used in the archdiocese of Milan and its surroundings as far north as parts of Switzerland and the Mozarabic in Spain, mostly in the vicinity of Toledo.
[51] Alan Griffiths, trans., *We Give You Thanks and Praise: The Ambrosian Eucharistic Prefaces of the Ambrosian Missal* (Franklin: Sheed & Ward, 2000), xiv–xv; Jordi Pinell i. Pons, "History of the Liturgies in the Non-Roman West," in *Handbook for Liturgical Studies Volume 1: Introduction to Liturgy*, ed. Anscar J. Chupungco, 179–95 (Collegeville: Liturgical Press, 1997), 182.
[52] Griffiths, trans., *We Give You Thanks and Praise*, xvi.
[53] Ibid., 42.
[54] Edward G. C. F. Atchley, trans., *The Ambrosian Liturgy: The Ordinary and Canon of the Mass according to the Rite of the Church of Milan* (London: Cope & Fenwick, 1909), 100.
[55] For another similar reading of Romans 8 in relation to the massacre, see Arthur Vööbus, ed., *A Syriac Lectionary from the Church of the Forty Martyrs in Mardin, Ṭūr ʿAbdīn, Mesopotamia*, CSCO 485 (Lovanii: E. Peeters, 1986), xviii–xxvii.
[56] Pons, "History of the Liturgies in the Non-Roman West," 183.
[57] Marco Magistretti, ed., *Manuale Ambrosianum ex codice saec. XI olim in usum canonicae Vallis Travaliae*, part 2: *Monumenta veteris liturgiae ambrosianae* 3 (Milan: Hoepli, 1904), 73.

2. Mozarabic Rite

Largely developed during the sixth and seventh centuries in three different areas in the Iberian Penninsula (Tarragona, Seville, and Toledo), this Hispanic liturgy survives only in Toledo today.[58] There, liturgical creativity developed relatively later than in other Mediterranean churches, but still outlasted them.[59] Its survival is remarkable considering Arab domination, suspicion of adoptionism, and Roman attempts at its suppression from the eighth to the eleventh century.[60] At the suggestions of Cardinals Francisco Ximénes de Cisneros and Marcelo González Martín, the Mozarabic rite would be practiced and be revised for a printed edition.[61]

The Office book for liturgical prayers and the Mass formulary are replete with familiar martyrdom vocabulary of the Roman rite, such as the palm, crowns, white robes, Mount Zion, and cries for vindication (Ps 8:2; 79:3, 10; Jer 31:15; Rev 6:9; see Chapter 4, VI. A–C).[62] But the Mozarabic rite also treats the *Feast of the Innocents* differently, presenting the same general ideas with some creative variations. In one antiphonal, for instance, the victims are examples of moral purity, a key quality of those who wash their hands and surround God's altar.[63] This cross-reference to Ps 26:6 (25:6 in the Vulgate) is possible due to the word *innocentes*.

Unlike the Roman church, the Mozarabic memorial is on January 8. The lectionary prescribes for that day: Jer 31:15-20; Ps 79:3, 10; Heb 2:9–3:2; Matt 2:16-23; and Ps 26:6.[64] The epistolary reading Heb 2:9–3:2 resembles the Ambrosian reading of Rom 8:14-21: Hebrews teaches about the glory of God's sons (2:10-13) and the suffering they share with Christ (2:14-18). The victims' suffering is an occasion to reflect upon the struggles of Christian life.

Also of interest is the festal title in the Mass formulary: the "dashing" (*allisio*) of the infants.[65] While Matt 2:16 does not explain how Herod's men kill the infants, hurling them against the ground is one possible mode of execution, often depicted in graphic art (see Chapter 6). It is also possible that "dashing" was an imprecatory code word against the Church's enemies and an allusion to Ps 137:9 (Ps 136:9 in the Vulgate). There, while the post-exile psalmist is condemning the daughter of Babylon

---

[58] Pons, "History of the Liturgies in the Non-Roman West," 187.
[59] Ibid.
[60] Ibid., 189–92.
[61] Ibid., 193.
[62] José Vives and Jerónimo Claveras, eds., *Oracional Visigótico*, Monumenta Hispaniae sacra: Serie litúrgica 1 (Barcelona: Consejo Superior de Investigaciones Científicas, Escuela de Estudios Medievales, Sección de Barcelona, Balmesiana: Biblioteca Balmes, 1946), 141–8.
[63] Ibid., 146.
[64] "Leccionario Hispano-Mozárabe-Liber Commicus," *Rito Hispano Mozárabe*, accessed March 17, 2018, http://www.mercaba.org/LITURGIA/Mozarabe/cartel_rito_hispanomozarabe.htm.
[65] Marius Férotin, Anthony Ward, and Cuthbert Johnson, eds., *Le Liber Mozarabicus Sacramentorum: Et Les Manuscrits Mozarabes*, Biblioteca Ephemerides Liturgicae, Subsidia 78, Instrumenta Liturgica Quarreriensia 4 (Roma: C.L.V.-Edizioni Liturgiche, 1995), 229.

for atrocities against Judah, he blesses "the one who will grasp and dash your children against the rock." (*qui tenebit et adidet parvulos tuos ad petram*). Other ideas of the psalm are complementary to the themes of Matthew 2: Judah's lamentations at Babylon (vv. 1-2), their captors' mockery (v. 3), and homesickness (vv. 5-6). The greatest contributions of the Ambrosian and the Mozarabic rites in the reception history of Matt 2:16-18 are arguably intertextual, bridging verses and words together to evoke a new perspective on the same event.

D. Eastern Orthodox *Menaion*

In 2003, the Orthodox Church, "one of the three major branches of Christianity," had over three hundred million followers from Greece, Georgia, Russia, and the United States.[66] Due to schisms with Rome and persecutions (esp. Ottoman Empire and Communism), only recently in the twentieth century did the West become better acquainted with its rich tradition.[67] An important representative source of Eastern Orthodoxy is the *Menaion* (Gk. Μηναῖον), a large liturgical book containing propers for the Byzantine rite.[68] The content can be divided into two distinct categories: (1) "Scriptural 'stratum' " and (2) "non-Scriptural 'stratum,' " consisting in religious poetry.[69] In reality, however, even the latter is scripturally rich, containing various biblical images and phrases.[70]

Such is the case in the memorial for the massacre victims on December 29.[71] Their high casualty toll of fourteen thousand and designation as martyrs reveal the strong influence of the Apocalypse that is paralleled in the Western rites and the early church. Elizabeth hides her son John the Baptist (see PJ in Chapter 3, V. A) and the weeping Rachel is happy to see the victims resting in Abraham's bosom (see Basil of Seleucia in Chapter 3, IX. H) while Herod laments with the Jews, the slayers of the prophets (see Origen and Hilary of Poitiers in Chapter 3, VIII. A and B). The infants are esteemed as sacrifices (see Chapter 3, X), but the language of Eastern Orthodoxy advances beyond mere respect. Just as John of Euobea argued for Bethlehem's sanctifications through

---

[66] Carl S. Tyneh, ed. *Orthodox Christianity: Overview and Bibliography* (New York: Nova Science, 2003), vii.
[67] "Orthodox Church," *ODCC*, 1205-6.
[68] The present author is indebted to Fr. Stefanos Alexopoulos for pointing him to this work.
[69] *The Festal Menaion*, trans. Mother Mary and Archimandrite Kallistos Ware, Introduction by Georges Florovsky (London: Faber, 1969), 16.
[70] Ibid. Technicalities of Eastern Orthodox hymnody do not need full explanation here to understand how this tradition has received Matt 2:16-18. Originally, *kontakia* (poetical sermons) of Romanos the Melodist were the most important in Byzantine hymnody from fifth to seventh century, but from eighth century onwards other forms began to occupy space and the *kontakia* were abbreviated. See Chapter 4, Introduction and I; and Alexander Lingas, "The Liturgical Place of the Kontakion in Constantinople," in *Liturgy, Architecture and Art of the Byzantine World: Papers of the XVIII International Byzantine Congress (Moscow, 8-15 August 1991) and Other Essays Dedicated to the Memory of Fr. John Meyendorff*, 50-7 (St. Petersburg: Publications of the St. Petersburg Society for Byzantine and Slavic Studies, 1995); and John Baggley, *Festal Icons for the Christian Year* (Crestwood: St. Vladimir's Seminary Press, 2000), 175.
[71] ΤΗι ΚΘ' ΤΟΥ ΑΥΤΟΥ ΜΗΝΟΣ ΔΕΚΕΜΒΡΙΟΥ Μνήμη τῶν Ἁγίων Νηπίων, τῶν ὑπὸ Ἡρῴδου ἀναιρεθέντων, ὧν ὁ ἀριθμός χιλιάδες ιδ' Μνήμη τοῦ Ὁσίου Πατρὸς ἡμῶν Μαρκέλλου, Ἡγουμένου τῆς Μονῆς τῶν Ἀκοιμήτων, accessed March 21, 2018, http://glt.goarch.org/texts/Dec/Dec29.html.

the innocents' sacrifice (see Chapter 4, VII. A), here their blood purifies and beautifies the Church.

The *Menaion* also contributes to the reception history of Matt 2:16-18 new scriptural associations. Augmenting the already-existing thematic connections with Exodus, allusions to the Red Sea miracle in Exodus 14 heighten the innocents' triumph. Also interesting is the allusion to Daniel 3, which describes the plight of Daniel's friends thrown into the fiery furnace for their stance against idolatry. Like the readings of Western rites, the Byzantine counterpart recontextualizes the massacre for an optimistic perspective.[72] The Orthodox rite, however, creatively employs OT narratives to serve the same purpose.

II. Verse

"Verse" is a broad category encompassing a wide range of forms and contexts.[73] Subcategories include hymns, prayers, poems, and songs. Within the reception history of Matt 2:16-18, hymns from the fourth and fifth centuries are good starting points. In subsequent centuries similar works follow, embellishing the massacre's details or repeating common readings and closely linked to church festivals or personal devotion.[74] For example, the Devonshire poet and Rector of Holsworthy Daniel Cudmore composed five sacred poems or "prayer songs" (*Euchodia* 2-6, ca. 1657) based on Matt 2:16-18. He relies on Macrobius and connects Herod and the victims with the pharaoh and sacrificial lambs, respectively. Yet, in addition to such familiar ideas, Cudmore also imagines the victims as (1) saplings that provide relief for Christ the Branch (Isa 4:2; 11:1; Jer 23:5; 33:15; Zech 3:8; 6:12) and (2) grafts in the tree of life (Genesis 1–3; Rom 11:11-24; Rev 2:7; 22:2, 14, 19) with "Herodian cicatrices" that bloom like Aaron's rod (Numbers 17).[75] Cudmore is perhaps the first known poet to string together verses in a horticultural theme in prayers.

---

[72] See discussion of recontextualization in Chapter 4, II.
[73] For a discussion of poetry's definition, see Anna C. Ribeiro, "Intending to Repeat: A Definition of Poetry," *Journal of Aesthetics and Art Criticism* 65:2 (2007): 189–201.
[74] For previous discussions, see Chapter 3 on Prudentius (IX. E; X. C) and Ephrem the Syrian (X. A and B); Chapter 4 on hymns (Introduction), the Roman antiphonals (VI. C), and liturgical drama (VI. F; VIII. F and G.)
[75] See other reiterations of familiar ideas in the Irish carol *Seacht Ndólas Na Maighdine Muire*; the motet *Vox in Rama Audita Est* by Jacobus Clemens non Papa (ca. 1553); oratori *L'enfance du Christ, Part One: Le songe d'Hérode (Herod's Dream)* by Hector Berlioz (ca. 1853); *The Light of the World* by Arthur Sullivan (1873); *The Passion of Mary* by Howard Blake (2006); the poems of George Wither (ca. 1622), Edward Sherburne (ca. 1651), Samuel Speed (1677), Ken Thomas (1721), Joseph Beaumont (1749), John Fellow (1778), Reginald Heber (ca. 1826), John Keble (1827), Isaac Williams (1857), and Christina Rosetti (1877, 1893); and the hymns of Carolyn W. Gillette, *Abraham Journeyed to a New Country* (2004) and *A Voice Was Heard in Rama* (2010). There are also poetic productions that modernize Matt 2:16-18 by exploring the symbolic potential of Herod. For example, Charles Causley's *Innocent's Song* (1961) reimagines Herod as a boogeyman who invades homes around Christmas time. Amy Witting's *A Curse on Herod* (1991) presents a tortured tyrant hemmed in by children and haunted by sounds of "birdcries from the playground," whines of "weewee" and ice cream. The antagonist hardly resembles the king from the antiquity; without the poem title, the imprecation could just as well apply to a child abuser or murderer.

In this section, attention is given to two innovative works of verse: *Coventry Carol* and Giambattista Marino's *La Strage degli Innocenti*.[76] For different reasons, both are worthy of full discussion in the reception history, the former for its ubiquity as a common song and the latter for its poetic grandeur. Both had (1) widespread and lasting influence and (2) reinterpreted Matt 2:16-18 in innovative and creative forms. Specifically, the massacre was cast in the mode of (1) the simple and popular lullaby and (2) Marino's more complex Italian poetry.

A. *Coventry Carol*

Before their decline in the 1500s (see Chapter 4, I), popular mystery plays from Coventry, England left behind the *Coventry Carol* from the *Shearmen and Tailors' Pageant*.[77] The unique combination of historical factors (the lyrics, post-fourteenth-century editing and rewriting, and Thomas Mawdyke's music from 1591 consisting of three male voice parts (alto, tenor, bass)) endue the carol with a unique identity and independent form different from its original late-fourteenth-century dramatic context and source.[78] It likely influenced the composition of William Byrd's more complex *Lulla, My Sweet Little Baby*.[79] The carol's lasting popularity is evident in the covers of many more recent popular recording artists.[80] In the 2006 film *The Nativity Story*, the

---

[76] Marino's work should not be linked closely with the genealogy of religious poetry just mentioned. Marino is primarily a secular poet and adapted "the post-Tridentine style of religious poetry" as only a part of his repertoire. James V. Mirollo, *The Poet of the Marvelous* (New York: Columbia University Press, 1963), 249.

[77] In addition, the young William Shakespeare likely gained much of his Bible knowledge from these regular performances. Howard Clarke notes how the raging Herod lingered in Shakespeare's mind in his composition of *Hamlet* (see Chapter 1, II. D). It is, however, impossible to juxtapose Shakespeare's words with the Coventry scripts for critical examination of influence, because most of the latter have not survived. Only two, the *Shearmen and Tailors' Pageant* and the *Weaver's Paegeant*, survive today. Beatrice Groves, *Texts and Traditions: Religion in Shakespeare 1592-1604*, Oxford English Monographs (Oxford: Clarendon Press, 2006), 36–41; Hannibal Hamlin, "William Shakespeare," in *The Blackwell Companion to the Bible in English Literature*, eds. Rebecca Lemon, Emma Mason, Jonathan Roberts, and Christopher Rowland, 225–38 (Oxford: Blackwell, 2009), 227.

[78] Pamela M. King, "Faith, Reason and the Prophets' Dialogue in the Coventry Paegeant of the Shearmen and Taylors," in *Drama and Philosophy*, ed. James Redmond, 37–46, Themes in Drama (Cambridge: Cambridge University Press, 1990), 37–8; Rastall, *Minstrels Playing*, 194; David N. Klausner, "19. Vernacular Drama," in *A Performer's Guide to Medieval Music*, ed. Ross W. Duffin, 253–63, Music: Scholarship and Performance (Bloomington: Indiana University Press, 1996), 259. As with visual exegesis, space could be devoted to treatment of audio exegesis in a separate chapter. The lyrics, however, inspired the music, so it is prudent to consider them together here.

[79] For the full text see Robert Atwan and Laurance Wieder, eds., *Chapters into Verse: Poetry in English Inspired by the Bible, Volume 2: Gospels to Revelation*. (Oxford: Oxford University Press, 1993), 45–6. Byrd structures his poem with the refrain "Lulla, la lulla, lulla lullaby. My sweet little baby, what meanest thou to cry?" and concludes verses 1-3 with a lament: "Oh woe, and woeful heavy day, when wretches have their will!" In verse 4, however, the last words are "Oh joy, and joyful day, when wretches want their will!" Within these frames, Byrd maintains a christological focus and includes ideas of the victims' innocence (verse 1), visitation of the magi (verse 2), flight to Egypt (verse 3), and conquest of the innocents (verse 4). Thus, compared to the *Coventry Carol*, Byrd's *Lulla, My Sweet Little Baby* is an elaborate work more akin to a hymn, lacking the simplicity of a lullaby. See John Harley, *William Byrd: Gentleman of the Chapel Royal* (London: Routledge, 2017), 289.

[80] Some notable examples include John Denver, Elaine Paige, Sting, and Annie Lennox.

composer Mychael Danna incorporates the carol's melody into scenes where Herod plots and executes the massacre. The lyrics are as follows:

Refrain:
Lully, lulla, thou little tiny child,
By by, lully, lullay.

Verse 1:
O sisters too, how may we do,
For to preserve this day
This poor youngling for whom we sing,
"By by, lully, lullay"?

Refrain

Verse 2:
Herod, the king, in his raging,
Charged he hath this day
His men of might in his own sight,
All young children to slay.

Refrain

Verse 3:
That woe is me, poor child, for thee!
And ever mourn and sigh,
For thy parting neither say nor sing,
"By by, lully, lullay."[81]

Prior to its widespread popularity as a carol, it was fundamentally a lullaby, as it repeats "By by, lully, lullay."[82] Its steady rhythm and simple repetitive melody are also characteristic of lullabies.[83] Composed by unknown people, their simplicity served to "to ease the drop into oblivion" for babies struggling to sleep.[84] A secondary function is to soothe the emotional burdens of the mothers or caregivers.[85]

---

[81] The modernized spelling of the lyrics is from Mark Lawson-Jones, *Why Was the Partridge in the Pear Tree? The History of Christmas Carols* (Stroud: History Press, 2011), 52–3.

[82] William E. Studwell broadly defines a Christmas carol as "a song used to celebrate Christmas and its adjacent events (including Advent, Epiphany, the New Year, and to some extent the winter season)," sung by all kinds of persons, generally obscure in origins but lasting due to its sociocultural influence. In contrast, classical, non-carol folk, religious, national, and patriotic songs appeal to limited portions of the Western audience. In the history of carols, the earliest well-known piece "O Come, O Come, Emmanuel" dates from the twelfth century. So then, *Coventry Carol* is relatively early, around the fifteenth century when the song type flourished. William E. Studwell, *Christmas Carols: A Reference Guide*, indexes by David A. Hamilton (New York: Garland, 1985), xi–xiii.

[83] Marina Warner, "'Hush-a-Bye Baby': Death and Violence in the Lullaby," *Raritan* 18 (1998): 93.

[84] Ibid.

[85] David Bosworth writes, "Due to the universality of infant cries and adult stress, lullabies often seek to soothe baby through music, even while expressing the adult's frustration in words." *Infant Weeping in Akkadian, Hebrew, and Greek Literature*, Critical Studies in the Hebrew Bible 8 (Winona Lake: Eisenbrauns, 2016), 27; Warner, "Hush-a-bye Baby," 93; Elizabeth MacKinlay and

Yet the images of the *Coventry Carol* are hardly soothing. In the first verse, the women wonder how to preserve their children. The second verse introduces the raging Herod who charges his mighty men to kill the children before him.[86] In the third verse, the women grieve, mourn, and sigh for children they can no longer lull to sleep. Marina Warner believes that the *Coventry Carol* signals a "decisive change from an allegorical threnody—Rachel weeping over the slaughter—to a lullaby, from a biblical, quasi-symbolic figure remote in time and place to an ordinary crowd of contemporaries in a situation they might encounter."[87] Unlike the Rachel-Mary-Church typology which elevates powerful matriarchs (see Chapter 4, VIII), at the carol's center are common women who struggle daily and worry over their children.[88]

This emotional link, however, extends beyond empathy with day-to-day maternal grief to extraordinary loss (i.e., bereavement, kidnapping, etc.) due to the subject matter of Matt 2:16-18. The *Coventry Carol* ironically and poetically combines the functions of the lament (the babes' death and the mothers' grief) and the lullaby (the babes' sleep and the mothers' comfort) to create a "lullament."[89] The overlap between death/laments and sleep/lullabies is readily apparent in different cultures and the Bible.[90] In this carol, however, the children are dead and the carol's secondary function that addresses the mothers' needs becomes primary as the lyrics encase their grief in a final goodbye.[91] Instead of a tool to soothe the child, this lullaby is a form of self-comfort. The grieving mothers rest in the resurrection hope as their children "sleep" until their future awakening (John 11:11; 1 Cor 15:6, 18-20; Eph 5:14; 1 Thess 4:14-15). This eschatological expectation, which scholarly prose of Rupert of Deutz makes explicit (see Chapter 4, VIII. D), is implicit in simple lullaby of the *Coventry Carol*.

Felicity Baker, "Nurturing Herself, Nurturing Her Baby: Creating Positive Experiences for First-time Mothers through Lullaby Singing," *Women and Music: A Journal of Gender and Culture* 9 (2005): 69–89.

[86] Unusual here is how the massacre takes place in Herod's presence, "in his own sight." Perhaps Bertram of Minden's Grabow Altarpiece, made for the St. Petri in Hamburg, inspires this idea. In the same panel depicting the massacre are Herod, the soldiers, the victims, and the bereaved women, without regard for the geographical distance between Jerusalem and Bethlehem. Perhaps the soldiers bring the children to Herod or he leads the campaign. The implied urgency and the note that Herod "sent" (ἀποστείλας) his soldiers make both scenarios unlikely (Matt 2:16). Either way, Herod's implication in the crime is clear. See full discussion in Chapter 6.

[87] Warner, "'Hush-a-Bye Baby,'" 100.

[88] Ibid.

[89] For an analysis of lullabies in relation to beginning-of-life, life, and end-of-life problems, see Clare O'Callaghan, "Lullament: Lullaby and Lament Therapeutic Qualities Actualized through Music Therapy," *American Journal of Hospice and Palliative Medicine* 25 (2008): 93–9.

[90] Dan 12:2; Matt 9:24 (cf. Mark 5:39; Luke 8:23); John 11:11; 1 Cor 11:30; 15:6, 18-20; Eph 5:14; 1 Thess 4:14-15; Aaron J. Atsma, "Hypnos," *Theoi Greek Mythology*, accessed October 18, 2017, http://www.theoi.com/Daimon/Hypnos.html; Scheherazade Hassan, "Female Traditional Singers in Iraq: A Survey," *International Journal of Contemporary Iraqi Studies* 4 (2010): 25–39; Aaron Kramer and Saul Lishinsky, eds. *The Last Lullaby: Poetry from the Holocaust* (Syracuse: Syracuse University Press, 1998); Luisa Del Giudice, "Ninna-nanne-nonsense? Fears, Dreams, and Falling in the Italian Lullaby," *Oral Tradition* 3 (1988): 270–93.

[91] Ironically, lullabies of different cultures often express resentment and frustration at children for the inconveniences they bring with their existence, but here their departure causes grief for the mothers. For examples, see Bosworth, *Infant Weeping in Akkadian, Hebrew, and Greek Literature*, 27–33.

Two features of Mawdyke's music may also hint at this resurrection hope. First, its ¾ time signature is common in dance music such as the waltz.[92] If the meter suggests dancing, perhaps it looks forward to more festive times in heaven. The other musical feature is the so-called Picardy Third (*Tierce de Picardie*).[93] It is "the major chord ending a composition in a minor key" or in any mode in which the third above the final or tonic is properly a minor chord."[94] Percy A. Scholes describes its effect in the following: "pleasant, as of a bright ray breaking through the clouds as the sun sinks."[95] Such a feature perhaps hints at the forthcoming respite and comfort.

B. Giambattista Marino's *La Strage degli Innocenti*

Giambattista Marino (1569–1625) is considered by some to be the greatest poet of the seventeenth century and one of the best Italian poets ever.[96] Perhaps no previous work of verse matches the intensity and ambition of his *ottava rima*, *La Strage degli Innocenti*, †Poetry_Extract written in four books. Posthumously published in 1632, it embodies Marino's strange yet reverent style. Despite his troubles with the law, peers, and the Church, he rose in prominence and conformed to orthodoxy in his religious works, albeit in an unconventional manner.[97] The influential Italian poet, who bridged two periods of literary history (sixteenth- and seventeenth-century Mannerism and seventeenth- and eighteenth-century Baroque), used an ornate and witty approach that employed unconventional combinations, metaphors, paradoxes, and comparisons alongside traditional imageries and their dominant traits.[98] Thus, this verse style, known as "Marinism" (*marinismo*) or "conceptism" (*concettismo*), is synonymous with "the seventeenth century" (*seicentismo*), since many seventeenth-century poets attempted to imitate Marino.[99]

In *La Strage degli Innocenti*, Marino avers that he attempts to do with the pen what his contemporary and fellow Mannerist Giuseppe Cesari did with the paintbrush

---

[92] "Waltz, Walzer, or Valse," in *The Oxford Companion to Music*, ed. Percy A. Scholes, 1110 (Oxford: Oxford University Press, 1970). Features of a "carol" may also suggest dancing. William E. Studwell notes, "Although there were some songs called carols before the 1400, the carol really began to develop in the 15th century. Around 1400 in England, and somewhat earlier on the continent, the carol evolved as a popular dance form and soon flourished. (The word 'carol' was probably derived from the word 'choros,' meaning 'dance.') This new type of song was a reaction to the strictness and puritanism of the Middle Ages, and was fostered by the more secular and humanistic spirit of the late Middle Ages and Renaissance." Studwell, *Christmas Carols*, xiii.

[93] For a discussion of this name and its origins, see Robert J. Hall, "How Picard Was the 'Picardy Third?'" *Current Musicology* 19 (1975): 78–80.

[94] "Tierce de Picardie or Tierce Picarde," in *The Oxford Companion to Music*, 1024.

[95] Ibid.

[96] Peter Brand and Lino Pertile, eds., *The Cambridge History of Italian Literature* (Cambridge: Cambridge University Press, 1999), 305.

[97] Ibid., viii–xi.

[98] David Sharp, "Inheriting Antiquity: Giambattista Marino's Rime Boscherecce, Luis de Góngora's La fábula de Polifemo y Galatea and the Baroque Literary Aesthetic," *Journal Language & Literature* 3 (2008); Maria R. Maniates, *Mannerism in Italian Music and Culture, 1530–1630* (Chapel Hill: University of North Carolina Press, 1979), 75–6; Mirollo, *The Poet of the Marvelous*, 153–9.

[99] Erik Butler, "The Garden of Earthly Delights and the Cult of the Martyrs," in *Massacre of the Innocents*, ed. Giambattista Marino, trans. Erik Butler, vii–xv (Cambridge: Wakefield, 2015), vii; Mirollo, *The Poet of the Marvelous*, 116–17.

(Book III: 1-2, 59).[100] Though Cesari did not paint a scene from Matt 2:16-18, Marino's work of homage and verbal imitation is in a sense a "speaking picture" (poetry) in place of the missing "mute poem" (painting).[101] Marino uses his picturesque style and illustrates the gruesome horrors of sin to affirm and glorify good in converse.[102] A project inspired by a painter cyclically became an inspiration for at least one painter, Peter Paul Rubens, who probably borrowed some of ideas from Marino's poem.[103]

Book I, known as *Herod's Suspicion* (*Sospetto d'Herode*), often finds the most attention because of Richard Crashaw's early English interpretation (*ca.* 1630s).[104] Crashaw's efforts partly demonstrate how rapidly Marino's influence spread throughout Europe. It begins in a Dantean hell where the fearful Satan laments Christ's nativity, but he is bound and helpless to hinder God's plan. He does have minions so he orders his fiercest maiden to execute a cruel plan.[105] The maiden in turn locates Fury (Erinye) to execute the massacre scheme. Fury disguises herself as Herod's brother, visits Herod who is asleep in Bethlehem, warns the king about Christ, and guides the snake Amphisbaene into Herod's heart. Perhaps Marino intends to foreshadow Herod's doom here since Homer states that Erinyes punish men for sacrilege.[106] In panic and anger, the poisoned king awakes and summons his ministers early in the morning.

Perhaps Marino finds inspiration from Syriac sources to invite readers to a vast hellish realm, where the devil grieves, schemes, and delegates duties. For example, Satan's lament and soliloquy is not unlike Jacob of Serugh's *Second Homily on the Nativity* (see Chapter 3, VI. C). Furthermore, just as evil kings of OT appear in Ephrem the Syrian's *Commentary on Tatian's Diatessaron* (see Chapter 3, V. B), Ahab, the pharaoh, and Nebuchadnezzar appear in the deeper parts of hell portending Herod's demise. Yet Marino moves further with his unusual combinations: Jezebel dwells in hell with creatures like harpies, Medusa, minotaurs, hydras, and chimera.

In Book II, Marino creatively and selectively departs from Matt 2:16-18 in certain details. He does not mention the Magi. The setting is not Jerusalem, but Bethlehem, where Herod sits on a throne "intended for those who have been fashioned in King David's mold" (4) and stays throughout *La Strage degli Innocenti*. Marino likely concentrates the action there to highlight Herod's unworthiness as a Jewish ruler,

---

[100] Butler, "The Garden of Earthly Delights and the Cult of the Martyrs," xii.
[101] Maniates, *Mannerism in Italian Music and Culture*, 30. This oft-cited idea originates from Simonides of Ceos, cited in Plutarch, *De gloria Atheniensium* 3.346: ζωγραφίαν ποίησιν σιωπῶσαν προσαγορεύει τὴν δὲ ποίησιν ζωγραφίαν λαλοῦσαν.
[102] Butler, "The Garden of Earthly Delights and the Cult of the Martyrs," xii-xiii.
[103] Willibald Sauerländer, *The Catholic Rubens: Saints and Martyrs*, trans. David Dollenmayer (Los Angeles: Getty, 2014), 239-48.
[104] One should hesitate to call this work a "translation." Crashaw's *Sospetto* did not woodenly translate Marino's Italian Book I into English, though the former is completely dependent on the latter's structure (sixty-six stanzas), topic, and content. Due to this dependence, the two works are treated together. D. R. M. Wilkinson, "*Sospetto d'Herode*: A Neglected Crashaw Poem," in *Studies in Seventeenth-Century English Literature, History and Bibliography: Festschrift for Professor T. A. Birrell on the Occasion of His Sixtieth Birthday*, ed. G. A. M. Janssens and Flor G. A. M. Aarts, 233-44, Costerus 46 (Amsterdam: Rodophi, 1984).
[105] All translations of Giambattista Marino are Erik Butler's.
[106] "Erinyes, who from under earth punish men, whoever swears a false oath" (Ἐρινύες, αἵ θ' ὑπὸ γαῖαν ἀνθρώπους τίνυνται, ὅτις κ' ἐπίορκον ὀμόσσῃ). Homer, *Il.* 19.259-60.

clearly prove Herod's blameworthiness, and foreshadow the appearance of Jesse's son himself in Book IV.[107] Marino narrates Herod's hysteria, vision, and his order to massacre thousands, in accordance with early church tradition that associated the victims with the 144,000.[108]

Marino then introduces two royal advisors. A pious and wise priest named Urizeus discourages such a hasty act before Herod halts him, and a cruel advisor named Baruch provides his own guidance. He flatters the king, legitimizes his worries, flatly contradicts Urizeus (cf. 22 with 45), and justifies the massacre. Marino narrates that Herod applauds Baruch and "lashed by Fury" (62), he "roves like Maenad" (64), again using unusual combination of word pictures. He decrees and summons all the Bethlehemite mothers with their children before him early next day.[109]

Marino's nuanced OT knowledge explains the choice of Baruch as the corrupt advisor's name. It recalls Neriah's faithful son who helped Jeremiah the prophet (Jeremiah 36 and 42), but Baruch is hardly a "blessed" character here. In contrast, Urizeus, whose name is not in the Bible, is the only voice of reason.[110] Herod's rejection of this older advisor and acceptance of Baruch recalls Rehoboam's rejection of his father Solomon's counselors in favor of his peers (1 Kings 12).

Marino's Bible knowledge also extends beyond minute details to broader strokes of theology. Next, the scene shifts to heaven, where Rachel, "the voice of Piety" (78), pleads for her sons, tearfully appealing to God's justice, sovereignty, and might. The heavenly host joins in intercession to avert the disaster. Here, Marino intensifies the old etymological idea of Ramah, so that not only does Rachel's voice reach "on high" (see Chapter 3, XII. B and C), the heavenly hosts join in the pleading.

God, "the tripartite Oneness, the Trinity single," on whose brow dwells Life, responds (78-79). He retraces history beginning from Creation, the Fall, and the Incarnation. He declares, "On high stands written that his blood be spent and that the innocents too, should be spilt" (90). The offering of babes' lives as blameless sacrifices will shame the evildoers as "woe will yield joy" and "glory will rise up from shame" (91). Here, Marino combines the two major readings: the victims as triumphant martyrs and sacrifices (see Chapter 3, IX and X). As for Herod, he is destined to join Satan in damnation, while the children await resurrection and Christ retreats to Egypt. After this divine decree, a herald locates Vision and together they warn Joseph. The remainder of Book II relates their sojourning.

---

[107] As early as Irenaeus, the massacre has been perceived with a Davidic focus (see Chapter 3, III. B).

[108] See discussion in Jerome's *Commentary on Isaiah* (Chapter 3, III. C); Prudentius's *Discourse of the Martyr St. Romanus against the Pagans* (Chapter 3, IX. E); and Quodvultdeus's *de Symbolo 2* (Chapter 3, IX. J).

[109] Sauerländer believes that Peter Paul Rubens borrowed this idea for his painted version of the scene (ca. 1635-7). A decree written in Hebrew but illegible is posted on a pillar near Herod seating in a shaded area. *The Catholic Rubens*, 243-8. Without understanding the message Sauerländer's theory is impossible to prove without dispute.

[110] Urizeus is a strange name and its etymological origins are mysterious. Since Marino is fond of mixing mythological and biblical concepts in a syncretistic fashion, perhaps the name is a compound from Uri ("my light"; אורי) and Zeus, the Greek God, but such conjecture is difficult to substantiate.

In Book III, Herod's soldiers gather at a fortress in Bethlehem to carry out the massacre. From a shaded portico, the decorated Herod waves his hand, the bugle sounds, and the slaughter commences. Like Gregory of Nyssa (see Chapter 3, XI. A), Marino describes the scene in shockingly horrid details, mixing metaphors from nature and myth. Though one of them sheds a tear, soldiers in general act like beasts (boar, bear, etc.) and monsters (ogre, giant). They employ a variety of weapons (flail, axe, knife), mock the protective mothers, and kill the children. Like prey (heifer and young) and tragic heroes (Trojan, Niobe), the mothers die with the children while courageously defending them or praying for deliverance. All the while, the children are ignorant of evil, playing and even extending love to their executioners, a scene similar to the one described in Peter Chrysologus's Sermon 152 (see Chapter 3, IX. G). Afterwards, the serpentine Herod inspects the horrid scene, where "geysers and fountains of welling blood spray" (83).

Book IV begins on the same night of the slaughter. Herod is pleased but not content, so he summons a Jebusite killer named Malachi to continue the massacre in Bethlehem's vicinity as the cries reach as far as Ramah. Again, Marino skillfully uses biblical allusions. Jebusites were inhabitants of Canaan, marked for elimination, and David's enemies.[111] Yet, Herod who sits in David's throne is in league with one. When Malachi kills a recently circumcised boy, Marino comments, "Unlike the first cut, which the Law fulfills, the next incision is sinful and kills" (15). The poet again employs metaphors from nature: a woman who became a "wife, orphaned mother, and widow in one" year, loses her children in deaths by the four elements of fire, earth, air, and water. Furies stalk and cruelty runs wild as Satan intended (see Book I: 36).

Back in Herod's court, a messenger arrives with terrible news for the king. He narrates the account: Malachi's scout locates a woman with two children in a shack. She hides her son in a cask but leaves the other in the open. Malachi, however, sees through the ploy when the crying son betrays his location. When Malachi throws the entire cask into a fire, the raging woman kills the child in the open. She then reveals that she is a royal nurse who has just killed Herod's only son, Alexander, and so avenged her son killed in the cask.[112] Stunned, Malachi imprisons her. Like Baruch in Book II, Malachi's name (meaning "my messenger" or "my angel") is tragically apt as he brings Herod terrible news.

While Herod reacts in rage, Doris his queen appears and sees her son's corpse. She mourns and sarcastically accuses her husband of being a "venomous spirit with a bear's soul" (73) and an offspring of hellish creatures (Chimera, Sphinx, Cerberus, etc.). Herod sheds a tear during Doris's dirge before the queen suddenly takes her own life. Herod grieves over his house, blames himself, and deems himself as an unworthy king. Marino imitates Eusebius of Caesarea's combination of Josephus and Matt 2:16-18 to

---

[111] See Exod 3:8, 17; 13:5; 23:23; 33:2; 34:11; Deut 20:17; Josh 24:11; and 2 Sam 5:6–10.
[112] See the discussion of the earliest texts that narrate the downfall of Herod's immediate family in Chapter 3, VII. A. They include Eusebius of Caesarea's *Ecclesiastical History 1*, 8; Ephrem the Syrian, *Commentary on the Diatessaron* 3:1; Macrobius, *Saturnalia* 2.4.11 and *Opus Imperfectum: Second Homily*.

depict justice (Chapter 3, VII. A), but by limiting Herod's family members to Doris and Alexander, Marino completely eradicates Herod's house.

In the last section of Book IV, Marino balances the darkness of hell, horrors of the massacre, and Herod's despair with the beauty of heaven. The unexpected pairings of Bible and myth, earthly and heavenly, continue: "to Elysian mansions, the Innocents soar" (92) like fireflies, bees, and a fiery cloud. King David observes this spectacle which appears as "a spiraling ladder—a bright chain of light" (98). He declares, "Justice no longer will be deferred" (99) as he wishes peace and glory upon the saved children.

Marino also heaps on familiar appellations with rhetorical flourish. For example, he combines and intensifies the honor of the innocents as preeminent officers of the church (see Chromatius, Chapter 3, IX. D) and flowers of martyrdom (see Prudentius, Chapter 3, IX. E) The "sacred, holy, dear, blessed martyrs" are chosen to die for Christ before Christ dies for them, "like fragrant roses between piercing thorns" (102). They are select lilies and jasmines in God's garden and though they are like disconnected branches, "a new Church takes root" in them (103). Marino continues to weave together images of sacrifice, nature, conquest, and victory in the rest of Book IV.[113]

All throughout *La Strage degli Innocenti*, Marino poetically adopts biblical and extra-biblical ideas and images to mold Matt 2:16-18 in his own vision. His purposeful arrangement of various ideas results in the heightened vilification of Herod as the cruel (he kills many), sadistic (he is present at the massacre), and demonic antithesis of King David (Herod weeps in Bethlehem, while David welcomes the innocents). In addition, the victims' dramatic exultation is even so satisfying because their earthly suffering is so terrible. The work cannot be overlooked in the reception history of the massacre.

III. Novels

Much of Matt 2:16-18's reception history up to 1517 centered on a dimension of Christian life, either ecclesial (e.g., sermons, liturgical readings, hymns), devotional/individual (e.g., commentaries, pilgrimages), or both (e.g., drama, visual art). Only a few without Christian interests such as Josephus and Macrobius have commented directly on Herod the Great or matters tangential to Matt 2:16-18. It can be inferred from Tertullian's *de Carne Christi* (*ca.* 205; see Chapter 3, II. A) and *Acts of Pilate* (fourth century; see Chapter 3, IV), however, that opponents of Christianity raised moral objections to Matt 2:16-18 or questions concerning its historicity.

Eventually, the novel would become a particularly important conduit of controversial ideas surrounding the massacre. In Europe, for example, Albert Camus revives the idea

---

[113] The victims bear the Redeemer's name on their brows and like "gentle lambs" and "doves without blame" burn as sacrifices in flame fueled by their own blood (104) (see Chapter 3, X). Their wounds and blood are "stars and rubies" that adorn Christ and the Church (105) and the Father has prepared them "arches of triumph and crowns" for their victory "bearing the Son as their shield" (109). "A banner made out of swaddling clothes" (110) await them as they safely arrive in heaven like a ship landing on the port. The champions reach "God's bosom" (112) and the arms of patriarchs who mourn the pain they endured. This last image of "God's bosom" intensifies Basil of Seleucia's image of Abraham's bosom (see Chapter 3, IX. H).

that Jesus should be blamed for the tragedy in his philosophical novel, *The Fall* (*La Chute*).[114] While sharing details of his personal life to a stranger at Amsterdam, a man named Jean-Baptiste Clamence at one point elaborates on innocence. He anticipates that the stranger is thinking of Jesus and asks why he may have been crucified.[115] Clamence then cites a major reason that has been "so carefully hidden": Jesus knew that he was not completely innocent because innocent children died because of him.[116] Haunted by their deaths and Rachel's weeping, Jesus accepted the cross.[117] Thus, Camus expands on the idea hinted in *Acts of Pilate*. Camus's notion that Jesus found it "impossible to justify his living" becomes the major theme of the Portuguese author José Saramago's *O Evangelho Segundo Jesus Cristo*.

In America, the reception history of Matt 2:16-18 leads to Herman Melville's *Moby Dick*. In it, Melville employs images from Matt 2:16-18 (among many other biblical allusions) to raise subtle but subversive questions about God's goodness. Thus, this book and *O Evangelho Segundo Jesus Cristo* are worth discussion here for two reasons: (1) the authors' great influence and (2) the importance of Matt 2:16-18 in shaping the stories (more than a passing allusion such as is found in most works).[118]

A. Herman Melville

Herman Melville's *Moby Dick* (1851) is a story about a seafarer named Ishmael, who joins the vengeful Captain Ahab in his hunt for a whale that dismembered his leg.[119] Despite his own dissatisfaction with the work and the scarcity of its mention in print during his lifetime, the novel would elevate him to "the highest literary realms" within three decades of his passing.[120] There is, however, a dark side to the novel. In a letter to Nathaniel Hawthorne, to whom he dedicated *Moby Dick*, he confessed: "I have written a wicked book." Based on this statement, Henry A. Murray cautions that

---

[114] All English translations are from Albert Camus, *The Fall*, trans. Justin O'Brien (New York: Knopf, 1956).
[115] Ibid., 111–12.
[116] Ibid., 112.
[117] Ibid., 112–13.
[118] Mark Twain makes a single terse allusion to Matt 2:16-18 in *The Adventures of Tom Sawyer* (1876). Tom convinces Ben to whitewash the fence for him and as the victim "worked and sweated in the sun, the retired artist sat on a barrel in the shade close by, dangled his legs, munched his apple and planned the slaughter of more innocents" (cited in "Slaughter of the Innocents," in DBTEL, 718). Certainly, there is little to explore here.
[119] There are various differences between the British and American editions, including unauthorized typographical changes, censorships, and omissions in the latter. The most significant difference is the epilogue, missing in the British version. Since the epilogue contains material directly relevant to Matt 2:16-18, the American edition will be used. See full discussion of textual issues in Herman Melville, *Moby Dick or the Whale*, ed. Harrison Hayford, Hershel Parker, and G. Thomas Tanselle, The Writings of Herman Melville 6, The Northwestern-Newberry ed. (Evanston: Northwestern University Press and Newberry Library, 1988), 581–929.
[120] A few contemporaries, however, such as Henry T. Tuckerman and William C. Russell praised the work for its poetic eloquence. Hershel Parker, *Melville Biography: An Inside Narrative* (Evanston: Northwestern University Press, 2012), 481–97.

"all interpretations which fail to show that *Moby-Dick* is, in some sense, wicked have missed the author's avowed intention."[121]

According to one line of interpretation, Melville mocks the Christian God either overtly in the narration or subtly through symbols.[122] Symbolism includes the whale as God, a whaling vessel as free thinkers' man-made effort and approach to divine mysteries, and a merchant as the futile Christian striving toward heaven.[123] Lest the critics trace blasphemies back to Melville and mar his reputation, Lawrence R. Thompson thinks the author strategically "projected one aspect of himself into his narrator Ishmael, and then projected another contrasting aspect of self into his hero, Captain Ahab."[124] Thereby, Melville's most controversial sentiments find expression in the insane, outspoken, and doomed Ahab while the author remains under the guise of the cowardly and unassuming narrator Ishmael, present from the beginning to the end. From this sheltered vantage point, "Melville's entire artistic contrivance in *Moby Dick* is his own esoteric and cabalistic commentary on God."[125]

Melville's use of biblical names contributes to his satirical ploy and symbolism. For example, the main character Ishmael is a disillusioned and nominal Presbyterian who subtly and cynically undermines Christianity.[126] His name corresponds well with Abraham's son who became an outcast (Gen 16:12).[127] A mysterious man named Elijah warns Ishmael before he boards Ahab's ship (ch. 19). Ahab is a wicked king of Israel, but also a victim of God's sovereignty (1 Kgs 22:22). More subtly, Melville aligns Job with the ivory-legged captain, who defies the inscrutability of God his dismemberer.[128] Ahab ignores the warnings of a man named Gabriel from a ship named *Jeroboam* (ch. 71) and contests a German ship called *Jungfrau*, which lacks oil like the unprepared foolish virgins (Matt 25:1-13) (ch. 81).

Most relevant to this chapter is Melville's use of Matt 2:16-18 to intensify Ahab's defiance. In chapter 126, Ahab's ship *Pequod* continues its course toward the equator and approaches Moby Dick's abode. During the night, the crew awakes from strange screams resembling "half-articulated wailings of the ghosts of all Herod's murdered Innocents," mermaids, or drowning men. Next day, Ahab laughs and surmises that

---

[121] Henry A. Murray, "'In Nomine Diaboli': *Moby Dick*," in *Herman Melville's Moby-Dick*, ed. Harold Bloom, 39–48, Modern Critical Interpretations (New York: Chelsea, 1986), 39.

[122] Lawrence R. Thompson, *Melville's Quarrel with God* (Princeton: Princeton University Press, 1952), 150.

[123] Ibid., 158.

[124] Ibid., 151.

[125] Ibid., 188. Not-so-subtle taunting include the following instances: Bildad, the part-owner of the ship *Pequod*, sends the crew off on Christmas Day with a blessing and exhortation to rest from whaling on the Lord's Day, unless there is a good chance for a profit (ch. 22); as a whaleman minces blubber into thin slices called "bible leaves," Melville narrates, "Arrayed in decent black; occupying a conspicuous pulpit; intent on bible leaves—what a candidate for an archbishopric, what a lad for a Pope, this mincer" (ch. 95); Captain Ahab baptizes his harpoon in blood while chanting a twisted formula: "Ego non baptizo te in nomine patris ... sed nomine diaboli" (ch. 113).

[126] Brian Yothers writes, "The central characters of the novel are fraught with religious complexity." *Sacred Uncertainty: Religious Difference and the Shape of Melville's Career* (Evanston: Northwestern University Press, 2015), 75.

[127] Thompson, *Melville's Quarrel with God*, 151–2. In chapter 10, Ishmael says, "I'll try a pagan friend since Christian kindness has proved hollow courtesy."

[128] Ibid., 152–5. See chs. 24, 32, the epilogue, and esp. 41.

they heard cries of nearby bereaved mother seals or orphaned young seals, but the superstitious crew remains disturbed. Their fears worsen in the early morning. At the first watch in the White Whale's territory, a crew member mysteriously falls overboard from *Pequod* and is lost.

Nearer to the whale, *Pequod* encounters the Nantucket ship *Rachel*. This ship provides Ahab an opportunity to relent from the dangerous enterprise for a charitable cause (ch. 128). *Rachel*'s Captain Gardiner begs Ahab to help in the search for his son and other survivors of a boat that attempted to capture Moby Dick a day earlier. Ahab, in a rush, refuses to assist and says, "May I forgive myself." Thompson concludes that Ahab is a monomaniacal sovereign whose "first responsibility is to the divine in himself."[129] Melville poignantly describes the departure of the forlorn *Rachel*: "by her still halting course and winding, woful [sic] way, you plainly saw that this ship that so wept with spray, still remained without comfort." In the epilogue, after the White Whale destroys *Pequod*, *Rachel* arrives just in time to save Ishmael, *Pequod*'s sole survivor and "orphan," but fails to locate any of her own children. Ishmael lives to tell the story, and the entirety of *Moby Dick* should be read with this knowledge that he survived not only the dangers of the sea but also myriads of religious ideas, including Christianity.[130]

Melville uses Matt 2:16-18 in the late chapters to amplify the ominous feeling and hopelessness as Ahab and Ishmael near the White Whale. Instead of depicting the innocents as crowned martyrs in heaven, Melville associates them with the ghostly and portentous wailings at the threshold of Moby Dick's territory. Reinforcing the bereavement theme and foreshadowing *Pequod*'s own destruction is the loss of *Rachel*'s crew, including Captain Gardiner's son. While the ship *Rachel* saves Ishmael, he is only a consolation prize; the story ends with her unresolved bereavement. In the end, God as the White Whale is the cause of *Rachel*'s pain, not its reliever. In accordance with "the heretical line of his hermeneutics," Melville ends the novel with deliverance, not from God but from *Rachel* who preserves Ishmael, a son of a rival nation.[131] There is no resolution or comfort for *Rachel*. So then, Matt 2:16-18 is key passage in *Moby Dick* Melville uses to discredit the goodness of God, who makes ships and their crew bereaved mothers and orphans, respectively.

B. José Saramago

The Portuguese 1998 Nobel Prize winner José Saramago is the author of the controversial 1991 novel *O Evangelho Segundo Jesus Cristo* (*The Gospel according to Jesus Christ*).[132] According to J. Robert C. Cousland, "Saramago inverts the traditional moral polarities of the Bible, namely, that God is good and the devil is bad, to expose

---

[129] Ibid., 213.
[130] Yothers, *Sacred Uncertainty*, 86–8.
[131] Ilana Pardes, *Melville's Bibles* (Berkeley: University of California Press, 2008), 144.
[132] The self-professed atheist and communist admitted that it is a "heretical Gospel" and the Portuguese government tried to exclude it from consideration for the 1992 European Literary Prize due to its anti-Christian message. J. Robert C. Cousland, "José Saramago's *Kakagellion*: The 'Badspel' according to Jesus Christ," in *Jesus in Twentieth Century Literature, Art, and Movies*, ed. Paul C. Burns, 55–74, UBC Studies in Religion 1 (London: Continuum, 2007), 55–6.

the oppressive systems he sees as lying at the heart of the Christian evangel."[133] Saramago presents Jesus as a victim of these systems and "a faulty religious impulse," not God's Son.[134] God is a human invention and he ought to be judged based on his effects on humanity.[135] Saramago was perturbed by "the commodification of human beings" and "the implicit disregard for human life" which is "intrinsic to Christianity and the Scriptures."[136] His communism also emerges: God, who "wants the entire world for himself" (368), represents the excessive greed of capitalism, while Satan, who in disguise of the selfless shepherd trains Jesus and claims "nothing belongs to me" (190), represents communism.[137]

Herod's massacre occupies a place of "paradigmatic importance" in his condemnation of Christianity, since Christ's advent precipitates the tragedy.[138] Saramago's Herod is rapidly declining because of age, pain, rage, and haunting memories of his murdered family members (60-1).[139] Adding to his tortured conscience are repeated nightmares, in which Micah the prophet condemns him (61-3) and the words of Micah 5:2 are revealed (75). He orders a priest to read the passage and concludes much to his dismay that Christ's birth has already passed (76-7). There is no mention of the magi or the star.

In contrast to Joseph in Matthew, Saramago's Joseph learns of the massacre plot coincidentally and does not receive angelic revelations in dreams. While visiting Jerusalem, Joseph overhears soldiers discuss Herod's order (79-80). He runs back to a cave near Bethlehem, where the family resides, and ensures Jesus's survival (83-90). While Joseph is away securing the area, an angel appears to Mary and brings a message of the family's doom, not preservation (Matt 1:18-25). Tragedy is inevitable because of "Joseph's crime" of concealing the plot from others, and thus his guilt will hang over the family (87-8). Joseph begins to dream nightmares in which he takes on the role of Herod's soldier in the massacre (91-2). He attempts to overcome his guilt and compensate by having many children (102-3). Still, the nightmares continue and Mary notices "the look of wistful tenderness in Joseph's face" when he addresses Jesus, but she is convinced that her husband is a good man like Job (104-6).

Jesus, who begins to be disturbed by his own dreams, matures and asks his parents about Joseph's nightmares (111-13). Here Saramago inserts his thoughts on theodicy:

> If Jesus continues as well as he has started, one day he will get around to asking why God saved Isaac and did nothing to protect those poor children, who were as innocent as Abraham's son yet were shown no mercy before the throne of the Lord. And then Jesus will be able to say to Joseph, "Father, you mustn't take all the

---

[133] Ibid., 55.
[134] Ibid.
[135] David G. Frier, "José Saramago's 'O Evangelho Segundo Jesus Cristo': Outline of a Newer Testament," *Modern Language Review* 100 (2005): 370.
[136] Cousland, "José Saramago's *Kakagellion*," 65.
[137] Ibid., 62-4. All translations are from José Saramango, *The Gospel According to Jesus Christ*, trans. Giovanni Pontiero, Harvest in Translation (New York: Mariner Books, 1994).
[138] Cousland, "José Saramago's *Kakagellion*," 65.
[139] Many revive the ancient link between the massacre and deaths in Herod's family. See Giambattista Marino's *La Strage degli Innocenti* above (II. B) and commentators that cite Josephus (Appendix B).

blame," and deep down, who knows, he might dare to ask, "When, O Lord, will You come before mankind to acknowledge Your own mistakes" (113).

After another year, a neighbor named Ananias confides in Joseph and reveals that he will join the revolution of Judas the Galilean (114–17). When Joseph later learns that Ananias lies wounded in Sepphoris, a town near Nazareth, he attempts to rescue him but fails because a thief steals his donkey (120–7). Joseph despairs as the last thirteen years of burdens, tears, and guilt swell up to hopelessness and realizes "God does not forgive the sins He makes us commit" (127–8). Soon afterwards, Roman soldiers find Joseph and mistakenly associate him with the rebels condemned to crucifixion (128–32). Initially he protests and insists on his innocence, but eventually resigns himself to his fate and dies at the age of thirty-three (131–2), foreshadowing Jesus's own death.

The massacre of the innocents continues to haunt Jesus as it did Joseph. He inherits his father's nightmares, except he experiences the event from an infant's perspective (143–9). After learning the truth from Mary, he departs from his family disillusioned (149–57). Later, when Jesus returns to the very cave where he was hidden to avoid the massacre, he encounters and joins a Gentile shepherd who knows all about him (182–7). This shepherd is the angel who appeared to Mary earlier to announce the family curse (212).

Under the pastor's apprenticeship, Jesus has a chance to escape his father's fate, but fails.[140] During one Passover, Jesus spares a lamb from his flock when he sees "a vast sea of blood, the blood of the countless lambs and other animal sacrifices since the creation of mankind" (203–9). After that lamb matures, however, God forces Jesus to offer it in the wilderness to seal a covenant with him and the shepherd expels Jesus (217–22). By sacrificing the innocent lamb, Jesus secures his trajectory toward death like the first Adam.[141] The novel ends at the cross, where Jesus realizes that the egomaniacal and sovereign God has tricked and forced him to become an icon for Christianity (376–7). He implores, "Men, forgive Him, for he knows not what He has done" before remembering his conversations with Joseph, whose fate Jesus shares (377).

Saramango revisits and adopts a subversive idea from Camus's *The Fall*: Jesus, haunted daily by Rachel's weeping voice, believes he deserves the cross.[142] Thus, Avi Sagi's summary of Camus's thought equally applies to Saramango's: "Christianity does not rest on the suffering of the innocent, but on guilt."[143] In Saramago's mind, Jesus is not only guilty but also a tragic hero and a victim of God's evil design just like the innocents. The author does not discuss Jer 31:15 or the complex intertwining of God's will and human responsibility, but only deep sorrow for the innocent children (149–53).[144] There is no resurrection for Jesus or triumphant visions of martyred children,

---

[140] According to David G. Frier, Saramago's Jesus fails to wrest free from the force of traditional piety and completely escape from God's authority. "José Saramago's 'O Evangelho Segundo Jesus Cristo,' " 381–2.
[141] Cousland, "José Saramago's *Kakagellion*," 66–7.
[142] Camus, *The Fall*, 111–13.
[143] Avi Sagi, *Albert Camus and the Philosophy of the Absurd*, Value Inquiry Book Series 125 (Amsterdam: Rodophi, 2002), 156.
[144] When Mary defends Joseph's character and cites Scriptures for support, Jesus retorts, "Don't speak of things you know nothing of" (150).

but only a God delighting in death that leads to his glory (377). This anti-theodical reading contributes to an atheistic satire of Christianity, which stands out in the reception history of Matt 2:16-18.

IV. Commentaries

As a genre, commentaries are important for their lasting existence from the second century onwards and their impact on the reception history of Matt 2:16-18. Many of the earliest and the most innovative commentary readings of the massacre stem from the second century to the fifth century and reemerge from the sixth century to modern times. Yet, as stated above, sixteenth-century exegesis marks a notable shift, from the medieval preference for the four senses to the preference for the historical-grammatical sense. This priority of original historical contexts and references has antecedents in the peak of the Antiochene school (the late fourth and early fifth centuries) under John Chrysostom and Theodore of Mospuetia.[145] From the sixteenth century onwards, the influence is much more widespread.

Surveys of commentaries from 1517 to the nineteenth century (see Appendix B) and modern commentaries from the twentieth and twenty-first centuries (see Appendix A, discussed in Chapter 2) reveal this transition. Broadly speaking, the two main concerns of these commentaries are historical-grammatical and moral.[146] Under these broad headings, many of the similar readings are grouped together thematically and highlight illustrative examples from a wide variety of traditions.

A. Historical-Grammatical Concerns

1. Corroborations and Harmonizations

As early as Eusebius of Caesarea (Chapter 3, VII. A), Josephus has been cited to help illuminate Matt 2:16-18. Desiderius Erasmus (1466–1536), the famous Catholic Dutch Renaissance humanist, follows this strategy to condemn Herod and explain his "fitting death."[147] Macrobius, though much later than Josephus, is another important extra-biblical source sought in support of the massacre's historicity. The influential French humanist, theologian, and translator Jacobus Faber Stapulensis (1455–1536) cite him, for example.[148] John Calvin also cites Macrobius but believes Matthew's testimony

---

[145] Hauser and Watson, "Introduction and Overview," 47.

[146] The specific purposes of certain commentaries (for personal use and/or preachers), when discernible, do not appear to largely affect the authors' interest in both historical-grammatical and moral matters. This equal attention may be due to the subject matter of Matt 2:16-18, which has moral issues (infanticide) at the forefront alongside historical-grammatical matters (fulfillment of prophecy, place names, etc.).

[147] Dean Simpson, trans., *Collected Works of Erasmus: Paraphrase on Matthew*, vol. 45 (Toronto: University of Toronto Press, 2008), 54–5.

[148] Jacques L. d'Étaples, *Commentarii initiatorii in quatuor Evangelia* (Meaux: Simon Colinaeus, 1522), 11; Guy Bedouelle, "Jacques Lefèvre d'Étaples (c. 1460–1536)," in *Reformation Theologians: An Introduction to Theology in the Early Modern Period*, ed. Carter Lindberg, 19–33 (Oxford: Blackwell, 2002).

is sufficient to prove the event took place after Jesus's presentation at the temple (Luke 2:22-39).[149] In *The Harmony, Chronicle, and Order, of the New Testament*, the Cambridge scholar John Lightfoot (1602–1675) agrees with this placement but also explains why the Holy Family returns to Galilee in Luke 2:39: since the third evangelist has no interest in narrating the events between Jesus's age of forty days to twelve years, he summarily recounts their movement to Nazareth.[150]

Not all inquirers, however, accept such nuanced approaches. Paul Henri Thiry d'Holbach, along with Denis Diderot and Voltaire, are major French innovators of anti-religious polemical works in late eighteenth century.[151] D'Holbach follows Calvin and Lightfoot and writes a biographical account of Jesus based on a harmony of the gospels, but believes that Matthew created stories to fit prophesies and the massacre is no exception.[152] The silence of Luke and Josephus convinces him to reconstruct Jesus's life critically "by merely reducing the marvelous to its proper value." Though D'Holbach's rationalistic analysis and conclusions exceptional at this time, he anticipates similar discussions in the twentieth century. For example, Richard T. France supports the massacre's historicity while others observe in it legendary elements (see discussion in Chapter 2, II. B).[153]

2. Measurements of the Two Years and the Death Toll

In relation to the massacre's veracity, Matt 2:16-18 raises questions concerning the calculation of two years and the death toll. These inquiries reveal a preoccupation with harmonizing with Luke and filling "historical interpretative space" created by the text (see Chapter 2, II. C). The Italian cardinal and Dominican master Thomas Cajetan (1469–1534) offers his explanation of the two years: Herod does not act immediately after the magi depart for their country but after the presentation of Jesus at the temple and the flight to Egypt.[154] While the timing of star's appearance in relation to the Magi's arrival has been debated since the early church (see discussion of *Fragment* 23 in Chapter 3, II. B), the nineteenth-century American Baptist John A. Broadus thinks the phrase "two years" proves little about the exact time the star appeared because a

---

[149] A. W. Morrison, trans., *John Calvin: A Harmony of the Gospels Matthew, Mark and Luke* (Edinburgh: St. Andrew's Press, 1972), 1:102.

[150] John R. Pitman, ed., *The Whole Works of the Rev. John Lightfoot: Master of Catharine Hall, Cambridge* (London: JF Dove, 1825), 3:27.

[151] Andrew Hunwick, "Introduction," in *Ecce homo! An Eighteenth Century Life of Jesus by Paul T. d'Holbach: Critical Edition and Revision of George Houston's Translation from the French*, ed. Andrew Hunwick, 1–38 (Berlin: Walter de Gruyter, 1995), 23.

[152] Paul T. d'Holbach, *Ecce homo!: An Eighteenth Century Life of Jesus by Paul T. d'Holbach: Critical Edition and Revision of George Houston's Translation from the French*, ed. Andrew Hunwick (Berlin: Walter de Gruyter, 1995), 83–4; François Rosset, "'False' and 'True' Infancy and Apocryphal Gospels in the Century of Voltaire," in *Infancy Gospels: Stories and Identities*, ed. Claire Clivaz, Andreas Dettwiler, Luc Devillers, Enrico Norelli, and Benjamin Bertho, 628–40, WUNT 281 (Tübingen: Mohr Siebeck, 2011).

[153] France, *The Gospel of Matthew*, 84–5; Brown, *Birth of the Messiah*, 204.

[154] Thomas Cajetan, *Evangelia cum Commentariis: In quatuor evangelia & Acta Apostolorum ad Graecorum codicum veritatem castigata ad sensum que vocant literalem Comentarii* (Venetiis: In aedibus Luceantonii Iunctae Florentini, 1530), 2:5.

child only beginning his second year would be labeled two years old and the paranoid Herod would have inflated the range.[155] Even so, many commentators after him have continued in speculations (see Appendix A).

As for the death toll, the association with the 144,000 of the Apocalypse is early and profound in reception history (see Chapter 3, IX). But with the emphasis on the historical sense, the high count reflected in liturgy gives way to smaller numbers. The bifurcation into the high numbers in pre-Vatican liturgical readings (see I. A above) and the low number in most commentaries today (see Appendix A) probably began with figures like the famous Flemish Jesuit and exegete Cornelius à Lapide (1567–1637). He highly doubts that 14,000 infants (cited in Abyssinian and Greek liturgy), let alone 144,000, is plausible in Bethlehem and its horizons, when significantly larger cities like Rome, Naples, or Milan cannot yield such a high amount.[156] Remarkably, à Lapide expresses these disagreements while still indebted to the church fathers for the traditional interpretation of the children as innocent martyrs.[157]

3. Fulfillment and Wider Context of Jeremiah 31

The lean toward the literal-historical sense also invites certain hermeneutical questions concerning Matt 2:17-18. For example, how does Matthew understand Jer 31:15? The Spanish humanist Juán de Valdés (*ca.* 1490–1541) comments tersely that "Ramah is a Hebrew word signifying height," and "Rachel is generic and representative of all the Jewish people."[158] When compared to earlier elaborate studies of Ramah's etymological significance and representative ecclesial roles of the matriarch (see Chapter 4, VIII), de Valdés's thoughts appear meager. Erasmus comments that Jeremiah employs the "*persona*" of Rachel who was buried nearby to give expression to the bereaved women.[159] Interestingly, Erasmus only considers the fulfillment of Jer 31:15 in Jesus's time, not in the captivity.

Like Erasmus, John Calvin views Rachel as a personification (προσωποποιία), aptly depicting sorrow reminiscent of sufferings at the Babylonian exile.[160] While he maintains a clear distinction between the first calamity of the exile and the second calamity of Herod's massacre, both Jer 31:15 and Matt 2:18, in the contexts of Jeremiah 31 and Matthew 2, respectively, hint at salvation to come.[161] Evoking the happier portions of Jeremiah 31 is a common interpretative strategy discussed today but dates from the times of Dionysius Exiguus and Rupert of Deutz (*ca.* sixth century and *ca.* late eleventh/early twelfth century, respectively), whose commentary is perhaps most

---

[155] John A. Broadus, *Commentary on the Gospel of Matthew*, An American Commentary on the New Testament (Philadelphia: American Baptist Publication Society, 1886), 23.
[156] Mossman, trans., *The Great Commentary of Cornelius à Lapide: S. Matthew's Gospel—Chaps. I. to IX*, 83.
[157] Ibid., 83-4.
[158] John Betts, trans., *Juán de Valdés' Commentary upon the Gospel of St. Matthew: Now for the First Time Translated from the Spanish and Never before Published in English* (London: Trübner, Ludgate Hill, 1882), 24.
[159] Simpson, trans., *Collected Works of Erasmus: Paraphrase on Matthew*, 55.
[160] Morrison, trans., *John Calvin: A Harmony of the Gospels Matthew, Mark and Luke*, 1:103.
[161] Ibid.

intricate.[162] W. D. Davies and Dale C. Allison Jr., for example, wonder whether Matthew expected his readers to recognize the hopeful outlook of Jeremiah 31.[163]

But by restricting much of the discussion to these two specific situations in biblical history, relatively less space is devoted to Rachel's representation as the suffering church. This idea began in the early church (see Chapter 3, XIII) and continued to a climax in the first half of the second millennium (see Chapter 4, VIII), when dramatic works displayed Rachel-Mary typology and anagogical readings of Matt 2:16-18. The German Calvinist Johann Peter Lange (1802–1884) is exceptional because he reads the text tropologically and envisions Rachel as the church grieving over hypocrisy: "the wail of Rachel is renewed in the Church as often as the witnesses of the truth are put to death by carnal and worldly men, who profess to be the representatives of the Church."[164] This reading is similar to Gregory of Nazianzus's interpretation of the massacre as the necessary end of spiritual immaturity (see Chapter 3, VIII. D).

4. Textual and Redactional Discussion of Matthew 2:18

Another consequence of the rise of the historical-grammatical sense is the interest in textual critical matters and redactions of the Jeremiah text. The Spanish Jesuit Juan Maldonato (1533–1583) compares the phrase in Matt 2:18, "weeping and great mourning" (κλαυθμὸς καὶ ὀδυρμὸς πολύς), with its counterpart in Jer 31:15 from the MT (Jer 31:15) and the LXX (Jer 38:15). He finds that Matthew's use of two nouns with an adjective is closer to the Hebrew (נהי בכי תמרורים) than the LXX's use of three nouns (θρήνου καὶ κλαυθμοῦ καὶ ὀδυρμοῦ). Yet, "great" (πολύς) in Matt 2:18 is not exactly the same as "bitter" (תמרורים) either.[165] Ultimately, Maldonato deems these differences in wording inconsequential.[166]

More interesting are his comments on the difference between the איננו and οὐκ εἰσίν, both with the English translation of "they are no more." He explains that the third person singular Hebrew word can be translated as plural because it is a Hebraism.[167] Furthermore, he finds that איננו elsewhere describes a swift and complete end that both godly men like Enoch (Gen 5:24) and the wicked in Ps 36:36 alike ultimately face.[168] Like Enoch, the massacred victims are suddenly carried away to Abraham's bosom.[169]

---

[162] See discussion in Chapter 4, VIII. D and commentators under "Hope and Comfort" in Appendix A, the Lutheran *Evangelical Lutheran Worship* (ELW; 2006), and the Episcopal *Book of Common Prayer* (BCP, 1979).
[163] Davies and Allison, *Matthew 1-7*, 269.
[164] Philip Schaff, trans., *A Commentary on the Holy Scriptures: Critical, Doctrinal, and Homiletical, with Special Reference to Ministers and Students by John Peter Lange. Vol. I. of the New Testament: Containing a General Introduction and the Gospel according to Matthew* (New York: Charles Scribner, 1865), 65.
[165] George J. Davie, trans., *A Commentary on the Gospels by John Maldonatus: S. Matthew's Gospel, Chapters I. to XIV* (London: John Hodges, 1888), 74.
[166] Ibid.
[167] Ibid., 75.
[168] Ibid.
[169] Ibid.

Later, the Lutheran textual critic Johann A. Bengel (1687–1752) makes similar textual comparisons.[170] He, however, adds that "bitter" (תמרורים) in the MT is plural and better understood as "bitternesses."[171] So then, the "much" (πολύς) is an appropriate expression of the Hebrew.[172] Bengel and Maldonato pose theories concerning translation techniques set precedence for later textual/source critical studies. For example, J. J. Menken and Joseph Fitzmyer systematically study these textual differences in attempts to locate a pre-Matthean *Vorlage* and/or a list of Christological OT passages created by a school or an individual.[173]

5. Geography

Location names such as Bethlehem and Ramah also invite commentators to geographical studies. The French Benedictine monk Antoine Augustin Calmet (1672–1757) traces the history of Ramah through the OT passages such as Judg 18:25; 19:13; and Jer 40:1.[174] In addition to the Joshua passages, Bengel gathers from other data (Gen 35:19; Ezra 2:21, 26) that Bethlehem and Ramah are "very near together" in proximity and association.[175] He does not grapple with problematic passages such as 1 Sam 10:2 that suggest another location of Rachel's tomb (see Chapter 2, IV. A).

The American Presbyterian Albert Barnes (1798–1870) is perhaps most descriptive, adding that the city was upon a hill and identical to Arimathea, hometown of Joseph (Matt 27:57) and the prophet Samuel (1 Sam 1:1, 19; 2:11; 8:4; 19:18; 25:1).[176] Barnes includes contemporaneous eyewitness accounts of a Muslim mosque there and beautiful summit views that extend to the Mediterranean Sea.[177] He surmises that Ramah was conveniently close to Jerusalem and became a favorite retreat place for kings, perhaps even inspiring one to write poetry from there (cf. Ps 104:25).[178] Similar geographical study is also a standard practice of modern commentators such as Daniel A. Carson, Raymond Brown, and Richard C. H. Lenski.[179] Locating Rachel's tomb in Matthew's day is an important step toward understanding the matriarch's representative

---

[170] Ernest Bengel, Johann C. F. Steudel, and Andrew R. Fausset, trans. and eds., *Gnomon of the New Testament by John A. Bengel, Now First Translated into English with Original Notes Explanatory and Illustrative*, vol. 1 (London: T&T Clark, 1858), 132.
[171] Ibid.
[172] Ibid.
[173] Luz, *The Theology of the Gospel of Matthew*, 38; Menken, "The Quotation from Jeremiah 31 (38).15 in Matthew 2.18: A Study of Matthew's Scriptural Text," 106–25; Fitzmyer, "4Q Testimonia and the New Testament," 513–37.
[174] Augustin Calmet, *Commentaire littéral sur tous les livres de l'Ancien et du Nouveau Testament: L'Evangile de S. Matthieu* (Emery Saugrain : Pierre de Martin, 1715), 40–1.
[175] Bengel, Steudel, and Fausset, trans. and eds., *Gnomon of the New Testament by John A. Bengel*, 133. Perhaps Bengel does not consider twelve miles a long distance by ancient standards.
[176] Albert Barnes, *Barnes' Notes on the New Testament, Complete and Unabridged in One Volume* (Grand Rapids: Kregel, 1962), 9.
[177] Ibid.
[178] Ibid.
[179] Carson, "Matthew," 122; Brown, *The Birth of the Messiah*, 205–6; Lenski, *The Interpretation of St. Matthew's Gospel*, 81–2.

significance, whether she stands for the victims of Assyrian captivity, the Babylonian captivity, the massacre, or all three.[180]

B. Moral Concerns

1. Theodicy and Providence

Many works throughout the reception history of Matt 2:16-18 defend God's providence and sovereignty over the massacre. This type of commentary originates in early church figures such as Gregory of Nyssa and John Chrysostom (see Chapter 3, IV) and continues throughout. One persistent idea is the futility of Herod's plan. The famous *Geneva Bible* (1560) records in a note to Matt 2:18: "Herod renewed the sorrowe which Benjaminites had suffered long before yet for all his crueltie he colde not bring to passe, that Christ shulde not reigne."[181] The influential nineteenth-century collaborative scholarly project of Robert Jamieson (St. Paul's, Glasgow, Scotland), Andrew R. Fausset (St. Cuthbert's York, England), and David Brown (St. James, Glasgow, Scotland), *Commentary Critical and Explanatory on the Whole Bible* (1871), is more emphatic: "Heaven and earth shall sooner pass away than thou shalt have that Babe into thy hands."[182]

Another idea is that Bethlehem is not innocent. Cornelius à Lapide thinks that through divine providence, the adult Bethlehemites are punished, because they refused hospitality to Joseph and Mary in labor and leading them to settle in the stable.[183] As for the massacred young victims, the infant Christ has the full use of reason to experience deep grief for them and the bereaved parents.[184] The famous nonconformist Matthew Henry (1662–1714) adds that Bethlehem is guilty because it did not receive the shepherd's good news.[185] But Christ eventually grows up and sheds his blood for those who shed their blood for him.[186] William Hendriksen, a twentieth-century commentator, directly responds to some of these ideas. In his opinion, the parents are not responsible for the children's deaths and more must be said about how original sin relates to the young victims.[187]

Others ground their theodical arguments on the use of τότε in Matt 2:17. Broadus is among the earliest commentators to detect Matthew's "instinctive reluctance" here and 27:9 "to associate directly the divine purpose with a deed of enormous wickedness."[188]

---

[180] Lenski, *The Interpretation of St. Matthew's Gospel*, 81–2.

[181] *The Bible and Holy Scriptures Conteined in the Olde and Newe Testament. Translated according to the Ebrue and Greke, and conferred with the best translations in divers languags. With moste profitable annotations upon all the Lord places, and other things of great importance as may appear in the Epistle to the Reader* (Geneva: Rouland Hall, 1560), 957.

[182] Robert Jamieson, Andrew R. Fausset, and David Brown, *Commentary Critical and Explanatory on the Whole Bible*, accessed December 6, 2017, https://www.biblestudytools.com/commentaries/jamieson-fausset-brown/.

[183] Mossman, trans. *The Great Commentary of Cornelius à Lapide: S. Matthew's Gospel—Chaps. I. to IX*, 83–4.

[184] Ibid.

[185] Matthew Henry, *Commentary on the Whole Bible (Complete)*, accessed December 7, 2017, https://www.biblestudytools.com/commentaries/matthew-henry-complete/.

[186] Ibid.

[187] William Hendriksen, *Exposition of the Gospel According to Matthew*, 180–1.

[188] Broadus, *Commentary on the Gospel of Matthew*, 24.

Current commentators (see Chapter 2, III. B) such as Dale C. Allison and John Nolland make the same observation.[189] God is not directly linked to the tragedies that befall Bethlehem and Judas Iscariot. As Nolland asserts, "neither Herod nor Judas was interested in fulfilling Scripture!"[190]

2. Herod and His Representation

Aside from repeating ancient testimonies about Herod, commentators also directly criticize his character to the point that he is labeled demonically evil. Satan's use of the king as his pawn is a common insight among the early church interpreters such as Origen, Optatus, and Jacob of Serugh (see Chapter 3, VI). Oecumenius and John of Euobea heighten the drama by recontextualizing Matt 2:16-18 into a cosmic struggle between God and the dragon of Revelation 12 (see Chapter 4, IV). The German Franciscan Johann Wild (1497–1554) continues the idea, analogizing Herod's massacre of infants to Satan's attacks against the human race.[191] The English Baptist John Gill (1697–1771) employs another interesting demonic association: the infanticidal Herod resembles the Jewish mythological night demon named Lilith who steals babies.[192] Modern commentators like Floyd V. Filson find similar parallels.[193]

In addition to Herod's resemblance to the devil, Wild makes connections between Herod and other infamous rulers in history, such as Nebuchadnezzar.[194] David Turner continues this kind of reading in twenty-first century, noting parallels between Herod and the kings of Psalm 2.[195] Perhaps more interesting is the way Herod can symbolize evil authorities outside of the Scriptures. In the early church, Herod became a timeless symbol for evil authorities, and through actualization of Matt 2:16-18, Lucifer of Cagliari vilified the pro-Arian Emperor Constantius (see Chapter 3, VIII. C) as another Herod. Henry similarly reveals his nonconformist bias in his commentary: Herod not only resembles Doeg the Edomite (1 Samuel 21–22) and Nero but also the Church of Rome.[196] Actualizations of Matt 2:16-18 continue in a variety of ways today. For example, Stanley Hauerwas sees Herod as a representation of those who abandon and abuse children.[197]

---

[189] Allison, *Studies in Matthew*, 254–5; John Nolland, *The Gospel of Matthew: A Commentary on the Greek Text*, NIGTC (Grand Rapids: Eerdmans and Paternoster, 2005), 124.
[190] Ibid.
[191] Miguel de Medina, ed., *Commentariorum Ioannis Feri in sacro sanctum Iesu Christi Euangelium secundum Matthaeum libri quatuor* (Compluti: Andreas de Angulo, 1567), 14.
[192] John Gill, *Exposition of the Bible*, accessed December 7, 2017, https://www.biblestudytools.com/commentaries/gills-exposition-of-the-bible/. For a survey of the development of the Lilith legend, see Howard Schwartz, *Tree of Souls: The Mythology of Judaism* (Oxford: Oxford University Press, 2004), 218.
[193] Filson, *A Commentary on the Gospel According to St. Matthew*, 61.
[194] de Medina, ed., *Commentariorum Ioannis Feri in sacro sanctum Iesu Christi Euangelium secundum Matthaeum libri quatuor*, 14.
[195] David L. Turner, *Matthew*, BECNT (Grand Rapids: Baker Academic, 2008), 93.
[196] Henry, *Commentary on the Whole Bible (Complete)*.
[197] Hauerwas, *Matthew*, 41.

3. Victims

Just as Herod represents evil, the victims often represent good beyond Matt 2:16-18. The infants have been hailed as martyrs and sacrifices since the early church and their fame continues beyond the Reformation (see Chapter 3, IX and X; Chapter 4, VI and VII) in the works of key figures such as Stapulensis and the English Methodist Joseph Benson (1749–1821).[198] The latter writes, "Here observe, the first crown of martyrdom for Jesus was won by these infant sufferers, and the honour to which they are advanced infinitely repays the short pains they endured."[199] This type of eulogy is ubiquitous in the reception history of Matt 2:16-18.

Still, imagination plays a key role in restating old ideas in new ways, especially in interpreting the victims as sacrifices. For example, Jamieson, Fausset, and Brown use imagery from Genesis 22. In the massacre, the innocents take the role of the ram caught by its horn in the thicket and sacrificed for Isaac, who represents Jesus. Later, the roles are reversed so that Jesus offers his life like the ram for the sake of the victims.[200]

At other times, such imaginative commentating is controversial, especially among differing hermeneutical traditions. For example, in his *Matthew: A Commentary on His Literary and Theological Art*, Robert H. Gundry combines redaction criticism and the reading of the victims as sacrifices to deny the massacre's historicity.[201] Gundry believes the theological redactor allegorized the offering of two turtledoves or young pigeons (Luke 2:24) and created the massacre event.[202] As a result of his publication, Evangelical Theological Society asked Gundry to resign.[203]

V. Conclusion

This sample survey of liturgical works (I), works in verse (II), novels (III), and commentaries (IV) demonstrates the existence of many possibilities in the future direction of reception history of Matt 2:16-18. Since the readership of Matthew is wider than ever before, challenges come from many different directions. One can identify the following three types of particular kinds of challenges in the period from 1517: (1) formal, (2) theodical, and (3) hermeneutical.

First, form continues to dictate content in the last five hundred years of the massacre's reception history. Even though the literal sense became preeminent, liturgical texts (I) and commentaries (IV) still preserve major inspirational, moral, and allegorical readings, with some variations. Despite major theological divisions, major

---

[198] d'Étaples, *Commentarii initiatorii in quatuor Evangelia*, 11; Joseph Benson, *Commentary of the Old and New Testaments*, accessed December 8, 2017, http://biblehub.com/commentaries/benson/.
[199] Benson, *Commentary of the Old and New Testaments*.
[200] Jamieson, Fausset, and Brown, *Commentary Critical and Explanatory on the Whole Bible*.
[201] Gundry, *Matthew*, 34–5.
[202] Gundry also thinks the redactor transformed Jewish shepherds in Luke 2 into gentile magi in Matthew 2. Ibid., 31.
[203] Leslie R. Keylock, "Evangelical Scholars Remove Robert Gundry for His Views on Matthew," *Christianity Today*, November 1, 2003, accessed December 8, 2017, https://www.christianitytoday.com/ct/2003/novemberweb-only/11-17-42.0.html.

clergymen continue to draw from common traditions accrued for a millennium and a half. For example, despite their theological differences, a Lutheran Philip Melanchthon can share with the Counter-Reformer Charles Borromeo a reverence for the victims of the massacre (I. B) in their sermonic material. Similarly, a Franciscan Johann Wild and a Baptist John Gill see the devil behind Herod (IV. B. 2). Most of these ideas are familiar to the careful student of reception history.

Unfamiliar content, however, also appears through new media, especially as it relates to suffering. Through Herman Melville's novel (III. A), reception history takes a decidedly unexpected turn outside church walls. Melville recalls the victims not as innocent saints in heaven described in the Apocalypse but haunting ghosts of the sea. Furthermore, the weeping Rachel is wrested from the narrative flow of the good news, Matthew's Gospel, and the generally hopeful outlook of Jeremiah 31. Instead, she sails on as the perpetually bereaved victim of God and her unresolved search is Melville's final word on her. The novel presents opportunities to enclose biblical ideas and imageries in irreverent and controversial ways that commentaries, liturgical readings, or sermons have not typically allowed. So then, these allusions defy traditional categories such as historical and moral senses of Scripture. If anything, they are receptions of the "immoral sense."

Melville is not the first or the last writer to call attention to inherent theodical issues in Matt 2:16-18. Its reception history incites both new challenges to the Christian faith and invitation to sympathize in suffering. An example of the former occurs with philosophers such as José Saramago (III. B). In response, proponents of orthodoxy are challenged to be ready to give an answer to the problem of evil that emerges early in the NT canon. Yet such exploration of weighty moral concerns is also an opportunity for good. The popular *Coventry Carol* reminds Christendom that pain and suffering is a shared universal experience like the everyday lullaby (II. A).

The Christian response, however, can go beyond mere sympathy. Giambattista Marino's *La Strage degli Innocenti* is a poignant defense that is memorable precisely because he intensifies the problem of evil (II. A). Marino empowers Herod with hellish power and exacerbates the massacre with horrid details only to resolve the theodical issue in the end: God hears Rachel, Herod loses his entire family, and the patriarchs welcome the victims into heaven. Interestingly, Marino's work might be proof that historical-grammatical sense has certain limitations and an apt response to suffering is imaginative: one begins with the literal sense, but then move toward the realm of sadistic, fantastical, and mythological, by employing the moral, allegorical, and anagogical senses.

Finally, there are hermeneutical issues that originate from the text. Actualization of Matt 2:16-18 most often leads to *ad hominem* vilification of authorities and opponents. For example, John Calvin, Philip Melanchthon (I. B), and Matthew Henry (IV. B. 2) all actualize the text and lead their audience to picture their enemies as embodiments of a cruel Herod in a rhetoric that is more inflammatory than constructive. Drawing proper bounds for biblical interpretation may be more necessary when dealing with controversial passages such as Matt 2:16-18.

Responsible hermeneutics is especially important since reader-oriented approaches to the text are more analogous to a mirror than a window (see Chapter 1, n. 12).

Influential readers may not be aware of this reflection. An interpreter of Matt 2:16-18 may condemn Herod or Satan rightly but unjustly subject an enemy to rhetorical violence. In the post-Gutenburg age of social media, the ethics of hermeneutics is paramount to encourage fruitful discussions of faith. Such care in the presentation of readings is all the more relevant when considering the visual reception history of Matt 2:16-18, the topic of the next chapter, as one often moves beyond pages of books and worship gatherings to public artwork visible to the general public.

6

Visual Interpretations of the Massacre of the Innocents

Introduction

From as early as the fifth century, visual artists have contributed to the reception history of Matt 2:16-18 through diverse visual media, including sculpture reliefs, manuscript illustrations, altarpieces, and paintings (see Chapter 4, introduction). From this sundry abundance, this chapter features representative artworks that echo the major strands of reading discussed in earlier chapters and/or present ideas in innovative and influential ways (due to popularity or chronological priority). While these receptions could have been discussed alongside the textual receptions, visual exegesis is sufficiently distinctive to justify separate treatment.[1] For example, a single image can present several ideas "together in suspension," transcend language barriers via memorable symbols, and tacitly aid subversive propaganda.[2]

I. Visual Exegesis

Before beginning the survey, terminological clarity ("reading," "visual exegesis," and "beholder") and methodological orientation are in order. Up to this point, the term "reading(s)" have been used to describe various verbal interpretations of Matt 2:16-18. Certainly, visual artists are also readers and their interpretations as "readings" facilitate comparisons between this chapter and the previous chapters. Just as commentators and homilists reckon with the "interpretative space" of a given passage, so do the painter and the sculptor (see Chapter 2, introduction).[3] While interpreting Matt 2:16-18,

---

[1] The choice is determined by personal preference, not any inherent incongruence between visual works and texts.
[2] Boxall, *Patmos in the Reception History of the Apocalypse*, 177; Christopher Rowland, "Imagining the Apocalypse," *NTS* 51 (2005): 316–19; Andrew Finch, Wei Song, Kumiko Tanaka-Ishii, and Eiichiro Sumita, "Speaking Louder than Words with Pictures across Languages," *AI Magazine* 34 (2013): 31–47; Colin Moore, *Propaganda Prints: A History of Art in the Service of Social and Political Change* (London: A&C Black, 2010), 10–11.
[3] Boxall, *Patmos in the Reception History of the Apocalypse*, 3–4.

artists, just like their counterparts who produce verbal interpretations, fill voids left by the text: Herod's height, the number of his men, the weapons used, and women's attitudes, and so on.

Visual interpreters, however, do not fill the voids in exactly the same way as their verbal counterparts. The influential art historian Erwin Panofsky highlights how textual exegetes and visual artists primarily draw from different (though at times overlapping) sets of sources.[4] As an example, Panofsky presents the picture by the Venetian seventeenth-century painter, Francesco Maffei, depicting a woman wielding a sword in her left hand and a plate of a decapitated head in her right. At first glance, the image could be either Judith with Holofernes's head or Salome with the head of John the Baptist. The trained reception historian, however, discerns it as a picture of Judith for the following reasons. While no existing literary source depicts Salome with a sword or Judith with a plate, various other artworks contain the latter motif.[5] In addition, the sword was an established visual symbol of honorable martyrs and such virtues could not apply to Salome.[6] So then, Maffei expands on the text differently than his textual counterparts.[7]

Understanding such visual motifs in art history is akin to learning the distinctive terminology of theology and church history. One must move beyond the bounds of theological traditions and Israelite history into the world of art and even into the broader culture of the artist's day.[8] To simply say that a painting or a sculpture visualizes the text is an oversimplified truism. Reception historians should become conversant in the two different types of sources (text-based and art-based) to provoke enriching interdisciplinary dialogue.[9]

Recognizing such complexity, the technical term "visual exegesis" is necessary to describe intermediary processes between the text and the visual productions. According to Christopher Nygren, study of evocative picturesque writing (rhetography) should be separate from study of physical images.[10] Unlike Nygren, however, who defines "visual exegesis" as a general overarching category under which rhetography and study of physical images (graphic exegesis) exist as subcategories, for the sake of clarity it is

---

[4] Erwin Panofsky argues that textual exegetes and visual exegetes draw from three different sets of sources: (1) familiar experiences vs. history of artistic styles, (2) knowledge of literary sources vs. history of types, (3) erudite scholarship vs. trained layman's perspective, respectively. "Iconography and Iconology: An Introduction to the Study of Renaissance Art," in *Meaning in the Visual Arts: Papers in and on Art History by Erwin Panofsky*, 26–54 (Garden City: Doubleday, 1957), 35–41.
[5] Panofsky, "Iconography and Iconology," 36–7.
[6] Ibid., 37.
[7] Berdini, *The Religious Art of Jacopo Bassano*, 1–35; O'Kane, "The Artist as Reader of the Bible," 337–73.
[8] Panofsky, "Iconography and Iconology," 38–9.
[9] J. Cheryl Exum, "Beyond the Biblical Horizon: The Bible and the Arts," in *Beyond the Biblical Horizon: The Bible and the Arts*, ed. J. Cheryl Exum, 1–7 (Leiden: Brill, 1999), 1–4.
[10] Christopher J. Nygren, "Graphic Exegesis: Reflections on the Difficulty of Talking about Biblical Images, Pictures, and Texts," in *The Art of Visual Exegesis: Rhetoric, Texts, and Images*, ed. Vernon K. Robbins, Walter S. Melion, and Roy R. Jeal, 271–302, Emory Studies in Early Christianity 19 (Atlanta: SBL Press, 2017), 285–8.

best to preserve Berdini's classic definition of visual exegesis for this chapter's analysis of physical images.[11] Berdini writes,

> The painter reads the text and translates his scriptural reading into a problem in representation, to which he offers a solution—the image. In that image the beholder acknowledges, not the text in the abstract, but the painter's reading of the text so that the effect the image has on the beholder is a function of what the painter wants the beholder to experience in the text. This is the trajectory of visualization, and the effect of the text through the image is a form of exegesis.[12]

Berdini further specifies the intermediary processes of patrons, theological advisors, and/or artists as "discursive strategies" that expand on the text and intricately involve various religious, political, and social contexts.[13] These factors are logical starting points for visual exegesis, especially when available data allows for critical analyses (biography, provenance, purpose, culture, etc.).

At times, such factors reveal limitations to the artist's freedom of expression or shape the direction of the work.[14] For example, under the category of "liturgical art," some works are "integral and appropriate to the liturgical actions of a community's liturgy."[15] Barbara G. Lane explains how Robert Campin's panel painting *The Virgin and Child before a Fire Screen* (*ca.* 1440; currently at the National Portrait Gallery, London) teaches important theological lessons in its details: (1) a circular fire screen behind Mary's head resembles a halo, (2) the infant Christ rests near an elegant liturgical chalice, and (3) the fireplace is obscured behind the Virgin and the Child. From these details, a participant at Mass would understand visually (1) the primacy of the Virgin, (2) the correspondence of the Eucharist to Christ, and (3) the superiority of the New Testament "living bread" formed in Mary's womb over OT burnt offerings, respectively.[16] Such ritualistic connections and interplays between the artist, the setting, and worshipers are important for visual exegesis.

So then, as seen in Berdini's definition above and demonstrated in Campin's work, visual exegesis also considers the complex responses of the "beholder," a term reserved for viewers who experience art.[17] Careful consideration of beholders' participations is necessary because an experience of art is not merely a secondary "re-presentation" of

---

[11] Ibid., 287–8; Heidi J. Hornik and Mikeal C. Parsons, *Illuminating Luke: The Infancy Narrative in Italian Renaissance Painting* (Harrisburg: Trinity Press International, 2003), 6–7.

[12] Berdini, *The Religious Art of Jacopo Bassano*, 35.

[13] Berdini, *The Religious Art of Jacopo Bassano*, 35. Though admittedly, distinguishing between the inputs of artists, patrons, and theological advisors is a difficult process and is less relevant in the reception history of Matt 2:16-18.

[14] For example, Peter Paul Rubens requested to narrate the life of St. Bavo in a retable at Ghent on a single panel but was denied and forced to work on the more traditional albeit more restrictive triptych. Sauerländer, *The Catholic Rubens*, 142–5, 234–8.

[15] Eileen D. Crowley, *Liturgical Art for a Media Culture*, American Essays in Liturgy (Collegeville: Liturgical Press, 2007), 13.

[16] Barbara G. Lane, *The Altar and the Altarpiece: Sacramental Themes in Early Netherlandish Painting* (New York: Harper & Row, 1984), 1–5. See also Beth Williamson, "Altarpieces, Liturgy, and Devotion," *Speculum* 79 (2004): 341–406.

[17] Just as readers read texts and audiences hear homilies, beholders experience art.

reality (*Vorstellung*) but "a presentation of the essence itself" (*Darstellung*) in which the artist and the beholder share together.[18] Artists often intend to display their work for specific functions in specific locations to evoke certain responses from others, even if such intentions are at times difficult to ascertain, unrealized, or unknown in the present because of anonymity or displacement of the work. Unintended beholders who react to these works in new settings (e.g., art galleries) may provoke or encourage different types of responses. Both the intended and unintended beholders of art should be considered participants who "acknowledge" (Berdini's term) the painter's reading of the text and not merely as passive observers.[19] In summary, this present author will attempt to present and analyze the artists' readings, explain the visual exegeses involved (e.g., intended purposes, locations, audiences), and explore possible effects on the beholders, both intended and unintended.

II. Major Strands of Reading

It is possible to organize the selected artworks in a strictly chronological order, the format for Appendix C (a non-exhaustive sampling of visual exegetical works depicting Matt 2:16-18). For the purposes of this chapter, however, it is best to organize the material according to the major strands of reading discussed in earlier chapters: The Massacre in Relation to Other Biblical Stories (III), Herod as Symbol of Evil (IV), Victims as Martyrs (V), Mothers as Mourners (VI), and Vindicated Mothers (VII). This scheme allows for easy comparisons with previous chapters. This chapter ends with a conclusion (VIII).

III. Massacre in Relation to Other Biblical Stories

The earliest surviving artworks parallel verbal exegesis in interpreting Matt 2:16-18 in relation to other biblical events, especially other infancy narrative episodes (often harmonizing Luke and Matthew) and the wider life of Jesus. Especially interesting is how certain visualizations juxtapose the massacre with OT scenes, the flight into Egypt, and later events of Jesus's adult ministry, such as the Passion. These juxtapositions reveal that suffering would characterize Jesus's life from the beginning and Herod's actions are typical of ungodly powers that oppose the saints.

A. Tympanum of the Strasbourg Cathedral

The construction project of Strasbourg Cathedral (also known as the *Cathédrale Notre-Dame de Strasbourg*) spans four centuries (*ca.* 1176–1439). The famous west façade contains thousands of figures. Three tympana, however, are thematically united and

---

[18] Martin O'Kane, "*Wirkungsgeschichte* and Visual Exegesis: The Contribution of Hans-Georg Gadamer," *JSNT* 33 (2010): 149–51.
[19] Berdini, *The Religious Art of Jacopo Bassano*, 35.

display pivotal Christological events: Christ's nativity (left), Passion (central), and the last judgment (right). The north (left) portal tympanum (*ca.* 1275) is most relevant to this chapter and contains three registers from the nativity: (1) the bottom register with the magi before Herod and their adoration of Christ, (2) the middle register with the massacre and the flight to Egypt, and (3) the top register with the presentation in the temple. The bottom and the middle registers are distinct because each includes two scenes from Matthew 2 and the figure of Herod (Figure 1).

Figure 1 "The north (left) portal tympanum of the Strasbourg Cathedral" (*ca.* 1275). © Cea +, @centralasian (*ca.* 2006) "Strasbourg Cathedral—Left Door Arch—Detail," photograph available from Flickr, https://www.flickr.com/photos/centralasian/7684355624/ (accessed December 1, 2020), used with permission.

The pairing and splicing of the two pairs of Matthean nativity scenes, combined with the Lucan presentation in the temple, send a clear message: Herod fails to thwart God's plan for Christ. Moving from left to right, the viewer of the bottom register learns that the magi do not sympathize with Herod's ill feelings toward the child but instead adore him. Similarly, the middle register reveals that Herod's plot does not prevent the Holy Family from escaping to Egypt. The proximity of the massacre to the flight also gives the impression of a dramatic and urgent escape. Only a few previous works, such as the mid-ninth-century *Chludov Psalter*, have spliced the massacre with the flight, whereas later visualizations frequently conflate the two events.[20]

The struggles between the magi and Herod and the ensuing mayhem find resolution at the uppermost top register. It displays the presentation in the temple, celebrated forty

---

[20] See Appendix C.

days after the *Feast of the Nativity* since earliest times.[21] Christ has overcome Herod, and is held up at the center of an altar by his parents, foreshadowing his sacrificial death to come and linked to the babes who have already suffered. The overall message is that the viewers should not meditate on the massacre in isolation but in the context of Christ's survival.

B. Bertram of Minden's Grabow Altarpiece

Among several fixtures in worship settings is the altarpiece. As stated earlier, Lane contends that artistic altarpieces do not simply display the Eucharist but illustrate corporate rituals and intensify personal devotion (see I. Visual Exegesis). Images of sacrifice and martyrdom are especially poignant and exemplary as they remind participants of Christ's sacrifice and the sacrifice demanded of his followers. One notable example is Bertram of Minden's major work: the Grabow Altarpiece (1378–83; tempera on wood). Originally located in St. Peter's Church in Hamburg, this work of the influential and early Gothic painter, illuminator, and wood-carver is considered "one of the high points of late 14th-century north German art."[22] The altarpiece's wings opened and closed as occasions required, revealing its valuable interior.

The Grabow Altarpiece is distinct from other similar works such as the altars of Buxtehude (*ca.* 1410, also by Bertram of Minden) and Lüneburg (*ca.* 1418) for the scale of its coverage of biblical scenes. While all three devote a frame to the massacre among other NT infancy scenes, Bertram has painted it among twenty-four scenes, mostly from Genesis, by design visible only when the outermost wings are open.[23] At the center of the altarpiece is the crucifixion, flanked by rows of saints and prophets, identifiable from their salient features. The massacre appears at the lower right wing. In the upper row of the left wing, the biblical history begins with the Genesis 1 creation story and ends with the creation of man from the ground. The story continues in the upper row of the right wing, beginning with Eve's creation and ending with Adam and Eve at work outside of Eden. The Genesis account continues on the bottom row of the left wing, beginning with Cain and Abel's sacrifice and ending with Isaac's blessing of the deceiver Jacob.

Finally, in the lower horizontal sequence of the right wing between the presentation in the temple (left) and the flight to Egypt (right) is the massacre (center) (Figure 2). Like the creator of the north portal tympanum of Strasbourg Cathedral, Bertram harmonizes individual scenes of the infancy narratives. But this visualization also creates other interesting juxtapositions of scenes from the two testaments. Just above the presentation in the temple is God's judgment of Adam, Eve, and the serpent in Eden. Above the massacre is the expulsion of Adam and Eve, still covering their bodies

---

[21] See an early account in John H. Bernard, trans., *The Pilgrimage of S. Silvia of Aquitania to the Holy Places (Circ. 385 AD)* (London: Palestine Pilgrims' Text Society, 1896), 51–2.

[22] "Bertram [von Minden], Master," in *The Grove Encyclopedia of Medieval Art and Architecture, Volume 1: Aachen to Cecco di Pietro*, ed. Colum Hourihane, 321–3 (Oxford: Oxford University Press, 2012); Victoria Charles and Klaus H. Carl, *Gothic Art* (New York: Parkstone International, 2008), 96.

[23] "Bertram [von Minden], Master," 321.

Figure 2 "Grabow Altarpiece," Meister Bertram von Minden, 1378–83, Kuntstalle Hamburg. Source: The Yorck Project (2002), *10.000 Meisterwerke der Malerei* (DVD-ROM), distributed by Directmedia Publishing GmbH.

in shame. Above the rest during the flight to Egypt, Adam works the soil while Eve sits.[24]

Bertram likely intended these Genesis scenes to shape the beholder's experience of the nativity scenes. Parallel to the massacre scene on the right wing is the murder of Abel on the left wing. Both are the first manifestations of murderous depravity in their respective testaments.[25] Earlier works already pointed out analogies between the victims and Cain, Abel, Herod, and the victims (see Gregory of Nyssa (Chapter 3, IV. A), Ephrem the Syrian (V. B), Lucifer of Cagliari (VIII. C), Gregory of Nazianzus (VIII. D), John of Euobea (see Chapter 4, IV. B), and Lord Crawford's Sahidic MS 36 (see VII. B)). Bertram's arrangement is consistent with the previous argument that like Abel, the babes are innocent.

Nearer to the massacre scene, scholars have noted the connection between the massacre and the expulsion, evident from two pairs of parallels: (1) the architectural

---

[24] This altarpiece is the earliest known artistic depiction of the rest on the flight to Egypt. Schiller, *Iconography of Christian Art*, 1:122.
[25] The present writer is indebted to Dr. Ian Boxall for this suggestion.

structures of the gate of paradise and Herod's throne and (2) the upraised swords of the archangel and Herod's soldier.[26] By juxtaposing and visibly linking the expulsion with the massacre, Bertram has advanced a pictorial and theodical defense. Bertram would agree with Gregory of Nyssa and John Chrysostom (see Chapter 3, A and B) that the massacre is not the fault of God or Christ but is one of many manifestations of mankind's wickedness that began at the fall.[27] When beholders consider the massacre in context of the entire altarpiece, their eyes move from the consequences of sin at the margins of the altar to the crucifixion at the center. The eucharistic context and function of the altarpiece as a whole presents Christ's sacrifice as a solution to evil for the participants of the Mass.

C. Paupers' Bible

The Paupers' Bible (*Biblia Pauperum*; ca. fifteenth century) is a picture book with pages that contain a NT antitype scene at the center, flanked by two corresponding OT types, and short explanatory biblical texts and verses. Though many manuscript examples originate from the fourteenth century, the invention of the printing press in the fifteenth century increased this Bible's popularity in the Netherlands and Germany, when it was produced in xylographic block book editions.[28] In the depiction of the massacre, the artist incorporates ideas from various portions of the Scriptures both pictorially from historical narratives and verbally from prophetic oracles, wisdom literature, and apocalyptic visions. As discussed below, the juxtaposition of these OT narrative scenes with the massacre as well as the concatenation of condemnatory verses lessens the theodical tension present in an isolated reading of Matt 2:16-18.

On the page depicting the massacre, two OT rulers guilty of massacres are also shown: (1) Saul against the priests and other inhabitants of Nob (1 Sam 22:18-19) and (2) Queen Athaliah's vengeful purge of the royal family (2 Kgs 11:1). The suggested parallels are striking: (1) all three overreact to perceived threats to their reign with infanticide among other atrocities (1 Sam 22:19; 2 Kgs 11:2-3) and (2) all three fail to locate their intended targets, who will eventually usurp their positions (2 Sam 5:1-5; 2 Kgs 11:4-21; Matt 2:2; 27:11, 29, 37).[29] Comparing Herod with evil OT kings is not a novel reading strategy (it is already found in PJ, Ephrem the Syrian, and Augustine: see Chapter 3, V). The novel contribution of the artist of the Paupers' Bible is that queens can be just as cruel as their male counterparts.

Accompanying verses also assist the viewer in understanding the typology. The words of Hosea 8:4, "they set up kings and not from me" (*Ipsi regnaverunt, et non ex*

---

[26] Elizabeth H. Dube, "The Grabow Altar of Master Bertram von Minden (Germany)" (PhD diss., Brown University, 1982), 106; Paul Portmann, *Meister Bertram* (Zürich: Verlag, 1963), 165.

[27] See also the capitals in the doorjambs of the Porte Miègeville in St. Sernin, Toulouse (ca. 1110–20). The capital of the massacred innocents is not only adjacent to the capital of the Annunciation and the Visitation, it is juxtaposed with the inner capital across the doorway that narrates the Expulsion from Eden. Nolan, "Ploratus et Ululatus," 113–15.

[28] "Biblia Pauperum," ODCC, 206.

[29] The rulers do not all exhibit the familiar outstretched hand motion that implicates them. While Herod and Athaliah are pointing a scepter and a finger, respectively, Saul is not gesturing with his hand.

me), implicate the people for setting up evil authorities like Herod. The words of Prov 28:15, "Like a roaring lion and a hungering bear is a wicked ruler over poor people" (*leo rugiens et ursus esuriens princeps impius super populum pauperem*), correspond to Herod's oppression of the innocent babes and their mothers. While citing the text of Matt 2:18, the artist omits Matt 2:17, thus deemphasizing God's providence in prophetic fulfillment and divine speech. The result is an efficient interpretative display of pain and suffering as the consequences of human sin rather than divine sovereignty.

But victims under wicked rulers are not without hope. The artist includes the familiar imprecatory prayer based on Ps 78:10, Deut 32:43, and Rev 19:2: "Vindicate, Lord, the blood of your saints" (*Vindica, Domine, sanguinem sanctorum tuorum*) from the antiphonary, *Under the Altar of God* (*Sub altare Dei*) of the Roman Office's Matins of the Innocents (see Chapter 4, VI. C). When read together with Matt 2:18, the voice of Ramah moves in a heavenward direction, to plead for divine intervention. So then, this unique combination of verses and pictures on a single page of the Paupers' Bible effectively communicates scriptural typology (Saul-Athaliah-Herod), moral condemnation of corrupt authorities (Prov 28:15; Hosea 8:4), and the recontextualization of the massacre in the flow of eschatological drama (Rev 19:2). Similarly, the anonymous illuminator of the *Book of Hours* of Bruges, Belgium (*ca.* 1480), juxtaposes the massacre scene with hopeful words from Psalms (Ps 126:1-2a) as also the earlier mid-ninth-century *Chludov Psalter* (Psalm 90).

D. Giovanni Pisano's Pulpits

While tourists, scholars, and art historians have paid more attention to the popular frescoes of his famous contemporary Giotto, Giovanni Pisano's sculpted marble pulpits at Pistoia (1301) and Pisa (*ca.* 1302–11) are important works that convey some interesting interpretations of Matt 2:16-18.[30] Jules Lubbock explains a major contributing factor in their previous neglect: "This account of relief sculpture is based upon the incorrect assumption that we look at these reliefs at eye-level. Seeing them obliquely from beneath has major implications for high relief sculpture which Giovanni exploited to great effect, not only technically and spatially ... but also dramatically."[31] Pisano's pulpits uniquely combine his artistry with familiar readings from reception history to produce creative interpretations of the massacre.

Three panels of the Pistoia pulpit are relevant: (1) the nativity; 2) a combined scene featuring the Magi's adoration, the angelic dreams warning both the magi and Joseph; and (3) the massacre. At the lower foreground of the second panel, the winged messengers lean over the magi (left) and Joseph (right) but point in different directions, likely because Joseph would flee west to Egypt while the magi would return home eastward. The adoration occupies the upper background. The impression is that the adoration ought to be viewed with the upcoming wrath of Herod in mind,

---

[30] Jules Lubbock, *Storytelling in Christian Art from Giotto to Donatello* (New Haven: Yale University Press, 2006), 85.
[31] Ibid., 85–7.

Figure 3 Giovanni Pisano "Pistoia Pulpit," *ca.* 1297–1301, Massacre of the Innocents, relief from the pulpit. Photo credit: Scala/Art Resource, NY, used with permission.

literally around the corner in the next panel.[32] This arrangement is a sobering recontextualization of the Magi's joyful arrival at the star's resting place (Matt 2:10). The frantic scene of the second panel directly foreshadows the chaos that ensues in the third panel: Herod's massacre (Figure 3).

An important salient feature of the Pisa counterpart is the curvature of each panel.[33] The curved shape of one panel serves to effectively invite the beholder into the succeeding panel. If the beholders view the massacre is properly and centrally from below, with the Passion in the right panel (with the flight to Egypt on the left), they can preview Judas Iscariot's kiss of Jesus obliquely.[34] So then, by means of the pulpit's three-dimensional artistry, the terrible massacre of the innocents adumbrates the Passion, a foreshadowing motif present already in Matthew's infancy narrative and a common reading among the early church receptors of Matt 2:16-18, including Origen, Hilary of Poitiers, Ephrem the Syrian, Theodore of Mopsuetia, Augustine, and Jacob of Serugh (see Chapter 3, VIII. A).[35]

---

[32] Ibid., 106–8. See also Jean Pucelle's illumination in the prayer book, *The Hours of Pucelle* (*ca.* 1324), in which the adoration of the magi and the massacre occupy the same page.

[33] Lubbock, *Storytelling in Christian Art from Giotto to Donatello*, 117.

[34] Ibid., 119–20. See figures 76–80 in 121–4.

[35] Two-twelfth century capitals, one in St. Pierre at Moissac (*ca.* 1115–30) and another in the cathedral of Notre Dame des Doms in Avignon (*ca.* 1160) also require viewing from various angles to fully appreciate the massacre's relationship to other biblical scenes. See discussion in Nolan, "Ploratus et

E. Pietro Testa's *The Massacre of the Innocents*

A friend of Nicolas Poussin and a principal artist of his patron Cassiano dal Pozzo, Pietro Testa (ca. 1612–1650) possessed talent, but his skills as a painter were unappreciated.[36] Better known as a draftsman and a printmaker, Testa incorporated classical themes into his works, at times eccentrically as evident in his etchings of the *Death of Sinorix* (from Plutarch, *Moralia* 4.257–8; date unknown) and Plato's *Symposium* (ca. 1648).[37] While a pen and chalk etching of the massacre exists (date unknown; currently at the National Galleries of Scotland, Edinburgh), his painting of the same scene in oil on canvas (ca. 1630–40), currently at the Galleria Spada, Rome, is better known and may be his best known painting.

Immediately relevant here is the flight to Egypt unfolding on the right side of the painting. The escape takes place on a boat floating on a stream with verdant trees in the background and the blue sky and white clouds above. The serene mini-scene contrasts drastically with the dark, earthy, and mostly monochrome painting of the massacre on the left. Not only does Testa combine the massacre with the flight (a common strategy in visual reception history; see Appendix C), but he also enhances the contrast through colors.

One detail of Testa's work makes an exceptional theodical statement: the Holy Family, huddled together, sits under a cross on the boat. The wooden structure could be a mast, but that is not likely because it is not centrally placed in the boat and there are no sails. The intention is likely to foreshadow the Passion that will take place in the future. Like Giovanni Pisano, Testa accomplishes visually what the early Church fathers have done with words (see D above), justifying Christ's exemption from the mass suffering of infants: he lives to die another day. Similarly, Poussin's oil-on-canvas painting, *The Return of the Holy Family from Egypt* (ca. 1628–38; currently at the Dulwich Picture Gallery, London), shows the Holy Family boarding a boat with a ferryman, with four angels directly above, carrying a cross.

F. William Holman Hunt's *Triumph of the Innocents*

Since the flight to Egypt repeatedly appears in massacre visualizations, one might inquire conversely concerning flight scenes that include the massacre. The English painter William Holman Hunt (ca. 1827–1910), one of the founders and "the most forceful proponent of Pre-Raphaelitism," does just that in his oil painting on canvas, *Triumph of the Innocents* (ca. 1883–4), with three versions at three locations: Tate Britain, London (Figure 4); Walker Art Gallery, Liverpool; and Harvard Art Museums, Cambridge, MA.[38]

Ululatus," 109–15. But the lack of curves and the sharp angles of the capitals do not communicate narrative foreshadowing as effectively as Pisano's pulpits.

[36] Nancy T. de Grummond, ed., *Encyclopedia of the History of Classical Archaeology* (Abingdon: Routledge, 1996), 1091.

[37] Ibid., 1091–2.

[38] Pre-Raphaelitism, a movement formed by a brotherhood of young artists in the late 1840s, did not have a formal charter; its members were likely united in "their dislike of the conventionality and insipidity of most of the painting they saw being produced and exhibited around them" and

Figure 4 William Holman Hunt, "The Triumph of the Innocents," *ca.* 1883–4. Tate Gallery, London, used with permission.

All three versions share some commonalities. While the title *Triumph of the Innocents* suggests that the victims of the massacre are the focal point, at the center is the Holy Family: Joseph is stepping over a placid shallow stream, carrying the load on his back, reining a donkey carrying Mary with the Christ child in her arms, with a colt close behind. According to Hunt himself, Joseph's face is turned away, vigilantly watching distant signal fires and signs of pursuing soldiers.[39] But the other two are smiling with the mother's attention on the infant.

Apparitions of the massacred infants are all around the Holy Family, taking the lead, the rear, or the flank. Gradually and in varying degrees, the infants experience the resurrection, the fruit of martyrdom, with more angelic babes on the left and the more corporeal ones on the right. A group of babes (three in the UK versions and eight in Harvard), progressively awaking to new life levitate behind Christ.[40] A group of nine (one is partially obscured in the UK versions but clearly seen in the Harvard one) is fully awake and follows the donkey on the ground in a semicircle, their arms locked together and adorned in floral adornments. A lone child flanks Mary and Christ, dressed in white inspecting a tear in his garment where the deathblow landed. Finally, another group of three take the lead in front of Joseph, with one of them holding palms and dressed in white. Also near the ground are magnified water globes that arise from

strove for "a conscious emulation of early Italian art" (fourteenth and fifteenth century; hence their name "Pre-Raphaelite Brotherhood"). Allen Staley, *The Pre-Raphaelite Landscape*, 2nd ed. (New Haven: Yale University Press, 2001), 1–2, 73.

[39] Wiliam H. Hunt, *The Triumph of the Innocents* (London: R. Clay, 1885), 3.
[40] Ibid., 4.

the stream, the largest one dimly reflecting Jacob's ladder (Gen 28:10-19), a symbol of the millennial hope of God's heavenly kingdom on earth.[41]

While the flight to Egypt is the foundation for this painting, the innocents literally shine in triumph. The artist has removed the infants from scenes of bloodbath to place them together with the Holy Family in their journey to Egypt. Hunt explains to his friend William Bell Scott that he avoided depicting the babes as angels and preferred to designate them as figures in a vision of Mary, who "sees the glory of their new birth."[42] The painter envisioned that she would with closer inspection receive consolation that these infants are indeed the victims of the recent massacre in their supernatural effulgence.[43]

There is also an important Christological and theodical message in *The Triumph of the Innocents*. The presence of the colt alongside the mother donkey likely anticipates Matthew's version of Christ's entry into Jerusalem and foreshadows the Passion. In the two UK versions, Christ looks behind him with a wheat sheaf in his hand and an amused gaze intent on a number of infants behind him. The sheaf, which symbolizes the Eucharist, readily identifies the centrally located babe as the Bread of Life.[44] Just as Pietro Testa's painting foreshadows Christ's sacrifice with a cross on a boat, Hunt does the same with the wheat sheaf in Jesus's hand. Christ survives the massacre to die for the innocents.

IV. Herod as Symbol of Evil

Herod's leading role in the massacre has led to speculation about his motives, often substantiated by materials from Josephus or other extra-biblical sources (see Chapter 3, VII). Besides historical-grammatical concerns, earlier chapters traced how interpreters placed the blame on Herod, not God (see Chapter 3, IV). They also saw supernatural forces standing behind Herod or Herod symbolically standing for earthly rulers (see Chapter 3, VI and VIII, respectively). The latter reading is an instance of actualization, in which the text functions as "a lens through which one can see one's own situation afresh."[45] Similar interpretative strategies appear in the visual reception history.

A. Gallic Sarcophagus at St. Maximin

According to an eleventh-century legend first mentioned in documents from the Abbey of Vézelay, Mary Magdalene, Martha, Lazarus, their servant Marcella, and Maximin, one of the seventy-two disciples, fled persecution in Palestine to preach the gospel to

---

[41] Ibid., 10–11.
[42] William Minto, ed., *Autobiographical Notes of the Life of William Bell Scott and Notices of His Artistic and Poetic Circle of Friends, 1830 to 1882*, 2 vols. (London: Osgood, McIlvaine, 1892), 2:228–9.
[43] Ibid., 2:229.
[44] John P. Lenox, "The Triumph of the Innocents," *The Biblical World* 11 (1898): 45.
[45] Kovacs and Rowland, *Revelation*, 9–10.

the Gauls.[46] Their efforts led to the founding of a community of believers, named after Maximin (Saint-Maximin-la-Sainte-Baume, France), but the discovery of a tomb there on December 9, 1279, purported to be Mary Magdalene's gave her priority above all others.[47] The crypt, located under a basilica, contains four marble sarcophagi.

One of these sarcophagi, by an anonymous artist, originates from the early fifth century and its relief carvings depict two scenes from Matthew 2 symmetrically: the massacre and the adoration of the magi.[48] Each scene contains four adults. On the right side, three magi bring gifts in their hands, almost identical in posture as they approach the infant Jesus in the manger, surrounded by animals. The first magus is looking behind his back, as if to lead the other two. Above the child is the star and sitting behind him is Mary, hand on her chin, as if contemplating the event unfolding before her. On the left side, two soldiers approach Herod's throne with babes in their hands. The first one is poised to throw the child overhead, while the second still has the infant near his chest. The fourth adult is a mother whose hands are empty but folded around her chest in agony. Herod is seated but points a finger close to the first soldier.

This early artwork communicates some key motifs in the visual exegesis of Matt 2:16-18. First, as Gertrud Schiller says, "this juxtaposition represents the antithesis between the false and the true kings," Herod and Jesus, respectively.[49] While the latter receives noble gifts worthy of a king, the former accepts lives gored on his behalf. Justin Martyr, Irenaeus of Lyons, and Jerome all speak of the rivalry between the kings Jesus and Herod, both vying for the magi's loyalty (Chapter 3, III). Also, the contrast between the magi's piety and Herod's wickedness is in the sermons of Optatus and Augustine (Chapter 3, VI. B and VIII. F).

More can be said about other aspects not found in such extant written works. For example, the contemplative posture of Mary contrasts well with Herod's violent and tyrannical gesture. Since both are seated at the extremes of their respective frame, the artist may have intended these two figures to represent two kinds of passions: one vehemently opposed to Christ's rule and the other reflecting positively upon it. This contrast between Herod and Mary is not attested elsewhere in the reception history, likely due to Mary's passive role in the Matthean infancy narratives.

Also, Herod's distance from the massacre is also visually close. Matthew 2:16 is silent about soldiers bringing the victims before Herod while a bereaved woman follows them. The context of Matthew 2 suggests that Herod gives this command from Jerusalem and the dispatched soldiers carry out the deed in Bethlehem and nearby areas. But the artist foregoes historical congruity and tolerates anachronism for moral

---

[46] By the thirteenth century, "there is an alarming confusion of versions of the voyage of our saint." Jean Misrahi, "A Vita Sanctae Mariae Magdalenae (B.H.L. 5456) in an Eleventh-Century Manuscript," *Speculum* 18 (1943): 335–6.
[47] See full discussion in Katherine L. Jansen, *The Making of the Magdalen: Preaching and Popular Devotion in the Later Middle Ages* (Princeton: Princeton University Press, 2001).
[48] For a discussion of relief carvings on sarcophagi and their importance in pre-Constantine and early Christian art history, see Robin M. Jensen, *Understanding Early Christian Art* (London: Routledge, 2000), 12.
[49] Schiller, *Iconography of Christian Art*, 1:115.

emphasis: the order and the execution are synchronized so that the final depiction clearly communicates Herod's responsibility. Herod's finger shows the origin of this evil. The blame belongs to the one pointing the finger, a frequently revisited visual motif in reception history.[50]

B. Tympanum on the Northern Façade of the *Notre-Dame de Paris*

The Cathedral of Paris (also known as *Notre-Dame de Paris*), a massive project that took about eighty-five years to complete (*ca.* 1160–1245), is monumental in Gothic architecture for several reasons, including its sheer gigantism and the earliest usage of flying buttresses.[51] In relation to the massacre's reception history, the thirteenth-century tympanum on its northern façade includes the scene in stone relief.[52] As in earlier works, soldiers are executing the command of the enthroned king. Here, however, they are dressed in chain mail of the thirteenth century, not tunics of antiquity. The artist is likely attempting to actualize the text in present circumstances.[53] One of the two mothers is on her knees with her child, begging a soldier for mercy and grasping the blade with her hands.[54]

Finally, Herod has a small demon at his ear. This creature distinguishes this French work from others. The idea that Satan is behind Herod's massacre is not new, but appears as early as Origen (see Chapter 3, VI) and in more recent works of Oecumenius and John of Euobea (see Chapter 4, IV). Though Herod is commonly said to be the devil's pawn, here the demon takes the role of a subordinate advisor, a depiction less subtle than the mere finger pointing of Herod.[55] The sculptor provides insights into the spiritual realm and still communicates that Herod is the main culprit.

---

[50] See Appendix C. The illuminated manuscript Book of Hours (*ca.* 1460) currently in the Euing Collection at the University of Glasgow shows Herod's advisor pointing instead.
[51] Caroline Bruzelius, "The Construction of Notre-Dame in Paris," *Art Bulletin* 69:4 (1987): 540–69.
[52] Schiller, *Iconography of Christian Art*, 1:116.
[53] Similarly, Hans Memling in his painting stages the massacre in a medieval town. Ibid.
[54] See also the initial C in a French breviary (*ca.* 1320–5) currently at the J. Paul Getty Museum, Los Angeles; Giusto di Giovanni Menabuoi's fresco in the baptistery of the cathedral in Padua (*ca.* 1370); Fra Angelico's tempera on wood (*ca.* 1451–3) currently at the Museo di San Marco, Florence; Ludovico Mazzolino's oil painting (*ca.* 1510–30) currently at the Rijksmuseum, Amsterdam; and Jacopo Robusti Tintoretto's oil painting on canvas (*ca.* 1582–7) currently at the Scuola Grande di San Rocco, Venice; Aegidius Sadeler's engraving (*ca.* 1580–1629) currently at the Rijkmuseum, Amsterdam; Pacecco de Rosa's oil painting on canvas (*ca.* 1640) currently at the Philadelphia Museum of Art; Peter Paul Rubens's two paintings. In Hendrik Goltzius's unfinished engraving (*ca.* 1584) currently at the Museum of Fine Arts, Boston, a man is seen grasping a dagger's blade while shielding a mother from a soldier.
[55] Like the designer of the tympanum, other artists attempt to depict the demonic influences that lay behind Herod's order. They do so through their design of the throne. Among the forty-six full-page pictures in a fourteenth-century English Psalter currently at St. John's College, University of Cambridge, the illustration of the massacre shows a distraught Herod seated on a throne that appears to be animated and alive. It has the hairy legs of a beast and hand rests formed of a monster's head that delights in the carnage. A similar idea is found in Giovanni Pisano's Pisa pulpit which shows Herod supported by a chaotic mob scene and the first and second Sienese paintings of Matteo di Giovanni where the hand rests' design is that of a sphinx's head (see B and C below).

C. Giovanni Pisano's Pulpits

One must return to Pisano's two pulpits to discuss Herod. In a panel of the Pistoia pulpit, the king's enthroned position at the top right-hand corner parallels Mary's position in the adoration scene in the second panel, similar to the juxtaposition of the adoration and the massacre in the Gallic sarcophagus at St. Maximin (IV. A).[56] His outstretched arm is a familiar sight, but it looks limp, perhaps reflective of his anxiety, and his countenance betrays his uncertainty (Figure 3).[57]

The king's highly elevated position, however, differs from most other depictions of the massacre and may have influenced Pisano's peers. For example, Herod executes the order from a nearby tower in Giotto's fresco cycle of the life of Christ at the middle tier of the south wall of the Scrovegni Chapel at Padua (*ca.* 1304–6) and the Basilica of St. Francis of Assisi (*ca.* 1310s).[58] Duccio di Buoninsegna's painted panel on the front of the Maestà altarpiece (*ca.* 1308–11) also elevates Herod above the action. Many other later artists also follow this technique.[59]

Pisano, however, adds some interesting nuances. The panel lacks a central focal point but depicts the massacre as an irreversible chaos unleashed by Herod. All around, violence has commenced: Herod's men are carrying out the command all over the panel with only a few advisors near the throne; mothers are begging for mercy and protecting their babes, and some grieve for the dead while others attempt to protect their young. Unlike most artworks up to this point, the mothers, the victims, the soldiers are not neatly grouped together by class, occupying distinct positions in the scene. Amorphous mass violence fills the panel from corner to corner and top to bottom, lacking symmetry or tactical formation. Many other later works follow this method of presentation.[60] Such pictorial presentation of disorder and turmoil is comparable to the written exegesis of Gregory of Nyssa, Prudentius, and others (Chapter 3, IX. A).

Similarly, the Pisa version depicts the massacre as an unleashed "wild carnage," with a "multiplicity of figures and dramatic presentation" (Figure 5).[61] Herod again occupies a throne near the top, with his hand stretched outward with some uncertainty. He appears largely unaware of the mayhem under and around his throne, initiated at his behest. This placement of Herod and resulting ignorance of the violence at his eye level somewhat absolves the tyrant, but the resulting damage is tremendous: mothers protest and weep over their children as the soldiers execute the command. Similar disorder characterizes the preceding panel that combines the presentation in the temple with Joseph's dream warning and Herod's plot (Matt 2:13-15).

This pulpit, however, showcases some developments in Pisano's craft since Pistoia. Herod's seat is comparatively more distinct and looms over the smaller figures involved in the massacre. Underneath it is a stocky administrator who carries out Herod's desire. The uncompassionate indifference of this servant is readily apparent, as his back is

---

[56] Lubbock, *Storytelling in Christian Art from Giotto to Donatello*, 108.
[57] Ibid., 110.
[58] Ibid.
[59] See Appendix C.
[60] Ibid.
[61] Schiller, *Iconography of Christian Art*, 1:116.

Figure 5 Giovanni Pisano "Pisa Pulpit," *ca.* 1297–1301, Massacre of the Innocents, relief from the pulpit. Photo credit: Scala/Art Resource NY, used with permission.

turned away from a soldier about to deliver a death blow and he has no remorse for the mother in front of him, vainly attempting to fight off a soldier. The seven advisors at Herod's eye level may symbolize the apparent perfect (as seven is the number of perfection) stability of his royal throne, but its unsteady foundation is evident from its tilt, Herod's uneven posture, and the violent movements of his subjects below.[62] The overall effect is that Herod's own evil actions undermine and undo him.

D. Matteo di Giovanni's Sienese Paintings

Matteo di Giovanni (*ca.* 1435–1495) was a prolific artist born in Borgo Sansepolcro, exceptional among his contemporaries, although there are very few historical references to him.[63] The massacre in particular captivated the artist, as the existence of four depictions prove, three for Sienese churches (1481-2) and one for the pavement of the Duomo as an inlaid stone (1481).[64] Some familiar and common features unite all four works: Herod sits elevated on a throne with his finger directing the butchery

---

[62] Ibid., 136.
[63] Keith Christiansen, Laurence B. Kanter, and Carl B. Strehlke, *Painting in Renaissance Siena: 1420-1500* (New York: Metropolitan Museum of Art, 1988), 270.
[64] *Art in Tuscany*, accessed April 24, 2018, http://www.travelingintuscany.com/art/matteodigiovanni.htm.

(Appendix C) amidst the chaotic outbreak of the massacre, akin to Pisano's pulpit (see IV. B. above).

While the marble floor mosaic conventionally depicts the ideas above, the three church compositions are exceptional for their actualizations of the text with respect to the xenophobia of Giovanni's times. To be specific, when seen in chronological order, the three church artworks reveal a progression of "the contemporary fears of Muslim expansion, made especially pressing by the Turkish fleet's destruction of Oranto only two years earlier."[65] On July 28, 1480, the Ottoman statesman Gedik Ahmed Pascha and some eighteen thousand men landed on the shores of Apulia in southern Italy and headed toward Oranto burning and looting along the way. Unequipped for a siege and with reinforcements too far away, the city fell by August 2 and the Turks occupied it for over a year.[66] Various legends have developed from this invasion, including reports of mass slaughter, Pascha's offer to spare life in exchange for conversion to Islam, and martyrdom.[67] While the veracity of these accounts has been questioned, the fear of a complete takeover was alarmingly real as the Turks captured key portions of Apulia.[68]

Such terror is palpable in Giovanni's artistry: (1) the skin and hair color differences between the aggressors (Herod and his men) and the victims (mothers and the infants), (2) Herod's imposing size, and (3) Giovanni's choice of the tyrant's monarchial headgear (Figure 6). First, Herod and his men are not only distinguishable from the victims because of their weapons, garb, and menacing looks but also their swarthy appearance. Secondly, in some cases, even while sitting, Herod is disproportionally large, compared with other characters (about twice as tall in the first two paintings).[69] While Herod is very frequently marked off by appearance and posture, he does not appear as gigantic in most other works.[70] The natural result is that details like his face are amplified. While artists usually enlarge the sizes of important positive beings like Jesus and Mary, here Herod's monstrosity is stressed.[71]

---

[65] Laura Jacobus, "Motherhood and Massacre: The Massacre of the Innocents in Late-Medieval Art and Drama," in *The Massacre in History*, ed. Mark Leven and Penny Roberts, 39–54 (New York: Bergahn, 1999), 52–3.

[66] Nancy Bisaha, *Creating East and West: Renaissance Humanists and the Ottoman Turks* (Philadelphia: University of Pennsylvania Press, 2004), 157–8.

[67] Ibid., 158. Biasha nonetheless concludes that these stories are likely fictional. She gathers this from earliest contemporary sources and the silence of humanists and preachers who would have undoubtedly seized on the opportunity to speak about such an awful and inspiring account of cruelty and courage.

[68] Ibid., 158–9.

[69] In the first and second paintings, the throne's hand rest also has a sphinx décor. See discussion of a similar depiction in IV. A above.

[70] Herod in the detail of the St. Michael's altarpiece at the Church of St. Nicholas in Burgos, Spain (*ca.* 1163), is one of the few examples where the tyrant dwarfs and marginalizes everyone else. In this work, Herod is seated at the center with the massacre taking place all around him. Most other works are more realistic in their presentation. In fact, Matteo di Giovanni's contemporary, Bernardino Jacopi Butinone (*ca.* 1450–1510) presents Herod in the background (though slightly elevated) in his tempera on poplar panel. Though he sits at the center of the painting in his royal regalia, his size is smaller than the soldiers and the mothers at the forefront.

[71] See, for example, the relatively larger sizes of Jesus in the ivory Magdeburg Panel depicting the raising of the widow's son from the dead (*ca.* 962–8, currently at the British Museum, London) and the Virgin Mary in the front panel of Duccio di Buoninsegna's tempera and gold on wood altarpiece Maestà (*ca.* 1308–11, currently at Siena Cathedral).

Figure 6 *Massacre of the Innocents*, Matteo di Giovanni, 1482, Museo Nazionale di Capodimonte. Source: The Yorck Project (2002), *10.000 Meisterwerke der Malerei* (DVD-ROM), distributed by Directmedia Publishing GmbH.

Thirdly and perhaps most importantly, the clear difference between the first painting of Herod (Figure 6) and the second one (Figure 7) is the change from a plain crown to an oriental turban, reflecting the fear of Turks.[72] In addition, Herod's face has been transformed into that of Pascha or the Sultan Mehmed II himself.[73] Giovanni's actualization is unmistakable in this artistic decision. The third painting differs from the second only in this respect: Herod donning a turban sits at the center above the fray, not at the right side.[74] The cumulative effect of these three artistic choices is one of menacing terror. In the backdrop of these details are contemporary Italian architecture, landscape, flooring, and people that further reinforce the dire message to the locals: the invaders are here and they are a threat to life.[75]

---

[72] Jacobus, "Motherhood and Massacre," 52–3.
[73] David Kunzle, "Spanish Herod, Dutch Innocents: Bruegel's *Massacres of the Innocents* in Their Sixteenth-Century Political Contexts," *Art History* 24:1 (2001): 56–7.
[74] For other images of Herod donning a turban, see Appendix C. Whether they, like Matteo di Giovanni, are actualizing a contemporary fear of foreigners is more difficult to ascertain.
[75] Kunzle, "Spanish Herod, Dutch Innocents," 56–7.

Figure 7 Matteo di Giovanni, "Massacre of the Innocents," Palazzo Pubblico, Siena, Italy. Photo credit: Scala/Art Resource, NY, used with permission.

Giovanni was not the first to combine factors as diverse as Matt 2:16-18 and political/ethnical struggles together. His caricature of Turkish authority is not far from the reading strategy of the early church figure Lucifer of Cagliari, who saw the pro-Arian Emperor Constantius as Herod the Great (see Chapter 3, VIII. C). But beyond the ruling figure(s), Giovanni vilifies an entire people group in the same way Hilary of Poitiers did with the Jews (see Chapter 3, VIII. B). At the same time, these late-fifteenth-century Italian pictorial works do offer more commentary on clashes of international politics and ideologies. While earlier struggles were largely doctrinal, Giovanni's actualization takes on a grander scale with warring nations of opposing religions: Christian Italy versus the Muslim Turks. Such bold political statements foreshadow the works of Pieter Bruegel the Elder and Peter Paul Rubens (see V. D, F, and VII. B.).

V. Victims as Martyrs

Commonplace in the massacre's reception history in all media (verbal or visual) is the depiction of the victims as martyrs. In art, this motif recurs in innovative ways that reflect the biblical knowledge, imagination, and historical contexts of artists, patrons, and theological advisors.

A. Triumphal Arch of *Basilica di Santa Maria Maggiore* in Rome

The *Basilica di Santa Maria Maggiore* in Rome (432–440) is significant for several reasons. First, its fifth-century mosaics represent the oldest surviving plan of Christian church mosaic decoration.[76] Secondly, the building has a political-religious purpose. In the fifth century, after power veered east, paganism was censured, and Alaric sacked Rome, Sixtus III endeavored to promote the religious primacy of Rome through various means, including the building of the basilica as a visible symbol of papal authority.[77]

This hegemony not only extends over paganism but also Christological dissensions. Another possible underlying motive for the construction was to promulgate the Council of Ephesus' (431) declaration of the Virgin Mary as *Theotokos*.[78] At the top left portion of the triumphal arch, an unfolding scene clearly elevates the Virgin: angels surround Mary, enthroned and adorned in empress' garments with a pigeon representing the Holy Spirit descending upon her while Joseph stands some distance away from her in ordinary clothes, with three angels between him and the Virgin.

On another front, the basilica also has a triumphal message over Judaism.[79] OT scenes outnumber NT and fill the nave mosaics. The inclusion and subordination of OT key characters in NT scenes signals both fulfillment and supersession caused by the incarnation: Sarah and Abraham are at Joseph's and Mary's betrothal while David and Isaiah greet the infant Christ, in accordance with the fulfillment tenor of Matthew (1:1, 2, 6, 17, 20, 22-23). Covenants, promises, and prophecies belong not to the triumphant Christianity, not the increasingly marginalized Jews.

The mosaic depicting the massacre does not detract from this overall exultant theme. It is relatively more serene than other artworks since violence has not yet commenced.

---

[76] Margaret R. Miles, "Santa Maria Maggiore's Fifth-Century Mosaics: Triumphal Christianity and the Jews," *HTR* 86 (1993): 155.

[77] Ibid., 155–6.

[78] David M.Gwynn, "Archaeology and 'the Arian Controversy' in the Fourth Century," in *Religious Diversity in Late Antiquty*, ed. David M. Gwynn and Susanne Bangert, 229–64 (Boston: Leiden, 2010), 235.

[79] During their reign, Emperor Theodosius II and co-emperor Valentinian III commissioned *Codex Theodosianus* (438–9), a compilation of Roman Empire rules under Christian Emperors since 312 to impose Christianity as the official religion and undermine heretics and rival religions, like Judaism. So then, if Theodosius II's decree is a direct rhetorical attack on Jewish public life, the art of *Santa Maria Maggiore* is a stealthy hermeneutical siege on their Scriptures. The unfolding drama of the OT history culminates at the triumphal arch, with a throne at its center and nativity scenes all around it. On the left from top to bottom are the annunciation to Joseph and Mary; their betrothal; the Epiphany, the massacre, and the city of Jerusalem. On the right are (top to bottom) presentation in the temple, the flight to Egypt, the magi before Herod, and the city of Bethlehem. William K. Boyd, *The Ecclesiastical Edicts of the Theodosian Code*, Studies in History, Economics, and Public Law 24, no. 2 (New York: Columbia University Press, 1905), 53, esp. n. 1; Miles, "Santa Maria Maggiore's Fifth-Century Mosaics," 156–60. For a discussion of other motifs and themes from apocryphal gospels and sermons found in the presentation in the temple and the adoration of the Magi, see Rainer Warland, "The Concept of Rome in Late Antiquity Reflected in the Mosaics of the Triumphal Arch of S. Maria Maggiore in Rome," *Acta ad archaeologiam et artium historiam pertinentia* 17 (2003): 127–41.

With three spearmen behind him, the seated Herod, uncertainty and apprehension in his face, points toward a soldier between him and a crowd of mothers with their children. The Roman clothing of the persecutors may reflect the vain attempts of earlier emperors to extinguish Christianity, logging another victory for the religion in the triumphant arch.[80] The very placement of nativity scenes involving Herod (namely the massacre and the magi before Herod) at the third level down from the top where it is inscribed, "Sixtus, the bishop to the people of God" (*Sixtus Episcopus plebi Dei*), indicates the papal primacy over earthly rulers.

The women and the children on the right side also reinforce the motif of Christian triumph. Though the women's hair is disheveled, their expressions are serene, with several pairs of eyes gazing upward to heaven. A small cross, the sign of the early ritual of baptism, marks a child's forehead. This sign confirms his seal of martyrdom and baptism with blood.[81] The mosaic artist(s) under Sixtus III depict(s) pictorially what fourth- and fifth-century homilists like Chromatius and Peter Chrysologus have asserted with words: the victims are rightfully innocent saints destined for heaven.[82]

B. Ivory Plaques from Lorraine or Northeastern France

Ivory plaques from Lorraine or Northeastern France (*ca.* second half of the eleventh century) once covered a gospel book. Ivory was a favored material for early Christian book covers, since it could handle minute detailed artwork and outlast gold, silver, and jeweled counterparts that were fragile and frequently recycled.[83] Display, not protection, was the main function these diptychs, whether they were permanently displayed on the altars, carried regularly in the liturgical procession, or used to prop up the gospel book, with the words on the page facing away from the worshipers.[84] As "a locus for public affirmation of orthodox belief," book covers, despite their names, had greater connection with other more permanent public images (i.e., altar decorations, the cross, etc.) than with the book contents.[85]

At first glance, these plaques do not appear to be significant in the visual reception history of the massacre. On the first panel, Herod sits upon a throne on the left, pointing his finger while helpless women watch soldiers dash their infants to the ground. In the second panel, the women mourn over their dead children. But through gestures and positioning, this artist economically communicates familiar ideas in innovative yet efficient ways. Laura Jacobus observes that in the first panel in which the massacre occurs, two infants suspended in the air have their arms outstretched in a cross

---

[80] Schiller, *Iconography of Christian Art*, 1:115.
[81] Ibid. Another way to mark off the victims as saints and martyrs was to dress them in white. For an example, see the left panel of the Jerusalem Triptych by a Netherlandish or Northern German painter (*ca.* 1497–1500; currently at the National Museum in Warsaw).
[82] See Chapter 3, IX. D and G.
[83] For a full discussion, see John Lowden, "The Word Made Visible: The Exterior of the Early Christian Book as Visual Argument," in *The Early Christian Book*, ed. William E. Klingshirn and Linda Safran, 13–47 (Washington, DC: Catholic University of America Press, 2007).
[84] Ibid., 45.
[85] Ibid., 46–7.

position.⁸⁶ In the split second before their deaths, these children imitate their peer, Christ, who will face the cross as an adult, though he escapes to Egypt in the present. Thus, Herod's slaughter is analogous to the later persecution of Jesus that culminates in the crucifixion, an idea attested as early as Origen (see Chapter 3, VIII. A). The artist, like Pope Leo the Great, also exalts the victims as martyrs as they participate in Christ's suffering as his peers (see Chapter 3, IX. I). A similar depiction also appears on an earlier ivory plaque from Metz (*ca.* mid-ninth century) and in a panel in the twelfth-century Incarnation Window of Chartres Cathedral.⁸⁷ This crucifix pose of the massacre victims was likely a familiar visual motif in northern France.⁸⁸

C. Winchester Psalter

A twelfth-century English illuminated manuscript known as the *Winchester Psalter* contains thirty-eight full-page miniatures, a calendar, the Psalms, the Song of Songs, prayers, and creeds. Its patron is likely Henry of Blois, Bishop of Winchester from 1129 to 1171.⁸⁹ It was probably intended for private usage at a Benedictine priory.⁹⁰ The exceptional feature of the psalter's miniature of the massacre is not the helpless women or even Herod pointing his guilty finger, but his gigantic male agent on the right side. With a monstrous face, he bites into a child he is simultaneously piercing with a sword.⁹¹ In her iconographical study, Kristine Haney suggests that the picture "evokes contemporary descriptions of the ubiquitous climate of violence during King Stephen's reign."⁹² The Anarchy (the civil war between England and Normandy caused by the rivalry between Stephen of Blois and Empress Matilda), internal revolts, and external invasions led to the breakdown of law and order and the devastation of the populace. The impaled and cannibalized child may represent the many innocents who suffered as a result of this warfare. So then, the gruesome scene is actualized in contemporary atrocities.

It is also credible that this violent image not only defends innocents generally, but children specifically. While English ecclesiastical authorities had long condemned infanticide, secular legislators did not treat it as equal to adult homicide until a law of Henry I (*Leges Henrici Primi*; ca. 1115) came into effect.⁹³ Though centuries

---

⁸⁶ Jacobus, "Motherhood and Massacre," 41.
⁸⁷ Malcolm Miller, Sonia Holladay, and Laura Lushington, *Chartres Cathedral* (New York: Riverside Book, 1997), 34.
⁸⁸ Schiller, *Iconography of Christian Art*, 1:116.
⁸⁹ The internal evidence for that provenance and a date from the first half of the twelfth century include the Psalter's inclusion of feasts connected with the Abbey of Cluny and the absence of the feast of Edward the Confessor, canonized in 1161. Kristine E. Haney, *The Winchester Psalter: An Iconographic Study* (Leicester: Leicester University Press, 1986), 8.
⁹⁰ Kathleen Nolan, "'Ploratus et Ululatus': The Mothers in the Massacre of the Innocents at Chartres Cathedral," *Studies in Iconography* 17 (1996): 105.
⁹¹ The closest parallel to this image is found in Charles LeBrun's oil painting on canvas (*ca.* 1665) currently at the Dulwich Picture Gallery, London. In the painting, a soldier is biting into the shirt of an infant, not his flesh.
⁹² Haney, *The Winchester Psalter*, 35.
⁹³ Mary M. McLaughlin, "Survivors and Surrogates: Children and Parents from the Ninth to the Thirteenth Centuries," in *The History of Childhood*, ed. Lloyd deMause, 101–82 (Oxford: Rowman & Littlefield, 1995), 121.

earlier Charlemagne issued a similar civil ordinance, no widespread condemnation and enforcement followed until after the twelfth century.[94] This visual expression likely reflects an attitudinal change toward children and those who kill them. If many have exalted the infants as martyrs in heaven, the artist of the *Winchester Psalter* has dignified them as full-status humans by vilifying their enemies. Thus, the artist not only repeats familiar past pictorial motifs but also creatively refashions the massacre account through actualization in a context of exaggerated violence.[95]

D. Pieter Brugel the Younger's Copy of the Elder's *The Massacre of the Innocents* in Kunsthistorisches Museum, Vienna

Like Matteo di Giovanni before him (see IV. D), the Flemish artist Pieter Bruegel the Elder (*ca.* 1525–1569) actualized the massacre scene to illustrate his people's plight under foreign occupation. During his fruitful last years, he produced an oil-on-panel painting of the massacre (*ca.* 1567–9) among other works.[96] One of the two surviving paintings of the massacre, the more famous version, in the Kunsthistorisches Museum in Vienna, is now believed to be by Pieter the Younger (*ca.* 1610; Figure 8). Though the other painting in Windsor Castle is the Elder's work, it has been overpainted.[97] A seventeenth-century owner (perhaps Queen Christina of Sweden) wished to replace the gory massacre with a plundering scene.[98] So then, the Younger's copy in Vienna is actually the closest to the original.

The uniqueness of the Viennese version consists in its departure from typical visual representations of Matt 2:16-18. Immediately noticeable is the snowy rural background. Its original composition date is likely *ca.* 1566 since (1) it is related to a group of winter scenes painted by Bruegel, among which is the *Census at Bethlehem* from that year, and (2) the winters in the second half of 1560s were acutely severe.[99] Bruegel's well-known fascination with the bucolic Netherlands, in contrast to the urban architectural background in works of his contemporaries like Maarten van Heemskerck, Frans Floris, and Pieter Vlerick, also emerges in this work.[100]

Beyond reflecting harsh climate conditions and rural peasant life, Bruegel may have intended to convey a subversive message. David Kunzle believes that, along with *The*

---

[94] Ibid., 157–8, n. 108.
[95] Haney, *The Winchester Psalter*, 34–5.
[96] He also traveled to Amsterdam before settling in Brussels, married his old master Pieter Coecke's daughter Mayken, and fathered more painters: Pieter the Younger and Jan. Jan is considered the better of the two, but in relation to the current chapter, Pieter's namesake is more important. The two sons in turn fathered more painters and perpetuated the name of their father through Pieter III and Jan the Younger. Émile Michel and Victoria Charles, *Pieter Bruegel* (New York: Parkstone International, 2012), 6–7, 52.
[97] Kunzle, "Spanish Herod, Dutch Innocents," 60.
[98] There is virtually no information concerning the patrons or earliest owners of these paintings. Ibid.
[99] Ibid.
[100] Larry Silver, *Peasant Scenes and Landscapes: The Rise of Pictorial Genres in the Antwerp Art Market* (Philadelphia: University of Pennsylvania Press, 2006), 161; Kunzle, "Spanish Herod, Dutch Innocents," 65–8. For examples of artists who like Bruegel favored the wintry peasant background, see Gillis Mostaert's two paintings (*ca.* 1554–98) and Lucas van Valckenborch's oil painting on panel (*ca.* 1586) currently at the Thyssen-Bornemisza Museum, Madrid.

Figure 8 Pieter Bruegel the Younger, "Massacre of the Innocents," *ca.* 1565, Kunsthistorisches Museum, Vienna, Austria. Photo credit: Eric Lessing/Art Resource, NY, used with permission.

Census of Bethlehem, The Massacre of the Innocents "surely stood as long-term vehicles of resentment against the Spanish administration, fiscal and military."[101] Spanish occupation of the Netherlands and widespread repression of rebels and heretics were deemed subhuman during the reigns of Charles V (*ca.* 1519–56), his successor Philip II (*ca.* 1556–98), and the local governorship of Margaret of Parma (*ca.* 1559–67). Their rule resulted in many thousands of slaughtered victims and exiles, peaking in the invasion of the Duke of Alba (*ca.* 1567).[102] In the 1560s, appointed inquisitors even overruled local jurisdictions and the traditional rights of the accused, much to the alarm of Netherland elites.[103]

In support of his theory, Kunzle notes that such "confrontational" art was not unprecedented among Bruegel's oeuvres before the *Census at Bethlehem* and the *Massacre of the Innocents*.[104] Furthermore, he points to similar polemical art works by

[101] Kunzle, "Spanish Herod, Dutch Innocents," 60–1.
[102] Ibid., 52–3.
[103] Helmut G. Koenigsberger, *Monarchies, States Generals and Parliaments: The Netherlands in the Fifteenth and Sixteenth Centuries* (Cambridge: Cambridge University Press, 2001).
[104] Svetlana Alpers, *The Making of Rubens* (New Haven: Yale University Press, 1995), 55. For some examples, see Kunzle, "Spanish Herod, Dutch Innocents," 61.

peers: (1) massacre paintings in a Flemish landscape unrelated to Bruegel, (2) various painted scenes of plundering in the countryside, and (3) the increasing popularity of the flight to Egypt and the parable of the good Samaritan as art subjects (evoking memories of exiles and looting victims, respectively) by late-sixteenth-century artists like Hans Bol and Abel Grimmer.[105]

So evidently, Bruegel was not the only subversive artist, although his *Massacre of the Innocents* is comparatively subtle. A less subtle work comes from his contemporary Frans Hogenberg who caricatured the Duke of Alba in a print in which the latter sits on a throne with his distinctive pointy beard, trampling decapitated bodies underfoot, devouring a child in his hand, with Cardinal Antoine Perronot Granvelle joining him in the eating.[106] Playwrights, songwriters, and William I of Orange (also known as William the Silent, *ca.* 1533–1584) had already made the unmistakable connection between Herod and the Duke of Alba and inspired artists like Hogenberg and Bruegel.[107]

The visual details of Bruegel's work further reflect such state of affairs: the imperial insignia on the herald's tabard and men with red coats, the uniform of the *bandes d'ordonnance*.[108] As "aristocratic provincial militias" and the Netherlands' version of the French *gens d'armes*, *bandes d'ordonnance* were infamous for their brutality and were integral to the military until Alba's arrival and the beginning of the Eighty Years War (1568).[109] In the painting, the Spaniards even unleash dogs on the villagers, just as they did with Indians, if one believes the accounts of Bartolomé de las Casas.[110] Bruegel vilifies the enemy through the actualization of Matt 2:16-18, condemning foreign powers and sympathizing with the struggles of the common folk.

E. Guido Reni's *The Massacre of the Innocents*

The influence of Guido Reni (*ca.* 1575–1642) extends beyond his Bologna home, as he became both Pope Paul V Borghese's favorite and Italy's leading painter, eventually rivaling even Raphael.[111] His oil painting on canvas of the massacre (*ca.* 1610–11) currently at the Pinacoteca Nazionale, Bologna, is notable for two reasons (Figure 9).

First is the mother at the center, modeled after the ancient marble sculpture *Niobe* currently at the *Galleria degli Uffizi*, Florence, and sitting on the ground with her hands folded in prayer as the violence swells all around her.[112] Before her are two corpses. Her eyes are turned upward and her lips are parted as if she is addressing God. Her ambiguous enraptured and/or pained countenance is "pivotal in the allure of Reni's art" and familiar in other works that deal not only with martyrdom, but also with suicide,

---

[105] Kunzle, "Spanish Herod, Dutch Innocents," 71–4.
[106] Ibid., 67–9.
[107] Ibid., 67–9, 75–6.
[108] Ibid., 63.
[109] Koenigsberger, *Monarchies, States Generals and Parliaments*, 78; Kunzle, "Spanish Herod, Dutch Innocents, 63.
[110] Kunzle, "Spanish Herod, Dutch Innocents," 69.
[111] Richard E. Spear, *The "Divine" Guido: Religion, Sex, Money and Art in the World of Guido Reni* (New Haven: Yale University Press, 1997), 2.
[112] Ibid., 78.

Figure 9 *Massacre of the Innocents*, Guido Reni, 1611, Pinacoteca Nazionale, Bologna. Source: The Yorck Project (2002), *10.000 Meisterwerke der Malerei* (DVD-ROM), distributed by Directmedia Publishing GmbH.

penance, and ecstasy.[113] John Drury thinks that Reni's painting reflects the constant efforts of religion to unify contradicting forces of pain and pleasure with an underlying unified purpose.[114] So then, the central mother through her expression communicates a twofold message: suffering is indeed terrible but there is ultimate good in directing it to God's purposes.

The other salient feature of this artwork is the heavenly scene that meets the praying mother's gaze. In the blue sky are two cherub angels riding on the clouds, each with sheaves of palms. One of them extends a palm with his left hand as if responding to the central woman. As early as Origen (see Chapter 3, IX. B), the palm has been a typical symbol of martyrdom associated with the innocents. While earlier artists have normally depicted martyrdom through subtler means (e.g., crucifixion pose, see V. A above), Reni clearly adjoins the disaster of earth with the vision of heaven, the prayer of the mother at the center functioning as the bridge.

---

[113] Ibid., 96.
[114] John Drury, *Painting the Word: Christian Pictures and Their Meanings* (New Haven: Yale University Press, 1999), ix–x.

Figure 10 Peter Paul Rubens, "The Massacre of the Innocents," *ca.* 1610, oil on panel. The Thomson Collection at the Art Gallery of Ontario, 2014, © Art Gallery of Ontario.

F. Peter Paul Rubens' Two Paintings Both Named *The Massacre of the Innocents*

So great is the influence of Peter Paul Rubens (*ca.* 1577–1640) that one biographer writes, "In him … the great Renaissance of Flemish art dawned on the horizon."[115] For a long time, a single painting on the massacre bore his authorship (*ca.* 1635–7; currently at Alte Pinakothek, Munich) until Sotheby's art expert George Gordon identified an earlier work (*ca.* 1609–11), previously attributed to Jan van den Hoecke.[116]

The first painting exhibits all of the typical post-Raphael stylistic features of visualizing the massacre: classical architecture in the background with nude soldiers (Figure 10). Due to the influence of Raphael (*ca.* 1483–1520) and later Pieter Bruegel the Elder, a great bifurcation occurred in the visual reception history of the massacre: soldiers are either (1) nude muscular athletes who kill naked babes against a classical architectural

---

[115] Jacob Burckhardt, *Recollections of Rubens* (New York: Phaidon, 1970), 20.
[116] "Unknown Rubens discovered in time for auction," *The Guardian*, February 28, 2002, https://www.theguardian.com/uk/2002/feb/28/2. The exact provenance and the commissioning of the two works are somewhat confusing with sources citing both Antoon Triest (1576–1657), the seventh bishop of Ghent and Anthonio de Tassis (1584–1651), a canon in the Antwerp Cathedral, as patrons. See Sauerländer, 236–8.

Figure 11 Marcantonio Raimondi, "Massacre of the Innocents," *ca.* 1512–13, Rijksmuseum, Amsterdam, used with permission.

backdrop or (2) contemporary men in contemporary settings (the Bruegel strategy; see V. C above).[117] Furthermore, Raphael's successful collaborative engraving project with the Bolognese printmaker Marcantonio Raimondi (currently at the Hermitage Museum, St. Petersburg; ca. 1512–13) incorporated Matt 2:16 with two most often revisited artistic motifs of his era: (1) Leonardo's "depiction of the savagery of war" and (2) Michelangelo's "dynamic mastery of the male nude in action," a common sight in ancient Greek art (Figure 11).[118] The popularity of this work led to increasing numbers of visual works on the massacre from the days of Raphael to the mid-seventeenth century.[119] Rubens follows in this line of influence, though there are fewer nude soldiers in Rubens' later painting.

More importantly, this later version stresses the veneration of the infants as martyrs, especially evident on the left side of the painting (Figure 12). One of the babes, stabbed through the chest, looks in pain toward heaven in the crucifixion pose, a motif of the infants' martyrdom (see V. B above). Furthermore, in the child's direct line of sight, a heavenly scene unfolds in the sky above. Three angels fly in the clear sky, an

---

[117] Kunzle, "Spanish Herod, Dutch Innocents," 57. For examples of other works that depict the soldiers as nude (or close to nude and bare chested) in the Raphaelesque fashion, see Appendix C.
[118] Hugo Chapman, Tom Henry, and Carol Plazzotta, *Raphael: From Urbino to Rome* (London: National Gallery, 2004), 182. For a full discussion of technique, see 244–51.
[119] Sauerländer, *The Catholic Rubens*, 239–42. Also vital to this growth of interest is Giambattista Marino's influential poetic treatise on the same topic, *La Strage degli Innocenti*. See discussion in Chapter 5, II. B.

Figure 12 Peter Paul Rubens, "The Massacre of the Innocents," *ca.* 1635–7, Alte Pinakothek, Bayerische Staatsgemaeldesammlungen, Munich, Germany. bpk Bildagentur/Art Resource, NY, used with permission.

image more prominent in seventeenth-century works indebted to Guido Reni.[120] Yet Rubens distinguishes himself with some key information regarding martyrdom. While Reni and Turchi paint angels hovering over the fray ready to distribute palms and crowns, Rubens's angels carry wreaths of roses and lilies, which symbolize the blood of martyrdom and purity, respectively.[121] Willibald Sauerländer opines that Rubens's use of the floral gifts is an allusion to early Christian works that referred to the children as flowers of martyrdom (see Chapter 3, IX. E).[122]

VI. Mothers as Mourners

The portrayal of bereaved mothers of the infants occurs early in the visual reception history. Their facial expressions, arm posture, and attire all communicate a sorrow that evokes sympathy on the part of the viewers. Some artworks specifically emphasize the mothers' roles as mourners.

---

[120] See Appendix C.
[121] Anca Husti and Maria Cantor, "Sacred Connection of Ornamental Flowers with Religious Symbols," *ProEnvironment Promediu* 8 (2015): 74–5.
[122] Sauerländer, *The Catholic Rubens*, 267–8.

A. The Miniature in the Rabbula Gospels

One of the earliest illuminated biblical manuscripts is the Syriac Rabbula Gospels. Its commissioner is unidentified, but it was produced at the Beth Zagba monastery near Apamea, Syria (*ca.* 586).[123] Doubts, however, persist concerning the exact date and provenance of the accompanying illuminated folios (containing miniatures, Eusebius of Caesarea's letter to Carpianus, Eusebian canon tables adorned with NT vignettes and prophets' portraits, and full-page illustrations) but they are likely contemporaneous with the text.[124] One page includes the Eusebian canon I table 3, containing numbers linked to passages found in all four gospels. On the same page are two miniatures, unrelated to the accompanying numerical information: (1) on the left, the seated Herod commanding the execution with a hand gesture; and (2) on the right, a soldier grasping a child by the ankle while his other hand is poised to strike with a sword, and a mother also grasping the babe's ankle and hurling herself forward in defense of her child (Figure 13). Just above Herod is a depiction of Jesus's baptism and above the massacre is the nativity scene.[125] At the top of the page are David on the left and Solomon on the right.[126]

By splitting the action in Matt 2:16 into two scenes, the struggle for the child's life receives separate attention on one side of the page. With this subtle artistic decision, the illuminator has created a precedent for later artists to follow: devoting separate attention to the mothers at the massacre. For example, ninth-century miniatures in Bishop Drogo's Sacramentary (*ca.* 844–55) does not include Herod at all but instead show a pair of soldiers slaughtering the children; three seated mothers, each dressed

---

[123] Only *The Vienna Genesis* (*ca.* early third of sixth century) and *Codex Purpureus Rossanensis* (*ca.* early or mid-sixth century), both with a possible provenance in Syrian Antioch, precede the Rabbula Gospels. The Rossano book is a gospel book and thus shares similarities with the Rabbula Gospels, but only fragments and fifteen miniatures survive. Ingo F. Walther and Norbert Wolf, *Codices Illustres: The World's Most Famous Illuminated Manuscripts 400–1600* (Köln: Taschen, 2001), 58–63.

[124] David H. Wright, "The Date and Arrangement of the Illustrations in the Rabbula Gospels," *Dumbarton Oaks Papers* 27 (1973): 199–208; Massimo Bernabò, "The Miniatures in the Rabbula Gospels: Postscripta to a Recent Book," *Dumbarton Oaks Papers* 68 (2014): 343–58.

[125] This sequence of images may reflect the chronological order of the Syriac liturgical calendar: (1) Christmas, (2) Feast of the Innocents, and (3) Epiphany. One historian notes, "The Eastern Syrian liturgical calendar is believed to have taken shape at about the beginning of the seventh century, while nothing that survives in the Syrian Orthodox tradition is earlier than the late seventh century." Another possible intention is to contrast the murderous King Herod on the left lower corner with King David, who sits placidly on a more ornate throne at the upper corner on the same side. Clearly the better king is visually "above" and superior to the false one. As for the scholarly Solomon on the right upper left corner and the struggle for the infant at the left bottom, perhaps the king invokes the wise discernment he makes between the two prostitutes concerning the true identity of the baby's mother (1 Kgs 3:16-28). Herod, however, lacks such acuity. There are also similarities between the two events: just as the true mother threw herself before Solomon's sword, the mother reveals her genuine maternity before Herod's sword. Michael G. Morony, "History and Identity in the Syrian Churches," in *Redefining Christian Identity: Cultural Interaction in the Middle East since the Rise of Islam*, ed. J. J. van Ginkel, H. L. Murre-van den Berg, and Theo M. van Lint, 1–34, OLA 134 (Leuven: Uitgeverij Peeters en Departement Oosterse Studies, 2005), 29.

[126] Schiller, *Iconography of Christian Art*, 1:115–16; Massimo Bernabò opines that this overcrowding may indicate a change in commission and/or illuminators. "The Miniatures in the Rabbula Gospels," 354.

Figure 13 "The Rabbula Gospels," Florence, The Biblioteca Medicea Laurenziana, ms. Plut.1.56, f. 4v. Reproduced with permission of MiBACT. Further reproduction by any means is prohibited.

in torn clothes and mourning over a pair of infant corpses on their laps; and another group of dead babes on the ground nearby.[127] The disturbing aftermath of the massacre leaves the mothers in deep anguish: one has her hands around her face; another lifts her right arm into the air; and the third has hers folded around her heart.[128]

B. The Miniature in *Codex Egberti*

Egbert, archbishop of Trier from 977 until his death in 993, and chancellor to Emperors Otto I and Otto II, commissioned a Gospel lectionary from Reichenau's workshop (*ca.*

---

[127] Schiller, *Iconography of Christian Art*, 1:116. The Sacramentary is an exceptional representative of Carolingian art made for the personal use of Drogo, Charlemagne's son and the bishop of Metz. The extensive use of artistic initials is a unique feature of this work, with twenty-nine out of thirty-eight depicting biblical scenes. Charles R. Dodwell, *The Pictorial Arts of the West, 800–1200* (New Haven: Yale University Press, 1995), 60. For other examples of artistic works without Herod, see Appendix C.

[128] Schiller thinks the three mothers allude to Sarah, Rebekah, and Rachel, since Matt 2:18 refers to the last matriarch. *Iconography of Christian Art*, 1:116. See also ivory plaques from Lorraine or Northeastern France (see VI. A and VII. B).

Figure 14 "Codex Egberti," folio 15v, ca. 980, Stadtbibliothek, Trier. Source: The Yorck Project (2002), *10.000 Meisterwerke der Malerei* (DVD-ROM), distributed by Directmedia Publishing GmbH.

980).[129] It contains sixty full-page miniatures illustrating the gospel accounts of Jesus's life, making it the largest pictorial cycle in any manuscript up to this point.[130] The miniaturist is a monk conveniently known as "Gregory master" (*Gregorius meister*), famous for clarity, abstract background, efficient delivery of the narrative, and vivid expression of the figures.[131]

This miniature of the massacre has a simple and spacious background that does not detract from the main central action where the massacre takes place (Figure 14). On the right where the women mourn, Bethlehem looms over the tragic sight.[132] The city resembles a medieval walled town, not a village from antiquity.[133] Herod is on the offensive in a battle, clearly excessive considering his helpless targets.

---

[129] Barbara Baert, "Pentecost and the Senses: A Hermeneutical Contribution to the Visual Medium and the Sensorium in Early Medieval Manuscript Tradition," in *Preaching after Easter: Mid-Pentecost, Ascension, and Pentecost in Late Antiquity*, ed. Richard W. Bishop, Johan Leemans, and Hajnalka Tamas, 346–70 (Leiden: Brill, 2013), 350.

[130] Christoper de Hamel, *A History of Illuminated Manuscripts*, 2nd rev. ed. (London: Phaidon, 1994), 58.

[131] Baert, "Pentecost and the Senses," 350.

[132] The identity of the city is confirmed by the Latin word written near the image: *BETHLEEM*. Over Herod is *HERODES* and the children are *PUERI OCCIDUNTUS*.

[133] For examples of similar interpretative filling, see Appendix C.

The illustration includes familiar details: Herod in his royal regalia with his guardsmen on the left, the commissioned soldiers meeting the victims in the middle, and the grieving mothers on the right. One swordsman has grasped a child's wrist and is poised to strike. One mother reaches out her hands to a child who mimics her hand motions, but his head is turned toward an approaching attacker. Another mother has her back turned away from the gore, covering her face with her hands.

The miniature, however, departs from other works mentioned thus far in several ways. Herod is outside his throne room, standing with legs crossed and leaning upon a staff while pointing toward his foes, soldiers deploy swords and spears to attack the babes, whose wounds discharge blood, and some mothers mourn with disheveled hair and bare chests.[134] Schiller believes some of the women in the scene are not mothers but ceremonial mourners accompanying them, but another possibility is that a progression is in view.[135] First, among two fully clothed mothers one is trying to save her child while another turns away, unable to look. Two other mothers have begun their ceremonial mourning, stripping their head coverings and their dresses. Various stages of the mourning correspond to the multiple stages of the massacre action, as some children already lie dead, others dying, and still others just at the brink of death. Like the miniature in the Rabbula Gospels (see VI. A above), greater attention to the victims and their mothers results in a broader range of emotions.

C. Ivory Plaques from Lorraine or Northeastern France

The second panel of the ivory plaque (see V. B.) from Lorraine or northeastern France subtly yet creatively exhibits interpretations known in textual counterparts. For example, the artist chose to concretize the idea of Jer 31:15 in a separate space for the grieving women.[136] Like the miniature in *Codex Egberti* above (see VI. B. above), several women mourn their dead in this second panel, but there is one central grieving woman, who likely represents the matriarch Rachel, surrounded by others who vainly attempt consolation.[137]

While a depiction of a bereaved mother with a corpse on her lap is not unprecedented, its centrality here is striking for two reasons.[138] First, thus far in the reception history the artistic strategy to focus on one child's death and one mother's grief is generally uncommon until Nicolas Poussin (see VI. D below). Secondly, just as the young victims in the first panel foreshadow the crucifixion with their pose, Rachel here anticipates the grief to come for Mary. These ideas directly parallel the medieval plays from Limoges, Freising and Fleury (see Chapter 4, X. F and G).

---

[134] For other images of Herod outside of his throne room, see Appendix C.
[135] Schiller, *Iconography of Christian Art*, 1:116.
[136] Jacobus, "Motherhood and Massacre," 41.
[137] See also an oil painting on canvas attributed to Jean-Baptiste Marie Pierre (*ca.* 1763) in which a woman is attempting to help a bereaved mother who may have stabbed herself in the chest.
[138] Though a genealogical dependence is difficult to assume, perhaps it anticipates a later subject in Christian art, the *Pietà* in which the Virgin holds the lifeless Christ on her lap. Ibid.

D. North Frieze of Chartres Cathedral

Chartres Cathedral or the *Cathédrale Notre-Dame de Chartres* is a World Heritage Site that houses the famous twelfth-century stained glass windows and the veil of Mary (*Sancta Camisa*).[139] In the north frieze of its west portal (also known as the Royal Portal, *ca*. 1140), which contains several infancy narrative episodes such as the adoration of the magi and the flight to Egypt, the massacre scene occupies three large and three small historiated capitals.[140] Taking up more space than any other single episode in the frieze, the high number of victimized mothers in this visualization, and the variety of their interactions with the children, make this work worthy of comment.[141] In its grand scale and attention to the massacre, it is similar to the contemporary work on the south portal of Le Mans Cathedral dedicated to St. Julian, also in Northern France, where seven of its forty-two self-contained voussoirs (wedged-shaped or tapered stones used in the construction of an arch) depict individual murders that collectively make up the massacre (*ca*. 1150).[142]

Kathleen Nolan attempts to explain the reason for this disproportional amount of interest in the massacre. She rejects the notions that the frieze artist mostly reflected the nearby public violence of the twelfth century (in reality it was relatively pacific compared to the thirteenth century).[143] Instead, she believes the primary motivation originates with the cult of the Virgin of Chartres. The Virgin was believed to have special compassion and affinity for suffering mothers. More cures of children are attributed to the Virgin of Chartres than to the Virgins of other pilgrimage sites, such as Rocamadour (6 out 126, about 5 percent).[144] In preexisting Chartres traditions that record her miracles, seven of thirty-two accounts (about 22 percent) deal with a mother's anguish, violent death of a child, prayers to the Virgin, and the child's restoration.[145] Indeed, the Virgin of Chartres appears as a sympathetic savior and advocate of children and mothers.

Also contributing to this local preoccupation with maternal love are the Marian sermons and liturgical works of Bishop Fulbert of Chartres (*ca*. 970–1028). Combined with the local cultic material, they invite the laity of the city not only to revere past saints but also to partake in suffering and live godly lives.[146] The experience of the bereaved

---

[139] For further background information, see Miller, Holladay, and Lushington, *Chartres Cathedral*, 24–41.
[140] Ibid., 27.
[141] Nolan, "Ploratus et Ululatus," 95; Margot E. Fassler, *The Virgin of Chartres: Making History through Liturgy and the Arts* (New Haven: Yale University Press, 2010), 298–9.
[142] Ibid., 114–19.
[143] Ibid., 119–22. *Contra* Fassler and Rachel Dressler, who believe the work reflects contemporary liturgical dramas, the cruelties of King Louis VII, and denunciation of Muslims. *The Virgin of Chartres*, 299; Rachel Dressler, "Deus Hoc Vult: Ideology, Identity and Sculptural Rhetoric at the Time of the Crusades," *Medieval Encounters* 1 (1995): 188–218.
[144] Nolan, "'Ploratus et Ululatus,'" 122–4.
[145] See miracles 6–9, 13, 16, and 19 in Jean le Marchant, *Miracles de Notre-Dame de Chartres*, ed. Pierre Kunstmann (Ottawa: University of Ottawa Press, 1973), 94–111, 127–31, 140–4, and 151–4.
[146] Tennyson Wellman, "Apocalyptic Concerns and Mariological Tactics in Eleventh-Century France," in *The Year 1000: Religious and Social Response to the Turning of the First Millennium*, ed. Michael Frassetto Palgrave, 133–163 (New York: Macmillan, 2002), 136–40; Fassler, *The Virgin of Chartres*, 316–18; "Fulbert, St.," in *ODCC*, 648–9.

mothers in Matt 2:16-18 therefore also connects to the struggles and piety of medieval motherhood. The sundry suffering women depicted in the frieze allow beholders to access the shared experience of suffering and hope in the Virgin of Chartres.

E. Nicolas Poussin's *The Massacre of the Innocents* in Chantilly

Nicolas Poussin (*ca.* 1594–1665) is considered to be "the father of French painting."[147] His surviving works consist of nearly 220 paintings and 400 drawings on the Bible, ancient history, and mythology.[148] In the 1620s, he formed crucial relationships with the poet Giovanni Battista Marino in Paris and Cardinal Francesco Barberini, who employed Cassiano dal Pozzo.[149] Eventually the cardinal took interest in Poussin's artistry and around this time two oil paintings on canvas of the massacre emerged. The authenticity of the first one in the Musée du Petit Palais in Paris is questioned but the later one in the Musée Condé, Chantilly is accepted without reservations.[150]

The Chantilly version focuses on one main struggle involving a bare-chested soldier (a depiction owing to the influence of Raphael), one mother, and her baby (Figure 15).[151] Poussin's artistic decision to emphasize a single act of massacre is less chaotic in presentation and as a result more focused on conveying strong individual suffering. Poussin was certainly capable of conveying widespread mayhem to accomplish "a pathos of death and violence," as in *The Plague of Ashdod* completed just a few years later (*ca.* 1630–1).[152] That OT work depicts masses of people tending to their dead. In this NT massacre, however, only one impending death occupies the space, confronting the viewers with the intense emotions of the child and his mother just before the fatal blow.[153] Through Poussin's influence later artists will return to the simplicity and neatness found in earlier visualizations prior to Pisano and foreground the emotions of few mothers and victims.[154]

VII. Vindicated Mothers

While a scene with weeping mothers is not difficult to imagine from reading Matt 2:16-18, another more striking idea emerges in its visual reception history that garners attention: vindicated mothers. Either the unarmed bereaved mothers seek to

---

[147] Richard Verdi, *Nicolas Poussin 1594–1665* (London: Zwemmer, 1995), 16.
[148] Ibid.
[149] Ibid., 11–12.
[150] David Carrier, *Poussin's Paintings: A Study in Art-Historical Methodology* (University Park: Pennsylvania State University Press, 1993), 100, n. 79.
[151] Verdi, *Nicolas Poussin 1594–1665*, 147.
[152] Louis Marin, *Sublime Poussin*, trans. Catherine Porter, Meridian: Crossing Aesthetics (Stanford: Standford University Press, 1999), 146–7.
[153] Schiller, *Iconography of Christian Art*, 1: 117.
[154] See Appendix C. That is not to say that great emotional distress cannot be expressed in background characters. For example, in Julius Schnorr von Carolsfeld's illustration in the *Picture Bible* (*ca.* 1860), a woman in the distance appears to reach forward to the edge of a building while another woman attempts to restrain her.

Visual Interpretations of Massacre of Innocents 197

Figure 15 Nicolas Poussin, "The Massacre of the Innocents," *ca.* 1625. Photo credit: Michel Urtado, © RMN-Grand Palais/Art Resource, NY, used with permission.

immediately avenge their loss as they fight the soldiers with their hands, nails, and/or teeth, or they seek vengeance from heaven.

A. *St. Albans Psalter* of Christina of Markyate

Christina (*ca.* 1097–1161), the daughter of a rich guild merchant of Huntingdon, took a vow of chastity during her visit to St. Albans Abbey and eventually settled in Markyate as an influential hermit, prioress, needlewoman, and possible owner of the famous *St. Albans Psalter*, regarded as a "masterpiece of Romanesque illumination."[155] Geoffrey Gorron, the Norman abbot and a close advisee/friend of Christina commissioned the English manuscript at the same location *ca.* 1120–40.[156] Consisting of five separate sections, it contains a calendar, the Alexis Quire, the Psalms, and a diptych of St. Alban

---

[155] David H. Farmer, *The Oxford Dictionary of Saints*, rev. ed. (Oxford: Oxford University Press, 2011), 88–9.
[156] For external and internal evidence (though not without certainty) that Geoffrey Gorron gifted this psalter to Christina, see Kristen Collins, Peter Kidd, and Nancy K. Turner, *The St. Albans Psalter: Painting and Prayer in Medieval England* (Los Angeles: J. Paul Getty Museum, 2013), 9–19.

and David, and one of the first completely painted narrative picture cycles of Christ's life available in history.[157] No correlation exists between the various parts.[158]

The narrative cycle consists of thirty-seven scenes from the annunciation to Pentecost; three OT scenes of the fall, the expulsion from Eden, and King David as a musician; and one of St. Martin of Tours. After the two Genesis scenes, Luke 1:28–2:14 furnishes the data for four NT accounts: the annunciation, the visitation, the nativity, and the annunciation to shepherds. Five more infancy narrative scenes from Matt 2:1–12 follow: the magi before Herod, the Magi's journey to Bethlehem, their adoration, dream, and return. After the presentation in the temple (Luke 2:22–28), the cycle returns to the events of Matthew 2: the flight to Egypt, the massacre, and the return from Egypt, before concluding Christ's pre-baptism life phase. As early as Tertullian, readers of Matthew 1–2 have attempted to harmonize individual episodes therein with the events of Luke 1–2 (see Chapter 3, II). While such ordering of events is not new, the two early and dark moments of Genesis 3 in this psalter largely prepares the reader(s) for the narratives of the Gospel, the good news (see IV. B for an elaborate example).

The massacre scene itself mixes familiar ideas with novel ones (Figure 16). For example, on the left side, Herod is seated on the throne with his finger pointing forward to a soldier who looks behind his back to receive the order. On the right side, the massacre has already commenced, as swordsmen deliver their death strokes against the babes in their mothers' arms. But the salient feature of this work is the lone woman without a child, presumably already dead. She is biting the leg of one soldier about to kill another infant. The significance of this counterattack should not be understated. Up to this point, most visual representations of the massacre show the mothers as distraught and helpless victims and at best sacrificially placing themselves between the weapons and the babes (see II. D and VII). But here and in later works, the bereaved mother is violently resisting or avenging her loss.[159]

This vengeful woman may reflect Christina's empathies for mothers and determination to avoid marriage with a man. Two facts give weight to this biographical actualization: (1) the commissioner Geoffrey Gorron's respect for Christina as a celibate mystic and (2) the Psalter's inclusion of the *Chanson de St. Alexis*, who renounced marriage by the bedside on her wedding night to become a hermit. Early in her life, the prioress experienced visions of Christ initially as her bridegroom, but later when he came in the guise of small child, she was his nursemaid for an entire day.[160] So even though Christina never became a mother, she understood mystically the joy of caring for a child and in part the sorrow of these bereaved women.

---

[157] Whether the psalter is the very first or among the first depends on its exact date of composition, which scholars have tried to specify as much as possible. Ibid., 13.

[158] See discussion in Jane Geddes, "The St. Albans Psalter: The Abbot and the Anchoress," in *Christina of Markyate: A Twelfth-century Holy Woman*, ed. Samuel Fanous and Henrietta Leyser, 197–216 (Abingdon: Routledge, 2005).

[159] See Appendix C.

[160] C. H. Talbot, Samuel Fanous, and Henrietta Leyser, eds. and trans., *The Life of Christina of Markyate: Revised with an Introduction and Notes*, Oxford World Classics (Oxford: Oxford University Press, 2008), xiii–xiv.

Figure 16 "St Albans Psalter," ca. 1120–40, Dombibliothek Hildesheim, HS St. God. 1 (Property of the Basilica of St. Godehard, Hildesheim), p. 30.

In addition, the illumination of the massacre might be a window into her struggles to keep her private vow of chastity against the wishes of her parents and suitors. When a nobleman named Beorhtred was pledged to be married to Christina, she avoided intercourse one evening by talking with him about religious topics all night and, on another occasion, hid from his sight behind a tapestry before a hermit helped her escape. So then, Christina's antipathy toward passionate men and authority parallels the vengeful woman's attack of Herod's soldier.[161] Gorron and others at the abbey knew these details and relayed them to the artists who expressed them in their work. They also included St. Alexis's story that strongly parallels Christina's. Like Apponius (see Chapter 3, VIII. E) and Hildegard of Bingen (see Chapter 4, VIII. E), the author of *St. Albans Psalter* could reflect spiritual struggles against worldly forces in opposition to faith. Unlike her female mystic peer Hildegard who envisioned the bereaved merely as victims (see Chapter 4, VIII. E), Christina may be advocating a fierce counterattack.

---

[161] Nolan, "Ploratus et Ululatus," 105.

Figure 17 Peter Paul Rubens, "The Horrors of War," ca. 1637–8, Gabinetto Fotografico delle Gallerie degli Uffizi, used with permission.

B. Peter Paul Rubens's *The Massacre of the Innocents* at Alte Pinakothek

In both of his works on the massacre, Peter Paul Rubens feature women who counterattack the soldiers, clawing, biting, holding back the blade with their bare hands, and mourning their dead. But the 1630s production shows some development (Figure 12). While Herod recedes into the shadowy background on the right side, at the center is the woman personifying Rachel.[162] Sauerländer describes her features: her ornate dress, disarrayed overgarment of black color of liturgical mourning, relatively larger size, tear-soaked face, eyes lifted to heaven, parted lips expressing lamentation, and isolated position.[163]

But more can be said about the central female character. Even a cursory skim through a catalog of Rubens's oeuvre would lead a beholder to detect the same lady figure in a work completed just after the *Massacre of the Innocents*: *The Horrors of War* (ca. 1637–8).[164] In *The Horrors of War* Rubens decries the wars in Europe, especially the crippling Thirty Years' War (1618–48), with his brush (Figure 17).[165] In a letter to the

---

[162] Sauerländer also points out Rubens's filling of background space with the tomb of Rachel in a mausoleum fashioned after the design of rotunda common since the antiquity, perhaps in imitation of Dirck Volckertsz Coornhert's engraving after Maarten van Heemskerck (ca. 1551) currently at the Rijksmuseum, Amsterdam or Philip Galle's engraving after Frans Floris (ca. 1569) currently at the Rijksmuseum, Prentenkabinet. It appears again in *The Martyrdom of Saint Thomas* on the High Altar of the Barefoot Augustinians in Prague (ca. 1637–9). Sauerländer, *The Catholic Rubens*, 253–7. See Appendix C.

[163] Sauerländer, *The Catholic Rubens*, 259.

[164] It was painted for Ferdinand de Medici the Grand Duke of Tuscany and his court painter and commissioner Justus Sustermans.

[165] Kristin L. Belkin, *Rubens* (London: Phaidon, 1998), 285–8.

commissioner Justus Sustermans, dated March 1638, Rubens explains the painting as an allegory of European struggles: with the Temple of Janus open in the background, the Fury Alekto, Pestilence, and Famine spur on Mars, who inevitably marches toward destruction against Venus, Amors, Cupids, Harmony, Concord, and Peace, with babes, mothers, and angels watching.[166]

Behind Venus the familiar woman from the *Massacre of the Innocents*, now appears as the "unfortunate Europe" (*l'infelice Europa*).[167] The resemblances are readily apparent: red silk dress with ermine trim, gold-lined black overgarment, exposed chest, arms and eyes heavenward in mourning, and tear-soaked pallid face. The adaptation and reprise are telling: mother Rachel is easily transformed into mother Europe, and she moves fluidly from the biblical scene to a mythical one. Yet, even while drawing from different source materials, Rubens's poignant and relevant political statement is one and the same: no one should ignore the current bloodsheds in Europe.

But Rachel in *The Massacre of the Innocents* is hopeful for change. Both women have their hands raised to heaven and mouths open in petition, but the biblical matriarch holds in her hand a white bloodstained swaddling cloth. With it, Rachel plays a representative role linking all the major protagonists in the scene to heaven. As she stands at the center between the darker right side where Herod sits and the brighter left side where the sky is visible, she tearfully sympathizes with the bereaved mothers, raises her hand toward the angels floating midair, and interposes the infants' blood between the cruel earth and the restful heaven.[168]

VIII. Conclusion

This chapter has surveyed the visual reception history of Matt 2:16-18, organized thematically (II), including the massacre in relation to other biblical stories (III), Herod as symbol of evil (IV), victims as martyrs (V) mothers as mourners (VI), and vindicated mothers (VII). A final integrative analysis of both the textual and the visual reception history will be undertaken in the next, final chapter.[169]

For now, this chapter concludes with three oft-revisited visual exegetical strategies in the reception history of Matt 2:16-18 to invite further inquiry: (1) collapsing events to communicate complex ideas, (2) intensifying individual and corporate piety through art, and (3) using subtle visual motifs to promote controversial ideas. First, many artists collapse two or more narrative events, otherwise separated by space and time, into a singular visual presentation that holds different ideas "together in suspension."[170] For example, most of the earliest representative works, from the fifth and sixth centuries, include Herod in the massacre, though his proximity to it seems unlikely.[171] Also, the

---

[166] Ibid., 288-91. The English translation of the letter is Belkin's.
[167] Ibid., 289; Sauerländer, *The Catholic Rubens*, 263.
[168] Sauerländer, *The Catholic Rubens*, 263-5.
[169] This approach is similar to the one discussed in O'Hear, *Contrasting Images of the Book of Revelation in Late Medieval and Early Modern Art*, 199.
[170] Boxall, *Patmos in the Reception History of the Apocalypse*, 177; Christopher Rowland, "Imagining the Apocalypse," *NTS* 51 (2005): 316-19.
[171] See Appendix C.

most enduring image of Herod is the moment from the past when he extends his finger to order the kill, a decree that defines him and his character. Even more dramatically, heaven and earth meet in one picture, as Guido Reni paints angels over the scene, welcoming the victims (see V. E). In Hunt's painting, heavenly beings descend on earth as the infant martyrs accompany the Holy Family and earthly surroundings transform to reflect the heavenly (see III. F).

This type of artistic splicing instantly fills an important "interpretative space" left by the text, namely the need to bring clarity and closure to moral issues raised by the text: Herod's guilt and the victims' innocence. Textual receptions also convey the same ideas but in less immediate ways, through detailed arguments. But artists "move" time and space to lead the beholders to confront multiple ideas at once, to immediately implicate Herod as the villain and revere the babes as innocent. In agreement with Berdini's definition, this common splicing is the visual solution to the moral problems in the representation of Matt 2:16-18.[172] Thus, the artist not only invites the beholder to experience suffering, but also answers questions like "Why did this happen?" and "Who is responsible?"

Secondly, one notes how visual exegesis of Matt 2:16-18 can intensify piety. Works like the Pauper's Bible (III. C) teach readers to consider not only OT parallels to Herod but also imprecatory prayers from Psalms. From them, persecuted Christians could learn to vocalize their pain to God. The characters also become examples of faithfulness during suffering. During Mass in northeastern France, a worshiper might hear a reading of Christ's demand to take up the cross and follow him while viewing the ivory plaques that show slaughtered victims suspended midair in a crucifix pose (V. B). Or in Tuscany, central Italy, a sermon on abuse of power may doubly convict a public official when preached from one of Pisano's pulpits. He would both hear and see the destabilizing effect of sin on a ruler like Herod, leading him to fear (IV. C). These images adorn liturgical fixtures so worship at times might be rightly deemed "multimedia." Altarpieces, pulpits, diptychs, and other similar works, combined with the words of a preacher or the lyrics of hymns, would create experiences that stimulate more than one sense.

Later unintended beholders who encounter such religious art in museums or photographs may enjoy richer experiences by understanding these original contexts. Reception history not only provides such beholders with sources from the past for informed analyses, they can contribute to its continuing progress with their own interpretations. All beholders in all contexts are invited to the shared experience of visual exegesis. While beyond the scope of this chapter, another study might include the inputs of various museums and curators alongside the modern beholders.

Thirdly, artists subtly use their skills to promote controversial points of view. William J. T. Mitchell observes how a violent image can become a "weapon" in service of revolution in addition to its role as a representative art that merely imitates and memorializes.[173] Certainly, artists knew how to wield art to protest against established

---

[172] Berdini, *The Religious Art of Jacopo Bassano*, 35.

[173] Mitchell also notes how violence in images can itself be an act of violence, such as vandalism or demolition. William J. T. Mitchell, *Picture Theory: Essays on Verbal and Visual Representation* (Chicago: Chicago University Press, 1994), 381–2.

patterns of thought or at least raise awareness of controversial issues of the day through actualization. Matteo di Giovanni's Sienese paintings heightened the dread of foreign Turks invasion with his depiction of Herod (IV. D). Pieter Bruegel the Elder similarly revealed the commonplace Dutch resentment of Spanish powers by painting them as soldiers in the scene (V. D). Peter Paul Rubens, though not a direct victim of violence, used his artistry to decry wars elsewhere in Europe by dressing the lamenting Rachel as Mother Europe (VII. B).

In all these works, Herod and Rachel are more than ancient figures; they are symbols, acting as caricatures in disguise or secret embodiments of heavenward hope. To the attentive eye of the reception historian, the turban on Herod's head or the garments of Rachel can powerfully communicate attitudes of the artists. But at the same time, precisely because such symbols are understated or hidden, artists can protest or take up a cause in noncontroversial ways. These artists in some ways imitate Jesus the parable teller because they present images that may be seen by all but understood by few (Matt 13:10-18). As Panofsky has demonstrated, these artists' secrets are often obtained via access to visual motifs in art history parallel to the way scholars become conversant in theological traditions.[174] For these reasons, visual exegesis contributes to a fuller perspective of the reception history of Matt 2:16-18.

---

[174] Panofsky, "Iconography and Iconology," 38–9.

7

Concluding Reflections

Introduction

As stated in Chapter 1, the goal of this reception-historical study was to enrich one's reading of the massacre of the innocents through engagement with other viewpoints, forgotten and fresh readings, and older interpretative strategies. Due to the importance of Matthew 2 and the depths of meaning behind, within, or in front of the text of verses 16-18, devotion to just one method or approach may not be adequate to explore all the potentialities of the text.[1] Another approach, namely reception history, better promotes "both ... and" instead of "either ... or." In other words, reception history may help to overcome the limitations and the fragmentations that result without "discussion across methods."[2]

Reception history's dual nature, implied in its name as (1) history and (2) reception is the reason for its effectiveness. First, reception history is a thoroughly historical task, because in it the "history of the text" is tied to the "history of culture."[3] Because Matthew has been read through many centuries beyond its original audience, its impact on culture is available for historical-critical analysis. As Nicholls writes, "examining the interpretation of the text is simply a lens through which to conduct a broader historical study."[4] Secondly, reception history considers receptions from the genesis of the text to the present. Like a dragnet, it collects interpretations from many centuries indiscriminately, without favoring recent approaches.

The benefits of reception history are numerous. It allows access to more data across textual and non-textual receptions (beyond the narrower history of interpretation) and older readings hitherto unknown to many interpreters (beyond most recent critical scholarship). While the large number of available sources is overwhelming, this research has allowed one in biblical studies to venture into atypical fields of liturgical studies and art history. Even within the more familiar areas of church history and

---

[1] For example, often historical-critical works lack modern relevance, while narrative criticism and reader- or audience-oriented readings inevitably depend on historical criticism for basic understanding. Luz, *Matthew in History*, 6; Boxall, *Discovering Matthew*, 29.
[2] Nicholls, *Walking on Water*, 1. See Chapter 1, n. 32.
[3] Gillingham, "Biblical Studies on Holiday?," 18.
[4] Nicholls, *Walking on Water*, 4.

biblical studies, one may encounter hitherto unfamiliar interpretations. For example, John Chrysostom defends Christ's escape from the massacre by juxtaposing it to Peter's escape from prison (Acts 12:18-19; see Chapter 3, IV. B). One may also discover how modern readings were frequently anticipated in premodern readings, some of them ancient. For example, the use of Josephus to understand Herod the Great better is hardly a "new" idea since it is found in Eusebius of Caesarea in the fourth century (see Chapter 3, VII. A).

The aim in this current chapter is to (1) reconsider the present writer's initial close reading of Matt 2:16-18 from Chapter 2 in light of reception history, (2) reflect on three major reading strategies identified in later chapters, and (3) point out some implications for ongoing Matthean scholarship. In Chapter 2, as the goal was to achieve a Gadamerian "historically effected consciousness," it was assumed that the initial reading of Matt 2:16-18 was limited in scope (Chapter 1, III. A).[5] That reading is best defined as a "horizon," "the total extent of what someone can envision from a particular point in space and time," by its very nature limited and circumscribed by "pre-judgments," "anticipations," or "pre-understandings."[6] The details of the horizon form the contents of the second chapter.

One of the main assumptions of this current project is that an individual horizon can change through encounters with past history.[7] Each subsequent chapter studied various horizons organized either chronologically (Chapter 3: the second to fifth centuries; Chapter 4: the sixth century to 1516; Chapter 5: from 1517 to the present) or generically (Chapter 6: visual receptions). When selecting materials for analysis, attempts were made to identify influential authors or readings possessing lasting strength, problem-solving qualities, and widespread reception.[8] To limit bias, this work included influential receptions of a non-Western provenance (e.g., Jacob of Serugh, Chapter 3, VI. C and Sahidic MS 36, Chapter 4, VII. B). Additionally, secular novels (e.g., Herman Melville and the atheist José Saramago, Chapter 5, III) were included and even an entire chapter on visual receptions (Chapter 6) to emphasize the artistic intuitions of talented laymen alongside the insights of clergymen and scholars.[9] This final chapter is a reflection on how the reception-historical data in Chapters 3 to 6 corresponds to, exceeds, or falls short of the expectations and initial impressions of Matt 2:16-18 (Chapter 2).

Beginning and ending the analysis of reception-historical data with the present writer's own close reading has certain methodological limitations. Thus, the second aim of this chapter is to organize the data from Chapters 3 to 6 according to broad categories. Given such a preponderance of material, the three most important reading strategies are identified: the massacre (1) juxtaposed with other biblical tragedies, (2) recontextualized with reference to the Apocalypse, and (3) actualized as an interpretative lens for understanding tragic events. This is the task of "delineating the

---

[5] Gadamer, *Truth and Method*, xv, xxxiv, 306-7.
[6] Ibid., 270, 277, 306; Nicholls, *Walking on Water*, 8.
[7] Gadamer, *Truth and Method*, 306.
[8] Parris, *Reception Theory and Biblical Hermeneutics*, 216–22.
[9] Panofsky, "Iconography and Iconology," 38.

range of possible meanings in a text."[10] Though by no means covering every aspect of the reception history of Matt 2:16-18, these three major strategies are the most definitive.

Finally, this chapter closes with implications for ongoing Matthean scholarship. As stated in the first chapter, the concluding chapter would constitute the return trip to the present, to connect a reception historically informed understanding of Matt 2:16-18 with its implications for the twenty-first-century study of Matthew (Chapter 1, III. A). Rachel Nicholls calls this task "contextualization," and it "involves making sense of a text by connecting it with contemporary philosophical and theological tradition and culture."[11] It is essentially a revisitation of the text with a historically effected consciousness, in the hope of gaining insights about Matt 2:16-18 and how it can inform other readers of the text. The present writer's role here resembles that of a guide in a boat on the stream of history, inviting other interested participants to embark, assessing the present location, and anticipating what is to come.[12] The two areas of potential foreseen as important for the future of Matthean scholarship are (1) reception history and philosophy of suffering and (2) twenty-first-century actualizations.

I. Revisiting the "Potential of the Text"

The initial close reading of Matt 2:16-18 in Chapter 2 largely produced the same observations and typical insights as modern critical commentators. Here is a summary of findings from Chapter 2 and five major possibilities identified there for further inquiry:

1. Matthew's portrayal of Herod the Great foreshadowing other secular rulers in the narrative (e.g., Herod Antipas' unequivocal desire to kill John the Baptist (14:5; cf. Mark 6:19-20); Jewish leaders who later persecute Jesus as an adult; Pontius Pilate's reaction to Jesus (Matt 27:14); and the mockery of Jesus (27:29-31, 41)).
2. A dramatic change of tone from joyful worship (2:9-12) to anger and death in Matt 2:13-23, a section formed by narratives of the Holy Family's movement to (2:13-15) and from Egypt (2:19-23) that bracket the massacre story (2:16-18).
3. Parallels between Exodus, the pharaoh, and Moses and Matthew, Herod, and Jesus, respectively (e.g., between the killing of Hebrew babes and the massacre, movement to and from Egypt, and support from unnamed protagonists (the Hebrew midwives and the magi)).
4. Interpretative space in Matt 2:16 that allows for speculation about logistics (e.g., number of soldiers, weapons used, or death toll) and questions related to the

---

[10] Nicholls, *Walking on Water*, 24.
[11] Ibid.
[12] This explanation is based on parable of Luz, which assumes that interpreters in reception history "resemble men, who must investigate the water of a stream while they sit in a boat, which is carried and driven by this very same stream." *Das Evangelium nach Matthäus (Mt 1–7)*, 110.

massacre's historicity (e.g., its impact as being too small or too great for Josephus to ignore).
5. Interpretative space in Matt 2:17-18 that invites inquiries about geography (e.g., the location of Ramah, Rachel's burial site, and whether she represents northern Israel, southern Judah, or both) and theodicy-related problems (e.g., comparison of 2:17 with other Christologically significant fulfillment citations, use of τότε, and the citation from Jeremiah).[13]

Author-focused and text-focused concerns mainly motivated the identification of these possibilities of Matt 2:16-18, in seeking to understand both original contexts and the world within the text. These agendas are closely aligned with the critical methodologies of current Matthean scholarship (see Chapter 1, I. B). For example, textual/redaction criticism (e.g., Greek and/or Hebrew source(s) behind the citation of Jer 31:15) and narrative criticism (e.g., foreshadowing of the Passion narrative) have been especially relevant in the close readings.

A. Treatment in Past Interpreters

Past receptions not only anticipate these five insights but also present a rich variety of readings that modern interpreters have often forgotten. First, interpreters of the distant past have noted the potentiality of Herod's role in Matthew as the prototypical antagonist in the NT (if reading in canonical order). Among the earliest receptions of this kind was Origen's *Commentary on Matthew* (*ca.* 248; see Chapter 3, VIII. A). He notes that the tenants in Jesus's parable who knowingly plot against the vineyard owner's son (Matt 21:38) correspond to the Jews who plot to take Jesus's life, and they in turn resemble Herod who knew the messianic prophecies, yet attempted to kill him anyway. Origen is a careful reader of the text, not unlike a modern narrative critic who treats Matthew "as a complete tapestry, an organic whole" and studies "the formal features of a text in its final form."[14] Modern narrative critical readings make similar connections between persecutors of Jesus at the beginning and the end of Matthew.[15]

Secondly, a few receptions reckon with dramatic changes in the narrative, such as the dissonance between (1) the joyful and reverent occasion of the Magi's visit and the angry and disturbed reaction of Herod and (2) the safety of Jesus in Egypt and the atrocity against the unfortunate victims at and near Bethlehem. Among the early representatives of the first type of dissonance is the early-fifth-century Gallic sarcophagus at St. Maximin which juxtaposes the scenes of the adoration of the magi and the massacre (see Chapter 6, IV. A). The artist makes some important and creative interpretative decisions that establish firm symmetry between the two scenes that are otherwise completely different in tone: (1) four adults are present in each scene;

---

[13] See the discussion of interpretative space in Boxall, *Patmos in the Reception History of the Apocalypse*, 3–4.
[14] Resseguie, *Narrative Criticism of the New Testament*, 18–19.
[15] Kingsbury, *Matthew as Story*, 46; Heil, *Death and Resurrection of Jesus*, 16; Garland, *Reading Matthew*, 30–1.

(2) Herod sits on one end, while Mary sits at the other end with Christ; and (3) three magi bring gifts in their hands, while two soldiers bring babes in their hands, with a grieving mother following them. At the close of Chapter 6 (VIII.), it was noted how visual receptions like this one can present multiple ideas with greater immediacy than textual receptions. This artwork invites the beholder to contemplate the true, gentle king viewed at the same level as the false, violent king.[16] The "gifts" that their subjects bring in their hands incriminate Herod and defend Christ.

Thirdly, the tendency to invite comparisons with the Exodus narratives is evident in the reception history. Ephrem the Syrian in his *Commentary on Tatian's Diatessaron* (*ca.* 369) identifies Herod as the antitype of the pharaoh who also failed to kill one Hebrew redeemer among many children (see Chapter 3, V. B). Closer to the present is the Eastern Orthodox *Menaion*, a large liturgical book containing propers for the Byzantine rite (see Chapter 5, I. D). The *Menaion* combines reflections on the massacre with allusions to the Red Sea crossing, to assure readers of the innocents' victory over Herod.

Fourthly, the interpretative space in Matt 2:16 is exploited in different ways. Here the role of the imagination is crucial. For example, the author of the ninth-century Infancy Gospel in the *Speckled Book* dramatizes the flight to Egypt by narrating it with the Holy Family still in Judea during the massacre (Chapter 4, III. B). When soldiers apprehend them, Jesus and Mary work together to ensure a narrow escape, while Joseph plays a marginal role (121–3). The author does not necessarily contradict Matt 2:13-18, but works within the interpretative space to add dramatic, unfolding scenes. So then, even if the text seemingly limits interpretative options, just as often the imagination permits creative activity in reception history.[17] Even more dramatically imaginative than the *Speckled Book* is Giambattista Marino's *La Strage degli Innocenti*, written in four books of poetry (1632; see Chapter 5, II. B) that includes gory details of the variety of weapons employed and the modes of death. This imaginative expansion is not qualitatively unlike the type of imaginative reconstruction in historical criticism.[18]

Fifthly, the interpretative space in Matt 2:17-18 has prompted interpreters to attempt to alleviate tensions inherent in the text, such as the possible geographical distance between Ramah and Bethlehem and the apparent absence of God. The anonymous author of the *Opus Imperfectum* circumvents both problems as he or she (1) assumes the etymological meaning of Ramah, as "on high" (*in excelso*), and (2) thematically connects Rachel's weeping with the humble prayer of the righteous of Sir 35:21: "the voice of the poor pierces the clouds, and it does not depart until it is heard" (see Chapter 3, XII. C). The effect of this reading of Matt 2:18 is that Ramah need not be a distant geographical location, and that God in heaven heard Rachel's weeping. Thus, the author of the *Opus Imperfectum* addresses both the historical and moral interpretative spaces left behind by Matt 2:18.

---

[16] Schiller, *Iconography of Christian Art*, 1:115.
[17] Lyons, "Hope for a Troubled Discipline?," 215–16.
[18] See, for example, Raymond Brown's hypothetical Johannine community in *The Community of the Beloved Disciple* (New York: Paulist, 1979).

B. Limitations of the Previous Close Reading

In locating past interpreters of Matt 2:16-18, it became apparent how often the present writer's reading strategies were not original. In fact, they were prevalent in very ancient works. For example, one could argue that thematic and linguistic parallels between Matthew 2 and Exodus (LXX) encourage a theodicy: God answering Rachel's cry by sending Jesus back to the land, just as God answered the enslaved Israelites' cry by sending Moses back to Egypt (see Chapter 2, IV. C).

In other cases, predecessors did not share such preoccupations. The Exodus-Matthew connections that seemed so important and mentioned often in recent commentators were not discussed as frequently or specifically in earlier receptions.[19] Instead, second-century writers such as Justin Martyr (*ca.* 100–165), Irenaeus of Lyons (*ca.* 130–200) and the author of the *Protevangelium of James* (*ca.* 145) retell the story of the massacre by incorporating material from other OT works, such as Isaiah 7–8 (due to the fulfillment of Isa 7:14 in Matt 1:23, frequent citations of Isaiah in the Gospel, and the popularity of Christological typology in the second century; Chapter 3, III. A. B) or 2 Chronicles: King Joash's plot and murder of prophet Zechariah (24:20-22; see Chapter 3, V. A). In *de Anima* (*ca.* 210), Tertullian connects Matt 2:16 to Ps 8:2 via Matt 21:16 to argue that the victims sensed the violence against them and offered worship with their voices (Chapter 3, IX. A). Many more intertextual connections with the Psalms would follow.[20] While Ephrem the Syrian later brands Herod as "a second pharaoh," this title is only one among a series of other names such as "a seed of Canaan," and Ephrem also makes comparisons with Cain, Gehazi, Judas Iscariot, and King Saul (see Chapter 3, V. B). Also encountered is the tendency to look forward in time to discover future parallels between Herod and ruler to come. At times, Herod's symbolic value extends beyond the text as it is actualized in extra-biblical circumstances, times, and settings. For example, Matthew Henry sees parallels between Herod and Nero (Chapter 5, IV. B. 2).

Among "new" readings of Matt 2:16-18, most noteworthy is the interpretation of the victims as martyrs, familiar to modern Catholic readers of Matthew, but outside most Protestant traditions. From as early as Irenaeus of Lyons (Chapter 3, III. B), this motif appears consistently and abundantly in a variety of sources. In the fifth century, it begins to appear in visual reception as well.[21] Recent works are more interested in matters historical (e.g., the calculation of the two years and the death toll) than hagiographical (e.g., martyrdom and heavenly destiny).[22]

---

[19] See Appendix A.

[20] See for example, Origen's *Homily 4 on Psalm 37 (36 LXX)* (*ca.* third century; see Chapter 3, IX. B); Augustine's *Exposition of Ps 48 (LXX 47)* (*ca.* 400; see Chapter 3, V. C); Roman antiphonals (*ca.* eighth to ninth centuries; see Chapter 4, VI. C); Rupert of Deutz's *Concerning the Glory and the Honor of the Son of Man, Commentary on Matthew* (*De Gloria et Honore Filii Hominis super Mattheum, ca.* 1127; see Chapter 4, VIII. D); the Ambrosian rite (*ca.* fifth century; see Chapter 5, I. C. 1); and the Mozarabic rite (*ca.* sixth and seventh centuries; see Chapter 5, I. C. 2).

[21] See discussion in Chapter 3, IX and *Basilica di Santa Maria Maggiore* in Rome (432–40; Chapter 6, V. A).

[22] See Appendix A.

Also, the frequent appearances of fulfillment citations in the Matthean infancy narratives (four out of ten: 1:22-23; 2:15, 17-18, 23; see Chapter 2, III), a salient feature of Matthew, contribute to the overall emphasis on Christological fulfillment of Scripture. With the two preceding citations (1:22-23; 2:15) clearly delineated as Christ-centered, whether relating to Jesus's name or his sojourning in Egypt, one would be inclined to approach Matt 2:16-18 with a similar interest.

Such horizon, however, should not be deemed inferior or superior to past receptions but simply different. As stated above, this present writer was mainly motivated by historical-critical concerns, agendas set by the majority of Matthean scholarship in the last century, searching for original contexts and exploration of the worlds behind and within Matt 2:16-18. While earlier interpreters do not dismiss such concerns, they bring other questions into the text. As expected, a proper survey of reception history indiscriminately gathers both familiar and forgotten readings while eschewing the "chronological snobbery" that favors more recent interpretations.[23]

II. Important Reading Strategies

In this section, attention is given to the most prevalent reading strategies in the reception history of Matt 2:16-18. The data could have been organized according to the traditional four senses of Scripture: literal, allegorical, tropological, and anagogical.[24] This approach, however, does not account for repeated actualizations of the text, a recurring reading strategy that does not neatly fall into just one of the three nonliteral senses.[25] Also difficult to fit into a single category is recontextualization (see Chapter 4, II.).[26] Often in reception history, both the victims (2:16) and Rachel (Matt 2:18) appear alongside diverse passages that serve as interpretative lens that recast the horrific tragedy in a more positive light. At different times, this reading strategy develops the tropological and/or anagogical sense(s). In addition, certain motifs employ multiple senses simultaneously. For example, the visual motif of Herod pointing his finger to execute the command with the victims nearby not only aligns with the literal sense of Matt 2:16: "he sent and killed all the children."[27] The gesture and the horrific violence unfolding in his presence confront Herod and condemn him to reveal the moral sense of the text to the beholders.

Thus, a better organizing principle is to divide up the data into three major reading strategies of juxtaposition, recontextualization, and actualization, not according to the four senses. Also, more attention is drawn to recurring ideas in reception history not anticipated in the initial close reading of the text. Provided here are three illustrations of these major reading strategies: (1) the massacre juxtaposed to other biblical

---

[23] Kealy, *Matthew's Gospel and the History of Biblical Interpretation: Book 1*, i–iii; Lewis, *Surprised by Joy*, 207.
[24] See Henri de Lubac, *Medieval Exegesis: Vol 1: The Four Senses of Scripture*, trans. Mark Sebanc (Grand Rapids: Eerdmans; Edinburgh: T&T Clark, 1998).
[25] Kovacs and Rowland, *Revelation*, 7–11.
[26] See Blackstone, "The Hermeneutics of Recontextualization in the Epistle to the Hebrews."
[27] See Appendix C.

tragedies, (2) the massacre recontextualized into the Apocalypse, and (3) the massacre as interpretative lens of tragic events.

A. The Massacre Juxtaposed to Other Biblical Tragedies

Following the lead of Eusebius of Caesarea (see Chapter 3, VII. A), modern works appeal to secular sources like Josephus and Macrobius for a better historical understanding of Herod the Great.[28] In the broader scope of reception history, however, many more interpreters are interested in answering moral questions left by the text through reading through the canon in search of similar situations. Juxtaposition is a frequently employed reading strategy used to compare and contrast the massacre with other negative events found in the Scriptures. These cross-references are not mere recognitions of parallels, but active arguments that serve to fill interpretative space in the text.

Earlier initial exegetical instincts led to other passages in Matthew and Exodus, but different biblical books have often suggested themselves to older interpreters. For example, in the fourteenth-century Grabow Altarpiece, Bertram of Minden deliberately arranges painted scenes from Genesis together with the massacre scene to produce two effects (Chapter 6, III. B). First, the massacre, which is on the right wing, is placed in symmetry with the murder of Abel on the left wing. They are the first bloodsheds of the OT and NT. The second, more immediate and innovative comparison is the scene just above the massacre: the expulsion from Eden. The similarities in design between (1) Herod's throne and the gate of paradise and 2) the soldier's sword and the angel's sword invite the beholder to consider the two tragedies together.[29] The resulting visual idea is that the burden of responsibility for the massacre is on the fallen man, not on God.

Other interpreters utilize stories later in the OT, especially those that involve despots. As stated earlier, Ephrem the Syrian compares Herod to King Saul who, while pursuing David, murdered the innocent priests of Nob and allowed Abiathar to escape (1 Sam 22:6-23; see Chapter 3, V. B). David's movements as a fugitive, the priests' death, and Abiathar's escape are details that parallel the flight to Egypt, the massacre, and John the Baptist's survival.[30] The artist of the fifteenth-century Pauper's Bible builds on the similarities between Herod and Saul by adding Queen Athaliah's purge (2 Kgs 11:1; see Chapter 6, III. C). The accompanying verses, Prov 28:15 and Hosea 8:4, guide the readers/viewers toward understanding the terrible consequences of ungodly reigns. Perhaps the most dramatic allusion to the OT is in the aforementioned *Protevangelium of James*. Herod kills Zechariah the father of John the Baptist in the same way King Joash killed another earlier martyr by the same name (2 Chr 24:20-22; see Chapter 3,

---

[28] See Appendices A and B.
[29] Dube, "The Grabow Altar of Master Bertram von Minden (Germany)," 106; Portmann, *Meister Bertram*, 165.
[30] The early account of John the Baptist's survival of the massacre is in the *Protoevangelium of James* (see Chapter 3, V. A).

V. A). All of these allusions and associations to past atrocities reinforce the timeless idea that rejecting God's rule in favor of human rule has severe consequences (1 Samuel 8).

In addition to looking backward into the OT, other interpreters look forward for patterns of tyrannical rule later in the NT. As mentioned earlier, connections between Herod who persecuted Jesus as an infant and the Jewish leaders who persecuted Jesus as an adult occur as early as Origen (see Chapter 3, VIII. A). More interesting are the various links made with other Herods in the NT such as Herod Antipas and Agrippa I. The author of the fourth- or fifth-century *History of Joseph the Carpenter* (see Chapter 3, VII. B) blames Herod the Great for the death of John the Baptist (Antipas's doing in Matt 14:1-12; Mark 6:14-29; Luke 9:9) and reports that the tyrant was eaten by worms (actually Agrippa I's demise in Acts 12:19-23). In his ninth homily on Matthew (*ca.* 393; see Chapter 3, IV. B) John Chrysostom advances a theodical defense with an exposition of Peter's miraculous escape from prison in Acts 12:1-19. Chrysostom argues that if Peter is not blamed for Herod Agrippa I's execution of the guards, then neither should Jesus be blamed for Herod the Great's massacre of the babes.

Thus, the violence of sinful leaders is a persistent theme in the Scriptures and many interpreters in the reception history of Matt 2:16-18 point to it. Various interpreters are interested in filling the moral interpretative space by looking into redemption history for patterns, insights, and sympathetic connections with others who have suffered. Though this strategy does not provide a completely satisfactory solution to the problem of evil, it is used for a reminder that the massacre is not the first instance of innocent suffering.

B. The Massacre Recontextualized into the Apocalypse

Another major reading strategy for Matt 2:16-18 in reception history is to recontextualize the passage in the happier or more triumphant setting of Revelation. This reading differs from juxtaposition in that interpreters are more interested in the fates of the characters involved, the outcomes of their choices and sufferings, than finding similarities and differences with other tragedies. Often this type of recontextualization creates new associations that derive meaning from the tropological and anagogical senses.

Among the earliest recontextualizations of Matt 2:16-18 in relation to the Apocalypse is Origen's *Homily 4 on Psalm 37 (36 LXX)* (*ca.* third century), in which Christians are encouraged to overcome occasions of stumbling by emulating the saints in the Bible, even younger saints such as the massacred victims who received crowns and palms of martyrdom for their suffering (see Chapter 3, IX. B). Later writers such as Quodvultdeus (died *ca.* 450) expand this connection. In his *De Symbolo* 2, he explicitly locates the victims in the scene of Rev 7:9, the throng of countless saints from every tribe in God's presence wearing white robes and carrying palms (see Chapter 3, IX. J).

Liturgical works are especially rich with examples of this type of recontextualization. The oldest extant witness to the Roman lectionary system, the *Comes of Würzburg* (*ca.* 600–50), prescribes the reading of Rev 14:1-5 on the *Feast of the Innocents* (see Chapter 4, VI. B).[31] So then, the unfortunate massacred victims from the Bethlehem

---

[31] Folsom, "The Liturgical Books of the Roman Rite," 256.

area are reckoned as the blessed 144,000 saints upon Mount Zion. But not all liturgical texts present the victims as standing among the saints. The Ambrosian rite (*ca.* fifth century; see Chapter. 5, I. C. 1), the Mozarabic rite (*ca.* sixth and seventh centuries; see Chapter 5, I. C. 2), and the Office antiphonal *Under the Altar of God* (*Sub altare Dei*) of the Matins of the Innocents (*ca.* eighth and ninth centuries) situate the victims under the heavenly altar (Rev 6:9-11) awaiting future vindication (see Chapter 4, VI. C).[32] *Under the Altar of God* also likens them to the twenty-four elders of Rev 4:10-11.[33]

The storyline of Revelation also absorbs Herod. Accordingly, Oecumenius, in his sixth-century commentary on the Apocalypse (see Chapter 4, IV. A), decodes Rev 12:3-6 as the unfolding events of the Matthean infancy narratives: the dragon uses Herod's massacre in an attempt to kill the child (12:5), but the Holy Family escapes into the wilderness, that is Egypt, for three and a half years (12:6). In his mid-eighth-century *Sermon on the Innocents Killed in Bethlehem and Rachel*, John of Euobea similarly perceives the schemes of the dragon of the Apocalypse behind the massacre (see Chapter 4, IV. A). The overall effect of such absorption is that Herod's massacre takes on cosmic significance as the forces of good and evil clash.

This type of recontextualization is not only unidirectional in the transfer of ideas from Matt 2:16-18 to Revelation but also bidirectional, as ideas from the latter move into the former. The most important and pervasive idea is the high death toll of the infants that the earliest interpreters from the late patristic period and early medieval ages calculate without qualms about historical accuracy.[34] As stated above, liturgical works such as the seventh-century *Comes of Würzburg* would have been a major source for the figure of 144,000 from Rev 14:1-5. But there were certainly detractors. In the exposition of Rev 7:4 in his eighth-century Apocalypse commentary, Ambrose Autpert explicitly answers criticisms against 144,000 as the number of victims (see Chapter 4, VI. D). He explains the high figure in its anagogical sense: the 144,000 count is not literal, but the anticipated total number of elect that the victims represent.

Thus, at every turn of this reception-historical survey, various readings recontextualize Matt 2:16-18 by combining it with passages of Revelation. Next to the Apocalypse, only the Psalms come close to providing such an abundance of material. In addition, not only does Revelation inform the reader of Matthew 2:16-18, the latter informs readings of the Apocalypse, as seen in the commentaries of Oecumenius and Ambrose Autpert. Such long-established connections do not continue as abundantly in

---

[32] See also *Homily 86* in Charles Borromeo, *Sancti Caroli Borromei S.R E. Cardinalis Archiepiscopi Mediolani Homiliae CXXVII. Ex MSS. Codicibus Bibliothecae Ambrosianae Ordine Chronologico In Lucem Productae* (Veith: Augustae Vindelicorum, 1758), 823-34.

[33] For more recent examples of recontextualization into the Apocalypse, see Daniel Cudmore's *Euchodia*, 2-6 (*ca.* 1657; see Chapter 5, II); the discussion of the *Book of Common Prayer* in Ramshaw, "The Holy Innocents, Martyrs, December 28," 46-7; and the Pauper's Bible (*ca.* fifteenth century; see Chapter 6, III. C).

[34] See for example, Jerome's *Commentary of Isaiah* (*ca.* 410; Chapter 3, III. C); Prudentius's *Discourse of the Martyr St. Romanus against the Pagans* (*ca.* 405; Chapter 3, III and IX. E); and *Martyrdom of Matthew* (*ca.* early medieval era; Chapter 4, VI. E). See also Hayward, "Suffering and Innocence in Latin Sermons for the Feast of the Holy Innocents, *c.* 400-800," 67-8; Brown, *Birth of the Messiah*, 205; and discussion in the introduction of Chapter 4.

more recent works.³⁵ Because these typically display more concern for historical-critical matters, their interests in the victims are more biographical than hagiographical. The accompanying effect is that less interpretative imagination is devoted to the massacred victims and the significance of their deaths. But Revelation is a source material accessible via canonical reading that potentially offers a theodically satisfying epilogue for their suffering and a glimpse into the Satanic forces at work behind Herod. Thus, the frequent recontextualizations of Matt 2:16-18 into its various passages reveal an urge to fill its moral interpretative space.

C. The Massacre as Interpretative Lens for Tragic Events

The potential of the massacre to evoke questions about innocent suffering has been evident throughout reception history. As seen above, interpreters have frequently noted parallels with tragedies in biblical history and attempted some satisfying closure via recontextualizations into the Apocalypse. Arguably more interesting are receptions that consider Matt 2:16-18 as actualized in extra-biblical historical atrocities.³⁶ While juxtapositions and recontextualizations certainly imply that the text could apply to some real-life situation, the interpreter through actualization makes sense of his contemporary situation through the passage.³⁷

Perhaps one of the best examples of actualization is found in Lucifer of Cagliari, who strongly opposed the Arian sympathizer Emperor Constantius II (see Chapter 3, VIII. C). His public disapproval of Athanasius of Alexandria's condemnation was so intense that the Arians convinced the emperor to imprison him for three days in the Imperial Palace (ca. 354).³⁸ Lucifer soon afterwards wrote vindictive treatises that lionized advocates of orthodoxy and denigrated pro-Arians, including his *de S. Athanasio* II 3:45-53 (ca. 358), in which Constantius reprised Herod's role while the victims represented the anti-Arians. Gregory of Nazianzus is another fourth-century bishop that opposes his enemies. In reaction to their disapproval of his appointment as Archbishop of Constantinople, he associates them with Herod in the massacre, specifically condemning them for their envy (see Chapter 3, VIII. D). Though relatively little is known about Apponius, he, like Lucifer of Cagliari, actualizes Matt 2:16-18 to combat contemporary heretics (ca. 410; see Chapter 3, VIII. E). Later, Protestants such as John Calvin, Philip Melanchthon, and Matthew Henry would also actualize the text to inform their struggles with the Roman Church or other fringe groups such as the Anabaptists (see Chapter 5, I. B and IV. B. 1).

---

[35] See Appendix A; Filson, *A Commentary on the Gospel According to St. Matthew*, 61. See also commentaries of Revelation that make similar connections, albeit without explicitly equating the dragon with Herod: Osborne, *Revelation*, 462; Sweet, *Revelation*, 196-7; and Ladd, *A Commentary on the Revelation of John*, 169.

[36] Kovacs and Rowland, *Revelation*, 7-11.

[37] Ibid., 9-10; O'Hear, *Contrasting Images of the Book of Revelation in Late Medieval and Early Modern Art*, 218. Later, Rowland expressed a preference for "analogy" over "actualization" to describe this process. "The Interdisciplinary Colloquium on the Book of Revelation and Effective History," 299.

[38] Flower, *Emperors and Bishops in Late Roman Invective*, 84.

Visual receptions also convey actualized readings of Matt 2:16-18 and place special emphases on characters besides the infants. For example, a miniature of the massacre in the twelfth-century *Winchester Psalter* features a soldier simultaneously chomping and piercing a child (see Chapter 6, V. C). This visual reception is decrying either the general climate of violence during the Anarchy or the perpetrators of infanticide at a time when it became equivalent to adult homicide and was widely condemned.[39] In a later example, the dark-skinned Herod in Matteo di Giovanni's second and third Sienese paintings dons a turban, effectively transforming him into one of the terrifying authorities of the Ottoman Empire, either Pascha or the Sultan Mehmed II (*ca.* 1481-2; see Chapter 6, IV. D). It reflects Italian fears of Turks who landed in Apulia and attacked Orantes.[40] Besides fear, resentment from foreign occupation is also evident. In Pieter Brugel the Younger's copy of the Elder's *The Massacre of the Innocents* in Kunsthistorisches Museum, Vienna (*ca.* 1610; see Chapter 6, V. D), Herod's soldiers appear in the garb of *bandes d'ordonnance* and unleash dogs on the villagers.[41] The art expresses antipathy toward the current Spanish occupation of the Netherlands, actualizing an ancient text in the process.

Another emotion that accompanies actualization is godly sorrow. Rachel, like Herod, his soldiers, and the victims, plays a prominent role. In Peter Paul Rubens's *The Massacre of the Innocents* at the Alte Pinakothek (*ca.* 1635-7), she represents not only the bereaved mothers but also all the innocents suffering during the Thirty Years' War (*ca.* 1618-48; see Chapter 6, VII. B). Her central location in the painting, her ornate dress, and her lifting a blood-stained cloth heavenward toward the angels suggest that the Catholic Rubens looked to God for change through the figure of Rachel (Matt 2:18).[42]

So, across the centuries and across textual and visual receptions, various interpreters project their experiences and attitudes by actualizing Matt 2:16-18. They see in the passage characters that symbolize the persecutors (Herod and his soldiers) and the persecuted (Rachel, the mothers, and the infants) in their own situations. Therefore, actualizations are particularly interesting receptions that act as portals into different worlds in front of the text.

III. Prospective: Wider Implications of the Present Study

As a consequence of this reception-historical study, the present writer's perspective on Matt 2:16-18 has been transformed and his horizon has shifted. In these four chapters there is a wide range of perspectives from different traditions (e.g., Roman Catholic and Orthodox), different eras (e.g., early church and the medieval age), and different disciplines (e.g., liturgy and art). Like Nicholls, a certain viewpoint of Matt 2:16-18 from the past has been now expanded.[43] With a consciousness that is now affected

---

[39] Haney, *The Winchester Psalter*, 34–5.
[40] Bisaha, *Creating East and West*, 157–9.
[41] Kunzle, "Spanish Herod, Dutch Innocents," 63, 69.
[42] Sauerländer, *The Catholic Rubens*, 263–5.
[43] Nicholls, *Walking on Water*, 11–12.

by reception history, and by way of prospective, two areas are proposed for further Matthean studies: (1) reception history in relation to philosophy of suffering and (2) twenty-first-century actualizations.

A. Reception History and Philosophy of Suffering

Even a narrow history of interpretation (*Auslegungsgeschichte*) of Matt 2:16-18 would reveal how Christian interpreters have often addressed its theodical issues. For example, as early as the fourth century, the *Acts of Pilate* blames Jesus for the death of the infants (Chapter 3, IV) while John Chrysostom defends Jesus's innocence (Chapter 3, IV. B). But without reception history, one is less likely to be aware that Albert Camus and others in the twentieth century revived major doubts about divine benevolence, at times mounting to antagonism (see Chapter 5, III). Herman Melville subversively incorporates Matt 2:18 into the last part of *Moby Dick*, presenting the uncomforted Rachel as a victim of deity as the final image of the novel (see Chapter 5, III. A). José Saramago is much more forthright and irreverent in his novel, *O Evangelho Segundo Jesus Cristo*. The guilt and responsibility for the massacre belongs to Joseph who knew about Herod's plot in advance, but failed to warn others (see Chapter 5, III. B). As this sin of omission haunts the family, Jesus questions his own existence and later accepts himself as an icon for Christianity, albeit begrudgingly as a victim of the Christian God who manipulated him. While Camus, Melville, and Saramago are fiction writers, they perceive real moral problems with Matt 2:16-18 as atheistic or agnostic readers of Scripture.

So then, a major benefit of reception history is that an individual from a specific tradition learns from not only similar traditions but also completely foreign ones and even rogue perspectives. Like the parable of the dragnet (Matt 13:47-50), reception history first catches all kinds of readings, good or bad, and then allows for thoughtful evaluation. Contemporary commentators and pastors, who are easily conversant with like-minded peers, ought to listen to voices from opposing religious, philosophical, and literary circles that have strong, even hostile, opinions about the tragedies of Scripture. Reception history can be that preparatory step, the process of listening to radically differing points of views. After hearing from them, they may better answer those who want to know the grounds for the Christian hope (1 Pet 3:15).

B. Twenty-First Century Actualizations

The massacre not only raises complex moral questions regarding innocent suffering in general, it can, via actualization, become the lens through which modern readers from diverse backgrounds make sense of their own pain. As long as infanticides, massacres, and tyranny remain in this world, Matt 2:16-18 continues to be a relevant passage for today, just as it was in the past.[44] By engaging with previous actualizations, Matthean

---

[44] For a recent news of infanticide, see Allyn Gaestel and Ricci Shryock, "Why Infanticide is a Problem in Senegel," National Public Radio, October 3, 2018, accessed October 30, 2018, https://www.npr.org/sections/ goatsandsoda/2018/10/03/631892291/why-infanticide-is-a-problem-in-senegal.

scholars can reflect on ways in which the text might appropriately be actualized. According to the Pontifical Biblical Commision's document *The Interpretation of the Bible in the Church*, "actualization is possible because the richness of meaning contained in the biblical text gives it value for all time and all cultures."[45]

This possibility has already been hinted in the large amount of space devoted to the subject of the massacre in the north frieze of *Cathédrale Notre-Dame de Chartres* (ca. 1140; see Chapter 6, VI. D). The cult of the Virgin of Chartres combined with the experience of medieval motherhood and the visual depictions of the massacre collectively discloses the piety and struggles of the mothers of Chartres. Another example is the *Coventry Carol* (ca. sixteenth century; see Chapter 5, II. A). It is both a lullaby and a lament, collectively a "lullament," that can no longer function to pacify a child, but primarily comforts grieving mothers.[46] Expressions of maternal grief and acknowledgment of the infants' departure into sleep are present in the lyrics and accompanied by the calm, soothing cadence. The story of the massacre invites empathy and camaraderie among mothers of diverse backgrounds who share similar struggles.

The two examples just mentioned demonstrate a key benefit of the reception history of Matt 2:16-18 for modern Matthean scholarship: the inclusion of the experiences of ordinary people. In reception history, hermeneutical authority is democratized to all types of readers instead of existing in an oligarchy of the literate and articulate few who write commentaries or preach homilies. Since reception historians need not favor clergy or learned scholars, the gathered bibliographical data will look different, at times dramatically so, than that of a typical historical-critical work. For example, the dialogues of the Solentiname *campesinos* (country inhabitants) on the Sunday Gospel Reading of Matt 2:16-18 would not be deemed inferior to exegetical commentaries.[47]

Hearing such popular readings and incorporating them into scholarly works will broaden the scope of Matthean scholarship with the diverse perspectives and interests of lay people. In most modern critical commentaries, scholars and theologians cite each other and converse among themselves in a perpetual cycle, preoccupied with meaning within and behind the text. Instead of actualizing the text in contemporary situations, they show the same type of historical-critical interests (e.g., in the historicity of the massacre, numerical figures, and geography).[48] Stanley Hauerwas is one of the few exceptions that actualize Matt 2:16-18 to include perspectives of the general public. This perspective is due to his background as a theological ethicist and the Brazos Commentary Series' inclusion of non-biblical scholars.[49] He perceives in Herod those who shrink from parenting to the point where they abandon children.[50] Today,

---

[45] Joseph A. Fitzmyer, *The Biblical Commission's Document "The Interpretation of the Bible in the Church": Text and Commentary*, Subsidia Biblica 18 (Rome: Editrice Pontificio Istituto Biblico, 1995), 171.

[46] O'Callaghan, "Lullament," 93–9.

[47] Ernesto Cardenal, *The Gospel in Solentiname*, trans. Donald D. Walsh (Maryknoll: Orbis, 1976), 73–83.

[48] See Appendix A.

[49] See Boston Collaborative Encyclopedia of Western Theology, "Stanley Haeurwas (1940-)," accessed April 13, 2016, http://people.bu.edu/wwildman/bce/hauerwas.htm; R. R. Reno, "Series Preface," in *1 & 2 Peter* by Douglas Harink, 9–14 (Grand Rapids: Brazos, 2009).

[50] Hauerwas, *Matthew*, 41.

interpreters of Matt 2:16-18 benefit from such readings that attest to the rich symbolic potential of the text to portray vividly the worlds in front of the text.[51]

So then, this study of Matt 2:16-18 has demonstrated reception history's value as a mediating discipline for twenty-first-century Matthean scholarship. Like the genealogy that begins the Gospel of Matthew (1:1-17), reception history can map out and trace the roots of traditions and reveal repetitions and patterns of readings in history. It invites marginalized voices to be heard alongside more well-known names, just as the women are included with the patriarchs of the genealogy. Finally, reception history promotes the universalist view of Matthew, hinted at in the genealogy and fully manifest in the Great Commission.[52] If current Matthean scholarship continues to profit from contributors from diverse cultures and backgrounds, reception history can be the means by which readings from all nations can be gathered and delineated.[53] As such diversity is celebrated and respected by reception historians who not only write reception history but also are transformed by it.

---

[51] For example, Rachel has already been utilized as a symbol of suffering faced by the abused, the homeless, and the aborted. See Denise M. Rowe, *The Voice of Rachel Weeping: A Creative Journey of Compassion, Healing, and Hope for Abused Women*; Jonathan Kozol, *Rachel and Her Children: Homeless Families in America*; and James T. Burtchaell, *Rachel Weeping and Other Essays on Abortion* (Toronto: Life Cycle Books, 1990).

[52] E. Anne Clements says it well: "the inclusion of these women serves to signal the importance of those on the margins in the ministry of the Messiah and to anticipate Matthew's rhetoric concerning the broadening of Israel's boundaries to include Gentile outsiders." *Mothers on the Margin? The Significance of the Women in Matthew's Genealogy*, 4.

[53] For an example of a work that attempts to assemble scholars from diverse backgrounds within the Lutheran tradition, see Kenneth Mtata and Craig Koester, eds., *To All the Nations: Lutheran Hermeneutics and the Gospel of Matthew*, Lutheran World Federation Studies 2015/2 (Leipzig: Evangelische Verlagsanstalt, 2015).

Appendix A

Massacre of the Innocents in Modern Commentaries

Interest in Historicity of the Event and Extra Biblical Corroborations

Lagrange (1927); Schlatter (1929); Lenski (1943); Lohmeyer (1956); Filson (1960); Bonnard (1963); Soares-Prabhu (1976); Hill (1981); Gundry (1982); Albright and Mann (1984); Gnilka (1986); Harrington (1991); Mounce (1991); Morris (1992); Blomberg (1992); Brown (1993); Boring (1995); Hagner (1998); Senior (1998); Green (2000); Hendriksen (2002); Schnackenburg (2002); Davies and Allison Jr. (2004); Wilkins (2004); Nolland (2005); France (2007); Turner (2008); Keener (2009); Osborne (2010); Evans (2012).

Interest in Numerical Figures

Calculation of two years	Allen (1912); Lagrange (1927); Lenski (1943); Filson (1960); Nellesen (1969); Gundry (1982); Mounce (1991); Harrington (1991); Blomberg (1992); Hagner (1998); Boice (2001); Hendriksen (2002); Davies and Allison Jr. (2004); Nolland (2005); Carson (2010); Osborne (2010)
Death toll	Lagrange (1927); Lenski (1943); Gundry (1982); Albright and Mann (1984); Mounce (1991); Blomberg (1992); Hagner (1998); Schnackenburg (2002); Hendriksen (2002); Wilkins (2004); Nolland (2005); France (2007); Turner (2008)
Interest in Christ and typology of ... Moses	Lohmeyer (1956); Filson (1960); Beare (1981); Broer (1981); Gnilka (1986); Patte (1987); Harrington (1991); Brown (1993); Knowles (1993); Boring (1995); Overman (1996); Senior (1998); Garland (1999); Carter (2000); Schnackenburg (2002); Bruner (2004); Davies and Allison Jr. (2004); Pregeant (2004); Nolland (2005); France (2007); Luz (2007); Kennedy (2008); Keener (2009)

David	Nolan (1979)
Solomon	Keener (2009)
Jeremiah	Harrington (1991); Knowles (1993); Davies and Allison Jr. (2004); France (2007); Keener (2009)
Recapitulation of Israel in Christ	Albright and Mann (1984); Patte (1987); Brown (1993); Knowles (1993); Boring (1995); Senior (1998); Bruner (2004); Davies and Allison Jr. (2004); Pregeant (2004); Nolland (2005); Kennedy (2008)

Interest in Adumbration of ...

Passion of Christ	Schlatter (1929); Gundry (1982); Gnilka (1986); Patte (1987); Harrington (1991); Overman (1996); Garland (1999); Carter (2000); Davies and Allison Jr. (2004); Kennedy (2008)
Jewish rejection and fate	Broer (1981); Gundry (1982); Gnilka (1986); Kingsbury (1988); Heil (1991); Knowles (1993); Davies and Allison Jr. (2004); Luz (2007)
Hope and comfort	Lenski (1943); Nellesen (1969); Broer (1981); Mounce (1991); Morris (1992); Brown (1993); Knowles (1993); Hagner (1998); Carter (2000); Boice (2001); Hendriksen (2002); Davies and Allison Jr. (2004); Wilkins (2004); Fiedler (2006); France (2007); Turner (2008); Keener (2009); Carson (2010); Osborne (2010)

Interest in Variations in Fulfillment Citation Formula and Theodicy

Lagrange (1927); Lenski (1943); Lohmeyer (1956); Gundry (1982); Gnilka (1986); Brown (1993); Knowles (1993); Boring (1995); Hagner (1998); Garland (1999); Carter (2000); Davies and Allison Jr. (2004); Pregeant (2004); Wilkins (2004); Nolland (2005); Fiedler (2006); France (2007); Luz (2007); Turner (2008); Carson (2010); Osborne (2010).

Interest in Textual-Critical and Redactional Details of Jeremiah 31:15

Allen (1912); Lagrange (1927); Schlatter (1929); Lenski (1943); Lohmeyer (1956); Bonnard (1963); Nolan (1979); Beare (1981); Gundry (1982); Albright and Mann

(1984); Gnilka (1986); Harrington (1991); Morris (1992); Brown (1993); Knowles (1993); Hagner (1998); Davies and Allison Jr. (2004); Nolland (2005); France (2007); Luz (2007); Turner (2008); Carson (2010).

Interest in Geographical Details of Bethlehem and Ramah

Lagrange (1927); Schlatter (1929); Lenski (1943); Lohmeyer (1956); Filson (1960); Bonnard (1963); Nellesen (1969); Beare (1981); Gundry (1982); Gnilka (1986); Patte (1987); Mounce (1991); Blomberg (1992); Morris (1992); Knowles (1993); Brown (1993); Senior (1998); Davies and Allison Jr. (2004); Hendriksen (2002); Schnackenburg (2002); Wilkins (2004); Nolland (2005); Luz (2007); Turner (2008); Keener (2009); Carson (2010); Osborne (2010).

Other Interpretations

Interest in Herod's parallelism to ...	
Those who fear and destroy children	Haeurwas (2006)
Kings of Psalm 2	Carter (2000); Hendricksen (2002); Turner (2008); Carson (2010)
Humanity's need	Bruner (2004)
Dragon of Revelation 12	Filson (1960)
Interest in bereaved women...	
pierced heart of Mary	Gundry (1982)
Parents not punished	Hendriksen (1973)

Interest in the Victims

Innocents as turtledoves and pigeons	Gundry (1982)
Slaughtered ones and original sin	Hendriksen (1973)

Appendix B

The Massacre of the Innocents in Commentaries from 1517 through the Nineteenth Century

All publication dates are approximate.

I. Historical-Grammatical Concerns

Interest in Historicity and Corroborations (E.g., Luke, Josephus, and Macrobius)

Stapulensis (1523); Cajetan (1530); Melanchthon (1544); Calvin (1555); Maldonato (1583); de Mariana (1620); a Lapide (1630); Hausted (1636); Lightfoot (1644); Trapp (1647); Poole (1685); Lamy (1689); Tillemont (1693); Burkit (1700); Brodick (1705); Hole (1716); Calmet (1717); Gill (1746); Crathorne (1749); Butler (1759); Thiry (1770); Challoner (1773); Horne (1779); Fleetwood (1795); Glasse (1797); Benson (1818); Clarke (1831); Sutcliffe (1838); Alford (1863); Meyer (1858); Lange (1865); Spurgeon (1865); Jamieson, Fausset, and Brown (1871); Whedon (1874); Ellicott (1878); Schaff (1879); Fouard (1880); Barnes (1884); Broadus (1886).

Interest in Measurements

Calculation of two years	Stapulensis (1523); Cajetan (1530); Calvin (1555); Maldonato (1583); de Mariana (1620); a Lapide (1630); Poole (1685); Henry (1710); Calmet (1717); Bengel (1742); Patrizi (1853); Meyer (1858); Bisping (1864); Fouard (1880); Barnes (1884); Broadus (1886)
Death toll	Stapulensis (1523); a Lapide (1630); Trapp (1647); Brodick (1705); Henry (1710); Hole (1716); Calmet (1717); Bengel (1742); Horne (1779); Fleetwood (1795); Alford (1863); Jamieson, Fausset, and Brown (1871); Whedon (1874); Ellicott (1878); Fouard (1880); Barnes (1884); Broadus (1886)

Interest in Fulfillment (E.g., Double Fulfillment, Four Senses) and Wider Context of Jeremiah 31

Stapulensis (1523); Cajetan (1530); de Valdes (1540); Calvin (1555); Maldonato (1583); de Sá (1596); de Mariana (1620); Menochio (1630); a Lapide (1630); Trapp (1647); Poole (1685); Burkit (1700); Brodick (1705); Henry (1710); Hole (1716); Calmet (1717); Bengel (1742); Gill (1746); Butler (1759); Thiry (1770); Horne (1779); Glasse (1797); Coke (1807); Benson (1818); Simeon (1819); Hawker (1826); Clarke (1831); Sutcliffe (1838); Meyer (1858); Darby (1860); Alford (1863); Bisping (1864); Lange (1865); Jamieson, Fausset, and Brown (1871); Whedon (1874); Abbott (1878); Schaff (1879); Fouard (1880); Broadus (1886).

Interest in textual-critical and redactional details of Jeremiah 31:15

Maldonato (1583); Bengel (1742); Clarke (1831); Bisping (1864); Lange (1865); Schaff (1879); Fouard (1880); Broadus (1886); Johnson (1891).

Interest in geographical details of Bethlehem and/or Ramah

Cajetan (1530); Melanchthon (1544); Maldonato (1583); Geneva Bible (1599); Drusius (1616); de Mariana (1620); Poole (1685); Burkit (1700); Henry (1710); Hole (1716); Calmet (1717); Bengel (1742); Butler (1759); Wesley (1765); Thiry (1770); Horne (1779); Benson (1818); Simeon (1819); Sutcliffe (1838); Meyer (1858); Bisping (1864); Lange (1865); Ellicott (1878); Abbott (1878); Schaff (1879); Fouard (1880); Barnes (1884); Broadus (1886); Johnson (1891).

II. Moral Concerns

Interest in theodicy (e.g., providence, Christ's ultimate sacrifice, punishment of Herod and/or Bethlehem)

Calvin (1555); Wild (1567); Geneva Bible (1599); Hausted (1636); Tillemont (1693); Wesley (1765); a Lapide (1630); Brodick (1705); Henry (1710); Hole (1716); Gother (1726); Bowes (1736); Butler (1759); Challoner (1773); Glasse (1797); Simeon (1819); Hawker (1826); Parker (1855); Jamieson, Fausset, and Brown (1871); Fouard (1880); Broadus (1886).

Appendix B

Interest in Herod's ...

Demonic and evil character	de Valdes (1540); Menochio (1630); a Lapide (1630); Wild (1567); Trapp (1647); Burkit (1700); Brodick (1705); Henry (1710); Bowes (1736); Bengel (1742); Gill (1746); Crathorne (1749); Butler (1759); Fleetwood (1795); Benson (1818); Simeon (1819); Hawker (1826); Parker (1855); Alford (1863); Lange (1865); Spurgeon (1865); Whedon (1874); Ellicott (1878); Schaff (1879); Barnes (1884); Broadus (1886)
Parallels with evil authorities	Wild (1567); Menochio (1630); Trapp (1647); Brodick (1705); Henry (1710); Gother (1726); Crathorne (1749); Glasse (1797); Coke (1807); Simeon (1819); Ryle (1856); Benson (1818); Parker (1855); Jamieson, Fausset, and Brown (1871)

Interest in innocence, martyrdom, and sacrifice of victims

Stapulensis (1523); Cajetan (1530); Maldonato (1583); a Lapide (1630); Tillemont (1693); Burkit (1700); Brodick (1705); Henry (1710); Hole (1716); Bingham (1721); Gother (1726); Bowes (1736); Crathorne (1749); Butler (1759); Challoner (1773); Horne (1779); Glasse (1797); Benson (1818); Simeon (1819); Hawker (1826); Clarke (1831); Sutcliffe (1838); Parker (1855); Haydock (1859); Lange (1865); Jamieson, Fausset, and Brown (1871); Whedon (1874); Schaff (1879); Fouard (1880).

Appendix C

Massacre of the Innocents in Art

Appendix C

Artist name, Providence and/āor title	Work type	Date (*ca.*)	Current location (if multiple, only one listed)	Modern background	Conflated with flight to Egypt	Herod not in the scene
Gallic Sarcophagi	Carving	Early fifth century	St. Maximin			
Ivory Diptych	Carving	Early fifth century	Berlin			
Triumphal Arch/*Basilica di Santa Maria Maggiore*	Mosaic	Fifh century	Rome			
Ivory Diptych	Carving	Late fifth/sixth century	Milan			
Rabbula Gospels	Miniature	586	Florence			x
Codex Purpureus	Miniature	Sixth century	St. Petersburg			
Historiated Initial/Bishop Drogo's Sacramentary	Miniature	844–55	Paris			x
Chludov Psalter	Miniature	Mid-ninth century	Moscow		x	
Gregory Master/*Codex Egberti*	Miniature	980	Trier	x		
Theodore Psalter	Miniature	Eleventh century	London			
Ivory Plaques/Lorraine or NE France	Carving	1050–99	London			
Incarnation Window/ Chartres Chapel	Stained Glass	Twelfth century	Chartres			
St. Albans Psalter	Illumination	1120–40	Hildesheim			
Wall/Råsted Church	Painting	1125–50	Råsted			
Picture Bible/Monastery of St Bertin, France	Illumination	1200	The Hague			x
Historiated Initial/*Ordo Officiaorum Ecclesiae Senensis*	Illumination	1215	Siena			x
North Portal Tympanum of the Strasbourg Cathedral	Carving	1275	Strasbourg		x	
Historiated Initial/ Antiphonal/Master of Gerona	Illumination	1275	Los Angeles			

Appendix C

Herod outside of throne room	Herod elevated	Herod points finger	Herod with Turban	Soldiers nude	Massacre fills scene |in chaos	Angelic beings present	Focus on one individual killing	Mother retaliating	Rachel's tomb in the background
		x							
		x							
		x							
		x							
		x							
	x	x							
	x	x							
x		x							
		x							
		x							
		x							
		x						x	
		x							
		x							

Artist name, Providence and/āor title	Work type	Date (*ca.*)	Current location (if multiple, only one listed)	Modern background	Conflated with flight to Egypt	Herod not in the scene
English Psalter	Illumination	Fourteenth	Cambridge			
Giovanni Pisano/Pulpit	Sculpture/ Marble	1301	Pistoia			
Giovanni Pisano/Pulpit	Sculpture/ Marble	1302–11	Pisa			
Giotto di Bondone	Fresco	1304–6	Padua	x		
Duccio di Buoninsegna/ *Maestà Altarpiece*	Tempera/ Gold/ Wood	1308–11	Siena			
Giotto di Bondone	Fresco	1310s	Assisi	x		
Andrea di Jacopo d'Ognabene/*St. James Altar*	Carving/ Gold	1316	Pistoia			
Church of the Holy Saviour	Fresco	1316–21	Chora	x		
Historiated Initial/French Breviary	Illumination	1320–5	Los Angeles			
Jean Pucelle/*Hours of Jeanne d'Évreux*	Illumination	1324	New York City			
Pietro Lorenzetti	Fresco	1330	Siena	x		
Maestro di Campli	Tempera/ Wood	1350–1400	Rome	x		
Giusto di Giovanni Menabuoi	Fresco	1370	Padua			x
Bertram of Minden/*Grabow Altarpiece*	Tempera/ Wood	1378–83	Hamburg			
Bartolo di Fredi	Tempera/ Gold Leaf	1380	Baltimore	x		
Pauper's Bible	Woodcut	Fifteenth	London			
Bertram of Minden/*Buxtehude Altarpiece*	Tempera/ Wood	1410	Buxtehude			
Gentile da Fabriano	Painting/ Wood	1425	Florence	x		
Bernardino Jacopi Butinone	Tempera/ Wood	1450–99	Detroit	x		

Appendix C

Herod outside of throne room	Herod elevated	Herod points finger	Herod with Turban	Soldiers nude	Massacre fills scene /in chaos	Angelic beings present	Focus on one individual killing	Mother retaliating	Rachel's tomb in the background
							x		
	x	x			x				
	x	x			x				
	x	x							
	x	x							
	x	x							
		x							
		x							
		x							
	x	x			x				
	x	x			x				
		x							
	x	x			x			x	
x									
		x							
	x								

Appendix C

Artist name, Providence and/āor title	Work type	Date (ca.)	Current location (if multiple, only one listed)	Modern background	Conflated with flight to Egypt	Herod not in the scene
Fra Angelico	Tempera/Wood	1451–3	Florence	x		
Flemish Artist/Bruges	Illustration/Parchment	1450s	Los Angeles	x		
Swabian Painter	Illumination	1450–70	New York City			x
Book of Hours	Illumination	1460	Glasgow	x		
Sano di Pietro	Tempera/Wood	1470	New York City	x		
Master of Freising Visitation	Tempera/Wood	1480	Nuremburg	x		
Hugo van der Goes(?)/Triptych	Oil	1480	St. Petersburg	x		x
Hans Memling	Oil	1480	Munich	x		x
Matteo di Giovanni	Tempera/Wood	1481	Naples	x		
Matteo di Giovanni	Mosaic Floor/Marble	1481	Siena			
Matteo di Giovanni	Tempera/Wood	1482	Siena	x		
Matteo di Giovanni	Tempera/Wood	1482	Siena	x		
Domenico Ghirlandaio	Fresco	1486–90	Florence	x		x
Master of the Virgo inter Virgines/Polyptych	Oil/Panel	1490–9	Salzburg			x
Jerusalem Triptych	Painting/Panel	1497-1500	Warsaw	x	x	
Collégiale Notre-Dame	Tapestry	1500	Beaune	x		
St. Blasius Church/Main Altar	Painting/Panel	1500	Kaufbeuren	x		x
Jean Poyet/*Hours of Henry VII*	Illumination	1500	New York City	x	x	x
Gerolamo Mocetto	Oil/Canvas	1500–25	London			
Amico Aspertini	Chalk	1510–20	Los Angeles			x
Ludovico Mazzolino	Oil/Wood	1510–28	Florence	x		

Appendix C

Herod outside of throne room	Herod elevated	Herod points finger	Herod with Turban	Soldiers nude	Massacre fills scene |in chaos	Angelic beings present	Focus on one individual killing	Mother retaliating	Rachel's tomb in the background
	x	x			x			x	
x									
		x						x	
	x	x	x		x				
					x				
	x	x	x		x				
	x	x	x		x				
							x		
x									
		x						x	
	x	x							
				x					
	x	x	x		x				

Artist name, Providence and/āor title	Work type	Date (ca.)	Current location (if multiple, only one listed)	Modern background	Conflated with flight to Egypt	Herod not in the scene
Marcantonio Raimondi/Raphael	Engraving	1512–13	St. Petersburg	x		x
Lucas Cranach the Elder	Oil/Tempera/Wood	1515	Warsaw	x	x	
Ludovico Mazzolino	Oil/Wood	1515–20	Amsterdam	x		
Domenico Campagnola	Woodcut/Block	1517	St. Petersburg			
Giovanni Angelo del Maino	Sculpture/Wood	1520	Boston	x	x	
Giovanni Francesco Caroto	Oil/Wood	1520–5	Bergamo	x	x	
Everhard Rensig or Gerhard Remisch	Stained Glass	1522–6	London			
Pieter Coecke van Aelst	Tapestry	1524–31	Vatican	x		x
Lambert Lombard/Triptych	Oil/Wood	1532–3	Private	x		x
Andreas Osiander/*Harmony of the Four Gospels*	Illustration	1540	n/a		x	x
Jan Swart van Groningen	Drawing	1550	London			
Dirck Volckertsz Coornhert/Maarten van Heemskerck	Engraving	1551	Amsterdam	x		
Daniele da Volterra (Ricciarelli)	Fresco	1555	Rome	x		x
Daniele da Volterra (Ricciarelli)	Oil/Panel	1557	Florence	x		x
Pieter Bruegel the Younger/the Elder	Oil/Panel	1567–9	Vienna			x
Philip Galle/Frans Floris	Engraving	1569	Amsterdam	x		
Bohemian Covered Tankard	Enamel	1578	Los Angeles	x		
Aegidius Sadeler	Engraving	1580–1629	Amsterdam			x
Jacopo Robusti Tintoretto	Oil/Canvas	1582–7	Venice	x		x
Hendrik Goltzius	Engraving	1584	Boston			
Lucas van Valckenborch	Oil/Panel	1586	Madrid			x
Giacomo Paracca	Sculpture/Clay	1587	Varallo	x		

Appendix C

Herod outside of throne room	Herod elevated	Herod points finger	Herod with Turban	Soldiers nude	Massacre fills scene |in chaos	Angelic beings present	Focus on one individual killing	Mother retaliating	Rachel's tomb in the background
			x						
	x	x							
	x	x	x		x				
	x	x	x	x	x				
	x	x			x				
		x		x					
x		x		x					
							x		
	x								
									x
				x			x		
x				x			x		x
				x					
				x			x		x
x		x		x					
	x	x			x				

Artist name, Providence and/āor title	Work type	Date (ca.)	Current location (if multiple, only one listed)	Modern background	Conflated with flight to Egypt	Herod not in the scene
Cornelis van Haarlem	Oil/Canvas	1590	Amsterdam	x		x
Gillis van Valckenborch	Oil/Copper	1590–5	Warsaw	x		
Cornelis van Haarlem	Oil/Canvas	1591	Haarlem	x		x
Peter Paul Rubens	Oil/Canvas	1609–11	Toronto	x		x
Guido Reni	Oil/Canvas	1611	Bologna	x		x
Frans Francken II	Oil/Copper	1620	Private	x		x
Jacques Callot	Etching/Engraving	1621--5	Amsterdam	x		
Paul Maupin	Woodcut/Buff Paper	1625	Boston	x		x
Nicholas Poussin	Oil/Canvas	1628	Chantilly			x
Pietro Testa	Oil/Canvas	1630–40	Rome		x	x
Peter Paul Rubens	Oil/Canvas	1635–7	Munich	x		
Alessandro Turchi	Oil/Copper	1640	Vienna	x		x
Pacecco de Rosa	Oil/Canvas	1640	Rouen			x
Jacques Stella	Grisaille	1640	Rouen	x		x
Sebastian Bourdon	Oil/Canvas	1640s	St. Petersburg	x		
Giovanni Cristoforo Storer	Oil/Canvas	1645	Milan	x		x
Valerio Castello	Oil/Canvas	1653	Paris	x		x
Valerio Castello	Oil/Canvas	1656–8	St. Petersburg	x		x
Nicolas Chevillard	Painting	1657	Beaune	x		x
Lucas Giordano	Oil/Canvas	1663	Madrid	x		x
Charles LeBrun	Oil/Canvas	1665	London	x		x
Pedro Atanasio Bocanegra	Oil/Canvas	1670	Córdoba	x		x
Cathedral of St. Mary	Carving/Wood	1687	Pamplona			x
Francesco Trevisani	Oil/Canvas	1700–10	Cambridge	x		x
Bertholet Flemalle	Oil/Canvas	1738	Liège	x		x
Jean-Baptiste Marie Pierre(?)	Oil/Canvas	1763	Private			x
Léon Cogniet	Oil/Canvas	1824	Rennes	x		x
Francois Joseph Navez	Oil/Canvas	1824	New York City	x		x

Appendix C

Herod outside of throne room	Herod elevated	Herod points finger	Herod with Turban	Soldiers nude	Massacre fills scene |in chaos	Angelic beings present	Focus on one individual killing	Mother retaliating	Rachel's tomb in the background
				x				x	
					x			x	
				x				x	
					x			x	
						x			
	x	x			x				
				x			x		
				x		x			
x					x			x	x
						x			
				x				x	
				x					x
x	x				x				
								x	x
									x
								x	
				x				x	x
								x	
				x					
				x				x	
						x			
						x			

Artist name, Providence and/āor title	Work type	Date (ca.)	Current location (if multiple, only one listed)	Modern background	Conflated with flight to Egypt	Herod not in the scene
Julius Schnorr von Carolsfeld/*Picture Bible*	Illustration	1860	Leipzig	x	x	
Angelo Visconti	Oil/Canvas	1860–1	Siena	x		x
Gustave Doré/*La Grande Bible de Tours*	Engraving/Wood	1866	Tours	x		x
Gustave Doré	Pen/Ink	1869	New York City	x		x
Carl H. Bloch	Oil/Copper	1875	Denmark			x
William Holman Hunt	Oil/Canvas	1876–87	Liverpool		x	x
William Holman Hunt	Oil/Canvas	1883–4	London		x	x
James Tissot	Watercolor	1886–94	New York City			x
Antonio Gaudi/Temple Expiatori de la Sagrada Família	Sculpture	1900–25	Barcelona			x
William Holman Hunt	Oil/Canvas	1903	Harvard		x	x
Eric Gill	Engraving/Wood	1914	London			x

Herod outside of throne room	Herod elevated	Herod points finger	Herod with Turban	Soldiers nude	Massacre fills scene |in chaos	Angelic beings present	Focus on one individual killing	Mother retaliating	Rachel's tomb in the background
						x		x	
							x		
							x		
					x				
					x				
							x		
					x				
							x		

Select Bibliography

Primary Sources and Reference Works

Alighieri, Dante. *The Divine Comedy, Purgatorio*. Translated by Dorothy Sayers. New York: Penguin Classics, 1962.

Allenbach, Jean, and Centre d'analyse et de documentation patristiques. *Biblia patristica: Index des citations et allusions bibliques dans la littérature patristique*. 5 vols. Paris: Éditions du Centre national de la recherche scientifique, 1980–91.

Art in Tuscany. Accessed in April 24, 2018. http://www.travelingintuscany.com/art/matteodigiovanni.htm.

Atchley, Edward G. C. F., trans. *The Ambrosian Liturgy: The Ordinary and Canon of the Mass according to the Rite of the Church of Milan*. London: Cope & Fenwick, 1909.

Atsma, Aaron J. "Hypnos." *Theoi Greek Mythology*. Accessed October 18, 2017. https://www.theoi.com/Daimon/Hypnos.html.

Atwan, Robert, and Laurance Wieder, eds. *Chapters into Verse: Poetry in English Inspired by the Bible*. 2 vols. Oxford: Oxford University Press, 1993.

Baggley, John. *Festal Icons for the Christian Year*. Crestwood: St. Vladimir's Seminary Press, 2000.

Baldi, P. Donatus. *Enchiridion Locorum Sanctorum*. Jerusalem: Tupis PP Franciscanorum, 1955.

Barclay, William B., trans. *St. Peter Chrysologus: Selected Sermons*. Vol. 3. The Fathers of the Church 110. Washington, DC: Catholic University of America Press, 2005.

Barnes, Albert. *Barnes' Notes on the New Testament, Complete and Unabridged in One Volume*. Grand Rapids: Kregel, 1962.

Baseley, Joel R., trans. *Festival Sermons of Martin Luther: The Church Postils: Sermons for the Main Festivals and Saints Days of the Church Year; Winter and Summer Selections*. Dearborn: Mark V, 2005.

Bauer, Walter, Frederick W. Danker, W. F. Arndt, and F. W. Gingrich, eds. *A Greek-English Lexicon of the New Testament and Other Early Christian Literature*. 3rd ed. Chicago: University of Chicago Press, 2000.

Bedjan, P., ed. *Homiliae selectae Mar-Jacobi Sarugensis*. 5 vols. Paris: Harrassowitz, 1905–10.

Bengel, Ernest, Johann C. F. Steudel, and Andrew R. Fausset, trans. and eds. *Gnomon of the New Testament by John A. Bengel, Now First Translated into English with Original Notes Explanatory and Illustrative*. Vol. 1. London: T&T Clark, 1858.

Benson, Joseph. *Commentary of the Old and New Testaments*. Accessed December 8, 2017. http://biblehub.com/commentaries/benson/.

Bernard, John H., trans. *The Pilgrimage of S. Silvia of Aquitania to the Holy Places (Circ. 385 AD)*. London: Palestine Pilgrims' Text Society, 1896.

Betts, John, trans. *Juán de Valdés' Commentary upon the Gospel of St. Matthew: Now for the First Time Translated from the Spanish and Never before Published in English*. London: Trübner, 1882.

The Bible and Holy Scriptures Conteined in the Olde and Newe Testament. Translated according to the Ebrue and Greke, and conferred with the best translations in divers languags. With moste profitable annotations upon all the Lord places, and other things of great importance as may appeare in the Epistle to the Reader. Geneva: Rouland Hall, 1560.

Bonnard, Émile, trans. *Saint Jérôme: Commentaire Sur S. Matthieu: Tome I: Livres I-II.* Sources chrétiennes 242. Paris: Cerf, 1977.

Borromeo, Charles. *Sancti Caroli Borromei S.R E. Cardinalis Archiepiscopi Mediolani Homiliae CXXVII. Ex MSS. Codicibus Bibliothecae Ambrosianae Ordine Chronologico In Lucem Productae.* Veith: Augustae Vindelicorum, 1758.

Boyd, William K. *The Ecclesiastical Edicts of the Theodosian Code.* Studies in History, Economics, and Public Law 24. No. 2. New York: Columbia University Press, 1905.

Braun, R. ed. *Opera Quodvultdeo Carthaginiensi Episcopo Tributa.* CCSL 60. Turnholt: Brepolis, 1976.

Brewer, Ebenezer C. *Brewer's Dictionary of Phrase & Fable.* Revised and enlarged edition. New York: Harper & Brothers, 1952.

Broadus, John A. *Commentary on the Gospel of Matthew.* An American Commentary on the New Testament. Philadelphia: American Baptist Publication Society, 1886.

Brodrick, Thomas. *Historia Sacra: Or, the Holy History: Giving an Exact and Comprehensive Account of All the Feasts and Fasts of the Church of England with Their Various Etymologies and Appellations, and the True Reasons and Grounds of their Celebration: Together with Practical Observations upon the Several Days, and Prayers Concluding Each Distinct Head to which is Added an Appendix, Wherein the Three Grand Solemnities Added to the Liturgy of the Church of England Are Clearly Expalin'd. The second, revis and correct; and the history illustrat with many new and curious cuts in copper. ed.* London: Printed for John Wyat at the Rose in St. Paul's Church-yard, 1720.

Budge, Ernest A. W., ed. and trans. *The Book of the Bee.* Oxford: Clarendon, 1886.

Budge, Ernest A. W., trans. *The Book of the Cave of Treasures: A History of the Patriarchs and the Kings Their Successors from the Creation to the Crucifixion of Christ Translated from the Syriac Text of the British Museum Ms. Add. 25875.* London: Religious Tract Society, 1927.

Budge, Ernest A. W.. *The History of the Blessed Virgin Mary and the History of the Likeness of Christ.* Luzac's Semitic Text and Translation Series 4 and 5. London: Luzac, 1899.

Burtchaell, James T. *Rachel Weeping and Other Essays on Abortion.* Toronto: Life Cycle Books, 1990.

Cajetan, Thomas. *Evangelia cum Commentariis: In quatuor evangelia & Acta Apostolorum ad Graecorum codicum veritatem castigata ad sensum que vocant literalem Comentarii.* Venetiis: In aedibus Luceantonii Iunctae Florentini, 1530.

Calmet, Augustin. *Commentaire littéral sur tous les livres de l'Ancien et du Nouveau Testament: L'Evangile de S. Matthieu.* Emery Saugrain: Pierre de Martin, 1715.

Camus, Albert. *The Fall.* Translated by Justin O'Brien. New York: Knopf, 1956.

Cardenal, Ernesto. *The Gospel in Solentiname.* Translated by Donald D. Walsh. Maryknoll: Orbis, 1976.

Carrier, David. *Poussin's Paintings: A Study in Art-Historical Methodology.* University Park: Pennsylvania State University Press, 1993.

Causley, Charles. *Collected Poems, 1951–2000.* London: Pan Macmillan, 2000.

Cawley, Arthur C. ed. *Everyman and Medieval Miracle Plays.* New York: Everyman's Library, 1961.

Clarke, G. W., trans. *The Letters of St. Cyprian of Carthage: Volume III: Letters 55–66*. Ancient Christian Writers: The Works of the Fathers in Translation 46. New York: Newman, 1983.

Collins Jr., Fletcher, ed. and trans. *Medieval Church Music-Dramas: A Repertory of Complete Plays*. Charlottesville: University of Virginia Press, 1976.

Cotes, Digby. *Fifteen Sermons Preach'd on Several Occasions*. Oxford: Printed at the Theatre for Ant. Peisley Bookseller and are to be sold by J. Knapton, W. Meadows, and T. Combes, Booksellers in London, 1721.

Cox, Patrick. "Christmas." In *The Wiley Blackwell Encyclopedia of Consumption and Consumer Studies*. Edited by Daniel T. Cook and J. Michael Ryan, 77–8. Oxford: John Wiley & Sons, 2015.

Davie, George J., trans. *A Commentary on the Gospels by John Maldonatus: S. Matthew's Gospel, Chapters I. to XIV*. London: John Hodges, 1888.

Deferrari, Roy J., trans. *Eusebius Pamphili: Ecclesiastical History, Book 1–5*. The Fathers of the Church: A New Translation 19. Washington, DC: Catholic University of America Press, 2005.

Deshusses, Jean, ed. *Le Sacramentaire Grégorien: Ses Principales Formes D'Après Les Plus Anciens Munscrits: Edition Comparative*. Fribourg: Editions universitaires, 1971.

de Grummond, Nancy T., ed. *Encyclopedia of the History of Classical Archaeology*. Abingdon: Routledge, 1996.

d'Étaples, Jacques L. *Commentarii initiatorii in quatuor Evangelia*. Meaux: Simon Colinaeus, 1522.

de Medina, Miguel, ed. *Commentariorum Ioannis Feri in sacro sanctum Iesu Christi Euangelium secundum Matthaeum libri quatuor*. Compluti: Andreas de Angulo, 1567.

de Sales, Francis. *Oeuvres Complètes de Saint François de Sales, Évêque et Prince de Genève et Docteur de L'Église: Tome Huitième: Sermons II*ᵉ *Volume*. Annecy: J. Niérat, 1892.

de Voragine, Jacobus. *The Golden Legend: Readings on the Saints: Translated by William G. Ryan with an Introduction by Eamon Duffy*. Princeton: Princeton University Press, 2012.

Diercks, G. F., ed. *Sancti Cypriani Episcopi Opera. Pars III, 2: Sancti Cypriani Episcopi Epistularium*. CCSL 3C. Turnholt: Brepolis, 1996.

Diercks, G. F., ed. *Luciferi Calaritani Opera Quae Supersunt: Ad Fidem Duorum Codium Qui Adhuc Extant Necnon Adhibitis Editionibus Veteribus*. CCSL 8. Turnholt: Brepolis, 1978.

Dodwell, Charles R. *The Pictorial Arts of the West, 800–1200*. New Haven: Yale University Press, 1995.

Doignon, Jean, trans. *Hilaire de Poitiers: Sur Matthieu: Tome I: Introduction, Texte Critique, Traduction et Notes*. Sources chrétiennes 254. Paris: Cerf, 1974.

Dronke, Peter, ed. and trans. *Nine Medieval Latin Plays*. Cambridge Medieval Classics I. Cambridge: Cambridge University Press, 1994.

Ehrman, Bart D., and Zlatko Pleše, eds. and trans. *The Other Gospels: Accounts of Jesus from Outside the New Testament*. Oxford: Oxford University Press, 2014.

Ehrman, Bart D. *Lost Scriptures: Books That Did Not Make It into the New Testament*. Oxford: Oxford University Press, 2003.

Elliott, James K. *A Synopsis of the Apocryphal Nativity and Infancy Narratives*. New Testament Tools and Studies 34. Leiden: Brill, 2006.

Elliott, James K., ed. *The Apocryphal New Testament: A Collection of Apocryphal Christian Literature in an English Translation*. Oxford: Oxford University Press, 1993.

Encyclopaedia Britannica Online. Accessed October 26, 2016. https://www.britannica.com/biography/Lucifer-bishop-of-Cagliari.

Étaix, R., and J. Lemarié, eds. *Chromatii Aquileiensis Opera*. CCSL 9a. Turnholt: Brepolis, 1974.

Evans, Ernest, ed. and trans. *Tertullian's Treatise on the Incarnation: The Text Edited with an Introduction, Translation, and Commentary.* London: SPCK, 1956.

Farmer, David H. *The Oxford Dictionary of Saints.* Revised edition. Oxford: Oxford University Press, 2011.

Feltoe, Charles L., ed. *Sacramentarium Leonianum: Edited, with Introduction, Notes, and Three Photographs.* Cambridge: Cambridge University Press, 1896.

Férotin, Marius, Anthony Ward, and Cuthbert Johnson, eds. *Le Liber Mozarabicus Sacramentorum: Et Les Manuscrits Mozarabes.* Biblioteca Ephemerides Liturgicae, Subsidia 78. Instrumenta Liturgica Quarreriensia 4. Roma: C.L.V.-Edizioni Liturgiche, 1995.

Finn, Thomas M., trans. *Quodvultdeus of Carthage: The Creedal Homilies: Conversion in Fifth-Century North Africa: Translation and Commentary.* Ancient Christian Writers 60. New York: Newman, 2004.

The Festal Menaion. Translated from the Original Greek by Mother Mary and Archimandrite Kallistos Ware, with an Introduction by Georges Florovsky. London: Faber, 1969.

Fitzmeyer, Joseph A. *The Biblical Commission's Document "The Interpretation of the Bible in the Church": Text and Commentary.* Subsidia Biblica 18. Rome: Editrice Pontificio Istituto Biblico, 1995.

Flower, Robin, ed. *Catalogue of Irish Manuscripts in the British Museum.* Vol. 2. London: British Museum, 1926.

Fortunantius of Aquileia. *Commentary on the Gospels. English Translation and Introduction by H. A. G. Houghton.* CSEL Extra Seriem. Berlin: De Gruyter 2017.

Freeland, Jane P., and Agnes J. Conway, trans. *St. Leo the Great: Sermons.* The Fathers of the Church 93. Washington, DC: Catholic University of America Press, 1996.

Fuller, Thomas. *A Fast Sermon Preached on Innocents Day.* London: Printed by L.N. and R.C. for John Williams at the signe of the Crowne in Saint Pauls Church-yard, 1642.

Gilbert, Peter, trans. *On God and Man: The Theological Poetry of St. Gregory of Nazianzus.* Crestwood: St. Vladimir's Seminary Press, 2001.

Giles, John A., ed. *Codex Apocryphus Novi Testamenti: The Uncanonical Gospels and Other Writings.* London: D. Nutt, 1852.

Gill, John. *Exposition of the Bible.* Accessed December 7, 2017. https://www.biblestudytools.com/commentaries/gills-exposition-of-the-bible/.

Ginzberg, Louis. *The Legends of the Jews.* 4 vols. Philadelphia: Jewish Publication Society, 1969.

Griffiths, Alan, trans. *We Give You Thanks and Praise: The Ambrosian Eucharistic Prefaces of the Ambrosian Missal.* Franklin: Sheed & Ward, 2000.

Gryson, Roger, P.-A. Deproost, trans. *Commentaires de Jérôme sur le prophète Isaïe: Livres I-IV.* AGLB 23. Freiburg: Herder, 1993.

Harrington, Daniel J., and Anthony J. Saldarini, trans. *Targum Jonathan of the Former Prophets: Introduction, Translation and Notes.* Aramaic Bible 10. Edinburgh: T&T Clark, 1987.

Hausted, Peter. *Ten Sermons, Preached Vpon Seuerall Sundayes and Saints Dayes: 1 Vpon the Passion of our Blessed Savior. 2 Vpon His Resurrection. 3 Vpon S. Peters Day. 4*

Vpon S. Iohn the Baptists Day. 5 Vpon the Day of the Blessed Innocents. 6 Vpon Palme Sunday. 7 and 8 Vpon the Two First Sundays in Advent. 9 and 10 Vpon the Parable of the Pharisee and Publicane, Luke 18. Together with a Sermon Preached at the Assises at Huntington. by P. Hausted Mr. in Arts, and Curate at Vppingham in Rutland. London: Printed by Miles Flesher, Bernard Alsop, and Thomas Fawcet for John Clark, and are to be sold at his shop under S. Peters Church in Cornhill, 1636.

Henry, Matthew. *Commentary on the Whole Bible (Complete)*. Accessed December 7, 2017. https://www.biblestudytools.com/commentaries/matthew-henry-complete/.

Hesbert, René-Jean, ed. *Antiphonale Missarum Sextuplex: D'après le graduel de Monza et les antiphonaires de Rheinau, de Mont-Blandin, de Compiègne, de Corbie et de Senlis.* Herder: Rome 1967.

Hildegard of Bingen. *Homilies on the Gospels*. Translated with introduction and notes by Beverly M. Kienzle. Cistercian Studies 241. Collegeville: Liturgical Press, 2011.

Hill, Edmund, trans. *The Works of Saint Augustine: A Translation for the 21st Century: Part III—Sermons Volume 10: Sermons 341–400*. Hyde Park: New City, 1995.

d'Holbach, Paul T. *Ecce homo!: An Eighteenth Century Life of Jesus by Paul T. d'Holbach: Critical Edition and Revision of George Houston's Translation from the French*. Edited by Andrew Hunwick. Berlin: Walter de Gruyter, 1995.

Horne, George. *Discourses on Several Subjects and Occasions*. 5th ed. 2 vols. Oxford: Printed for J. Cooke and G. G. and J. Robinson, T. Cadell, and F. and C. Rivington, London, 1795.

Hourihane, Colum, ed. *The Grove Encyclopedia of Medieval Art and Architecture, Volume 1: Aachen to Cecco di Pietro*. Oxford: Oxford University Press, 2012.

Hunt, Wiliam H. *The Triumph of the Innocents*. London: R. Clay, 1885.

Jamieson, Robert, Andrew R. Fausset, and David Brown. *Commentary Critical and Explanatory on the Whole Bible*. Accessed December 6, 2017. https://www.biblestudytools.com/commentaries/jamieson-fausset-brown/.

Jeffrey, David L., ed. *A Dictionary of Biblical Tradition in English Literature*. Grand Rapids: Eerdmans, 1992.

Kaster, Robert A., ed. and trans. *Macrobius: Saturnalia Books 1–2*. Vol. 1. Loeb Classical Library 510. Cambridge: Harvard University Press, 2011.

ΤΗι ΚΘ' ΤΟΥ ΑΥΤΟΥ ΜΗΝΟΣ ΔΕΚΕΜΒΡΙΟΥ Μνήμη τῶν Ἁγίων Νηπίων, τῶν ὑπὸ Ἡρῴδου ἀναιρεθέντων, ὧν ὁ ἀριθμὸς χιλιάδες ιδ' Μνήμη τοῦ Ὁσίου Πατρὸς ἡμῶν Μαρκέλλου, Ἡγουμένου τῆς Μονῆς τῶν Ἀκοιμήτων. Accessed March 21, 2018. http://glt.goarch.org/texts/Dec/Dec29.html.

Kellerman, J. A., trans. *Incomplete Commentary on Matthew (Opus Imperfectum)*. Edited by Thomas C. Oden. 2 vols. Ancient Christian Texts. Downers Grove: IVP Academic, 2010.

Killingbeck, John. *The Blessedness and Reward of Charity Asserted: In a Sermon Preach'd in the Parish-Church of St. Peter's in Leeds, December 28. 1709. (Being Innocents-Day) for Promoting the Charity-School Erected There*. London: Printed for H. Clements, at the Half-Moon in St. Paul's Church-Yard, 1710.

King, Pamela M., and Clifford Davidson. *The Coventry Corpus Christi Plays*. Early Drama, Art, and Music Monograph Series 27. Kalamazoo: Medieval Institute, 2000.

Kirschbaum, Engelbert, Wolfgang Braunfels, Johannes Kollwitz, and Günter Bandmann, eds. *Lexikon der christlichen Ikonographie*. 8 vols. Freiburg: Herder, 1968–76.

Kollamparampil, Thomas, ed. and trans. *Jacob of Serugh, Select Festal Homilies*. Rome: Centre for Indian and Inter-Religious Studies and Dharmaram, 1997.

Kozol, Jonathan. *Rachel and Her Children: Homeless Families in America.* New York: Broadway, 2006.

Kramer, Aaron, and Saul Lishinsky, eds. *The Last Lullaby: Poetry from the Holocaust.* Syracuse: Syracuse University Press, 1998.

"Leccionario Hispano-Mozárabe-Liber Commicus." *Rito Hispano Mozárabe.* Accessed March 17, 2018. https://mercaba.org/LITURGIA/Mozarabe/cartel_rito_hispanomozarabe.htm.

Le Marchant, Jean. *Miracles de Notre-Dame de Chartres.* Edited by Pierre Kunstmann. Ottawa: University of Ottawa Press, 1973.

Lemon, Rebecca, Emma Mason, Jonathan Roberts, and Christopher Rowland, eds. *The Blackwell Companion to the Bible in English Literature.* Oxford: Blackwell, 2009.

Lequien, P. Michaelis, ed. *John of Damascus, John of Nicæa, Patriarch John VI of Constantinople, Joannes of Eubœa.* Patrologiae cursus completus, series graeca 46. Paris: Petit-Montrouge, 1864.

Lewis, Wyndham. *The Childermass.* London: Chatto and Windus, 1928.

Litwa, M. David, trans. *Refutation of All Heresies: Translated with an Introduction and Notes.* Writings from the Greco-Roman World. Atlanta: SBL Press, 2016.

Löfstedt, B., ed. *Rabanus Maurus: Commentarius in Matthaeum. I-IV.* CCSL 174. Turnhout: Brepols, 2001.

Long, Siobhán D., and John F. A. Sawyer. *The Bible in Music: A Dictionary of Songs, Works, and More.* Lanham: Rowman & Littlefield, 2015.

Louw, Johannes P., Eugene Albert Nida, Rondal B. Smith, and Karen A. Munson, eds. *Greek- English Lexicon of the New Testament: Based on Semantic Domains.* 2 vols. New York: United Bible Societies, 1989.

Maggioni, Giovanni P., ed. *Iacopo da Varazze: Legenda aurea.* Firenze: Sismel Edizioni del Galluzzo, 1998.

Magistretti, Marco, ed. *Manuale Ambrosianum ex codice saec. XI olim in usum canonicae Vallis Travaliae, part 2: Monumenta veteris liturgiae ambrosianae* 3. Milan: Hoepli, 1904.

Margoliouth, Moses. *A Pilgrimage to the Land of My Fathers.* London: Richard Bentley, 1850.

Marino, Giambattista. *The Massacre of the Innocents.* Translated by Erik Butler. Cambridge: Wakefield, 2015.

Martin, L. T., and D. Hurst, trans. *Bede: Homilies on the Gospels: Book One: Advent to Lent.* Kalamazoo: Cistercian Publications, 1991.

"Matthew 2," *The Pulpit Commentaries.* Accessed November 13, 2017. https://www.studylight.org/commentaries/tpc/matthew-2.html.

McCarthy, Carmel., trans. *Saint Ephrem's Commentary on Tatian's Diatessaron: An English Translation of Chester Beatty Syriac MS 709 with Introduction and Notes.* Journal of Semitic Studies Supplement 2. Oxford: Oxford University Press, 1993.

Meehan, Denis M. trans. *Saint Gregory of Nazianzus: Three Poems: Concerning His Own Affairs, Concerning Himself and the Bishops, Concerning His Own Life.* The Fathers of the Church 75. Washington, DC: Catholic University of America Press, 1987.

Melville, Herman. *Moby-Dick.* Edited by John Bryant and Haskell Springer. A Longman Critical Edition. New York: Pearson Longman, 2007.

Melville, Herman. *Moby Dick or The Whale.* Edited by Harrison Hayford, Hershel Parker, and G. Thomas Tanselle. The Writings of Herman Melville 6. The Northwestern-Newberry Edition. Evanston: Northwestern University Press and the Newberry Library, 1988.

Migne, Jacques-Paul, ed. *Origenes*. Patrologiae cursus completus, series graeca 11. Paris: Petit-Montrouge, 1857.

Minto, William, ed. *Autobiographical Notes of the Life of William Bell Scott and Notices of His Artistic and Poetic Circle of Friends, 1830 to 1882*. 2 vols. London: Osgood, McIlvaine, 1892.

Mohlberg, Leo C., Leo Eizenhöfer, and Petrus Siffrin, eds. *Liber Sacramentorum Romanae Aeclesiae Ordinis Anni Circuli: (Cod. Vat. Reg. Lat. 216/Paris Bibl. nat. 7193, 41/56): (Sacramentarium Gelasianum)*. Roma: Herder, 1960.

Moore, Colin. *Propaganda Prints: A History of Art in the Service of Social and Political Change*. London: A&C Black, 2010.

Morin, G. "Le Plus Ancien *Comes* ou Lectionnaire de L'Église Romaine." *RB* 27 (1910): 41–74.

Morin, G. "Liturgie et Basiliques de Rome au Milieu du VIIe Siècle d'après les Listes D'Évangiles de Würzburg." *RB* 28 (1911): 296–330.

Morrison, A. W., trans. *John Calvin: A Harmony of the Gospels Matthew, Mark and Luke*. Edinburgh: St. Andrew's Press, 1972.

Mossman, Thomas W., trans. *The Great Commentary of Cornelius à Lapide: S. Matthew's Gospel—Chaps. I. to IX*. London: John Hodges, 1876.

Moulton, James H., and George Milligan, eds. *The Vocabulary of the Greek Testament: Illustrated from the Papyri and Other Non-literary Sources*. London: Hodder and Stoughton, 1929.

Muraoka, Takamitsu, ed. *A Greek-English Lexicon of the Septuagint*. Leuven: Peeters, 2009.

Neusner, James, ed. and trans. *Lamentations Rabbah and Leviticus Rabbah. Scripture and Midrash in Judaism*. Vol. 3. Frankfurt: Peter Lang, 1995.

Neville, Robert. *Goodness Proved to Be the Best Protection from the Arrests of All Harmes: In a Sermon Preached before the University, upon Innocents Day, in Great St. Maries Church in Cambridge*. London: Printed for Benj. Billingsley, 1687.

New Documents Illustrating Early Christianity. Edited by Greg H. R. Horsley and Stephen Llewelyn. North Ryde: Ancient History Documentary Research Centre, Macquarie University, 1981–2012.

Olivar, Alexandri, ed. *Sancti Petri Chrysologi: Collectio Sermonum a Felice Episcopo Parata Semonibus Extravagantibus Adiectis*. CCSL 24B. Turnhout: Brepols, 1982.

The Oxford Dictionary of Art. Edited by Ian Chilvers and Harold Osborne. 2nd ed. Oxford: Oxford University Press, 1997.

The Oxford Dictionary of Byzantium. Edited by Alexander P. Kazhdan, Alice-Mary Talbot, Anthony Culter, Timothy E. Gregory, and Nancy P. Ševčenko. 3 Vols. Oxford: Oxford University Press, 1991.

The Oxford Dictionary of the Christian Church. Edited by Frank L. Cross and Elizabeth A. Livingstone. 3rd revised edition. Oxford: Oxford University Press, 2005.

Orthodox Study Bible. Edited by Alan Wallerstedt. Nashville: Thomas Nelson, 1993.

Pitman, John R., ed. *The Whole Works of the Rev. John Lightfoot: Master of Catharine Hall, Cambridge*. 11 vols. London: JF Dove, 1825.

Pope, R. Martin, trans. *The Hymns of Prudentius*. London: J. M. Dent, 2005.

Rahlfs, Alfred. *Septuaginta, Id est Vetus Testamentum graece iuxta LXX interpretes*. Stuttgart: Wüttembergische Bibelanstalt, 1971.

Reuss, Joseph, ed. *Matthäus-Kommentare aus der Griechischen Kirche*. Texte und Untersuchungen zur Geschichte der altchristlichen Literatur 61. Berlin: Akademie-Verlag, 1957.

Roberts, Alexander, and James Donaldson, eds. *The Ante-Nicene Fathers: Translations of the Writings of the Fathers down to A.D. 325*. 10 vols. Grand Rapids: Eerdmans, 1950.

Robinson, Forbes, trans. *Coptic Apocryphal Gospels: Translations Together with the Texts of Some of Them*. Texts and Studies: Contributions to Biblical and Patristic Literature 4. No. 2. Cambridge: Cambridge University Press, 1896.

Roca-Puig, Ramón, ed. *Himne a la Verge Maria "Psalmus Responsorius." Papir llatí del segle iv*. 2nd ed. Barcelona: Asociación de Bibliofilos de Barcelona, 1965.

Rose, Martial, ed. *The Wakefield Mystery Plays*. Garden City: Doubleday, 1963.

Rousseau, Adelin, and Louis Doutreleau, trans. *Irénée de Lyon: Contre les Heresies Livre III: Tome II: Introduction, Texte Critique, Traduction et Notes*. Sources chrétiennes 211. Paris: Cerf, 2002.

Rowe, Denise M. *The Voice of Rachel Weeping: A Creative Journey of Compassion, Healing, and Hope for Abused Women*. Maitland: Xulon, 2016.

Rusch, Adolph. *Biblia Latina cum glossa ordinaria: Facsimile Reprint of the editio princeps Adolph Rusch of Strassburg 1480/81*. Turnhout: Brepols, 1992.

Saramango, José. *The Gospel according to Jesus Christ*. Translated by Giovanni Pontiero. Harvest in Translation. New York: Mariner Books, 1994.

Schaff, Philip, trans. *A Commentary on the Holy Scriptures: Critical, Doctrinal, and Homiletical, with Special Reference to Ministers and Students by John Peter Lange. Vol. I. of the New Testament: Containing a General Introduction and the Gospel according to Matthew*. New York: Charles Scribner, 1865.

Scheck, Thomas P., trans. *Jerome-Origen: Commentary on Isaiah Including St. Jerome's Translation of Origen's Homilies 1–9 on Isaiah: Translated and with an Introduction*. Ancient Christian Writers: The Works of the Fathers in Translation 68. New York: Newman, 2015.

Scheck, Thomas P., trans. *Jerome: Commentary on Matthew*. The Fathers of the Church 117. Washington, DC: Catholic University of America Press, 2008.

Schiller, Gertrud. *Iconography of Christian Art*. Translated by Janet Seligman. 2 vols. Greenwich: New York Graphic Society, 1971–2.

Scholes, Percy A. ed. *The Oxford Companion to Music*. Oxford: Oxford University Press, 1970.

Selections from Ancient Irish Poetry. Translated by Kuno Meyer. London: Constable, 1911.

Sheridan, J. Mark. *Rufus of Shotep: Homilies on the Gospels of Matthew and Luke: Introduction, Text, and Commentary*. Corpus dei Manosritti Copti Letterari. Roma: Centro Italiano Microfiches, 1998.

Shoemaker, Stephen J., trans. *The Life of the Virgin: Maximus the Confessor: Translated with an Introduction and Notes*. New Haven: Yale University Press, 2012.

Simeon, Charles. *Horae Homileticae: Matthew*. Vol. 11. London: Holdsworth and Ball, 1832.

Simonetti, Manlio, ed. *Matthew*. 2 vols. Ancient Christian Commentary on Scripture: New Testament 1a-1b. Downers Grove: InterVarsity, 2001–2.

Simpson, Dean, trans. *Collected Works of Erasmus: Paraphrase on Matthew*. Vol. 45. Toronto: University of Toronto Press, 2008.

Spector, Stephen, ed. *The N-Town Play*. 2 vols. Early English Text Society Supplementary Series 11–12. London: Early English Text Society, 1998.

Strickert, Frederick M. *Rachel Weeping: Jews, Christians, and Muslims at the Fortress Tomb*. Collegeville: Liturgical Press, 2007.

Studwell, William E. *Christmas Carols: A Reference Guide*. Indexes by David A. Hamilton. New York: Garland, 1985.

Suggit, John N., trans. *Oecumenius: Commentary on the Apocalypse*. The Fathers of the Church 112. Washington, DC: Catholic University of America Press, 2006.

Talbot, C. H., Samuel Fanous, and Henrietta Leyser, eds. and trans. *The Life of Christina of Markyate: Revised with an Introduction and Notes*. Oxford World Classics. Oxford: Oxford University Press, 2008.

Thackeray, Henry St. J., trans. *Josephus: The Jewish War, Books 5–7*. Vol. 3. Loeb Classical Library 210. Cambridge: Harvard University Press, 1928.

Thomson, H. J., ed. and trans. *Prudentius*. 2 vols. Loeb Classical Library. Cambridge: Harvard University Press, 1949–53.

Unger, Dominic J., trans. *St. Irenaeus of Lyons: Against the Heresies: Book 3: Translated and Annotated with an Introduction and Further Revisions*. Ancient Christian Writers: The Works of the Fathers in Translation 64. New York: Newman, 2012.

van Banning, J. ed. *Opus imperfectum in Mattheum*. CCSL 87B. Turnhout: Brepols, 1988.

Verdi, Richard. *Nicolas Poussin 1594–1665*. London: Zwemmer, 1995.

Vives, José, and Jerónimo Claveras, eds. *Oracional Visigótico*. Monumenta Hispaniae sacra: Serie litúrgica 1. Barcelona: Consejo Superior de Investigaciones Científicas, Escuela de Estudios Medievales, Sección de Barcelona, Balmesiana: Biblioteca Balmes, 1946.

Walker, Alexander, trans. *Apocryphal Gospels, Acts, and Revelations*. Ante-Nicene Christian Library 16. Edinburgh: T&T Clark, 1870.

Walther, Ingo F., and Norbert Wolf. *Codices Illustres: The World's Most Famous Illuminated Manuscripts 400–1600*. Köln: Taschen, 2001.

Waszink, Jan H., *Tertullian De Anima mit Einleitung Übersetzung und Kommentar*. Amsterdam: H. J. Paris, 1933.

Williams, D. H., trans. *Hilary of Poitiers: Commentary on Matthew*. The Fathers of the Church 125. Washington, DC: Catholic University of America Press, 2012.

Secondary Sources

Albright, William F., and C. S. Mann. *Matthew*. Garden City: Doubleday, 1984.

Allen, Leslie C. *Jeremiah: A Commentary*. The Old Testament Library. Louisville: Westminster John Knox, 2008.

Allen, Willoughby C. *A Critical and Exegetical Commentary on the Gospel according to S. Matthew*. ICC. Edinburgh: T&T Clark; New York: Charles Scribner's Sons, 1912.

Allison, Dale C. *Resurrecting Jesus: The Earliest Christian Tradition and Its Interpreters*. London: T&T Clark, 2005.

Allison, Dale C. *Studies in Matthew: Interpretation, Past, and Present*. Grand Rapids: Baker, 2005.

Allison, Dale C. *The New Moses: A Matthean Typology*. Minneapolis: Fortress, 1993.

Alpers, Svetlana. *The Making of Rubens*. New Haven: Yale University Press, 1995.

Anderson, Janice C. "Life on the Mississippi: New Currents in Matthean Scholarship 1983–1993." *Currents in Biblical Research* 3 (1995): 169–218.

Andrews, Lew. *Story and Space in Renaissance Art: The Rebirth of Continuous Narrative*. Cambridge: Cambridge University Press, 1998.

Authors on the Line. "Christmas and the Sting of Personal Loss: An Interview with John Piper and Paul Maier." In *Authors on the Line*, a podcast by Tony Reinke, Paul Maier, and John Piper in desiringgod.org.

Avni, Gideon. *The Byzantine-Islamic Transition in Palestine: An Archaelogical Approach.* Oxford Studies in Byzantium. Oxford: Oxford University Press, 2014.

Bacon, Benjamin W. *Studies in Matthew.* New York: Henry Holt, 1930.

Baert, Barbara. "Pentecost and the Senses: A Hermeneutical Contribution to the Visual Medium and the Sensorium in Early Medieval Manuscript Tradition." In *Preaching after Easter: Mid-Pentecost, Ascension, and Pentecost in Late Antiquity.* Edited by Richard W. Bishop, Johan Leemans, and Hajnalka Tamas, 346–70. Leiden: Brill, 2013.

Barkhuizen, J. H. "Romanos Melodos, 'On the Massacre of the Innocents': A Perspective on *Ekphrasis* as a Method of Patristic Exegesis." *Acta Classica* (2007): 29–50.

Barton, John, and John Muddiman, eds. *The Oxford Bible Commentary.* Oxford: Oxford University Press, 2001.

Barton, Stephen C. "Can We Identify the Gospel Audiences?" In *The Gospels for All Christians: Rethinking the Gospel Audiences.* Edited by Richard Bauckham, 173–94. Grand Rapids: Eerdmans, 1998.

Bauer, David R. "The Interpretation of Matthew's Gospel in the Twentieth Century." *American Theological Library Association Summary of Proceedings* 42 (1988): 119–45.

Bauer, David R. "The Kingship of Jesus in the Matthean Infancy Narrative: A Literary Analysis." *Catholic Biblical Quarterly* 57 (1995): 306–23.

Beare, Francis W. *The Gospel of Matthew: A Commentary.* Oxford: Basil Blackwell, 1981.

Becker, Eve-Marie. "The Reception of 'Mark' in the 1st and 2nd Centuries C. E." In *Mark and Matthew II: Comparative Readings: Reception History, Cultural Hermeneutics, and Theology.* Edited by Eve-Marie Becker and Anders Runesson, 15–36. Wissenschaftliche Untersuchungen zum Neuen Testament 304. Tübingen: Mohr Siebeck, 2013.

Bedouelle, Guy. "Biblical Interpretation in the Catholic Reformation." In *A History of Biblical Interpretation. Volume 2: The Medieval through the Reformation Periods.* Edited by Alan J. Hauser and Duane F. Watson, 428–49. Grand Rapids: Eerdmans, 2009.

Bedouelle, Guy. "Jacques Lefèvre d'Étaples (c. 1460–1536)." In *Reformation Theologians: An Introduction to Theology in the Early Modern Period.* Edited by Carter Lindberg, 19–33. Oxford: Blackwell, 2002.

Behr, John. *Irenaeus of Lyons: Identifying Christianity.* Christian Theology in Context. Oxford: Oxford University Press, 2013.

Belkin, Kristin L. *Rubens.* London: Phaidon, 1998.

Berdini, Paolo. *The Religious Art of Jacopo Bassano: Painting as Visual Exegesis.* Cambridge: Cambridge University Press, 1997.

Bernabò, Massmo. "The Miniatures in the Rabbula Gospels: Postscripta to a Recent Book." *Dumbarton Oaks Papers* 68 (2014): 343–58.

Betsworth, Sharon. "The Child and Jesus in the Gospel of Matthew." *Journal of Childhood and Religion* 1 (2010): 1–14.

Bisaha, Nancy. *Creating East and West: Renaissance Humanists and the Ottoman Turks.* Philadelphia: University of Pennsylvania Press, 2004.

Billman, Kathleen D., and Daniel L. Migliore. *Rachel's Cry: Prayer of Lament and Rebirth of Hope.* Cleveland: United Church Press, 1999.

Bingham, D. Jeffrey. *Irenaeus' Use of Matthew's Gospel in Adversus Haereses.* Traditio Exegetica Graeca 7. Leuven: Peeters, 1998.

Bird, Mike. "Bauckham's *The Gospels for All Christians* Revisited." *European Journal of Theology* 15:1 (2006): 5–13.

Bird, Paul. "Living Liturgy: The Vision of Vatican II." *Australasian Catholic Record* 91:3 (2014): 334–49.

Black, Stephanie L. *Sentence Conjunction in the Gospel of Matthew: καί, δέ, τότε, γάρ, οὖν and Asyndeton in Narrative Discourse.* Journal for the Study of the New Testament Supplement Series 216. Sheffield: Sheffield Academic, 2002.

Blackstone, Thomas L. "The Hermeneutics of Recontextualization in the Epistle to the Hebrews." PhD diss., Emory University, 1995.

Blomberg, Craig. *Matthew.* The New American Commentary 22. Nashville: Broadman & Holman, 1992.

Bockmuehl, Markus. *Seeing the Word: Refocusing New Testament Study.* Studies in Theological Interpretation. Grand Rapids: Baker Academic, 2006.

Bordenstedt, Mary Immaculate. *The Vita Christi of Ludolphus the Carthusian: A Dissertation.* The Catholic University of America Studies in Medieval and Renaissance Latin Language and Literature 16. Washington, DC: Catholic University of America Press, 1944.

Boice, James Montgomery. *The Gospel of Matthew.* Grand Rapids: Baker, 2001.

Bonnard, Pierre. *L'évangile selon Saint Matthieu.* Commentaire du Nouveau Testament 1. Neuchâtel: Delachaux et Niestlé, 1963.

Bonanno, George, and Stacey Kaltman, "Toward an Integrative Perspective on Bereavement." *Psychological Bulletin* 125 (1999), 760–76.

Boring, M. Eugene. "Matthew." In *The New Interpreter's Bible: General Articles & Introduction, Commentary, & Reflections for Each Book of the Bible Including the Apocryphal/Deuteronocanonical Books. Volume 8: General Articles on the New Testament; Matthew; Mark,* 87–506. Nashville: Abingdon, 1995.

Bornkamm, Günther. "Die Sturmstillung im Matthäus-Evangelium." In *Überlieferung und Auslegung im Matthäusevangelium.* Edited by Günther Bornkamm, Gerhard Barth, and Heinz Joachim Held, 48–53. Vol. 1. Neukirchener: Verlag, 1960.

Boston Collaborative Encyclopedia of Western Theology. "Stanley Haeurwas (1940–)." Accessed April 13, 2016. http://people.bu.edu/wwildman/bce/hauerwas.htm.

Bosworth, David. "'David Comforted Bathsheba': Gender and Parental Bereavement." In *Seitenblicke: Literische und historische Studien zu Nebenfiguren im zweiten Samuelbuch.* Edited by Walter Dietrich, 238–55. Orbis Biblicus et Orientalis 249. Göttingen: Vandenhoeck and Ruprecht, 2011.

Bosworth, David. *Infant Weeping in Akkadian, Hebrew, and Greek Literature.* Critical Studies in the Hebrew Bible 8. Winona Lake: Eisenbrauns, 2016.

Bowker, John. *The Targums and Rabbinic Literature: An Introduction to Jewish Interpretation of Scripture.* Cambridge: Cambridge University Press, 1969.

Boxall, Ian. *Discovering Matthew: Content, Interpretation, Reception.* London: Society for Promoting Christian Knowledge, 2014.

Boxall, Ian. *Patmos in the Reception History of the Apocalypse.* Oxford Theology and Religion Monographs. Oxford: Oxford University Press, 2013.

Boxall, Ian. "Reception History." In *The New Cambridge History of the Bible: Volume 4: 1750 to the Present.* Edited by John Riches, 172–83. Cambridge: Cambridge University Press, 2015.

Boynton, Susan. "From the Lament of Rachel to the Lament of Mary: A Transformation in the History of Drama and Spirituality." In *Signs of Change: Transformations of Christian Traditions and Their Representation in the Arts, 1000–2000.* Edited by Nils Holger Petersen, Claus Clüver, and Nicolas Bell, 319–40. Textxet: Studies in Comparative Literature 43. Amsterdam: Rodopi, 2004.

Boynton, Susan. "Performative Exegesis in the Fleury Interfectio Puerorum." *Viator* 29 (1998): 39–64.

Brand, Peter, and Lino Pertile, eds. *The Cambridge History of Italian Literature*. Cambridge: Cambridge University Press, 1999.

Breed, Brennan W. *Nomadic Text: A Theory of Biblical Reception History*. Bloomington: Indiana University Press, 2014.

Broer, Ingo. "Jesusflucht und Kindermord—Exegetische Anmerkungen zum zweiten Kapitel des Mattäusevangeliums." In *Zur Theologie der Kindheitsgeschichten: Der heutige Stand der Exegese*. Edited by Rudolf Pesch, 74–96. Münich: Schnell & Steiner, 1981.

Brown, Raymond E. *The Birth of the Messiah: A Commentary on the Infancy Narratives in Matthew and Luke*. New updated edition. Anchor Bible Reference Library. New York: Doubleday, 1993.

Brown, Raymond E.. *The Community of the Beloved Disciple*. New York: Paulist Press, 1979.

Bruce, Frederick F. "Herod Antipas, Tetrarch of Galilee and Peraea." *Annual of Leeds University Oriental Society* 5 (1963/5): 6–23.

Brueggemann, Walter. *Texts that Linger, Words that Explode: Listening to Prophetic Voices*. Edited by Patrick D. Miller. Minneapolis: Fortress, 2000.

Bruner, Frederick D. *Matthew: A Commentary*. 2 vols. Revised and expanded edition. Grand Rapids: Eerdmans, 2004.

Bruzelius, Caroline. "The Construction of Notre-Dame in Paris." *Art Bulletin* 69:4 (1987): 540–69.

Bultmann, Rudolf K., ErnstLohmeyer, Julius Schniewind, Helmut Thielicke, and Austin Farrer. *Kerygma and Myth: A Theological Debate*. Edited by Hans Werner Bartsch. Revised edition by Reginald H. Fuller. New York: Harper, 1961.

Bultmann, Rudolf K. "Is Exegesis without Presuppositions Possible?" In *Existence and Faith: Shorter Writings of Rudolf Bultmann*. Translated by Schubert M. Ogden, 289–96. New York: Meridian Books, 1960.

Burckhardt, Jacob. *Recollections of Rubens*. New York: Phaidon, 1970.

Butler, Erik. "The Garden of Earthly Delights and the Cult of the Martyrs." In *Massacre of the Innocents* by Giambattista Marino. Translated by Erik Butler, vii–xv. Cambridge: Wakefield, 2015.

Cairns, Earle E. *Christianity through the Centuries: A History of the Christian Church*. Grand Rapids: Zondervan, 1996.

Camus, Albert. *The Fall*. Translated by Justin O'Brien. New York: Vintage Books, 1956.

Canellis, Aline. "Jerome's Heremenutics: How to Exegete the Bible?" In *Patristic Theories of Biblical Interpretation: The Latin Fathers*. Edited by Tarmo Toom, 49–76. Cambridge: Cambridge University Press, 2016.

Carrera, Elena. *Teresa of Avila's Autobiography: Authority, Power and the Self in Mid-sixteenth-Century Spain*. Legenda. London: Modern Humanities Research Association and Maney, 2005.

Carruthers, Mary. *The Craft of Thought: Meditation, Rhetoric, and the Making of Images, 400–1200*. Cambridge Studies in Medieval Literature 34. Cambridge: Cambridge University Press, 1998.

Carson, Daniel A., and Douglas J. Moo. *Introduction to the New Testament*. 2nd ed. Grand Rapids: Zondervan, 2005.

Carson, Daniel A. "Matthew." In *The Expositor's Bible Commentary: Matthew-Mark*. Edited by Tremper Longman III and David E. Garland, 23–670. Revised edition. Expositor's Bible Commentary 9. Grand Rapids: Zondervan, 2010.

Carter, Warren. *Matthew and the Margins: A Sociopolitical and Religious Reading*. The Bible & Liberation Series. Maryknoll: Orbis, 2000.

Case-Winters, Anna. *Matthew*. Belief: A Theological Commentary on the Bible. Louisville: Westminster John Knox, 2015.

Chambers, Ross. "Commentary in Literary Texts." *Critical Inquiry* 5 (1978): 323–7.

Chance, J. Bradley. *Jerusalem, the Temple, and the New Age in Luke-Acts*. Macon: Mercer University Press, 1988.

Chapman, Hugo, Tom Henry, and Carol Plazzotta. *Raphael: From Urbino to Rome*. London: National Gallery, 2004.

Charles, Victoria, and Klaus H. Carl, *Gothic Art*. New York: Parkstone International, 2008.

Chatman, Seymour. *Story and Discourse: Narrative Structure in Fiction and Film*. Ithaca: Cornell University Press, 1978.

Chilton, Bruce. "Justin and Israelite Prophecy." In *Justin Martyr and His Worlds*. Edited by Sara Parvis and Paul Foster, 77–87. Minneapolis: Fortress, 2007.

Christiansen, Keith, Laurence B. Kanter, and Carl B. Strehlke. *Painting in Renaissance Siena: 1420–1500*. New York: Metropolitan Museum of Art, 1988.

Clark, Kenneth W. "The Gentile Bias in Matthew." *Journal of Biblical Literature* 66:2 (1947): 165–72.

Clarke, G. W. "Introduction." In *The Letters of St. Cyprian of Carthage: Translated and Annotated: Volume III: Letters 55–66*. Translated by G. W. Clarke, 1–29. Ancient Christian Writers: The Works of the Fathers in Translation 46. New York: Newman, 1983.

Clarke, Howard. *The Gospel of Matthew and Its Readers: A Historical Introduction to the First Gospel*. Bloomington: Indiana University Press, 2003.

Clements. E. Anne. *Mothers on the Margin? The Significance of the Women in Matthew's Genealogy*. Eugene: Pickwick, 2014.

Coles, Blanche. *Shakespeare Studies: Hamlet*. New York: R. R. Smith, 1938.

Coles, Richard. *Bringing in the Sheaves: Wheat and Chaff from My Years as a Priest*. London: Weidenfeld & Nicolson, 2016.

Collins, Kristen, Peter Kidd, and Nancy K. Turner. *The St. Albans Psalter: Painting and Prayer in Medieval England*. Los Angeles: J. Paul Getty Museum, 2013.

Collins, Raymond. *Introduction to the New Testament*. Garden City: Doubleday, 1983.

Corcoran, Vanessa. "'With Your Speech, Mary, I Am Well Repaid': Understanding Gendered Expectations through the Corpus Christi Cycles." Unpublished manuscript, November 5, 2014, typescript.

Cosgrove, Charles H. "Justin Martyr and the Emerging Christian Canon: Observations on the Purpose and Destination of the Dialogue with Trypho." *Vigilae Christianae* 36 (1982): 209–32.

Cousland, J. Robert C. "José Saramago's *Kakagellion*: The 'Badspel' according to Jesus Christ." In *Jesus in Twentieth Century Literature, Art, and Movies*. Edited by Paul C. Burns, 55–74. UBC Studies in Religion 1. London: Continuum, 2007.

Crowley, Eileen D. *Liturgical Art for a Media Culture*. American Essays in Liturgy. Collegeville: Liturgical Press, 2007.

Crossley, James G. "The End of Reception History, a Grand Narrative for Biblical Studies and the Neoliberal Bible." In *Reception History and Biblical Studies: Theory and*

Practice. Edited by Emma England and William J. Lyons, 45–59. Scriptural Traces Critical Perspectives on the Reception and Influence of the Bible 6. London: T&T Clark, 2015.

Crossley, James G. *Reading the New Testament: Contemporary Approaches*. London: Routledge, 2010.

Crowe, Brandon D. "Fulfillment in Matthew as Eschatological Reversal." *Westminster Theological Journal* 75:1 (2013): 111–27.

Daley, Brian E. *Gregory of Nazianzus*. The Early Church Fathers. London: Routledge, 2006.

Davies, William D., and Dale C. Allsion Jr. *The Gospel according to Saint Matthew*. 3 vols. International Critical Commentary. London: T&T Clark, 2004.

Davis, Ellen F., and Richard B. Hays. *The Art of Reading Scripture*. Grand Rapids: Eerdmans, 2003.

de Claissé-Walford, Nancy, Rolf A. Jacobson, and Beth LaNeel Tanner. *The Book of Psalms*. New International Commentary on the Old Testament. Grand Rapids: Eerdmans, 2014.

de Hamel, Christopher. *A History of Illuminated Manuscripts*. 2nd revised edition. London: Phaidon, 1994.

de Lubac, Henri. *Medieval Exegesis: Vol 1: The Four Senses of Scripture*. Translated by Mark Sebanc. Grand Rapids: Eerdmans; Edinburgh: T&T Clark, 1998.

de Saussure, Ferdinand. *Course in General Linguistics*. Edited by Charles Bally and Albert Sechehaye. Translated by Wade Baskin. New York: McGraw-Hill, 1966.

Del Giudice, Luisa. "Ninna-nanne-nonsense?: Fears, Dreams, and Falling in the Italian Lullaby." *Oral Tradition* 3 (1988): 270–93.

Destro, Adriana, and Mauro Pesce. "The Cultural Structure of the Infancy Narrative in the Gospel of Matthew." In *Infancy Gospels: Stories and Identities*. Edited by Claire Clivaz, Andreas Dettwiler, Luc Devillers, Enrico Norelli, and Benjamin Bertho, 94–115. Wissenschaftliche Untersuchungen zum Neuen Testament 281. Tübingen: Mohr Siebeck, 2011.

Dobschütz, Ernst von. "Bible in the Church." In *Encyclopaedia of Religion and Ethics*. Edited by James Hastings, 2:579–615. Edinburgh: T&T Clark, 1909.

Dodd, Charles H. *According to the Scriptures: The Sub-structure of New Testament Theology*. London: Nisbet, 1952.

Dormeyer, Detlev. "A Catholic Reading of the Gospels of Mark and Matthew in the 20th Century." In *Mark and Matthew II: Comparative Readings: Reception History, Cultural Hermeneutics, and Theology*. Edited by Eve-Marie Becker and Anders Runesson, 169–88. Wissenschaftliche Untersuchungen zum Neuen Testament 304. Tübingen: Mohr Siebeck, 2013.

Dresner, Samuel H. *Rachel*. Minneapolis: Fortress, 1994.

Dressler, Rachel. "Deus Hoc Vult: Ideology, Identity and Sculptural Rhetoric at the Time of the Crusades." *Medieval Encounters* 1 (1995): 188–218.

Drumbl, Johann. *Quem quaeritis: teatro sacro dell'alto Medioevo*. Biblioteca teatrale 39. Roma: Bulzoni, 1981.

Drury, John. *Painting the Word: Christian Pictures and Their Meanings*. New Haven: Yale University Press, 1999.

Dube, Elizabeth H. "The Grabow Altar of Master Bertram von Minden (Germany)." PhD diss., Brown University, 1982.

Dudley, Martin R. "Natalis Innocentum: The Holy Innocents in Liturgy and Drama." *Studies in Church History* 31 (1994): 233–42.

Dunn, Geoffrey D. *Tertullian*. The Early Church Fathers. London: Routledge, 2004.
Dunn, James D. G. *Jesus Remembered: Christianity in the Making*. Grand Rapids: Eerdmans, 2003.
Dunn, James D. G. *The Living Word*. London: SCM, 1987.
Ebeling, Gerhard. *The Word of God and Tradition: Historical Studies Interpreting the Divisions of Christianity*. Translated by S. H. Hooke. Philadelphia: Fortress, 1968.
Ebeling, Gerhard. *Wort Gottes und Tradition: Studien zu einer Hermeneutik der Konfessionen*. Göttingen: Vandenhoeck & Ruprecht, 1964.
Edwards, James R. *The Gospel according to Mark*. The Pillar New Testament Commentary. Grand Rapids: Eerdmans, 2002.
Edwards, Mark U. *Printing, Propaganda and Martin Luther*. Berkeley: University of California Press, 1994.
Eisenman, Robert H. *James the Brother of Jesus: The Key to Unlocking the Secrets of Early Christianity and the Dead Sea Scrolls*. New York: Viking, 1997.
Elliott, Mark W. "Effective-History and the Hermeneutics of Ulrich Luz." *Journal for the Study of the New Testament* 33:2 (2010): 161–73.
England, Emma, and William J. Lyons. "Explorations in the Reception of the Bible." In *Reception History and Biblical Studies: Theory and Practice*. Edited by Emma England and William J. Lyons, 3–13. Scriptural Traces Critical Perspectives on the Reception and Influence of the Bible 6. London: T&T Clark, 2015.
Erickson, Richard J. "Divine Injustice? Matthew's Narrative Strategy and the Slaughter of the Innocents (Matthew 2:13–23)." *Journal for the Study of the New Testament* 64 (1996): 5–27.
Evans, Craig A. *Matthew*. New Cambridge Bible Commentary. Cambridge: Cambridge University Press, 2012.
Evans, Robert. *Reception History, Tradition and Biblical Interpretation: Gadamer and Jauss in Current Practice*. Library of New Testament Studies 510. Scriptural Traces: Critical Perspectives on the Reception and Influence of the Bible 4. London: Bloomsbury, 2014.
Exum, J. Cheryl. "Beyond the Biblical Horizon: The Bible and the Arts." In *Beyond the Biblical Horizon: The Bible and the Arts*. Edited by J. Cheryl Exum, 1–7. Leiden: Brill, 1999.
Exum, J. Cheryl. "Toward a Genuine Dialogue between the Bible and Art." In *Congress Volume Helsinki 2010*. Edited by M. Nissinen, 473–503. Supplements to Vetus Testamentum 148. Leiden: Brill, 2012.
Fackenheim, Emil. "New Heart and the Old Covenant: On Some Possibilities of a Fraternal Jewish-Christian Reading of the Jewish Bible Today." In *The Divine Helmsman: Studies on God's Control of Human Events*. Edited by James L. Crenshaw and Samuel Sandmel, 191–205. New York: KTAV, 1980.
Falkenberg, René. "Matthew 28:16-20 and the Nag Hammadi Library: Reception of the Great Commission in the *Sophia of Jesus Christ*." In *Mark and Matthew II: Comparative Readings: Reception History, Cultural Hermeneutics, and Theology*. Edited by Eve-Marie Becker and Anders Runesson, 93–104. Wissenschaftliche Untersuchungen zum Neuen Testament 304. Tübingen: Mohr Siebeck, 2013.
Farmer, William R. *The Gospel of Jesus: The Pastoral Relevance of the Synoptic Problem*. Louisville: Westminster John Knox, 1994.
Farrar, Frederic W. *The Life of Christ*. London: Cassell, Petter, and Galpin, 1874.
Farrer, Austin. "On Dispensing with Q." In *Studies in the Gospels: Essays in Memory of R. H. Lightfoot*. Edited by D. E. Nineham, 55–88. Oxford: Blackwell, 1955.

Fassler, Margot E. *The Virgin of Chartres: Making History through Liturgy and the Arts.* New Haven: Yale University Press, 2010.
Fiedler, Peter. *Das Matthäusevangelium.* Theologischer Kommentar zum Neuen Testament 1. Kohlhammer: Stuttgart, 2006.
Filson, Floyd V. *A Commentary on the Gospel according to St. Matthew.* London: Adam & Charles Black, 1960.
Finch, Andrew, Wei Song, Kumiko Tanaka-Ishii, and Eiichiro Sumita. "Speaking Louder than Words with Pictures across Languages." *AI Magazine* 34 (2013): 31–47.
Fish, Stanley E. *Self-consuming Artifacts: The Experience of Seventeenth-Century Literature.* Berkeley: University of California Press, 1972.
Fitzmyer, Joseph A. "4Q Testimonia and the New Testament." *Theological Studies* 18 (1957): 513–37.
Fitzmyer, Joseph A. *The Gospel according to Luke I-IX: Introduction, Translation, and Notes.* Anchor Bible 28. Garden City: Doubleday, 1981.
Flanagan, C. Clifford. "The Apocalpyse and the Medieval Liturgy." In *The Apocalypse in the Middle Ages.* Edited by Richard K Emmerson and Bernard McGinn, 333–51. Ithaca: Cornell University Press, 1992.
Flower, Richard. *Emperors and Bishops in Late Roman Invective.* Cambridge: Cambridge University Press, 2013.
Folsom, Cassian. "The Liturgical Books of the Roman Rite." In *Handbook for Liturgical Studies Volume 1: Introduction to Liturgy.* Edited by Anscar J. Chupungco, 245–314. Collegeville: Liturgical Press, 1997.
Forster, E. M. *Aspects of the Novel.* San Diego: Harcourt Brace Jovanovich, 1927.
France, Richard T. *The Gospel of Matthew.* The New International Commentary on the New Testament. Grand Rapids: Eerdmans, 2007.
Frier, David G. "José Saramago's 'O Evangelho Segundo Jesus Cristo': Outline of a Newer Testament." *Modern Language Review* 100 (2005): 367–82.
Froehlich, Karlfried. "Church History and the Bible." In *Biblical Hermeneutics in Historical Perspective: Studies in Honor of Karlfried Froehlich on His Sixtieth Birthday.* Edited by Mark S. Burrows and Paul Rorem, 1–15. Grand Rapids: Eerdmans, 1991.
Gadamer, Hans-Georg. *Truth and Method.* Reprint edition. Bloomsbury Revelations. London: Bloomsbury Academic, 2013.
Gadamer, Hans-Georg. *Truth and Method.* 2nd revised edition. London: Sheed and Ward, 1989.
Gaestel, Allyn, and Ricci Shryock. "Why Infanticide Is a Problem in Senegel." National Public Radio. October 3, 2018. Accessed October 30, 2018. https://www.npr.org/sections/goatsandsoda/2018/10/03/631892291/why-infanticide-is-a-problem-in-senegal.
Gardner, Howard. *Frames of Mind: The Theory of Multiple Intelligences.* New York: Basic Books, 1983.
Garland, David E. *Reading Matthew: A Literary and Theological Commentary on the First Gospel.* Macon: Smyth & Helwys, 1999.
Geddes, Jane. "The St. Albans Psalter: The Abbot and the Anchoress." In *Christina of Markyate: A Twelfth-Century Holy Woman.* Edited by Samuel Fanous and Henrietta Leyser, 197–216. Abingdon: Routledge, 2005.
Gibbs, Lee W. "Biblical Interpretation in Medieval England and the English Reformation." In *A History of Biblical Interpretation. Volume 2: The Medieval through the*

Reformation Periods. Edited by Alan J. Hauser and Duane F. Watson, 372–402. Grand Rapids: Eerdmans, 2009.

Gillingham, Susan. "Biblical Studies on Holiday? A Personal View of Reception History." In *Reception History and Biblical Studies: Theory and Practice*. Edited by Emma England and William J. Lyons, 17–30. Scriptural Traces Critical Perspectives on the Reception and Influence of the Bible 6. London: T&T Clark, 2015.

Gnilka, Joachim. *Das Matthäusevangelium: I. Teil: Kommentar zu Kap: 1, 1–13, 58*. Herders theologischer Kommentar zum Neuen Testament; Bd. 1. Freiburg: Herder, 1986.

Gomes, Jules F. *The Sanctuary of Bethel and the Configuration of Israelite Identity*. Beihefte zur Zeitschrift für die alttestamentliche Wissenschaft 368. Berlin: Walter de Gruyter, 2006.

Gómez, Raúl R. "Blurring the Line between Liturgy and Popular Religion: An Example from the Hispano-Mozarabic Rite." *Journal of Hispanic/Latino Theology* 10:1 (2002): 18–36.

Goodacre, Mark. *The Case against Q: Studies in Markan Priority and the Synoptic Problem*. Harrisburg: Trinity Press International, 2002.

Goodenough, Erwin R. *The Theology of Justin Martyr*. Jenna: Fromman, 1923.

Gorman, Michael M. "Frigulus: Hiberno-Latin Author or Pseudo-Irish Phantom? Comments on the Edition of the Liber Questionum in Euangeliis (CCSL 108F)." *Revue d'Histoire Ecclésiastique* 100 (2005): 425–56.

Guinness, Os. *Fool's Talk: Recovering the Art of Christian Persuasion*. Downers Grove: InterVarsity, 2015.

Goulder, Michael D. *Midrash and Lection in Matthew*. London: SPCK, 1974.

Grant, Michael. *Herod the Great*. New York: American Heritage, 1971.

Grant, Michael. *Jesus: An Historian's Review of the Gospels*. New York: Charles Scribner's Sons, 1977.

Green, Michael. *The Message of Matthew: The Kingdom of Heaven*. Downers Grove: InterVarsity, 2000.

Groves, Beatrice. *Texts and Traditions: Religion in Shakespeare 1592—1604*. Oxford English Monographs. Oxford: Clarendon Press, 2006.

Gundry, Robert H. *Matthew: A Commentary on His Literary and Theological Art*. Grand Rapids: Eerdmans, 1982.

Gundry, Robert H. *The Use of the Old Testament in St. Matthew's Gospel: With Special Reference to the Messianic Hope*. Supplements to Novum Testamentum 18. Leiden: Brill, 1967.

Gwynn, David M. "Archaeology and 'the Arian Controversy' in the Fourth Century." In *Religious Diversity in Late Antiquity*. Edited by David M. Gwynn and Susanne Bangert, 229–64. Boston: Leiden, 2010.

Hagner Donald A., and Stephen A. Young. "The Historical-Critical Method." In *Methods for Matthew*. Edited by Mark A. Powell, 11–43. Cambridge: Cambridge University Press, 2009.

Hagner, Donald A. *Matthew*. 2 vols. Word Biblical Commentary 33A–33B. Dallas: Word, 1998.

Hall, Robert J. "How Picard Was the 'Picardy Third'?" *Current Musicology* 19 (1975): 78–80.

Haney, Kristine E. *The Winchester Psalter: An Iconographic Study*. Leicester: Leicester University Press, 1986.

Harding, James E. "What Is Reception History, and What Happens to You if You Do It?" In *Reception History and Biblical Studies: Theory and Practice*. Edited by Emma England and William J. Lyons, 31–44. Scriptural Traces Critical Perspectives on the Reception and Influence of the Bible 6. London: T&T Clark, 2015.

Hare, Douglas R. A. "Current Trends in Matthean Scholarship." *Word and World* 18 (1998): 405–10.

Harkins, Franklin T. "Nuancing Augustine's Hermeneutical Jew: Allegory and Actual Jews in the Bishop's Sermons." *Journal for the Study of Judaism in the Persian, Hellenistic and Roman Period* 36 (2005): 41–64.

Harrington, Daniel J. *The Gospel of Matthew*. Sacra Pagina 1. Collegeville: Liturgical Press, 1991.

Harris, Max. *Sacred Folly: A New History of the Feast of Fools*. Ithaca: Cornell University Press, 2011.

Harley, John. *William Byrd: Gentleman of the Chapel Royal*. London: Routledge, 2017.

Hassan, Scheherazade. "Female Traditional Singers in Iraq: A Survey." *International Journal of Contemporary Iraqi Studies* 4 (2010): 25–39.

Hauser, Alan J., and Duane F. Watson. "Introduction and Overview." In *A History of Biblical Interpretation. Volume 1: The Ancient Period*. Edited by Alan J. Hauser and Duane F. Watson, 1–54. Grand Rapids: Eerdmans, 2003.

Hauerwas, Stanley. *Matthew*. Brazos Theological Commentary on the Bible. Grand Rapids: Brazos, 2006.

Hays, Richard B. *Reading Backwards: Figural Christology and the Fourfold Gospel Witness*. Waco: Baylor University Press, 2014.

Hayward, Paul A. "Suffering and Innocence in Latin Sermons for the Feast of the Holy Innocents, c. 400–800." In *The Church and Childhood: Papers Read at the 1993 Summer Meeting and the 1994 Winter Meeting of the Ecclesiastical History Society*. Edited by Diana Wood, 67–80. Studies in Church History 31. Oxford: Blackwell, 1994.

Heil, John P. *Death and Resurrection of Jesus: A Narrative-Critical Reading of Matthew 26–28*. Minneapolis: Fortress, 1991.

Henderson, George. *Studies in English Bible Illustration*. Vol. 2. London: Pindar Press, 1985.

Hendriksen, William. *Exposition of the Gospel According to Matthew*. New Testament Commentary. Grand Rapids: Baker, 1973.

Hengel, Martin, and Helmut Merkel. "Die Magier aus dem Osten und die Flucht nach Ägypten (Mt 2) im Rahmen der anitiken Religionsgesschichte und der Theologie des Matthäus." In *Orientierung an Jesus: Zur Theologie der Synoptiker, Für Josef Schmid*. Edited by Paul Hoffmann, Norbert Brox, and Wilheim Pesch, 139–69. Freiburg: Herder, 1973.

Hess, Andrew C. "The Ottoman Conquest of Egypt (1517) and the Beginning of the Sixteenth-Century World War." *International Journal of Middle East Studies* 4 (1973): 55–76.

Hill, David. *The Gospel of Matthew*. New Century Bible Commentary. Grand Rapids: Eerdmans, 1981.

Hope, David M. *Leonine Sacramentary: A Reassessment of Its Nature and Purpose*. Oxford Theological Monographs. London: Oxford University Press, 1971.

Hornik, Heidi J., and Mikeal C. Parsons. *Illuminating Luke: The Infancy Narrative in Italian Renaissance Painting*. Harrisburg: Trinity Press International, 2003.

Houlden, James L., ed. *The Interpretation of the Bible in the Church*. London: SCM, 1995.

Howell, David B. *Matthew's Inclusive Story: Study in the Narrative Rhetoric of the First Gospel*. Journal for the Study of the New Testament Supplement Series 42. Sheffield: Sheffield Academic, 1990.

Humphreys, Colin J. "The Star of Bethlehem: A Comet in 5 BC and the Date of Christ's Birth." *Tyndale Bulletin* 43 (1992): 31–56.

Hunwick, Andrew. "Introduction." In *Ecce homo!: An Eighteenth Century Life of Jesus: Critical Edition and Revision of George Houston's Translation from the French by Paul T. d'Holbach*, 1–38. Edited by Andrew Hunwick. History of Religions in Translation 1. Berlin: Walter de Gruyter, 1995.

Husti, Anca, and Maria Cantor. "Sacred Connection of Ornamental Flowers with Religious Symbols." *ProEnvironment Promediu* 8 (2015): 73–9.

Iggers, Georg G. *Historiography in the Twentieth Century: From Scientific Objectivity to the Postmodern Challenge*. Hanover: Wesleyan University Press, 1997.

Izdorcyzyk, Zbigniew. "Introduction." In *The Medieval Gospel of Nicodemus: Texts, Intertexts, and Contexts in Western Europe*. Edited by Zbigniew Izdorcyzyk, 1–20. Medieval & Renaissance Studies 158. Tempe: Medieval & Renaissance Texts & Studies, 1997.

Jacobus, Laura. "Motherhood and Massacre: The Massacre of the Innocents in Late-Medieval Art and Drama." In *The Massacre in History*. Edited by Mark Leven and Penny Roberts, 39–54. New York: Bergahn, 1999.

Jakobson, Roman O. "Linguistics and Poetics." In *Style in Language*. Edited by Thomas A. Sebeok, 350–77. Cambridge: MIT Press, 1960.

Janin, Hunt. *Four Paths to Jerusalem: Jewis, Christian, Muslim, and Secular Pilgrimages, 1000 B.C.E. to 2001 C.E.* New York: Harper & Row, 2002.

Jansen, Katherine L. *The Making of the Magdalen: Preaching and Popular Devotion in the Later Middle Ages*. Princeton: Princeton University Press, 2001.

Jauss, Hans-Robert. "Limits and Tasks of Literary Hermeneutics." *Diogenes* 109 (1980): 92–119.

Jauss, Hans-Robert. *Question and Answer: Forms of Dialogic Understanding*. Translated by Michael Hays. Minneapolis: University of Minnesota Press. 1989.

Jauss, Hans-Robert. *Toward an Aesthetic of Reception*. Translated by Timothy Bahti. Minneapolis: University of Minnesota Press, 1982.

Jensen, Robin M. *Understanding Early Christian Art*. London: Routledge, 2000.

Jones, Gareth L. "Jewish Folklore in Matthew's Infancy Stories." *Modern Believing* 52:4 (2011): 14–23.

Joyce, Paul M., and Diana Lipton. *Lamentations Through the Centuries*. Chichester: Wiley-Blackwell, 2013.

Kähler, Martin. *The So-Called Historical Jesus and the Historic, Biblical Christ*. Translated by Carl E. Braaten. Philadelphia: Fortress, 1964.

Kannengiesser, Charles. *Handbook of Patristic Exegesis: The Bible in Ancient Christianity*. The Bible in Ancient Christianity 1. Leiden: Brill, 2006.

Karnes, Michelle. *Imagination, Meditation, and Cognition in the Middle Ages*. Chicago: University of Chicago Press, 2011.

Kasher, Aryeh. *King Herod: A Persecuted Persecutor: A Case Study in Psychohistory and Psychobiography*. Studia Judaica 36. Berlin: Walter de Gruyter, 2007.

Kealy, Sean P. *Matthew's Gospel and the History of Biblical Interpretation: Book 1 and 2*. Mellen Biblical Press Series 55ab. Lewiston: Mellen Biblical Press, 1997.

Keener, Craig. *The Gospel of Matthew: A Socio-Rhetorical Commentary*. Grand Rapids: Eerdmans, 2009.

Kennedy, Joel. *The Recapitulation of Israel: Use of Israel's History in Matthew 1:1–4:11.* Wissenschaftliche Untersuchungen zum Neuen Testament 2. Reihe. 257. Tübingen: Mohr Siebeck, 2008.

Keylock, Leslie R. "Evangelical Scholars Remove Robert Gundry for His Views on Matthew." *Christianity Today.* November 1, 2003. Accessed December 8, 2017. http://www.christianitytoday.com/ct/2003/novemberweb-only/11-17-42.0.html.

Kidger, Mark. *The Star of Bethlehem: An Astronomer's View.* Princeton: Princeton University Press, 1999.

Kiley, Mark. "Why 'Matthew' in Matt 9, 9–13?" *Biblica* 65 (1984): 347–51.

King, Pamela M. "Faith, Reason and the Prophets' Dialogue in the Coventry Paegeant of the Shearmen and Taylors." In *Drama and Philosophy.* Edited by James Redmond, 37–46. Themes in Drama. Cambridge: Cambridge University Press, 1990.

Kingsbury, Jack D. *Matthew: Structure, Christology, Kingdom.* Philadelphia: Fortress, 1975.

Kingsbury, Jack D. *Matthew as Story.* Philadelphia: Fortress, 1988.

Klancher, Nancy. *The Taming of the Canaanite Woman: Constructions of Christian Identity in the Afterlife of Matthew 15:21–28.* Studies in the Bible and Its Reception, 1. Berlin: De Gruyter, 2013.

Klausner, David N. "19. Vernacular Drama." In *A Performer's Guide to Medieval Music.* Edited by Ross W. Duffin, 253–63. Music: Scholarship and Performance. Bloomington: Indiana University Press, 1996.

Klee, Paul. "Creative Credo." In *Theories of Modern Art: A Source Book by Artists.* Translated by Herschel B. Chipp, 182–6. California Studies in the History of Art. Berkeley: University of California Press, 1996.

Knight, Alan E. "Faded Pageant: The End of the Mystery Plays in Lille." *Journal of the Midwest Modern Language Association* 29:1 (1996): 3–14.

Knight, Douglas A., and Amy-Jill Levine. *The Meaning of the Bible: What the Jewish Scriptures and Christian Old Testament Can Teach Us.* New York: HarperCollins, 2011.

Knight, Mark. "*Wirkungsgeschichte*, Reception History, Reception Theory." *Journal for the Study of the New Testament* 33:2 (2010): 137–46.

Knowles, Michael P. *Jeremiah in Matthew's Gospel: The Rejected Prophet Motif in Matthean Redaction.* Journal for the Study of the New Testament Supplement Series 68. Sheffield: Sheffield Academic, 1993.

Koenigsberger, Helmut G. *Monarchies, States Generals and Parliaments: The Netherlands in the Fifteenth and Sixteenth Centuries.* Cambridge: Cambridge University Press, 2001.

Kozlova, Ekaterina E. *Maternal Grief in the Hebrew Bible.* Oxford Theology & Religion Monographs. Oxford: Oxford University Press, 2017.

Krieger, Murray. *A Window to Criticism: Shakespeare's Sonnets and Modern Poetics.* Princeton: Princeton University Press, 1964.

Kunzle, David. "Spanish Herod, Dutch Innocents: Bruegel's *Massacres of the Innocents* in their Sixteenth-Century Political Contexts." *Art History* 24:1 (2001): 51–82.

Ladd, George E. *A Commentary on the Revelation of John.* Grand Rapids: Eerdmans, 1972.

Lagrange, Marie-Joseph. *Évangile Selon Saint Mattieu.* Études bibliques. 3rd ed. Paris: Gabalda, 1927.

Lane, Barbara G. *The Altar and the Altarpiece: Sacramental Themes in Early Netherlandish Painting.* New York: Harper & Row, 1984.

Lawson-Jones, Mark. *Why Was the Partridge in the Pear Tree?: The History of Christmas Carols.* Stroud: History Press, 2011.

Lenox, John P. "The Triumph of the Innocents." *Biblical World* 11 (1898): 45–6.

Lenski, Richard C. H. *The Interpretation of St. Matthew's Gospel.* Columbus: Wartburg, 1943.

Levinsohn, Stephen H. *Discourse Features of New Testament Greek: A Coursebook on the Information Structure of New Testament Greek.* 2nd ed. Dallas: SIL International, 2000.

Lewis, Clive S. *Surprised by Joy: The Shape of My Early Life.* New York: Harcourt Brace, 1955.

Lindars, Barnabas. "'Rachel Weeping for Her Children'—Jeremiah 31:15-22." *Journal for the Study of the Old Testament* 12 (1979): 47-62.

Lingas, Alexander. "The Liturgical Place of the Kontakion in Constantinople." In *Liturgy, Architecture and Art of the Byzantine World: Papers of the XVIII International Byzantine Congress (Moscow, 8-15 August 1991) and Other Essays Dedicated to the Memory of Fr. John Meyendorff*, 50-7. St. Petersburg: Publications of the St. Petersburg Society for Byzantine and Slavic Studies, 1995.

Lohmeyer, Ernst. *Das Evangelium des Matthäus: Nachgelassene Ausarbeitungen und Entwürfe zur Übersetzung und Erklärung.* Edited by Werner Schmauch. Göttingen: Vandenhoeck & Ruprecht, 1956.

Longman, Tremper, III. *Jeremiah, Lamentations.* New International Biblical Commentary. Peabody: Hendrickson, 2008.

Lowden, John. "The Word Made Visible: The Exterior of the Early Christian Book as Visual Argument." In *The Early Christian Book.* Edited by William E. Klingshirn and Linda Safran, 13-47. Washington, DC: Catholic University of America Press, 2007.

Luz, Ulrich. "The Contribution of Reception History to a Theology of the New Testament." In *The Nature of New Testament Theology.* Edited by Christopher Rowland and Christopher Tuckett, 123-34. Malden: Blackwell, 2006.

Luz, Ulrich. *Das Evangelium nach Matthäus: 1. Teilband Mt 1-7.* Evangelisch-Katholischer Kommentar zum Neuen Testament; Bd. 1. 5., völlig neubearbeitete Auflage. Neukirchen-Vluyn: Neukirchener Verlag, 2002.

Luz, Ulrich. "Kann die Bibel heute noch Grundlage für die Kirche sein? Über die Aufgabe der Exegese in einer religiös-pluralistischen Gesellschaft." *New Testament Studies* 44 (1998): 317-39.

Luz, Ulrich. *Matthew 1-7: A Commentary.* Edited by Helmut Koester. Revised edition. Hermeneia: A Critical and Historical Commentary on the Bible. Minneapolis: Fortress, 2007.

Luz, Ulrich. *Matthew 1-7: A Continental Commentary.* Translated by Wilheim C. Linss. Minneapolis: Fortress, 1989.

Luz, Ulrich. *Matthew in History: Interpretation, Influence, and Effects.* Minneaplois: Foretress Press, 1994.

Luz, Ulrich. *Studies in Matthew.* Grand Rapids: Eerdmans, 2005.

Luz, Ulrich. *The Theology of the Gospel of Matthew.* New Testament Theology. Cambridge: Cambridge University Press, 1995.

Lyons, William J. "Hope for a Troubled Discipline? Contributions to New Testament Studies from Reception History." *Journal for the Study of the New Testament* 33:2 (2010): 207-20.

Lubbock, Jules. *Storytelling in Christian Art from Giotto to Donatello.* New Haven: Yale University Press, 2006.

Lundbom, Jack R. *Jeremiah 21-36: A New Translation with Introduction and Commentary.* Anchor Bible 21b. Garden City: Doubleday, 2004.

MacCulloch, Diarmaid. *Reformation: Europe's House Divided 1490–1700*. London: Penguin, 2003.
MacKinlay, Elizabeth, and Felicity Baker. "Nurturing Herself, Nurturing Her Baby: Creating Positive Experiences for First-time Mothers through Lullaby Singing." *Women and Music: A Journal of Gender and Culture* 9 (2005): 69–89.
Maier, Paul L. "Herod and Infants of Jerusalem." In *Chronos, Kairos, Christos II: Chronological, Nativity, and Religious Studies in Memory of Ray Summers*. Edited by E. Jerry Vardaman, 169–89. Macon: Mercer University Press, 1998.
Mâle, Emile. *Religious Art in France: The Late Middle Ages: A Study of Medieval Iconography and Its Sources*. Translated by Marthiel Matthews. Bollingen Series 90:3. Princeton: Princeton University Press, 1986.
Mamahit, Ferry Y. "Postcolonial Reading of the Bible: An Asian Evangelical Friend or Foe?" Paper presented at Asia Theological Association Theological Consultation Meeting. Malang, Indonesia. July 18–20, 2017.
Maniates, Maria R. *Mannerism in Italian Music and Culture, 1530–1630*. Chapel Hill: University of North Carolina Press, 1979.
Mann, Christopher S. *Mark: A New Translation with Introduction and Commentary*. Anchor Bible 27. Garden City: Doubleday, 1986.
Mans, M. J. "The Early Latin Church Fathers on Herod and the Infanticide." *Hervormde Teologiese Studies* 53 (1997): 92–102.
Marin, Louis. *Sublime Poussin*. Translated by Catherine Porter. Meridian: Crossing Aesthetics. Stanford: Standford University Press, 1999.
Mason, Steven. *Josephus and the New Testament*. Peabody: Hendrickson, 1992.
Massaux, Édouard. *The Influence of the Gospel of Saint Matthew on Christian Literature before Saint Irenaeus Book 2: The Later Christian writings*. Translated by Norman J. Belval and Suzanne Hect. New Gospel Studies 5/2. Macon: Mercer University Press, 1993.
Matera, Frank J. "The Plot of Matthew's Gospel." *Catholic Biblical Quarterly* 49 (1987): 233–53.
Mayeski, Marie A. "Early Medieval Exegesis: Gregory I to the Twelfth Century." In *A History of Biblical Interpretation Volume 2: The Medieval through the Reformation Periods*. Edited by Alan J. Hauser and Duane F. Watson, 86–112. Grand Rapids: Eerdmans, 2009.
Mayordomo-Marín, Moisés. *Den Anfang Hören: Leserorientierte Evangelienexegese am Beispiel von Matthäus 1-2*. Göttingen: Vandenhoeck & Ruprecht, 1998.
McGinness, Frederick J. "Preaching Ideals and Practice in Counter-Reformation Rome." *Sixteenth Century Journal* 11:2 (1980): 108–28.
McGinn, Bernard. *The Growth of Mysticism*. The Presence of God: A History of Western Christian Mysticism 2. New York: Crossroad, 1994.
McGrath, Alister E. *Christian Spirituality: An Introduction*. Oxford: Wiley-Blackwell, 1999.
McIvor, Robert S. "The Star of Messiah." *Irish Biblical Studies* 24 (2002): 175–83.
McLaughlin, Mary M. "Survivors and Surrogates: Children and Parents from the Ninth to the Thirteenth Centuries." In *The History of Childhood*. Edited by Lloyd deMause, 101–82. Oxford: Rowman & Littlefield, 1995.
McNamara, Martin, and Jean-Daniel Kaestli. "The Irish Infancy Narratives and Their Relationship with Latin Sources." In *Apocrypha Hiberniae I, 1: Evangelia Infantiae*. Edited by Martin McNamara, Caoimhín Breatnach, John Carey, Maíre Herbert, Jean-Daniel Kaestli, Brian Ó Cuív, Pádraig Ó Fiannachta, and Diarmuid Ó Laoghaire, 41–134. CCSA 13. Turnhout: Brepols, 2001.

Meier, John P. *A Marginal Jew: Rethinking the Historical Jesus*. Anchor Bible Reference Library. 4 vols. New York: Doubleday, 1991–2009.

Meier, John P. "Matthew, Gospel of." In *Anchor Bible Dictionary: K-N*. Vol. 4. Edited by David N. Freedman, 622–41. New York: Doubleday, 1992.

Meiser, Martin. "Protestant Reading of the Gospels of Mark and Matthew in the 20th Century." In *Mark and Matthew II: Comparative Readings: Reception History, Cultural Hermeneutics, and Theology*. Edited by Eve-Marie Becker and Anders Runesson, 151-67. Wissenschaftliche Untersuchungen zum Neuen Testament 304. Tübingen: Mohr Siebeck, 2013.

Menken, Maarten J. J. "The Quotation from Jeremiah 31 (38).15 in Matthew 2.18: A Study of Matthew's Scriptural Text." In *The Old Testament in the New Testament: Essays in Honour of J. L. North*. Edited by Steve Moyise, 106–25. Library of New Testament Studies 189. Sheffield: Sheffield Academic, 2000.

Metzger, Bruce M. *A Textual Commentary on the Greek New Testament*. 2nd ed. London: United Bible Socieites, 1971.

Michel, Émile, and Victoria Charles. *Pieter Bruegel*. New York: Parkstone International, 2012.

Middleton, Paul. *Martyrdom: A Guide for the Perplexed*. T&T Clark Guides for the Perplexed. London: T&T Clark, 2011.

Midgley, Emma. "Queen Victoria Popularised Our Christmas Traditions." *BBC Berkshire*. December 15, 2010. http://news.bbc.co.uk/local/berkshire/hi/people_and_places/history/newsid_9286000/9286971.stm.

Miller, Malcolm, Sonia Holladay, and Laura Lushington. *Chartres Chapel*. New York: Riverside Book, 1997.

Miles, Margaret R. "Santa Maria Maggiore's Fifth-Century Mosaics: Triumphal Christianity and the Jews." *Harvard Theological Review* 86:2 (1993): 155–75.

Minns, Denis. *Irenaeus: An Introduction*. London: T&T Clark, 2010.

Minns, Denis, and Paul Parvis, eds. *Justin, Philosopher and Martyr: Apologies: Edited with a Commentary on the Text*. Oxford Early Christian Texts. Oxford: Oxford University Press, 2009.

Mirollo, James V. *The Poet of the Marvelous*. New York: Columbia University Press, 1963.

Misrahi, Jean. "A Vita Sanctae Mariae Magdalenae (B.H.L. 5456) in an Eleventh-Century Manuscript." *Speculum* 18 (1943): 335–9.

Mitchell, William J. T. *Picture Theory: Essays on Verbal and Visual Representation*. Chicago: Chicago University Press, 1994.

Montanari, Shaena. "In This Town, the Weapons of War are Flour and Eggs." *National Geographic Society*. September 14, 2017. Accessed December 8, 2017. https://www.nationalgeographic.com/photography/proof/2017/09/you-won_t-believe-this-bizarre-celebration-in-spain/.

Monti, James. *The Week of Salvation: History and Traditions of Holy Week*. Our Sunday Visitor Books 532. Huntington: Our Sunday Visitor, 1993.

Morgan, Jonathan. "Visitors, Gatekeepers and Receptionists: Reflections on the Shape of Biblical Studies and the Role of Reception History." In *Reception History and Biblical Studies: Theory and Practice*. Edited by Emma England and William J. Lyons, 61–76. Scriptural Traces Critical Perspectives on the Reception and Influence of the Bible 6. London: T&T Clark, 2015.

Morgan, Robert. "*Sachkritik* in Reception History." *Journal for the Study of the New Testament* 33:2 (2010): 175–90.

Morony, Michael G. "History and Identity in the Syrian Churches." In *Redefining Christian Identity: Cultural Interaction in the Middle East since the Rise of Islam*. Edited by J. J. van Ginkel, H. L. Murre-van den Berg, and Theo M. van Lint, 1–34. Orientalia Lovaniensia Analecta 134. Leuven: Uitgeverij Peeters en Departement Oosterse Studies, 2005.

Morris, Leon. *The Gospel according to Matthew*. The Pillar New Testament Commentary. Grand Rapids: Eerdmans and InterVarsity Press, 1992.

Moss, Candida R. *Ancient Christian Martyrdom: Diverse Practices, Theologies, and Traditions*. New Haven: Yale University Press, 2012.

Mounce, Robert H. *Matthew*. New International Biblical Commentary 1. Peabody: Hendrickson, 1991.

Mtata, Kenneth, and Craig Koester, eds. *To All the Nations: Lutheran Hermeneutics and the Gospel of Matthew*. Lutheran World Federation Studies 2015/2. Leipzig: Evangelische Verlagsanstalt, 2015.

Müller, Morgens. "The Reception of the Old Testament in Matthew and Luke-Acts: From Interpretation to Proof from Scripture." *Novum Testamentum* 43 (2001): 315–30.

Murray, Henry A. "'In Nomine Diaboli: *Moby Dick*.'" In *Herman Melville's Moby-Dick*. Edited by Harold Bloom, 39–48. Modern Critical Interpretations. New York: Chelsea, 1986.

Nellesen, Ernst. *Das Kind und seine Mutter: Struktur und Verkündigung des 2. Kapitels im Matthäusevangelium*. Stuttgarter Bibelstudien 39. Stuttgart: Verlag Katholisches Bibelwerk, 1969.

Nicholls, Rachel. *Walking on Water: Reading Mt. 14:22-33 in the Light of Its Wirkungsgeschichte*. Bible Interpretation Series 90. Leiden: Brill, 2007.

Nicholls, Rachel. "Is Wirkungsgeschichte (or Reception History) a Kind of Intellectual Parkour (or Freerunning)?" In *Conference Paper, Society for the Study of the New Testament*. Available at http://bbibcomm.net. 2005.

Nolan, Brian M. *The Royal Son of God: The Christology of Matthew 1-2 in the Setting of the Gospel*. Orbis Biblicus et Orientalis 23. Göttingen: Vandenhoeck & Ruprecht, 1979.

Nolan, Kathleen. "'Ploratus et Ululatus': The Mothers in the Massacre of the Innocents at Chartres Cathedral." *Studies in Iconography* 17 (1996): 95–141.

Nolland, John. *The Gospel of Matthew: A Commentary on the Greek Text*. New International Greek Testament Commentary. Grand Rapids: Eerdmans and Paternoster Press, 2005.

Nygren, Christopher J. "Graphic Exegesis: Reflections on the Difficulty of Talking about Biblical Images, Pictures, and Texts." In *The Art of Visual Exegesis: Rhetoric, Texts, and Images*. Edited by Vernon K. Robbins, Walter S. Melion, and Roy R. Jeal, 271–302. Emory Studies in Early Christianity 19. Atlanta: SBL Press, 2017.

O'Callaghan, Clare. "Lullament: Lullaby and Lament Therapeutic Qualities Actualized through Music Therapy." *American Journal of Hospice and Palliative Medicine* 25 (2008): 93–9.

Ocker, Christopher. "Scholastic Interpretation of the Bible." In *A History of Biblical Interpretation. Volume 2: The Medieval through the Reformation Periods*. Edited by Alan J. Hauser and Duane F. Watson, 254–79. Grand Rapids: Eerdmans, 2009.

Ó Concheanainn, Tomás. "The Scribe of the Leabhar Breac." *Ériu* 24 (1973): 64–79.

O'Hear, Natasha F. H. *Contrasting Images of the Book of Revelation in Late Medieval and Early Modern Art: A Case Study in Visual Exegesis*. Oxford: Oxford University Press, 2011.

O'Kane, Martin. "The Artist as Reader of the Bible: Visual Exegesis and the Adoration of the Magi." *Biblical Interpretation* 13:4 (2005): 337–73.

O'Kane, Martin. "*Wirkungsgeschichte* and Visual Exegesis: The Contribution of Hans-Georg Gadamer." *Journal for the Study of the New Testament* 33:2 (2010): 147–59.

O'Keefe, John J., and Russell R. Reno. *Sanctified Vision: An Introduction to Early Christian Interpretation of the Bible*. Baltimore: John Hopkins University Press, 2005.

O'Neill, John C. "Jesus of Nazareth." *Jounral of Theological Studies* 50:1 (1999): 135–42.

Osborne, Grant R. *Matthew*. Zondervan Commentary on the New Testament. Grand Rapids: Zondervan, 2010.

Osborne, Grant R. *Revelation*. Baker Exegetical Commentary on the New Testament. Grand Rapids: Baker Academic, 2002.

Overman, J. Andrew. *Church and Community in Crisis: The Gospel according to Matthew*. New Testament in Context. Valley Forge: Trinity Press International, 1996.

Oxford Concise Companion to Irish Literature. Edited by Robert Welch. Oxford Paperback Reference. Oxford: Oxford University Press, 2000.

Oyer, John S. "The Writings of Melanchthon against the Anabaptists." *Mennonite Quarterly Review* 26 (1952): 259–279.

Palmer, Anne-Marie. *Prudentius on the Martyrs*. Oxford: Clarendon Press, 1989.

Panofsky, Erwin. "Iconography and Iconology: An Introduction to the Study of Renaissance Art." In *Meaning in the Visual Arts: Papers in and on Art History by Erwin Panofsky*, 26–54. Garden City: Doubleday, 1957.

Pardes, Ilana. *Melville's Bibles*. Berkeley: University of California Press, 2008.

Park, Eugene E. "Rachel's Cry for Her Children: Matthew's Treatment of the Infanticide by Herod." *Catholic Biblical Quarterly* 75:3 (2013): 473–85.

Parker, Hershel. *Melville Biography: An Inside Narrative*. Evanston: Northwestern University Press, 2012.

Parris, David P. *Reception Theory and Biblical Hermeneutics*. Princeton Theological Monograph Series 107. Eugene: Pickwick, 2009.

Patte, Daniel. *The Gospel according to Matthew: A Structural Commentary on Matthew's Faith*. Philadelphia: Fortress, 1987.

Pons, Jordi Pinell i. "History of the Liturgies in the Non-Roman West." In *Handbook for Liturgical Studies Volume 1: Introduction to Liturgy*. Edited by Anscar J. Chupungco, 179–95. Collegeville: Liturgical Press, 1997.

Portmann, Paul. *Meister Bertram*. Zürich: Verlag, 1963.

Powell, Mark A. "Introduction." In *Methods for Matthew*. Edited by Mark A. Powell, 1–10. Cambridge: Cambridge University Press, 2009.

Powell, Mark A. "Literary Approaches and the Gospel of Matthew." In *Methods for Matthew*. Edited by Mark A. Powell, 44–82. Cambridge: Cambridge University Press, 2009.

Powell, Mark A. "The Plot and Subplots of Matthew's Gospel." *New Testament Studies* 38 (1992): 187–204.

Powell, Mark A. *What Is Narrative Criticism?* Minneapolis: Fortress, 1990.

Pervo, Richard. "The Ancient Novel Becomes Christian." In *The Novel in the Ancient World*. Edited by Gareth Schmeling, 685–711. Leiden: Brill, 1996.

Petri, Sara. "Quodvultdeus of Carthage." In *The Oxford Guide to the Historical Reception of Augustine* 3. Edited by Karal Pollman and Willemien Otten, 1629–30. Oxford: Oxford University Press, 2013.

Pregeant, Russell. *Matthew*. Chalice Commentaries for Today. St. Louis: Chalice, 2004.

Johannes Quasten, *Golden Age of Latin Patristic Literature from the Council of Nicea to the Council of Chalcedon. Patrology.* Volume 4. Westminster: Christian Classics, 1986.

Räisänen, Heikki. "The 'Effective History' of the Bible: A Challenge to Biblical Scholarship." In *Challenges to Biblical Interpretation*. Edited by Heikki Räisänen, 263–82. Biblical Interpretation Series 59. Leiden: Brill, 2001.

Rall, Karen. *Medieval Mysteries: A Guide to History, Lore, Places and Symbolism of Twelve Medieval Mysteries.* Lake Worth: Nicolas-Hays, 2014.

Ramshaw, Gail. "The Holy Innocents, Martyrs, December 28." In *New Proclamation Commentary on Feasts, Holy Days, and Other Celebrations.* Edited by David B. Lott, 42–7. Philadelphia: Fortress, 2007.

Rastall, Richard. *Minstrels Playing.* Music in Early English Religious Drama 2. Cambridge: D.S. Brewer, 2001.

Reed, Roland. "The Slaughter of the Innocents." *Early Theatre* 3 (2000): 219–28.

Reno, R. R. "Series Preface." In *1 & 2 Peter*. Edited by Douglas Harink, 9–14. Grand Rapids: Brazos, 2009.

Repschinski, Boris. *The Controversy Stories in the Gospel of Matthew: Their Redaction, Form and Relevance for the Relationship between the Matthean Community and Formative Judaism.* Forschungen zur Religion und Literatur des Alten und Neuen Testaments 189. Göttingen: Vandenhoeck & Ruprecht, 2000.

Resseguie, James L. *Conflicting Mythologies: Identity Formation in the Gospels of Mark and Matthew.* Edinburgh: T&T Clark, 2000.

Resseguie, James L. *Narrative Criticism of the New Testament: An Introduction.* Grand Rapids: Baker Academic, 2005.

Ribeiro, Anna C. "Intending to Repeat: A Definition of Poetry." *Journal of Aesthetics and Art Criticism* 65:2 (2007): 189–201.

Ritter, Christine. *Rachels Klage im antiken Judentum und frühen Christentum.* Arbeiten zur Geschichte des antiken Judentums und des Urchristentums 52. Leiden: Brill, 2003.

Robbins, Vernon K. "New Testament Texts, Visual Material Culture, and Earliest Christian Art." In *The Art of Visual Exegesis: Rhetoric, Texts, and Images.* Edited by Vernon K. Robbins, Walter S. Melion, and Roy R. Jeal, 13–54. Emory Studies in Early Christianity 19. Atlanta: SBL Press, 2017.

Roberts, Jonathan. "Introduction." In *The Oxford Handbook of the Reception History of the Bible.* Edited by Michael Lieb, Jonathan Roberts, and Christopher Rowland, 1–8. Oxford: Oxford University Press, 2011.

Roberts, Jonathan, and Christopher Rowland. *The Bible for Sinners: Interpretation in the Present Time.* London: SPCK, 2008.

Roberts, Jonathan, and Christopher Rowland. "Introduction." *Journal for the Study of the New Testament* 33:2 (2010): 131–6.

Roberts, Robert E. *The Theology of Tertullian.* London: Epworth, 1924.

Rose, Els. *Ritual Memory: The Apocryphal Acts and Liturgical Commemoration in the Early Medieval West (c. 500–1215).* Mittellateinische Studien und Texte 40. Leiden: Brill, 2009.

Rosset, François. "'False' and 'True' Infancy and Apocryphal Gospels in the Century of Voltaire." In *Infancy Gospels: Stories and Identities.* Edited by Claire Clivaz, Andreas Dettwiler, Luc Devillers, Enrico Norelli, and Benjamin Bertho, 628–40. Wissenschaftliche Untersuchungen zum Neuen Testament 281. Tübingen: Mohr Siebeck, 2011.

Rowland, Christopher. "A Pragmatic Approach to *Wirkungsgeschichte*: Reflections on the Blackwell Bible Commentary Series and on the Writing of Its Commentary on the Apocalypse." Paper presented at Evangelisch-Katholischer Kommentar Biannual Meeting. Germany. March 21-3, 2004.

Rowland, Christopher. "Imagining the Apocalypse." *NTS* 51 (2005): 303-27.

Rowland, Christopher. "The Interdisciplinary Colloquium on the Book of Revelation and Effective History." In *The Way the World Ends? The Apocalypse of John in Culture and Ideology*. Edited by William J. Lyons and Jorunn Økland, 289-304. The Bible in the Modern World 19. Sheffield: Sheffield Phoenix, 2009.

Rowland, Christopher. "Re-imagining Biblical Exegesis." In *Religion, Literature and the Imagination: Sacred Worlds*. Edited by Mark Knight and Louise Lee, 140-9. London: Continuum, 2010.

Rowland, Christopher. "Reception History." In *Searching for Meaning: An Introduction to Interpreting the New Testament*. Edited by Paula Gooder, 111-13. London: SPCK, 2008.

Rowland, Christopher, and Judith Kovacs. *Revelation: The Apocalypse of Jesus Christ*. Blackwell Bible Commentaries. Oxford: Wiley-Blackwell, 2004.

Ruether, Rosmary R. *Faith and Fratricide: The Theological Roots of Anti-Semitism*. New York: Seabury, 1974.

Rummel, Erika. "The Renaissance Humanists." In *A History of Biblical Interpretation. Volume 2: The Medieval through the Reformation Periods*. Edited by Alan J. Hauser and Duane F. Watson, 280-98. Grand Rapids: Eerdmans, 2009.

Runesson, Anders. "Judging the Theological Tree by Its Fruit: The Use of the Gospels of Mark and Matthew in Official Church Documents on Jewish-Christian Relations," In *Mark and Matthew II: Comparative Readings: Reception History, Cultural Hermeneutics, and Theology*. Edited by Eve-Marie Becker and Anders Runesson, 189-228. Wissenschaftliche Untersuchungen zum Neuen Testament 304. Tübingen: Mohr Siebeck, 2013.

Runesson, Anders, and Eve-Marie Becker. "Introduction: Reading Mark and Matthew within and beyond the First Century." In *Mark and Matthew II: Comparative Readings: Reception History, Cultural Hermeneutics, and Theology*. Edited by Eve-Marie Becker and Anders Runesson, 1-12. Wissenschaftliche Untersuchungen zum Neuen Testament 304. Tübingen: Mohr Siebeck, 2013.

Runesson, Anders, and Eve-Marie Becker. "Preface." In *Mark and Matthew II: Comparative Readings: Reception History, Cultural Hermeneutics, and Theology*. Edited by Eve-Marie Becker and Anders Runesson, v-vi. Wissenschaftliche Untersuchungen zum Neuen Testament 304. Tübingen: Mohr Siebeck, 2013.

Sagi, Avi. *Albert Camus and the Philosophy of the Absurd*. Value Inquiry Book Series 125. Amsterdam: Rodophi, 2002.

Saito, Tadashi. *Die Mosevorstellungen im Neuen Testament*. Bern: Peter Lang, 1977.

Saldarini, Anthony J. *Matthew's Christian-Jewish Community*. Chicago Studies in the History of Judaism. Chicago: University of Chicago Press, 1994.

Sauerländer, Willibald. *The Catholic Rubens: Saints and Martyrs*. Translated by David Dollenmayer. Los Angeles: Getty Publications, 2014.

Sanders, Ed P. *The Historical Figures of Jesus*. London: Penguin, 1993.

Schalit, Abraham. *König Herodes: Der Mann und sein Werk*. Vol. 2. Auflage: De Gruyter, 2015.

Scheck, Thomas P. "Introduction." In *Jerome: Commentary on Matthew*. Translated by Thomas P. Scheck, 3–47. The Fathers of the Church 117. Washington, DC: Catholic University of America Press, 2008.

Scheck, Thomas P. "Introduction." In *Jerome-Origen: Commentary on Isaiah Including St. Jerome's Translation of Origen's Homilies 1–9 on Isaiah: Translated and with an Introduction*. Translated by Thomas P. Scheck, 1–65. ACW 68. New York: Newman, 2015.

Schlatter, D. Adolf. *Der Evangelist Matthäus: Seine Sprache, sein Ziel, seine Selbständigkeit: Ein Kommentar zum ersten Evangelium*. Stuttgart: Calwer Verlag, 1929.

Schnackenburg, Rudolf. *The Gospel of Matthew*. Translated by Robert R. Barr. Grand Rapids: Eerdmans, 2002.

Schofield, John. *Philip Melanchthon and the English Reformation*. St. Andrews Studies in Reformation History. Aldershot: Ashgate, 2006.

Schwartz, Howard. *Tree of Souls: The Mythology of Judaism*. Oxford: Oxford University Press, 2004.

Schwentzel, Christian-Georges. *Hérode le Grand: Juifs et Romains, Salomé et Jean-Baptiste, Titus et Bérénice*. Paris: Pygmalion, 2011.

Scott, Stuart O. "The Slaying of the Innocents: A Relational Treatise on Composition and Conducting." Doctor of Arts Thesis, Ball State University, 1986.

Seaver, James E. *The Persecution of the Jews in the Roman Empire (300–428)*. University of Kansas Publications. Humanistic Studies 30. Lawrence: University of Kansas Press, 1952.

Sekules, Veronica. *Medieval Art*. Oxford: Oxford University Press, 2001.

Senior, Donald. *Matthew*. Abingdon New Testament Commentaries. Nashville: Abingdon, 1998.

Senior, Donald. "The Lure of the Formula Quotations: Re-assessing Matthew's Use of the Old Testament with the Passion Narrative as Test Case." In *The Scriptures in the Gospels*. Edited by C. M. Tucket, 89–115. Bibliotheca Ephemeridum Theologicarum Lovaniensium 131. Leuven: Leuven University Press, 1997.

Senior, Donald. *The Passion of Jesus in the Gospel of John*. Collegeville: Liturgical Press, 1991.

Senior, Donald. *What Are They Saying about Matthew?* Revised and expanded edition. New York: Paulist, 1996.

Sered, Susan Starr. "Rachel's Tomb and the Milk Grotto of the Virgin Mary: Two Women's Shrines in Bethlehem." *Journal of Feminist Studies in Religion* 2 (1986): 7–22.

Sharp, David. "Inheriting Antiquity: Giambattista Marino's Rime Boscherecce, Luis de Góngora's La fábula de Polifemo y Galatea and the Baroque Literary Aesthetic." *Journal Language & Literature* 3 (2008): 1–9.

Sheppard, Lancelot C. *The Mass in the West*. New York: Hawthorn, 1995.

Sherwood, Yvonne. *A Biblical Text and Its Afterlives: The Survival of Jonah in Western Culture*. Cambridge: Cambridge University Press, 2000.

Silver, Larry. *Peasant Scenes and Landscapes: The Rise of Pictorial Genres in the Antwerp Art Market*. Philadelphia: University of Pennsylvania Press, 2006.

Sim, David C. *The Gospel of Matthew and Christian Judaism: The History and Social Setting of the Matthean Community*. Edinburgh: T&T Clark, 1998.

Smith, Wilfred C. *What Is Scripture? A Comparative Approach*. Minneapolis: Fortress, 1993.

Soares-Prabhu, George. *The Formula Citations in the Infancy Narrative of Matthew: An Enquiry into the Tradition History of Matthew 1-2*. Analecta Biblica 63. Rome: Biblical Institute, 1976.

Spear, Richard E. *The "Divine" Guido: Religion, Sex, Money and Art in the World of Guido Reni*. New Haven: Yale University Press, 1997.

Stafford, Barbara M. *Good Looking: Essays on the Virtue of Images*. Cambridge: MIT Press, 1996.

Staley, Allen. *The Pre-Raphaelite Landscape*. 2nd ed. New Haven: Yale University Press, 2001.

Stanton, Graham N. *The Gospels and Jesus*. 2nd ed. Oxford Bible Series. Oxford: Oxford University Press, 2004.

Stanton, Graham N. *A Gospel for a New People: Studies in Matthew*. Louisville: Westminster/John Knox, 1993.

Stendahl, Krister. *The School of St. Matthew and Its Use of the Old Testament*. Lund: Gleerup, 1954.

Stendahl, Krister. "*Quis et Unde?* An Analysis of Mt 1-2." In *Judentum, Urchristentum, Kirche: Festschrift für Joachim Jeremias*. Edited by W. Eltester, 94–105. Beihefte zur Zeitschrift für die neutestamentliche Wissenschaft 26. Berlin: Töpelmann, 1964.

Strauss, Valerie. "Howard Gardiner: 'Multiple Intelligences' Are Not 'Learning Styles.'" *Washington Post*. October 16, 2013. Accessed August 1, 2017. https://www.washingtonpost.com/news/answer-sheet/wp/2013/10/16/howard-gardner-multiple-intelligences-are-not-learning-styles/?utm_term=.ee7cede43814.

Strickert, Frederick M. *Rachel Weeping: Jews, Christians, and Muslims at the Fortress Tomb*. Collegeville: Liturgical Press, 2007.

Stronstad Roger. *The Charismatic Theology of St. Luke: Trajectories from the Old Testament to Luke-Acts*. 2nd ed. Grand Rapids: Baker Academic, 2012.

Studwell, William E. *The Christmas Carol Reader*. New York: Routledge, 2011.

Swartz, Michael D. *The Signifying Creator: Nontextual Sources of Meaning in Ancient Judaism*. New York: New York University Press, 2012.

Sweet, John. *Revelation*. TPI New Testament Commentaries. London: SCM, 1990.

Talbert, Charles H. *What Is a Gospel? The Genre of the Canonical Gospels*. Philadelphia: Fortress, 1977.

Temple, W. M. "The Weeping Rachel." *Medium aevum* 28:2 (1959): 81–6.

Theisen, Reinold. "The Reform of Mass Liturgy and the Council of Trent." *Worship* 40:9 (1966): 565–83.

Thiselton, Anthony C. "'Postmodern' Challenges to Hermeneutics: 'Behind' and 'In Front Of' the Text—Language, Reference and Indeterminacy" (2001). In *Thiselton on Hermeneutics: Collected Works with New Essays*, 607–24. Grand Rapids: Eerdmans, 2006.

Thompson, Lawrance R. *Melville's Quarrel with God*. Princeton: Princeton University Press, 1952.

Thompson, William G. *Matthew's Story: Good News for Uncertain Times*. New York: Paulinist Press, 1989.

Thompson, William G. *Matthew's Advice to a Divided Community: Mt. 17,22-18,35*. Analecta Biblica 44. Rome: Biblical Institute, 1970.

Tiessen, Paul. "Wyndham Lewis's *The Childermass* (1928): The Slaughter of the Innocents in the Age of Cinema." In *Apocalyptic Visions Past and Present*. Edited by JoAnn James and William J. Cloonan, 25–35. Tallahassee: Florida State University Press, 1988.

Toom, Tarmo. "Augustine's Hermeneutics: The Science of the Divinely Given Signs." In *Patristic Theories of Biblical Interpretation: The Latin Fathers*. Edited by Tarmo Toom, 77–108. Cambridge: Cambridge University Press, 2016.

Trexler, Richard C. *The Journey of the Magi: Meanings in History of a Christian Story*. Princeton: Princeton University Press, 1997.

Tuor-Kurth, Christina. *Kindesaussetzung und Moral in der Antike: Jüdische und christliche Kritik am Nichtaufziehen und Töten neugeborener Kinder*. Forschungen zur Kirchen- und Dogmengeschichte 101. Göttingen: Vandenhoeck & Ruprecht, 2010.

Turner, David L. *Matthew*. Baker Exegetical Commentary on the New Testament. Grand Rapids: Baker Academic, 2008.

Turner, Victor W. *Image and Pilgrimage in Christian Culture: Anthropological Perspectives*. New York: Columbia University Press, 1978.

Turner, Victor W. *The Ritual Process: Structure and Anti-structure*. Chicago: Aldine, 1969.

Twycross, Meg. "The Theatricality of Medieval English Plays." In *The Cambridge Companion to Medieval English Theatre*. Edited by Richard Beadle and Alan J. Fletcher, 26–74. 2nd revised edition. Cambridge: Cambridge University Press, 2008.

Tyneh, Carl S., ed. *Orthodox Christianity: Overview and Bibliography*. New York: Nova Science, 2003.

"Unknown Rubens Discovered in Time for Auction." *The Guardian*. February 28, 2002. https://www.theguardian.com/uk/2002/feb/28/2.

van Aarde, Andries G., and Yolanda Dreyer. "Matthew Studies Today—a Willingness to Suspect and a Willingness to Listen." *HTS Teologiese Studies/Theological Studies* 66:1 (2010) Article #820.

van Dodewaard, Johannes A. E. "La force évocatrice de la citation mise en lumière en prenant pour base l'Évangile de S. Matthieu." *Biblica* 36 (1955): 482–91.

van Engen, John H. *Rupert of Deutz*. Berkeley: University of California Press, 1983.

van Henten, Jan. "Matthew 2:16 and Josephus' Portrayals of Herod." In *Jesus, Paul, and Early Christianity: Studies in Honour of Henk Jan de Jonge*. Edited by Rieuwerd Buitenwerf, Harm W. Hollander, and Johannes Tromp, 101–22. Supplment to Novum Testamentum 130. Leiden: Brill, 2008.

van Oyen, Geert. "The *Protoevangelium Jacobi*: An Apocryphal Gospel?" In *Apocryphal Gospels within the Context of Early Christian Theology*. Edited by Jens Schröter, 271–304. Bibliotheca Ephemeridum Theologicarum Lovaniensium 260. Leuven: Peeters, 2013.

van Winden, J. C. M. *An Early Christian Philosopher: Justin Martyr's Dialogue with Trypho, Chapters One to Nine*. Philosophia Patrum 1. Leiden: Brill, 1971.

Verheyden, Joseph. "Reading Matthew and Mark in the Middle Ages: The *Glossa Orinaria*." In *Mark and Matthew II: Comparative Readings: Reception History, Cultural Hermeneutics, and Theology*. Edited by Eve-Marie Becker and Anders Runesson, 121–150. Wissenschaftliche Untersuchungen zum Neuen Testament 304. Tübingen: Mohr Siebeck, 2013.

Vermes, Geza. *The Nativity: History and Legend*. New York: Doubleday, 2006.

Vioque, Guillermo Galán. *Martial, Book VII: A Commentary*. Translated by J. J. Zoltowski. Leiden: Brill, 2002.

Viviano, Benedict T. "God in the Gospel according to Matthew." *Interpretation* 64 (2010): 341–54.

Vogel, Cyrille. *Medieval Liturgy: An Introduction to the Sources*. Revised and translated by William Storey and Niels Rasmussen. Portland: Pastoral, 1986.

Vööbus, Arthur, ed. *A Syriac Lectionary from the Church of the Forty Martyrs in Mardin, Ṭūr ʿAbdīn, Mesopotamia*. CSCO 485. Lovanii: E. Peeters, 1986.
Wainwright, Elaine. "Rachel Weeping for Her Children: Intertextuality and the Biblical Testaments—a Feminist Approach." In *A Feminist Companion to Reading the Bible: Approaches, Methods and Strategies*. Edited by Athalya Brenner and Carole R. Fontaine, 452-69. Feminist Companion to the Bible 11. Sheffield: Sheffield Academic, 1997.
Ward, Benedicta. *The Venerable Bede*. Cistercian Studies 169. Collegeville: Liturgical Press, 1998.
Warland, Rainer. "The Concept of Rome in Late Antiquity Reflected in the Mosaics of the Triumphal Arch of S. Maria Maggiore in Rome." *Acta ad archaeologiam et artium historiam pertinentia* 17 (2003): 127-41.
Warner, Marina. "'Hush-a-bye Baby': Death and Violence in the Lullaby." *Raritan* 18 (1998): 93-114.
Weiser, Francs X. *Handbook of Christian Feasts and Customs: The Year of the Lord in Liturgy and Folklore*. New York: Harcourt Brace, 1958.
Wellman, Tennyson. "Apocalyptic Concerns and Mariological Tactics in Eleventh-Century France." In *The Year 1000: Religious and Social Response to the Turning of the First Millennium*. Edited by Michael Frassetto Palgrave, 133-63. New York: Macmillan, 2002.
Whitters, Mark F. "Jesus in the Footsteps of Jeremiah." *Catholic Biblical Quarterly* 68 (2006): 229-47.
Wick, Peter. "Herodes im Matthäus-Evangelium: Messiasprätendent—Pharao—Antichrist," *Herodes und Jerusalem*. Edited by Linda-Marie Günter, 61-70. Stuttguart: Franz Steiner Verlag, 2009.
Widdicombe, Peter. "The Patristic Reception of the Gospel of Matthew: The Commentary of Jerome and the Sermons of John Chrysostom," In *Mark and Matthew II: Comparative Readings: Reception History, Cultural Hermeneutics, and Theology*. Edited by Eve-Marie Becker and Anders Runesson, 105-19. Wissenschaftliche Untersuchungen zum Neuen Testament 304. Tübingen: Mohr Siebeck, 2013.
Wilkins, Michael J. *Matthew*. The NIV Application Commentary. Grand Rapids: Zondervan, 2004.
Wilkinson, D. R. M. "*Sospetto d'Herode*: A Neglected Crashaw Poem." In *Studies in Seventeenth-Century English Literature, History and Bibliography: Festschrift for Professor T. A. Birrell on the Occasion of His Sixtieth Birthday*. Edited by G. A. M. Janssens and Flor G. A. M. Aarts, 233-44. Costerus 46. Amsterdam: Rodopli, 1984.
Williams, D. H. "Introduction." In *Hilary of Poitiers: Commentary on Matthew*. Translated by D. H. Williams, 3-38. The Fathers of the Church 125. Washington, DC: Catholic University of America Press, 2012.
Williamson, Beth. "Altarpieces, Liturgy, and Devotion." *Speculum* 79 (2004): 341-406.
Wilson, R. M. *The Lost Literature of Medieval England*. 2nd ed. London: Methuen, 1972.
Witherington III, Ben. *Matthew*. Smyth & Helwys Bible Commentary 19. Macon: Smyth & Helwys, 2006.
Witherington III, Ben. *New Testament Rhetoric: An Introductory Guide to the Art of Persuasion in and of the New Testament*. Eugene: Wipf & Stock, 2009.
Witherington III, Ben. "Primary Sources." *Christian History* 17:3 (1998): 12-20.
Wright, David H. "The Date and Arrangement of the Illustrations in the Rabbula Gospels." *Dumbarton Oaks Papers* 27 (1973): 199-208.

Wright, Edith A. *The Dissemination of the Liturgical Drama in France*. Geneve: Slatkline Reprints, 1980.
Wright, N. T. *The New Testament and the People of God*. London: SPCK, 1992.
Yothers, Brian. *Sacred Uncertainty: Religious Difference and the Shape of Melville's Career*. Evanston: Northwestern University Press, 2015.
Young, Frances. "Alexandrian and Antiochene Exegesis." In *A History of Biblical Interpretation. Volume 1: The Ancient Period*. Edited by Alan J. Hauser and Duane F. Watson, 334–54. Grand Rapids: Eerdmans, 2003.
Young, Karl. *The Drama of the Medieval Church*. 2 vols. Oxford: Clarendon Press, 1967.
Zerwick, Maximilian. *Biblical Greek: Illustrated by Examples*. 9th reprint. Subsidia Biblica 41. Rome: Gregorian & Biblical Press, 2011.

General Index

144,000 54, 78, 105–6, 129, 142, 152, 214

A' Lapide, Cornelius 125, 152, 155
Abel 54, 111–12, 166–7, 212
Abiathar 57, 212
Abraham 1, 28, 45, 75, 113, 135, 146, 148, 153, 181
Acts of Pilate 54, 144–5, 217
actualization 62, 66, 86, 130–1 156, 158, 173, 180, 206–7, 211, 215–18
Adam 66, 79, 149, 166
Ahab 65, 141, 145–7
allegory 50, 91, 94, 113, 117, 122, 157–8, 211
Allison, Dale C. 2, 16–17, 24, 33, 40, 153, 156
Ambrosian Rite 132–4, 210, 214
anagogy 94, 106, 117, 123, 125, 133, 158, 211, 213
antiphon 102–5, 109, 122, 128–9, 133–4, 136, 169, 210, 214
Apponius 59, 62, 66–7, 71, 86, 91, 114, 130, 199
Aquinas, Thomas 91, 112
Arabia 81–2, 112
Arabic Gospel of the Infancy of the Savior (AIG) 90, 96
Arius/Arian 63–5
Assyria 43–4, 51–2, 54, 155
Athaliah 168, 212
Augustine 14, 54, 58, 60, 62–3, 67, 69, 73, 75–8, 81, 84–6, 91, 103, 130–1, 168, 170, 174
Autpert, Ambrose 106, 123, 214

Babylon 40, 43–4, 98, 152, 155
Bar Salibi, Dionysius 112, 129
Basil of Seleucia 59–60, 71, 75, 79–80, 90, 135
Basilica di Santa Maria Maggiore 181–2, 210

beholder 161, 163–4, 168, 202
Benjamin 42, 81–4, 95, 106, 112
Berdini, Paolo 92, 163–4
Bertram of Minden 139, 166–8, 212
Book of Common Prayer 126, 129, 153, 214
Book of the Bee 94, 97–9
Borromeo, Charles 131, 133, 158, 214
Boxall, Ian 3, 8, 11, 161, 167, 201, 205
Broadus, John A. 151–2, 155–6
Brown, Raymond 5–6, 28–9, 38, 45, 154, 209, 214
Byzantine Rite 135, 209

Cain 54, 57, 65–6, 100, 166–7, 210
Calendar of Carthage 89, 130
Calvin, John 130, 150–2, 158
Camus, Albert 144–5, 149, 217
Cathédrale Notre-Dame de Chartres 195, 218
Catiline 101–2, 109, 123
Christina of Markyate 197–9
Christmas 6, 17, 58, 74, 79, 89–90, 108–11, 115, 146
Chromatius of Aquileia 9, 69, 71–2, 77, 106, 144, 182
Chrysologus, Peter 51, 60, 69, 71, 73–7, 80, 103, 143, 182
Chrysostom, John 14, 55–6, 69, 86, 96, 131, 150, 155, 168, 206, 213, 217
Clarke, Howard 15–16, 24, 137
Codex Egberti 192–4
Comes of Würzburg 104, 123, 133, 213
communism 135, 148
Constantine 14–15, 64
Constantius 63–5, 156, 180, 215
Counter-Reformation 129, 131, 158
Coventry Carol 126–7, 137–40, 158, 218
crown 54, 69–70, 75, 78, 86, 103, 107, 133–4, 213
Cudmore, Daniel 136, 214
Cyprian of Carthage 69–71, 75, 86

Damascus 51, 82
David 1, 28, 33, 35, 44, 52–3, 55, 57–8, 68, 108–9, 111, 114, 118, 141–4, 181, 191, 198, 212
Di Giovanni, Matteo 175, 177–80, 184, 203
Diocletian 72, 131
Docetism/Docetic 49, 53
dragon 35, 93, 97, 99–100, 122, 156, 214

Ebeling, Gerhard 7, 12–13
Egypt 2, 28–30, 33, 38, 45, 49, 54, 63, 73, 75, 97, 99, 109–10, 112, 119, 122–3, 125, 137, 151, 165–6, 170–1, 173, 195, 198, 207, 209, 212, 214
Elizabeth 56, 78, 94
Emmanuel/Immanuel 28, 44, 50, 53, 113
Ephrem the Syrian 56–8, 61, 63, 78, 80–1, 86, 90, 104, 116, 131, 136, 141, 143, 167–8, 170, 209–10, 212
Epiphanius of Salamis 49, 69–71
Epiphany 67, 72–3, 90, 117, 138, 191
Eucharist 107, 133, 163, 166, 168, 173
Eusebius of Caesarea 49, 60–1, 72, 86, 89, 92, 95–6, 98, 131, 143–4, 150, 191, 206, 212
Evangelical Lutheran Worship (ELW) 126, 129, 153
Evangelisch-Katholischer Kommentar zum Neuen Testament (EKK) 10, 12–13
Evans, Robert 13, 22–4
Exiguus, Dionysius 94, 112, 116, 129, 152

Feast of Fools (festum stultorum) 101–2, 108, 128
Festival of the Innocents 89, 101–2, 104, 121, 127–34, 191, 213–14
firstfruits 78, 80, 104, 109, 116, 129
Fitzmeyer, Joseph 27, 154, 218
Fleury 108–10, 119–22, 194
flower 72, 79, 190
Fortunatianus of Aquileia 83, 131
Fragment 23 (Frag. 23) 49, 62, 94
Fragment 34, 82–3
Freising 100–2, 109, 119–22, 194
Fulbert of Chartres 195–6
fulfillment citation 36–8, 41
Fulgentius of Ruspe 54, 71, 75, 77

Gadamer, Hans 8, 10, 12, 15, 17–18, 21, 206
Gehazi 57, 210
Gelasian Sacramentary 103–4, 133
genealogy 28, 36, 40, 44, 65, 137, 194, 219
Glossa Ordinaria 20, 91
Gorron, Geoffrey 197–9
Gospel of Pseudo-Matthew (GPM) 90, 96, 111
Grabow Altarpiece 139, 166–8, 212
Gregory of Nazianzus 49, 65–6, 79, 86, 91, 103, 112–13, 130, 153, 167
Gregory of Nyssa 54–5, 58, 80, 83, 86, 90, 131, 143, 155, 167–8, 176
Gundry, Robert H. 36, 42, 157

Haney, Kristine 183–4, 216
Hauerwas, Stanley 156, 218
Hendriksen, William 36, 46, 155
Henry, Matthew 155–6, 158, 210
Herod Agrippa I 55–6, 60, 213
Herod Antipas 30, 60–1, 66, 207, 213
Herod Archelaus 114
Hilary of Poitiers 63–5, 75, 77, 83–6, 91, 130, 135, 170, 180
Hildegard of Bingen 91, 117–18, 122, 199
historical criticism/critical method 11–15, 20, 22, 24, 27, 35–6, 44, 62, 86, 125, 205, 215
Historically Effected Consciousness (*wirkungsgeschichtliches Bewußtsein*) 21, 206–7
History of Interpretation (*Auslegungsgeschichte*) 8, 17, 205, 217
History of Joseph the Carpenter (HJC) 59, 61–2, 86, 213
Holy Family 30–1, 33, 36, 49, 61, 63, 95–7, 99, 110, 114, 121, 123, 132, 151, 165, 171–3, 202, 207, 209, 214
Horizon (*Horizont*) 17–19, 21, 206
Hostis Herodes impie 58, 120
Hunt, William Holman 171–3, 202

imagination 18, 22–3, 36, 45, 80, 85, 92, 123, 126–7, 157, 181, 209, 215
imprecation/imprecatory 105, 134, 136, 169, 202
Infancy or Birth Narrative 5–6, 28, 34, 38, 41, 50, 85, 94–5, 164

interpretative space 27, 35, 43, 46, 151, 161–2, 202, 212
intratextuality 2, 24
Irenaeus of Lyons 51–4, 68–9, 76, 85, 89, 131, 142, 174, 210
Ishodad of Merv 95, 112

Jacob of Serugh 23, 49, 53, 59–60, 63, 74, 78–80, 91, 141, 156, 170, 206
Jamieson, Robert, Andrew R. Fausset, and David Brown 155, 157
Jauss, Hans R. 9–10, 22–3
Jeremiah 2, 37, 39–40, 55, 69
Jerome 20, 53–4, 76, 82, 84, 91–2, 104, 113, 142, 174, 214
Jerusalem 3, 29–30, 40, 42
Joash 56–7, 98, 210, 212
John of Euobea 100, 110–11, 122–3, 135, 156, 167, 175, 214
John the Baptist 30, 41, 49, 52, 56–7, 61, 66, 78–9, 94, 97–8, 111, 162, 207, 212–13
Joseph 4, 31, 38, 54, 61, 63, 96–7, 99, 123, 148–9, 155, 169, 172, 176, 181, 209, 217
Josephus 28–9, 34, 57, 61, 86, 95–6, 131, 143–4, 148, 150, 206, 212
Judaism 67, 85, 98, 156, 181
Judas Iscariot 39, 57, 66, 107, 170, 210
Justin Martyr 50–1, 54, 58, 76, 82, 85, 131, 174, 210
juxtaposition (Strategy) 211–13

Kealy, Sean P. 1, 6–7, 14–15, 24, 211
Kerameus, Thomas 91, 95
Kunzle, David 179, 184–6, 189

lamb 78–9, 100, 105, 108–9, 111, 113, 118, 136, 144, 149
Lazarus 55, 75, 173
Leah 83–5, 103, 113
lectionary 102, 104, 128–9, 133–4
Leo the Great 54, 60, 69, 75–7, 79, 86, 89, 103, 183
Limoges 105, 118–21, 123, 194
literal sense 93, 103–4, 113, 122, 126, 129, 152, 158, 211
Lorraine, France 182, 194
Lucifer of Cagliari 64, 75, 86, 130, 156, 167, 180

lullament 139, 218
Luther, Martin 126–7, 130
Luz, Ulrich 3, 6, 7, 10–14, 24, 27, 37, 44, 154, 205, 207
Lyons, William John 8, 13, 22–4

Macrobius 34, 61, 131, 136, 143–4, 150, 212
Maher-Shalal-Hash-Baz 50, 53–4, 113
Marcion 14, 49, 114
Marino, Giambattista 137, 148, 158, 196, 209
Martyrdom of Matthew 106–8, 123, 214
Mary 2, 4, 36, 44, 54, 56, 79, 95–7, 99, 119, 121–3, 148–9, 153, 155, 163, 172–4, 176, 178, 181, 194–5, 209
Matins of the Innocents 169, 214
Matthean Community 4, 40
Maurus, Rabanus 91, 116
Mawdyke, Thomas 137, 140
Maximin 173–6, 208
Maximus the Confessor 95–6, 98, 110, 122
Melanchthon, Philip 130, 158
Melville, Hermann 8, 127, 145–7, 158, 206, 217
Menaion 135–6, 209
midwife 33, 61, 101, 207
milk 71, 74, 114
Moses 2, 28, 33, 35, 45–6, 57, 107, 123, 207, 210
Mozarabic Rite 132–5, 210, 214
Muslim/Islam 81, 154, 178
mystery play 92–3, 127

narrative criticism/critical 27, 35–6, 46, 86, 205, 208
Narsai 24, 80, 82
Nazareth 28–30, 38
Nebuchadnezzar 98, 156
Nero 64, 131, 210
Nicholls, Rachel 8, 10, 17–19, 21, 24, 205, 207, 216
Notker the Stammerer 90, 110, 120–1

Oecumenius 99, 122–3, 156, 175, 214
Optatus 59, 91, 156, 174
Opus Imperfectum 9, 51, 58, 61, 69, 81–2, 91, 143, 209

Origen 17, 49, 59–60, 62–5, 67, 69, 71, 82, 86, 91–2, 117, 135, 156, 170, 175, 187, 208, 210, 213
Ottoman Empire 125, 135, 178

palm 69, 74–6, 86, 97, 103, 105, 134, 187, 213
Panofsky, Erwin 162, 203, 206
Passion 32, 35, 38–9, 46, 57, 79, 95, 121, 164, 170, 171, 173
Paupers' Bible (*Biblia Pauperum*) 168–70, 202, 212
Pharaoh 33, 35, 45, 56–7, 141, 207
Pieter Bruegel the Elder 93, 180, 184, 203
Pieter Bruegel the Younger 93, 184
Pilgrimages 92, 94, 105, 114–15, 125–7, 144
Pisano, Giovanni 169–71, 176–8, 202
Plato 107, 171
Play of Rachel (Ordo Rachelis) 108–10, 119–22
Play of the Star (Officium Stellae) 100, 102, 109, 119, 121–2
Pontius Pilate 32, 66, 86, 207
Pope Paul VI 128, 186
Pope Peter I of Alexandria 51, 56, 62
Pope Pius V 128, 132
Pope Sixtus III 181–2
Poussin, Nicolas 93, 171, 194, 196
Presentation at/in the Temple 49, 95, 151, 165–6, 176, 181, 198
Protoevangelium of James (PJ) 49, 56–7, 90, 94–8, 101, 111, 168, 210, 212
Providence 95, 155–6
Prudentius, Aurelius Clemens 69, 72, 79–80, 90, 101, 104, 118, 136, 142, 144, 176, 214

Quid tu virgo 120–2
Quodvultdeus 54, 58, 60, 67, 69, 72, 75–7, 80, 86, 103–4, 142, 213

Rabbula Gospels 191–2, 194
Raphael 171–2, 186, 188–9, 196
reader-oriented method 4, 8, 20, 123, 158, 205
rrecontextualization 93–4, 104, 123, 136, 156, 169–70, 211–15
Reni, Guido 93, 186–7, 190, 202
responsory 104, 129

Romanos the Melodist 90, 135
Rowland, Christopher 6, 8, 22–3, 62, 161, 173, 201, 211
Rubens, Peter Paul 93, 141–2, 163, 175, 180, 188–90, 200–1, 203
Rufus of Shotep 91, 112–14, 119, 122
Runesson, Anders and Eve-Marie Becker 19–20, 24
Rupert of Deutz 116–17, 123, 129, 131, 139, 152, 210

Sahidic MS 36 111–12, 115–16, 167, 206
Samaria 51–2, 73
Samuel 123, 154
Saramago, José 145, 147–50, 158, 206, 217
Satan/Devil 32, 59–61, 64, 66, 75–6, 86, 91, 99, 118, 141, 143, 148, 156, 159, 175
Sauerländer, Willibald 142, 189, 200
Saul 56–8, 65, 131, 168, 210, 212
Sedulius, Caelius 58, 90
Shakespeare, William 16, 127, 137
Shepherd 52–3, 67, 78–9, 101
Simeon 51–2, 57, 95, 132
Solomon, King 66, 69, 191
Speckled Book (Leabhar Breac) 96–7, 119, 122–3, 209
St. Albans Psalter 197–9
Stapulensis, Jacobus Faber 150, 157
Strasbourg Cathedral 164–6
Summit-dialogue of Authors/*Gipfeldialog der Autoren*/Höhenkamm der Autoren 9–10
Synagogue 83, 102, 113, 121–2

Te Deum 102, 110, 121
Tertullian 49, 68–9, 73, 75, 78, 86, 105, 131, 144, 198, 210
Testa, Pietro 171, 173
theodicy 2, 40, 45–6, 48, 54–6, 85, 130, 148, 155–7, 168, 173
Theodore of Mopsuetia 9, 56, 63, 69, 150, 170
tropology 66, 82, 86, 91, 93–4, 103–4, 112–13, 117, 122–3, 125, 132, 211, 213
typology 50–4, 56, 58, 71, 85–6, 91, 117, 121–2, 139, 153, 168–9

Under the altar of God (Sub altare Dei) 105, 109, 118–19, 123, 169, 214

Vatican II 128–9, 132
Venerable Bede 90–1, 114–15
Veronese Sacramentary 89, 102–3, 133
Visual Exegesis 92, 161–3, 174, 202

Wirkungsgeschichte 10–13, 15, 18–19

Young, Karl 90, 100–1, 108, 118–21

Zechariah 56–7, 94, 97–8, 111, 210, 212

Scripture Index

Genesis
1 — 166
1–3 — 136
3 — 198
4 — 112
4:12 — 14 100
5:24 — 153
16:12 — 146
22 — 157
22:6-10 — 72
28:10-19 — 173
29:31 — 113
35:19 — 154
35:20 — 114
48:7 — 154

Exodus
1:16 — 116
1:22 — 45
2 — 45
2:15 — 57
2:23 — 45
2:23-24 — 45
2:23-25 — 57
2:24-25 — 45
2:25 — 45
3-4 — 45
3:1–4:31 — 45
3:8 — 143
3:17 — 143
4 — 107
4:18 — 45
4:19–20 — 33
13:5 — 143
14 — 136
17:16 (LXX) — 52
23:23 — 143
32:2 — 91
33:2 — 143
34:11 — 143

Leviticus
19:18 — 73

Numbers
17 — 107

Deuteronomy
6:5 — 73
17:6 — 73
19:15 — 73
20:17 — 143
32:43 — 169

Joshua
18–19 — 81
18:25 — 81, 154
19:29, 39 — 81
24:11 — 143

Judges
18:25 — 154
19–20 — 84
19:13 — 154

1 Samuel
1:1 — 154
1:19 — 154
2:11 — 154
8 — 213
8:4 — 154
10:2 — 42
19:18 — 154
21–22 — 156
22:6-23 — 212
22:18-19 — 168
22:19 — 168
24 — 58
25:1 — 154
26 — 58

2 Samuel

5:1-5	168
5:6-10	143
12:15-23	118
16:11	55

1 Kings

3:16-28	191
6–7	69
12:28-29	91
22:22	146

2 Kings

11:1	168, 212
11:2-3	168
11:4-21	168

1 Chronicles

3:16-17	40
12:32	9

2 Chronicles

24:20-22	57, 210, 212
36:21	37

Ezra

2:21	26, 154

Esther

2:6	40

Job

19:26	112
21:26	117

Psalm

2	56, 58, 60, 156
2:1-3	35
2:8-9	99
3:5	112
8	104–5
8:1	105
8:2	68–9, 73, 78, 86, 102, 104–5, 134, 210
8:3	133
8:9	105
18:8	133
24:21	133
25:6	133
25:18-19	55
26:6 (Vulgate 25:6)	134
28:7	112
30:20	133
36:36	153
37:23-29	69
37:24	69
42:3	116
48	58, 60, 77
48:4-7	58
48:6	58
63:8	133
63:10	66
68:23	66
78:10	169
79:3	105, 134
79:10	134
90	169
92:5	133
104:25	154
105	116
105:15	116
105:17-18	116
105:18	116
118:30	133
122:3	117
124	105, 129
124:2-3	129
124:4-5	129
124:7b-8	129
126:1-2a	169
126:6	105
137:1-2	135
137:3	135
137:5-6	135
137:9 (Vulgate 136:9)	134
148:1-4	17

Proverbs

8	118
21:18	91
28:15	169, 212

Song of Songs

1:15	71
2:15	66
5:12	71

Scripture Index

Isaiah
1:3	67
2:3	58
4:2	136
6:9-10	50
7-8	85, 210
7:2	53
7:10-17	51
7:13	53
7:14	50, 53-4, 210
7:15	53-4
8:3-4	54
8:4	51-2, 73, 99
9:1-2	50
11:1	136
13:10	50
16:1	109
19:1	75
26:19	109
29:13	50
40:3	50
42:1-4	50
49:6	67
53:4	50
56:7	50

Jeremiah
4:14	40
4:19	113
4:31	43
6:18	40
8:5	40
13:27	40
15:1	123
15:5	40
23:5	136
24:1	40
27:19-21	40
28:4	40
29:2	40
31	41, 115-17, 129, 152-3, 158
31:15 (LXX 38:15)	2, 4, 27, 40-5, 47, 82-3, 116, 122, 129, 134, 149, 152-3, 194, 208
31:15-17	43
31:15-20	133-4
31:15-22	2, 43
31:16	112, 116, 123, 129
31:16-17	131
31:16-22	131
31:17	117
31:22	116
32:6-15	39
33:15	136
36	142
40:1	42, 154
42	142

Lamentation
2:1	43
2:4	43
2:10	43
2:18	43

Ezekiel
40-41	69

Daniel
3	136
12:2	139
12:3	131

Hosea
8:4	168-9, 212
11:1	38, 45

Amos
6:5-6	116

Micah
5:2	42, 148

Zechariah
1:1	57
3:8	136
6:12	136
11:12-13	39

Malachi
4:2	111

Matthew
1	1-2, 29
1:1-17	28, 219
1:1	181
1:2	181

Scripture Index

1:6	181	2:14	29
1:11	40	2:14-15	30
1:11-12	40	2:14-15a	38
1:12	40	2:15	29, 31, 37–8, 45, 211
1:17	40, 181	2:15b	38
1:18-21	38	2:19	29
1:18-25	28, 31, 38, 44, 148	2:19-21	30, 33
1:18–2:12	49	2:19-23	30, 45, 207
1:20	181	2:20	29
1:21	35	2:20-21	
1:22	29, 37–8	2:21	
1:22-23	37–8, 181, 211	2:22	29
1:22-2:23	38	2:22-23	30
1:23	46, 50, 113, 210	2:23	29
1–2	28, 33, 38, 50, 53–4, 198	3:3	37, 41, 43, 50
		3:15	29
2	2, 4–5, 28–9, 33–5, 45, 50–1, 54, 58, 67, 82, 99, 135, 152, 157, 165, 174, 198, 205, 210	3:17	41, 43
		4:1	29
		4:3	86
		4:6	86
		4:8	32
2:1	29	4:9	29
2:1-2	16	4:10	29
2:1-8	30	4:12	29
2:1-12	28, 30, 53, 101, 198	4:14	29
2:2	29	4:14-16	37, 50
2:2-3	29	5:3-12	45, 74
2:3	29–30, 40, 54, 129	5:4	43
2:4	53	5:5	117
2:4-6	29	5:10	116
2:5	42	5:12	40
2:5-6	37	5:17	14, 29
2:6	29, 35	6:2	29
2:7	29–30, 39	6:4	29
2:7-12	29	6:5	29
2:8	29–30, 32	6:16	29
2:8-9	4, 29	6:18	29
2:9	29	8:2	29
2:9-12	30, 207	8:11	29
2:10	31–2, 115, 170	8:12	42
2:11	4, 29, 50, 94	8:17	29, 37, 50
2:12	29, 31	8:28	32
2:13	29	8:34	29
2:13-14	4	9:18	29
2:13-15	30–1, 49, 131, 176, 207	9:24	29, 139
		9:27	44
2:13-18	49, 69, 71, 129, 133, 209	10:8	35
		10:8-10	13–14
2:13-23	28, 30–1, 43, 104, 207	10:23	73

11:16-19	40	21:28-32	39
12:14	29–30	21:29	39
12:15	29	21:32	39
12:17	29	21:33-46	40
12:17-21	37, 50	21:38	62
13:10-18	203	21:46	30
13:14-15	37, 50	22:1-14	78
13:35	29, 37	22:13	42
13:42	42	22:15	29
13:47-50	217	22:40	73
13:48	29	22:41-46	44
13:50	42	23	57, 94
14:1-12	213	23:1	29
14:5	30, 207	23:32	29
14:13	29	23:33-39	60
14:22-33	6, 17	23:34-37	40
14:26	29	23:35	29, 57, 97
14:33	29	23:37	40
14:49	37	23:37-39	110
15:7-9	50	24:27	29
15:12	29	24:29	50
15:21	29	24:51	42
15:21-28	17	25:1-12	78
15:22	44	25:1-13	146
15:25	29	25:30	42
15:28	37	25:40	43
16:14	39–40	25:45	43
16:24	29	26:4	30, 109
17:5	41	26:14	29
17:19	29	26:49	109
18:1-5	108	26:54	29
18:3	75, 107	26:56	37
18:5	4	26:59	29
18:10	105	27:3	29, 39
18:16	73	27:3-10	39
18:21	29	27:4	39
18:26	29	27:5	29, 39
19:27	29	27:6-7	39
20:20	29	27:8	39
20:28	35	27:9	29, 155
20:30-31	44	27:9-10	37, 39–40
21:4	29	27:11	168
21:4-5	37	27:14	32, 207
21:8	69	27:25	3, 43
21:13	50	27:29	32
21:15	30, 44	27:27-31	32
21:15-16	44, 68, 78, 102	27:29	109
21:16	68–9, 86, 105, 210	27:29-31	207
21:23–22:33	62	27:31	32

27:37	168	9:9	213
27:38-44	32	12:50	71
27:40	86	13:28	42
27:41	32	13:32	66
27:46	42	13:34-35	110
27:50	42	16:19-22	75
27:54	97	16:19-31	55
27:57	154	16:22	113
27:62-64	30	16:23	75
27:63	30		
28:9	29	John	
28:11-15	3	1:29	109
28:13-14	30	1:48	98
28:16-20	20, 108	2:1-12	78
28:17	29	4:22	67, 77
		7:27	62
Mark		9:1-2	36
5:39	139	11:11	139
6:14-29	213	12:13	69
6:19-20	207	18:36	61
6:19	30	19:3	109
6:20	30		
11:8	69	Acts	
15:18	109	7:54-60	71
15:39	97	12:1-19	213
15:40	61	12:18-19	55, 206
16:1	61	12:19-23	213
		12:23	62
Luke		20:37	42
1–2	54, 198		
1:26–2:20	49	Romans	
1:28	109	2:20	66
1:28–2:14	198	8:13	91
1:52	102	8:14-21	133–4
2	157	8:18	133
2:7	53	8:35-36	79
2:8-20	101	11:11-24	136
2:12	53	15:4	131
2:21-38	49		
2:22-28	198	1 Corinthians	
2:22-39	151	2:12	116
2:24	157	3:1-4	66
2:25-35	51, 57	3:2	71
2:29-32	51	4:9-13	130
2:34	36	5:5	55
2:35	36	9:26	69
2:39	151	11:30	139
2:52	53, 91	13:11	66
8:23	139	14:20	75, 103

15:6	139
15:18-20	139

2 Corinthians

7:7	41
7:10	116
13:1	73

Galatians

4:1	66

Ephesians

2:14-17	67
2:20	58
4:14	66
5:14	139
6:12	69

Colossians

3:5	91

1 Thessalonians

4:13-14	117
4:14-15	76, 139
4:18	117

1 Timothy

4:7	69

2 Timothy

2:5	69
4:8	69

Hebrews

2:7	69
2:9	69
2:9–3:2	134
2:10-13	134
2:14-18	134
5:11-14	66, 91
11:11	44

James

1:12	69
3:2	69

1 Peter

3:6	44

3:15	217
4:12-19	129
5:4	69

1 John

1:5-2:2	129
3:2	117
3:12	100

Revelation

1:20	17
2:7	136
2:10	54, 69
3:4-5	105
3:11	54, 69
4:4	69
4:10	54
4:10-11	105, 214
6:9	105, 133–4
6:9-11	129, 214
6:10-11	131
7	106
7:4	106, 214
7:9	54, 69, 76, 105, 109, 129, 213
11:1-14	73
12	99–100, 156
12:1-6	35
12:3-6	99, 214
12:4	99
12:4-6	99
12:5	99, 214
12:5-6	99
12:6	99, 214
14:1-4	129
14:1-5	78, 104, 128, 133, 213–14
14:2-3	105
14:4	109
14:4-5	105
19:2	105, 169
19:7-10	78
21:1-7	129
21:2	129
22:2	136
22:14	136
22:19	136

Apocrypha

2 Maccabees
7	72–73
11:6	41

Sirach
35:21	82, 209

Pseudepigrapha

1 Enoch
18:11-14	17

Joseph and Asenath
14:1-7	17

Pseudo-Philo's Biblical Antiquities
9.9-15	33

Josephus

Jewish War
1:440	29
1.654-55	34

Antiquities
2.9.2	57
2:205-37	33
15:6	34
15:8-10	34
15:53-55	34
15:82	29
15:173-78	34
15:222-36	34
15:247-51	34
15:260-66	34
15:280-90	34
16:75	29
16:387-94	34
16:392-94	34
17:41-44	34
17:148-50	34
17:167	34
17:182-87	34

Church Fathers

1 Clement
24–27	112

www.ingramcontent.com/pod-product-compliance
Lightning Source LLC
Chambersburg PA
CBHW052153300426
44115CB00011B/1653